Use these handy Zagat bookmarks to mark your favorites and the places you'd like to try. Plus, we've included re-useable blank bookmarks for you to write on (and wipe off). Browsing through your Zagat guide has never been easier!

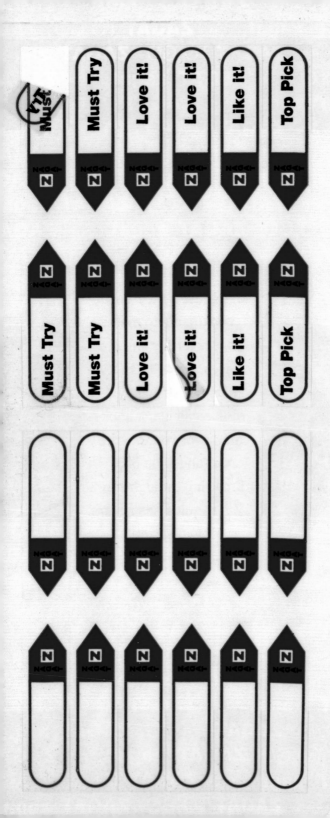

ZAGAT®

New Jersey
Restaurants
2008/09

LOCAL EDITORS
Cody Kendall and Brooke Tarabour with Andrea Clurfeld
and Robert Strauss
STAFF EDITOR
Sharon Gintzler

Published and distributed by
Zagat Survey, LLC
4 Columbus Circle
New York, NY 10019
T: 212.977.6000
E: newjersey@zagat.com
www.zagat.com

ACKNOWLEDGMENTS

We thank G. Fogelman, Lizzie Fuerst, Maria Gallagher, Larry Gershon, A.S. Gintzler, Phyllis Gintzler, Craig LaBan, Fran Levine, Rosalie Saferstein, Robert Seixas, Steven Shukow, Jennie Stein, Traci Turi and Nolan Willence, as well as the following members of our staff: Caitlin Eichelberger (assistant editor), Sean Beachell, Maryanne Bertollo, Catherine Bigwood, Sandy Cheng, Reni Chin, Larry Cohn, Carol Diuguid, Alison Flick, Jeff Freier, Karen Hudes, Roy Jacob, Natalie Lebert, Mike Liao, Dave Makulec, Andre Pilette, Kimberly Rosado, Becky Ruthenburg, Troy Segal, Sharon Yates, Anna Zappia and Kyle Zolner.

The reviews published in this guide are based on public opinion surveys. The numerical ratings reflect the average scores given by all survey participants who voted on each establishment. The text is based on direct quotes from, or fair paraphrasings of, participants' comments. Phone numbers, addresses and other factual information were correct to the best of our knowledge when published in this guide.

Contents

About This Survey

This **2008/09 New Jersey Restaurants Survey** is an update reflecting significant developments since our last Survey was published. It covers 931 restaurants in the New Jersey area, including 96 important additions. We've also indicated new addresses, phone numbers, chef changes and other major alterations to bring this guide up to the minute.

WHO PARTICIPATED: Input from 5,797 avid local diners forms the basis for the ratings and reviews in this guide (their comments are shown in quotation marks within the reviews). Collectively they bring roughly 911,000 annual meals worth of experience to this Survey. We sincerely thank each of these participants – this book is really "theirs."

HELPFUL LISTS: Whether you're looking for a celebratory meal, a hot scene or a bargain bite, our top lists and indexes can help you find exactly the right place. See Most Popular (page 7), Key Newcomers (page 7), Top Ratings (pages 9–14) and Best Buys (page 15). We've also provided 48 handy indexes.

OUR EDITORS: Special thanks go to our local editors for this update, Cody Kendall, a restaurant critic for *The Star-Ledger*, Brooke Tarabour, a food columnist also at *The Star-Ledger*, and to Andrea Clurfeld and Robert Strauss, who worked on the original Survey.

ABOUT ZAGAT: This marks our 29th year reporting on the shared experiences of consumers like you. What started in 1979 as a hobby involving 200 of our friends has come a long way. Today we have well over 300,000 surveyors and now cover dining, entertaining, golf, hotels, movies, music, nightlife, resorts, shopping, spas, theater and tourist attractions worldwide.

SHARE YOUR OPINION: We invite you to join any of our upcoming surveys – just register at **ZAGAT.com,** where you can rate and review establishments year-round. Each participant will receive a free copy of the resulting guide when published.

AVAILABILITY: Zagat guides are available in all major bookstores, by subscription at **ZAGAT.com** and for use on web-enabled mobile devices via **ZAGAT TO GO** or **ZAGAT.mobi.** The latter two products allow you to contact your choice among many thousands of establishments by phone with just one click.

FEEDBACK: There is always room for improvement, thus we invite your comments and suggestions about any aspect of our performance. Is there something more you would like us to include in our guides? Did we get anything wrong? We really need your input! Just contact us at **newjersey@zagat.com.**

New York, NY
May 7, 2008

Nina and Tim Zagat

What's New

It's been a banner year for New Jersey dining – from extravagant ethnic spots and chic restaurant-cum-nightclubs to star-chef outposts – as upscale eateries continue their influx statewide.

SOUTH JERSEY SCENE: Atlantic City is quickly becoming *the* NJ dining destination. Joining Bobby Flay Steak, Michael Mina's SeaBlue and Wolfgang Puck American Grille at the Borgata Hotel, Casino & Spa is Michael Schulson (ex-executive chef of Buddakan in Philadelphia and New York City), who's betting on Izakaya, a Japanese eatery with a serious sake bar (and sommelier) in a modern setting. The steaks are high for Stephen Starr (famed for Buddakan and Continental on the Pier at Caesars) as he readies the chophouse Chelsea Prime as well as Teplitzky's – a midcentury-inspired diner – at The Chelsea, the soon-to-debut hotel on the boardwalk.

A GRAZING WE WILL GO: The petite plate trend is no flash-in-the-pan, as evidenced by Daryl Wine Bar, celebrity chef David Drake's New Brunswick New American, where small (and large) plates allow patrons to sample a variety of dishes. At Cranford's A Toute Heure, an American with a French accent, a "bites" menu encourages tastings, while you can eat tapas-style at Havana, a Cuban in Highlands. Sampling is also the focus at the fish-centric New American Salt Water Beach Café in Asbury Park (where an upstairs supper club is scheduled for a summer 2008 debut).

DINNER AND A DANCE: Customers who want to feed their inner Fred Astaire after a meal can move to the groove of live entertainment at new restaurants-cum-nightclubs. By way of example, Union City's Latin fusion Park Avenue Bar & Grill, which offers four floors of nonstop action for wining, dining and, on weekends, dancing. Over in Bloomfield there's Prana, which fuses innovative Middle Eastern–Indian cuisine and post-11 PM dance parties.

EXOTIC EATS AND ENVIRONS: The central part of the state welcomed a duo of luxe Eastern-style newcomers. In North Brunswick, the Rupee Room's Bollywood set-like decor – fountains, lights, a table with swings instead of chairs – transports you far from its strip-mall locale, while a liveried doorman is posted at the entrance at Indigo Restaurant & Bar.

CHECK IT OUT: Though the average dinner costs $36.95 in New Jersey, compared to the $33.67 national average, and the state of the economy is uncertain, fine dining in New Jersey seems secure, given the numerous upper-crust spots that are setting up shop.

New Jersey
May 7, 2008

Cody Kendall
Brooke Tarabour

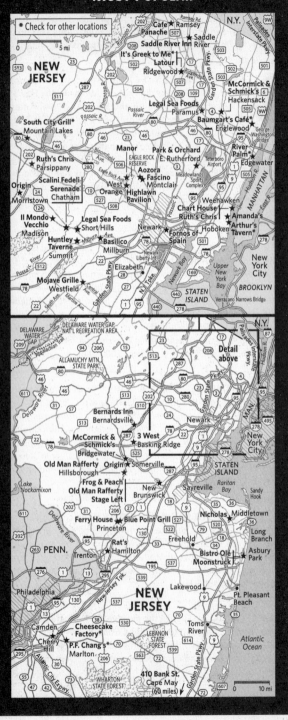

Most Popular

1	Nicholas | *American*	**21**	Huntley Taverne | *American*
2	Cheesecake Factory | *Amer.*	**22**	3 West | *American*
3	Legal Sea Foods | *Seafood*	**23**	P.F. Chang's | *Chinese*
4	River Palm | *Steak*	**24**	Ferry House | *American/French*
5	Amanda's | *American*	**25**	South City Grill | *American*
6	Origin | *French/Thai*	**26**	McCormick/Schmick | *Seafood*
7	Scalini Fedeli | *Italian*	**27**	Manor, The | *American*
8	Frog and the Peach | *American*	**28**	Old Man Rafferty's | *American*
9	Highlawn Pavilion | *American*	**29**	Bistro Olé | *Portuguese/Spanish*
10	Baumgart's | *Amer./Pan-Asian*	**30**	Il Mondo Vecchio | *Italian*
11	Serenade | *French*	**31**	It's Greek To Me | *Greek*
12	Saddle River Inn | *Amer./French*	**32**	Rat's | *French*
13	Fascino | *Italian*	**33**	Park & Orchard | *Eclectic*
14	Bernards Inn | *American*	**34**	Chart House | *Amer./Seafood*
15	Cafe Panache | *Eclectic*	**35**	Arthur's | *Steak*
16	Blue Point | *Seafood*	**36**	Aozora | *French/Japanese*
17	Basilico | *Italian*	**37**	Fornos of Spain | *Spanish*
18	Ruth's Chris | *Steak*	**38**	Mojave Grille | *Southwestern*
19	Moonstruck | *American/Med.*	**39**	Stage Left | *American*
20	Latour | *French*	**40**	410 Bank St. | *Creole*

It's obvious that many of the above restaurants are among New Jersey's most expensive, but if popularity were calibrated to price, we suspect that a number of other restaurants would join their ranks. Thus, we have added a list of 80 Best Buys on page 15.

KEY NEWCOMERS

Our editors' take on the main arrivals of the past year. For a full list, see page 187.

Daryl Wine Bar | *American*	Pearl of Lisbon | *Portuguese*
Due Terre | *Italian*	Prana | *Indian/Mideastern*
Equus | *American*	Sage | *Mediterranean*
Hotoke | *Pan-Asian*	Stonehouse | *American*
Indigo | *Indian*	Tabor Rd. Tavern | *American*
Kanji | *Japanese/Steak*	Undici | *Italian*
Manna | *American*	Vivas | *Nuevo Latino*

Ratings & Symbols

Zagat Top Spot	Name	Symbols	Cuisine	Zagat Ratings			
				FOOD	DECOR	SERVICE	COST

Area, Address & Contact

Z Tim & Nina's ◗ *Pizza*   ▽ 23 | 9 | 13 | $15

Atlantic City | 5678 Pacific Ave. (Atlantic Ave.) | 609-555-1212 | www.zagat.com

Review, surveyor comments in quotes

"Miles from the boardwalk but still not far enough away", this "never-closing" AC "eyesore" "single-handedly" started the "saltwater-taffy pizza craze" that's "sweeping the casino capital" like "a run of bad luck"; don't forget to "visit the all-you-can-stomach buffet" – "it's to die for" (or from) – but don't look for ambiance because "T & N don't know from design", or service, for that matter.

Ratings

Food, Decor and **Service** are rated on the Zagat 0 to 30 scale.

0	–	9	poor to fair
10	–	15	fair to good
16	–	19	good to very good
20	–	25	very good to excellent
26	–	30	extraordinary to perfection
	▽		low response	less reliable

Cost reflects our surveyors' average estimate of the price of a dinner with one drink and tip and is a benchmark only. Lunch is usually 25% less.

For **newcomers** or survey **write-ins** listed without ratings, the price range is indicated as follows:

I	$25 and below
M	$26 to $40
E	$41 to $65
VE	$66 or more

Symbols

Z	Zagat Top Spot (highest ratings, popularity and importance)
◗	serves after 11 PM
⑤	closed on Sunday
Ⓜ	closed on Monday
⊄	no credit cards accepted

Top Food Ratings

Excludes places with low votes.

<u>29</u> Nicholas | *American*

<u>28</u> DeLorenzo's | *Pizza*
Chef's Table | *French*
Cafe Panache | *Eclectic*
Bay Ave. Tratt. | *Amer./Italian*

<u>27</u> André's | *American*
SeaBlue | *Seafood*
Saddle River Inn | *Amer./French*
Serenade | *French*
Whispers | *American*
Scalini Fedeli | *Italian*
Latour | *French*
Lorena's | *French*
David Drake | *American*
CulinAriane | *American*
Cafe Matisse | *Eclectic*
Blue Bottle | *American*
Ebbitt Room | *American*
Chez Catherine | *French*
White House | *Sandwiches*
410 Bank St. | *Creole*

<u>26</u> Washington Inn | *American*
Le Rendez-Vous | *French*
David Burke | *American*
Sagami | *Japanese*
Ajihei | *Japanese*
Perryville Inn | *American*
Black Duck | *Eclectic*
Gables, The* | *Eclectic*
Augustino's | *Italian*
Fernandes Steak | *Steak*
Union Park | *American*
La Isla | *Cuban*
Fascino | *Italian*
Zoe's | *French*
Mélange Cafe | *Creole*
Peter Shields* | *American*
Stage Left | *American*
Le Fandy | *French*
Taka* | *Japanese*
Origin | *French/Thai*
Sono Sushi | *Japanese*

BY CUISINE

AMERICAN (NEW)

<u>29</u> Nicholas
<u>27</u> André's
Saddle River Inn
Whispers
David Drake

AMERICAN (TRAD.)

<u>28</u> Bay Ave. Trattoria
<u>26</u> Washington Inn
Perryville Inn
Ram's Head Inn
<u>25</u> Doris & Ed's

CARIBBEAN/CUBAN

<u>26</u> La Isla
<u>24</u> Casona
Rebecca's
<u>21</u> Cuba Libre
Martino's

CHINESE

<u>26</u> Far East Taste
<u>24</u> Chengdu 46
Lotus Cafe
Meemah
<u>23</u> Cathay 22

CONTINENTAL

<u>24</u> Madeleine's
<u>23</u> Black Forest Inn
Stony Hill Inn
<u>21</u> Court Street
Ho-Ho-Kus Inn

ECLECTIC

<u>28</u> Cafe Panache
<u>27</u> Cafe Matisse
<u>26</u> Black Duck
Gables, The*
<u>25</u> Anthony David's

FRENCH

<u>27</u> Saddle River Inn
Latour
Lorena's
Chez Catherine
<u>26</u> Zoe's

FRENCH (BISTRO)

<u>28</u> Chef's Table
<u>26</u> Le Rendez-Vous
Le Fandy
<u>24</u> Bienvenue
<u>23</u> Pierre's

---

* Indicates a tie with restaurant above

FRENCH (NEW)

27 Serenade
26 Origin
25 Le Petit Chateau
24 Rat's
22 Brothers Moon

INDIAN

25 Karma Kafe
24 Moghul
23 Aangan
   Passage to India
   Ming

ITALIAN

28 Bay Ave. Trattoria
27 Scalini Fedeli
26 Augustino's
   Fascino
   Chef Vola's
   Il Capriccio
25 Anthony David's
   Lu Nello
   Portofino
   Girasole
   Giumarello's*
   Laceno

JAPANESE

26 Sagami
   Ajihei
   Taka
   Sono Sushi
   Yumi

MEDITERRANEAN

25 Varka Fish House
24 Moonstruck
   Hamilton's Grill
   Frescos
22 Vine

MEXICAN

24 El Meson
   Charrito's
23 Los Amigos
   Tortilla Press
   Juanito's

PIZZA

28 DeLorenzo's
25 Grimaldi's Pizza
24 Tacconelli's

22 Reservoir Tavern
   Margherita's

SANDWICHES

27 White House
24 Kibitz Room
21 Sallee Tee's
20 Richard's
19 Jack Cooper's

SEAFOOD

27 SeaBlue
26 Dock's Oyster
25 Varka Fish House
   Shipwreck Grill
   Doris & Ed's

S. AMER./PAN-LATIN

26 Cucharamama
25 Casa Solar
24 Zafra
23 Brasilia Grill
22 Lua

SOUTHERN/CAJUN

23 Silver Oak Bistro
22 Delta's
   Indigo Smoke
20 Luchento's
19 Oddfellows

SPANISH/ PORTUGUESE

26 Fernandes Steak
25 Bistro Olé
24 Adega Grill
   Tony Da Caneca
   Casa Vasca

STEAKHOUSES

26 Fernandes Steak
25 River Palm
   Old Homestead
24 Ruth's Chris
   Palm

THAI

26 Origin
   Far East Taste
25 Thai Thai
   Siri's Thai French
   Mie Thai

BY SPECIAL FEATURE

BREAKFAST
- 24 Zafra
- 23 Meil's
- 21 Christopher's
- Mad Batter
- 19 Country Pancake

BRUNCH
- 26 Amanda's
- 25 Anthony David's
- Verjus
- 24 Rat's
- Zafra

BYO
- 28 Chef's Table
- Cafe Panache
- Bay Ave. Trattoria
- 27 Saddle River Inn
- Whispers

CHILD-FRIENDLY
- 27 White House
- 410 Bank St.
- 26 Mélange Cafe
- Far East Taste
- Dock's Oyster

HOTEL DINING
- 27 SeaBlue
  (Borgata Hotel)
- Whispers
  (Hewitt Wellington)
- Ebbitt Room
  (Virginia Hotel)
- 26 Gables, The
  (Green Gables Inn)
- Mia
  (Caesars)

NEWCOMERS (UNRATED)
- Daryl Wine Bar
- Due Terre
- Prana
- Tabor Rd. Tavern
- Undici

OFFBEAT
- 26 La Isla
- Taka

- Chef Vola's
- Yumi
- Cucharamama

PEOPLE-WATCHING
- 27 David Drake
- 26 Zoe's
- Bernards Inn
- Cucharamama
- Mia

POWER SCENES
- 28 Cafe Panache
- 27 SeaBlue
- Saddle River Inn
- Serenade
- Chez Catherine

SINGLES SCENES
- 26 Cucharamama
- Mia
- 25 Shipwreck Grill
- 24 Atlantic B&G
- Cenzino

TRENDY
- 28 DeLorenzo's
- 27 SeaBlue
- Scalini Fedeli
- Latour
- Lorena's

WINNING WINE LISTS
- 29 Nicholas
- 27 SeaBlue
- Serenade
- Scalini Fedeli
- David Drake

WORTH A TRIP
- 28 DeLorenzo's
  Trenton
- Cafe Panache
  Ramsey
- 27 André's
  Newton
- SeaBlue
  Atlantic City
- Saddle River Inn
  Saddle River

BY LOCATION

ATLANTIC CITY
27 SeaBlue
White House
26 Chef Vola's
Mia
Dock's Oyster

CAPE MAY AREA
27 Ebbitt Room
410 Bank St.
26 Washington Inn
Black Duck
Union Park Dining Rm.

CHERRY HILL
26 Mélange Cafe
25 Siri's Thai French
Bobby Chez
24 La Campagne
Kibitz Room

COLLINGSWOOD
26 Sagami
25 Bobby Chez
24 Water Lily
Casona
Word of Mouth

HOBOKEN
26 Augustino's
La Isla
Amanda's
Cucharamama
25 Anthony David's

LAMBERTVILLE
25 Manon
24 Hamilton's Grill
No. 9
23 Ota-Ya
22 Anton's/Swan

MIDDLETOWN
29 Nicholas
26 Sono Sushi
22 Crown Palace
Anna's Italian
18 Neelam

MONTCLAIR
27 CulinAriane
26 Fascino
25 Osteria Giotto
Aozora
Nouveau Sushi

MORRISTOWN
26 Origin
25 Grand Cafe
Tim Schafer's
Copeland
24 Sushi Lounge

NEWARK
26 Fernandes Steak
24 Adega Grill
Tony Da Caneca
Casa Vasca
23 Brasilia Grill

NEW BRUNSWICK
26 Stage Left
Frog & Peach
24 Panico's
23 Clydz
SoHo on George

PRINCETON
26 Ajihei
25 Blue Point
Ferry House
21 Lahiere's
Teresa Caffe

RED BANK
24 Bienvenue
23 Sogno
Siam Garden
Juanito's
Teak

RIDGEWOOD
27 Latour
25 Sakura-Bana
Village Green
23 Radicchio
Silver Oak Bistro

SOMERVILLE
26 Origin
25 Shumi
24 Wasabi
da Filippo
23 Chao Phaya

VOORHEES
25 Little Café
Laceno Italian
Bobby Chez
24 Ritz Seafood
Catelli

Top Decor Ratings

28	Rat's
27	Highlawn Pavilion
	Ombra
	Chakra
	Peter Shields
	Ram's Head Inn
26	Pluckemin Inn
	Taka
	Nauvoo Grill
	Avenue
	Nicholas
	CoccoLa
	Catherine Lombardi
	Washington Inn
	Sirena
	Serenade
25	Grand Cafe
	Chart House
	Il Capriccio
	SeaBlue

Molly Pitcher
Lua
Bernards Inn
Saddle River Inn
Manor
Scalini Fedeli
Stony Hill Inn
Specchio
Gables, The
Copeland
Cafe Matisse
Amanda's
Inn at Millrace
Liberty House
Harvest Bistro
Bobby Flay Steak
Raven & Peach
David Burke
Union Park Dining Rm.

24 Old Homestead

OUTDOORS

Anthony David's	Hamilton's Grill
Axelsson's	Latour
Bernards Inn	Lilly's on Canal
Frenchtown Inn	Peter Shields
Girasole	Tisha's

ROMANCE

Cafe Matisse	Le Rendez-Vous
CulinAriane	Perryville Inn
Ebbitt Room	Raven & Peach
Harvest Moon	Sergeantsville Inn
Le Petit Chateau	Washington Inn

ROOMS

Chakra	Makeda
Cucharamama	Nicholas
David Burke	Ombra
David Drake	Pluckemin Inn
Lorena's	Rat's

VIEWS

Arthur's Landing	Matisse
Atlantic B&G	McLoone's
Avenue	Molly Pitcher
Avon Pavilion	Union Park Dining Rm.
Inlet Café	Walpack Inn

Top Service Ratings

28	Nicholas

26
- Grand Cafe
- André's
- Ebbitt Room
- Saddle River Inn
- David Drake
- Serenade
- Cafe Panache
- Cafe Matisse
- Scalini Fedeli
- Washington Inn

25
- Benito's
- Union Park Dining Rm.
- Il Capriccio
- Peter Shields
- Capriccio
- Whispers
- Latour
- Amanda's
- Lorena's

- Ram's Head Inn*
- Bernards Inn
- SeaBlue
- Chef's Table
- Stage Left
- Chez Catherine
- Cenzino
- Le Petit Chateau

24
- Pluckemin Inn
- David Burke
- Specchio
- Il Villaggio
- Zoe's*
- Manor
- Black Duck
- Frog & Peach
- Rat's
- Ristorante Benito
- Panico's
- Taka

Best Buys

In order of Bang for the Buck rating.

1. Amazing Hot Dog
2. Surf Taco
3. Benny Tudino's
4. White House
5. DeLorenzo's
6. Pop Shop
7. Irish Pub
8. Grimaldi's Pizza
9. Fedora Cafe
10. Tacconelli's Pizzeria
11. Richard's
12. Aroma Royal Thai
13. Meemah
14. Pad Thai
15. Country Pancake
16. Skylark Diner
17. Far East Taste
18. Brooklyn's Pizza
19. Tick Tock
20. La Isla
21. Sri Thai
22. Thai Kitchen
23. Kibitz Room
24. Karma Kafe
25. Coconut Bay
26. Mie Thai
27. Hunan Chinese
28. El Meson
29. Ali Baba
30. Tortilla Press
31. Chao Phaya
32. P.J. Whelihan's
33. Eurasian Eatery
34. Senorita's
35. Bombay Gardens
36. Charrito's
37. Mr. Chu
38. Joe's Peking
39. Somsak/Taan
40. Juanito's

OTHER GOOD VALUES

Aby's Mexican
Allen's Clam
Anatolia's
Bamboo Leaf
Bistro San Miguel
Brickwall Tavern
Champa Laos
China Palace
Conte's
Creole Cafe
Dayi'nin Yeri
Doo Rae Myun Ok
Drew's Bayshore
Espo's
Gagan Bistro
GRUB Hut
Krakus
La Tapatia
Malabar House
Martino's
Mexico Lindo
Moksha
Mr. Bill's
Nobi
Passage to India
Pete & Elda's
Pho Binh
Pic-Nic
Pithari Taverna
Saffron
Seven Hills
Sister Sue's
Smokey's BBQ
Tashmoo
Thai Thai
Tony Luke's
Tony's Baltimore
West Lake
Wondee's Thai
Ya Ya Noodles

RESTAURANT
DIRECTORY

Aamantran Ⓜ *Indian*

$\triangledown$ 23 | 16 | 21 | $23

Toms River Township | Victoria Plaza | 1594 Rte. 9 S. (Churchill Rd.) | 732-341-5424 | www.aamantrancuisine.com

The open kitchen at this Toms River Indian BYO dispenses "great" Indian food in a "comfortable" environment; the "hospitable" service, "family"-friendly atmosphere and "value" of a lunch buffet trump the strip-mall surroundings; N.B. a Bordentown location is scheduled to open in spring 2008.

Aangan *Indian*

23 | 17 | 19 | $27

Freehold Township | A & M Plaza | 3475 Rte. 9 N. (Three Brooks Rd.) | 732-761-2900 | www.aanganrestaurant.com

Its lunch buffet is a "deal" and a "good introduction" to "excellent" Indian cooking say fans of this "kid-friendly" BYO "treasure" in a Freehold strip mall; given the "attentive" service, it's hard not to feel accommodated in the "comfortable" dining room.

Aby's Mexican Restaurant *Mexican*

$\triangledown$ 22 | 14 | 18 | $24

Matawan | 141 Main St. (Ravine Dr.) | 732-583-9119 | www.abysrestaurant.com

"All the basics" taste "good" at this Matawan Mexican BYO storefront whose menu is a "value", the decor "homey" yet "attractive" and the service "friendly", if sometimes "slow"; plus, the seasonal weekend guitar brings a touch of the festive.

Acacia Ⓜ *American*

25 | 20 | 22 | $47

Lawrenceville | 2637 Main St. (bet. Craven Ln. & Phillips Ave.) | 609-895-9885 | www.acaciacuisine.com

Now in its 16th year, this Lawrenceville BYO still supplies "joy", combining "excellent" New American cuisine, "knowledgeable, friendly" service and a "convivial" vibe; the redecorated dining room remains a "tight fit", but fans accede and keep squeezing in.

Acqua Ⓢ *Italian*

21 | 21 | 21 | $43

Raritan | 777 Rte. 202 N. (bet. 1st Ave. & Ortho Dr.) | 908-707-1777 | www.acquaristorante.com

"Active" bar fans hit this "noisy" Raritan Italian proffering a "predictably good" menu, weekend entertainment and a staff as "lively" as the setting; the scene's *bellissimo* – but it will cost you.

Acquaviva delle fonti *Italian*

23 | 21 | 21 | $46

Westfield | 115 Elm St. (Broad St.) | 908-301-0700 | www.acquaviva-dellefonti.com

Acolytes applaud the "consistently good" fare, "romantic" ambiance and "professional" service at this high-ceilinged Westfield Northern Italian in a renovated bank building; yes, it's "pricey", but "wonderful" experiences don't come cheap.

Adega Grill *Portuguese/Spanish*

24 | 24 | 23 | $37

Newark | 130-132 Ferry St. (bet. Madison & Monroe Sts.) | 973-589-8830 | www.adegagrill.com

Smitten surveyors dine on "delicious" "family-style" food at this "romantic" "special-occasion" Iberian in Newark's Ironbound; the

| | FOOD | DECOR | SERVICE | COST |

"vineyardlike" decor (*adega* means 'wine cellar' in Portuguese) and "comfortable" seating are as pleasing as the "good" service and the bar, where "you'll swear you were in Lisbon" once you sit down.

NEW Aglio Ⓢ *Italian* — | — | — | M

Metuchen | 140 Durham Ave. (Central Ave.) | 732-600-6231 | www.restaurantaglio.com

A rustic Tuscan look informs this dignified-but-down-to-earth new Metuchen BYO, where chef-owner John Harkness chats with customers when he's not preparing midpriced, French-influenced Italian fare like braised sweetbreads and porcini mushrooms; live entertainment accompanies your dinner on Thursday nights.

Z Ajihei *Japanese* 26 | 11 | 18 | $30

Princeton | 11 Chambers St. (Nassau St.) | 609-252-1158

It's all about the fish at this "little" Princeton Japanese BYO serving "superb" sushi that's "as fresh as can be"; put yourself "on autopilot and let the chef do the flying", and just remember that you're eating "top-flight" fare in "dorm-room" digs.

Akai Lounge *Japanese* 23 | 20 | 18 | $39

Englewood | 11 N. Dean St. (bet. Bergen St. & E. Palisades Ave.) | 201-541-0086 | www.akailounge.com

Enthusiasts embrace this "upscale" Englewood Japanese for its "inventive" sushi (some even call it "Nobu"-like) served within a "slick", "modern" space; while the "friendly" "service needs work", "delicious" drinks and a "loungey" vibe help distract.

Akbar *Indian* 18 | 17 | 17 | $29

Edison | 21 Cortland St. (Patrick Ave.) | 732-632-8822 | www.theakbarrestaurant.com

This super-sized Edison Indian is "a solid standby in a sea of choices"; though some say the restaurant "could use a little redecorating", the consensus is "you're not there for the wallpaper", just for the "good" food and a buffet that's "one of the best for lunch."

Alan@594 Ⓢ Ⓜ *Italian* 20 | 18 | 17 | $34

Upper Montclair | 594 Valley Rd. (Bellevue Ave.) | 973-744-4120

Dedicated diners endorse the "good", "reasonably" priced menu at this Upper Montclair regional Italian BYO whose "pleasant" dining room can be "crowded" on account of "tight" conditions; P.S. fresh-air fans can always opt for the "great" garden.

Alchemist & Barrister *American* 16 | 16 | 17 | $34

Princeton | 28 Witherspoon St. (Nassau St.) | 609-924-5555 | www.theaandb.com

"Stick with the pub and you won't be disappointed" aver patrons of this "100% old-school" Princeton American where three seating options (in the bar, patio or more formal room) draw preppies of all ages; it's "typical Ivy League", down to "chairs that creak", and correspondents concede if the food "isn't exciting" at least "it serves its purpose well."

	FOOD	DECOR	SERVICE	COST

Al Dente Ristorante *Italian* | 23 | 20 | 23 | $41 |

Piscataway | 1665 Stelton Rd. (Ethel Rd.) | 732-985-8220 | www.aldenteristorante.com

"Honest", "excellent" homemade pastas and "detailed" service are the draws of this "pricey" Piscataway Northern Italian "hidden" in a strip mall; if the decor proves a bit "over-the-top", it still seems to fit the food and "old-world" mood.

Aldo & Gianni *Italian* | 21 | 14 | 19 | $37 |

Montvale | A&P Shopping Ctr. | 108 Chestnut Ridge Rd. (Grand Ave.) | 201-391-6866

South Hackensack | 268 Huyler St. (bet. Dinallo & Hoffman Sts.) | 201-487-4220

www.aldoandgianni.com

"Good" and "garlicky" "homestyle" Italian is the bill of fare at these neighborhood storefronts that "cater to businesspeople" at lunch and a "casual crowd" at dinner; the atmosphere "may not be great", but "gracious" service compensates; N.B. South Hackensack is BYO.

Alessio 426 Ⓜ *Continental*   ▽ | 20 | 17 | 19 | $35 |

Metuchen | 426 Main St. (New St.) | 732-549-6464 | www.alessio426.com
Expect to "feel at home" in this Metuchen BYO storefront (formerly Dan's on Main), whose kitchen dishes up a variety of Northern Italian–influenced Continental specialties; a "generous" lunch buffet reinforces the notion that the food here is "well worth the cost."

Alexander's *French*   ▽ | 24 | 26 | 24 | $41 |

Cape May | Alexander's Inn | 653 Washington St. (bet. Franklin & Ocean Sts.) | 609-884-2555 | www.alexandersinn.com
Very Victorian in every way – right down to the "attentive", white-glove service – this longtime B&B restaurant provides a "great" Cape May experience for patrons who dine on the "wonderful" French food in "charming" quarters; not even the "pricey" tabs get in the way of "romantic" rendezvous; N.B. closed January.

Ali Baba *Mideastern* | 20 | 12 | 17 | $20 |

Hoboken | 912 Washington St. (bet. 9th & 10th Sts.) | 201-653-5319
"Delicious" food is what's kept this "tried-and-true" Middle Eastern Hoboken BYO a neighborhood eat-in/take-out staple since 1983; the reasonably priced menu and "friendly" service help smooth the edges over the "rough", "dour" digs.

Aligado Asian Restaurant *Japanese/Thai*   ▽ | 23 | 13 | 18 | $29 |

Hazlet | 2780 Rte. 35 (Miller Ave.) | 732-888-7568
Japanese and Thai specialties turn up at this Hazlet Asian BYO relied upon for its "well-prepared" fare, but not necessarily for its ambiance; still, most maintain it's a "cut above" the pack.

Alisa Cafe Ⓜ *French* | 22 | 19 | 21 | $35 |

Cherry Hill | Barclay Farms Shopping Ctr. | 112 Rte. 70 E. (Kings Hwy.) | 856-354-8807 | www.alisacafe.com
Capitalizing on his base of South Jersey fans, West Philly transplant Tony Kanjanakorn offers patrons this Cherry Hill strip-mall BYO,

where the "excellent" French dinners are influenced by a "touch of Thai"; given the "good" service, "repeat visits" are no surprise here.

Allendale Bar & Grill ● *Pub Food* | 16 | 12 | 16 | $24

Allendale | 67 W. Allendale Ave. (bet. Demercurlo Dr. & Maple St.) | 201-327-3197 | www.mahwahbarandgrill.com

Trekking to this 70-plus-year-old Bergen County American is "tradition" on account of its "reliable" pub fare (especially the "great" burgers), nice touches (fresh popcorn on the tables) and "friendly" staff; if the "old standby's" decor needs "a shot of Botox", overall, this "quintessential" bar "still holds its own."

Allen's Clam Bar Ⓜ⫽ *Seafood* | - | - | - | M

New Gretna | 5650 Rte. 9 (Garden State Pkwy.) | 609-296-4106

Take a trip down the Parkway for this seafood BYO destination in New Gretna that may be a half step above a shack in appearance but nevertheless is a sight for sore fresh-fish-seeking eyes; the fried fare here draws both fisher folk and Humvee-driving landlubbers.

🆕 Aloe Fusion *Thai* | - | - | - | M
(fka Champa Laos)

Cherry Hill | 219 Haddonfield-Berlin Rd. (Brace Rd.) | 856-795-0188 | www.aloefusion.net

This cheery new Cherry Hill Thai BYO strip-maller (formerly Champa Laos) is distinguished by its reasonably priced, veggie-friendly fare (tofu supreme) that supplements the usual edibles (chicken satay); N.B. the three-course lunch special (Mondays-Fridays, $8.95) makes it a popular midday stop.

🆕 Alstarz Sports Pub *Eclectic* | - | - | - | I

Bordentown | 140 Rte. 130 S (Hwy. 206) | 609-291-0200 | www.alstarzsportspub.com

A Bordentown first – this sizable, striking, industrial-style restaurant/bar with 24 TVs and an Eclectic menu offers nachos to niçoise – and is the latest venture of the Mastoris family, whose landmark diner is across the parking lot; the crowd's as lively as the televised sports – and word is the kitchen's got game.

☑ Amanda's *American* | 26 | 25 | 25 | $45

Hoboken | 908 Washington St. (bet. 9th & 10th Sts.) | 201-798-0101 | www.amandasrestaurant.com

"After all these years", this "serene", "romantic" Hoboken New American in a "beautiful" brownstone still epitomizes "upscale", "classy" dining with its "impeccably" prepared cuisine, "extensive" wine list, "attentive" service and "lovely" decor; an "amazing" brunch and early-bird special – a "steal" at $14 per person – affirm this winning spot's seemingly everlasting appeal.

Amarone *Italian* | 21 | 16 | 23 | $41

Teaneck | 63 Cedar Ln. (bet. Broad St. & Teaneck Rd.) | 201-833-1897 | www.amaroneristorante.net

"Attentive" service ("they treat newcomers like regulars") helps warm this "lovely" "neighborhood" Teaneck Northern Italian distinguished by "quality" home cooking; some say it's "formal", others insist it's "cozy", but just about everyone agrees "it's like eating at your friend's place."

Amazing Hot Dog *Hot Dogs*

22	11	19	$9

Verona | 148A Bloomfield Ave. (Pompton Ave.) | 973-433-3073
Bound Brook | 600 W. Union Ave. (Tea St.) | 732-469-0389 🛇 Ⓜ
www.amazinghotdog.com

"Top dogs" and bargain-basement prices lure aficionados to this Verona BYO (NJ's No. 1 Bang for the Buck), where fried franks accompanied by a "variety of toppings" and "crisp", "tasty" fries rule; sure, it's safe to say there's "no decor", "but who cares" when the wieners are "the best this side of Coney Island"?; N.B. a bigger Bound Brook branch opened post-Survey offering breakfast and dessert in addition to the tube steaks.

Amici Milano *Italian*

22	18	21	$36

Trenton | 600 Chestnut Ave. (Roebling Ave.) | 609-396-6300 |
www.amicimilano.com

Northern Italian food followers "keep coming back" to this "crowded" standby in Trenton's Chambersburg section for "delicious", "old-school", "copiously" portioned victuals; the "highlight" of an evening here may be the piano music, which helps sustain the "lively" setting.

Amiya *Indian*

21	18	18	$25

Jersey City | Harborside Financial Ctr. | 160 Greene St.
(Christopher Columbus Dr.) | 201-433-8000 |
www.amiyarestaurant.com

"Subtle twists on the classics" distinguish this contemporary Jersey City Indian located in the heart of the Financial District; the lunch buffet is "a cut-above" the rest – and "consistently packed" – so "go on the weekend when the workers are gone" and the restaurant becomes more of "a neighborhood place"; P.S. patio dining is a "treat."

🆕 Anatolia's Turkish Kitchen *Turkish*

-	-	-	M

(fka Nazmi's Turkish Kitchen)

Cliffside Park | 442 Anderson Ave. (bet. Edgewater Rd. & Fulton Terr.) |
201-941-6650

When new management recently took over this offbeat Turkish BYO in Cliffside Park (formerly known as Nazmi's Turkish Kitchen) it was given a fresh new look (artwork hung on apricot walls) – but it's the classic homestyle fare (hummus, salad, rice pudding) and affordable prices that keep customers contented.

Andaman Ⓜ *French/Thai*

23	14	17	$28

Morristown | 147 Morris St. (bet. Elm & King Sts.) |
973-538-5624

Those with a yen for East-West cuisine find "oh-so-good" Thai-French fare at this Morristown BYO; hence, it's "easy to ignore" the plain decor, even more so when you consider the "great" value of the lunch and dinner prix fixes.

	FOOD	DECOR	SERVICE	COST

Z André's M *American*
| | 27 | 22 | 26 | $53 |

Newton | 188 Spring St. (bet. Adams & Jefferson Sts.) | 973-300-4192 |
www.andresrestaurant.com

This "friendly" BYO "behind a storefront" in Newton is "always a delight" given the "crafty creations" of "talented" chef-owner André
de Waal, the man behind the "sublime" New American menu; if the
"pricey" tabs prove a bit daunting, budget-conscious fans go for the
"moderately" priced bistro menu on Sundays; another plus – wines
may be purchased Wednesdays–Sundays at the on-site boutique;
N.B. also closed Tuesdays.

Angelo's Fairmount Tavern *Italian*
| | 20 | 13 | 19 | $31 |

Atlantic City | 2300 Fairmount Ave. (Mississippi Ave.) | 609-344-2439 |
www.angelosfairmounttavern.com

The "hearty" down-home Italian food (i.e. "nonna"-approved) is
perfect for the *famiglia* say fans of this "nothing-fancy", 72-year-old
"red-gravy" warhorse in Atlantic City , aka "the best deal in town";
the wine is "homemade" and the joint's filled with "characters."

Anjelica's M *Italian*
| | 25 | 16 | 21 | $43 |

Sea Bright | 1070 Ocean Ave. (bet. Peninsula Ave. & River St.) |
732-842-2800 | www.anjelicas.com

While you "shouldn't count on conversation" (it's "loud"), expect
"consistently wonderful" food and an "enormous" menu at this Sea
Bright Italian BYO also proffering a handful of wines; they "aim to
please" here, which more than makes up for the "crowded" conditions
in the summer.

Anna's Italian Kitchen M *Italian*
| | 22 | 14 | 20 | $38 |

Middletown | Fountain Ridge Shopping Ctr. | 1686 Rte. 35 S.
(Old Country Rd.) | 732-275-9142 | www.annasitaliankitchen.com

Anna Perri fills her Middletown BYO by offering a "variety" of "good"
Italian food, including "the best gnocchi"; no, it's "not cheap" considering it's located in a shopping center, but the quality of the cooking stamps out any gripes about prices; N.B. weekly cooking classes
are offered March–May.

Anthony David's *Eclectic/Italian*
| | 25 | 19 | 21 | $42 |

Hoboken | 953 Bloomfield St. (10th St.) | 201-222-8399 |
www.anthonydavids.com

"Fantastic" fare emerges from the "tiny" kitchen within chef-owner
Anthony Pino's pocket-size Hoboken BYO whose Eclectic–Northern
Italian menu, "amazing" cheeses and widely touted brunch (among
the "best" in town) are served in "low-key" quarters, or in the more
casual, rustic front room, where prepared foods are sold; N.B. a
post-Survey renovation may outdate the above Decor score.

Anthony's M *Italian*
| | 23 | 19 | 20 | $39 |

Haddon Heights | 512 Station Ave. (White Horse Pike) | 856-310-7766 |
www.anthonyscuisine.com

A part of Downtown Haddon Heights' ongoing revival, this "quaint"
storefront BYO "doesn't strive to be cutting-edge", but does provide

"reliably" good Italian food considered a "value"; that you're "never rushed" seems to make the setting even more "inviting."

Anton's at the Swan 🅼 *American* | 22 | 22 | 21 | $49 |

Lambertville | Swan Hotel | 43 S. Main St. (Swan St.) | 609-397-1960 | www.antons-at-the-swan.com

"First-class food in a first-class setting" is a perfect excuse to try this "romantic" New American in a "charming" historic Lambertville hotel; whether you have a "drink by the fireplace with your sweetheart" or on the patio, this "low-key", leisurely dining mainstay is a "true destination for lovers – or for those with expense accounts."

ⓩ Aozora *French/Japanese* | 25 | 20 | 19 | $40 |

Montclair | 407 Bloomfield Ave. (Seymour St.) | 973-233-9400 | www.aozorafusion.com

"Eye-pleasing" delights that "look too nice to eat" are proffered at this "stylish" Montclair BYO, the showcase for Nelson Yip's "outstanding", "dreamy" Japanese-French handiworks that include "fabulous" sushi; if "somewhat pricey", the quality of the fare is pure "Tiffany's."

Aquila Cucina *Italian* | 21 | 17 | 20 | $40 |

New Providence | 30 South St. (Springfield Ave.) | 908-464-8383 | www.aquilarestaurant.com

For "reliably" good Italian, diners turn to this "steady" (the "menu never changes") New Providence BYO where a "friendly", "accommodating" staff and "comfortable" atmosphere "don't disappoint"; partisans propose it's perfect for a casual meal or "special occasion."

Aroma Royal Thai *Thai* | 22 | 21 | 21 | $24 |

Franklin Park | 3175 Rte. 27 (Delar Pkwy.) | 732-422-9300 | www.aromarestaurant.com

It's "well-named" note patrons of this BYO Thai tucked inside a Franklin Park strip mall, a sound option on account of "exquisitely crafted" food proffered by "eager-to-please" servers; the enthused agree this Asian "diamond" is also "easy on the wallet."

Arthur's Landing *American* | 20 | 24 | 20 | $53 |

Weehawken | 1 Pershing Rd. (Ferry Blvd.) | 201-867-0777 | www.arthurslanding.com

The "killer" views of Manhattan keep customers enthralled at this Weehawken waterside New American, as does the innovative cooking of executive chef Michael Haimowitz; as always, the staff "makes you feel special" and there's always that ever-popular pretheater $50 per person "deal" – a three-course meal and round-trip ferry service, making this a great "destination" spot.

ⓩ Arthur's Steakhouse & Pub *Steak* | 18 | 12 | 16 | $28 |
(fka Arthur's Tavern)

North Brunswick | 644 Georges Rd. (Milltown Rd.) | 732-828-1117 | www.arthurssteakhouse.org

ⓩ Arthur's Tavern *Steak*

Emerson | 214 Kinderkamack Rd. (Lincoln Blvd.) | 201-265-5180

(continued)

Arthur's Tavern

Hoboken | 237 Washington St. (3rd St.) | 201-656-5009
Morris Plains | 700 Speedwell Ave. (Littleton Rd.) |
973-455-9705 ☞
www.arthurstavern.com

For a "cholesterol fix that won't bankrupt you", try this chophouse quartet dishing out "monster"-size slabs of steaks along with "amazing" burgers; the "bare" decor surely doesn't impress, and the service is somewhat "spotty", but they're the best "beef-o-rama" deals around; N.B. the North Brunswick location, Arthur's Steakhouse & Pub, is separately owned.

Arturo's ⓜ *Italian*   22 | 19 | 20 | $45

Midland Park | 41 Central Ave. (bet. Godwin & Greenwood Aves.) |
201-444-2466 | www.arturos-restaurant.com

"Nice people, good food" attracts admirers to this "reliable" 25-year-old Midland Park Southern Italian known for its fare and "stand-up" servers; though now "pricey" thanks to a liquor license, fans can take solace in a "varied" wine list.

Asia Star Cafe *Pan-Asian*   – | – | – | E

Tinton Falls | 4060 Asbury Ave. (Greengrove Rd.) | 732-922-1119 |
www.asiastarcafe.com

Although mostly Japanese and Chinese, the fare at this Tinton Falls BYO also acknowledges Thailand and Malaysia on its diverse menu; the dark and sleek decor is a draw for locals along with visitors en route to the Shore.

Assembly Steak House *Steak*   16 | 17 | 17 | $50

Englewood Cliffs | 495 Sylvan Ave. (Palisades Ave.) | 201-568-2616 |
www.assemblysteakhouse.com

Surveyors are split on this "old-standard" Englewood Cliffs chophouse: while fans can't figure out why this "excellent", "pricey-but-worth-it" beef emporium "isn't more popular", contrarians claim it's "disappointing", citing "so-so" steaks while wondering "who goes here?"

A Tavola ⓜ *Italian*   23 | 14 | 18 | $30

Old Bridge | Deep Run Shopping Ctr. | 3314 Rte. 9 S. (Ferry Rd.) |
732-607-1120 | www.atavola1.com

"Fabulous food and friendly folks – what more could you want?" ask fans of this Old Bridge Italian strip-mall BYO distinguished by its "delicious" dishes prepared in an open kitchen; since you can expect a "good value", it's wise to "reserve" before showing up.

Athenian Garden ⓜ *Greek*   23 | 12 | 20 | $27

Galloway Township | 619 S. New York Rd. (bet. Holly Brook Dr. &
W. Brook Ln.) | 609-748-1818 | www.athenian-garden.com

The staff's "as nice as can be" at this rustic Greek BYO emphasizing "tasty" seafood and other savories in out-of-the-way Galloway; the open kitchen and fresh fish on display enhance the rustic, if basic digs ("from the look, you'd never expect such great food").

			FOOD	DECOR	SERVICE	COST

Atlantic Bar & Grill *American/Seafood*
24 | 22 | 22 | $48

South Seaside Park | Central & 24th Aves. | 732-854-1588 |
www.atlanticbarandgrillnj.com

At this Shore New American, the "awesome" view is a given thanks
to floor-to-ceiling windows and the fact that you're dining "as close
to the ocean as possible"; but aside from the sight of "waves crash-
ing against the shoreline", expect "well-prepared" seafood and a
"terrific" bar, the latter enhanced by live jazz on some nights.

NEW A Toute Heure Ⓜ *American*
- | - | - | M

Cranford | 232 Centennial Ave. (Lincoln Ave.) | 908-276-6600 |
www.atouteheure.com

The name translates as "anytime" in French, and when the occasion
calls for American cuisine served in a Gallic milieu, this new
Cranford BYO with an open kitchen and affordable, daily-changing
dishes spotlighting organic ingredients should do the trick; there's a
"bites" menu and Sunday brunch too, but whichever you choose, keep
in mind the no-reservations policy – and come early during prime time.

Ⓩ Augustino's Ⓢ⌀ *Italian*
26 | 17 | 23 | $43

Hoboken | 1104 Washington St. (bet. 11th & 12th Sts.) | 201-420-0104 |
www.augustinosrestaurant.com

"As good as it gets" for NJ homestyle Southern Italian say surveyors
about this "small" cash-only Hoboken storefront that's "stuffed like
a manicotti every night"; the staff will "charmingly bust your chops",
and "good luck" trying to get a reservation on any night.

Ⓩ Avenue *French*
22 | 26 | 20 | $59

Long Branch | 23 Ocean Ave. (Laird Ave.) | 732-759-2900 |
www.leclubavenue.com

Think "South Beach" – not Long Branch – at this "pricey" French
brasserie/lounge whose "spectacular" ocean views coupled with
famed London architect David Collins' "beautiful", "modern" design
(marble-tiled floors, floor-to-ceiling windows) are more than a
match for the "chic" crowd; despite "spotty" service, most seem sated
by Antonio Mora's "tasty" fare and "delicious" drinks at the "sexy" bar.

Avon Pavilion *American*
18 | 16 | 18 | $33

Avon-by-the-Sea | 600 Ocean Ave. (bet. Norwood & Woodland Aves.) |
732-775-1043 | www.avonpavilion.com

Although dinner is the time for "terrific" people-watching, "breakfast
is the real star" at this Boardwalk BYO American in Avon where eating
is a "fantastic way to enjoy food" since the backdrop is the beach and
the water ("just being by the ocean makes anything taste great");
N.B. breakfasts and lunches are cash only at this summer spot.

Axelsson's Blue Claw *Seafood*
22 | 20 | 20 | $43

Cape May | 991 Ocean Dr. (Rte. 109) | 609-884-5878 |
www.blueclawrestaurant.com

You "can't go wrong" at this "old-time" Cape May docksider
delivering "tasty" preparations of "fresh" seafood; the bar is
"beautiful" – and there's music on Saturday nights, to boot – though

it's important to note the "pricey" fare speaks to the place's "classy" ambiance (there's "no slurping clams out of the shell here").

Axia Taverna *Greek*
FOOD	DECOR	SERVICE	COST
21	22	19	$46

Tenafly | 18 Piermont Rd. (Central Ave.) | 201-569-5999 | www.axiataverna.com

Some consider this "upscale" bi-level Greek in Tenafly an "oasis in the heart of suburbia" thanks to its "sophisticated" menu, "beautiful" modern design (by famed architect Tony Chi), mostly Hellenic wine list and "friendly" staff; given its virtues, it seems "worth the detour."

Azúcar Ⓜ *Cuban*
FOOD	DECOR	SERVICE	COST
19	21	19	$36

Jersey City | 495 Washington Blvd. (Pavonia Ave.) | 201-222-0090 | www.azucarcubancuisine.com

When "looking for Cuban", it can't hurt to hit this Jersey Cityite whose "cool" decor and "lively" ambiance go hand in hand with the fare; P.S. they offer free salsa lessons, and some insist there's nothing like "relaxing with your pals over great cigars" in the lounge.

Bacari Grill *American*
FOOD	DECOR	SERVICE	COST
21	21	20	$44

Washington Township | 800 Ridgewood Rd. (Pascack Rd.) | 201-358-6330 | www.bacarigrill.com

"Reliably good" food and a country-inn setting folks "love" help explain the popularity and longevity of this "consistent" Washington Township New American; true, you may not find it a bargain outing, but the "sharp" staff, "spirited" vibe and bar scene keep the "crowds" happy.

Bahama Breeze *Caribbean*
FOOD	DECOR	SERVICE	COST
16	19	16	$26

Cherry Hill | Cherry Hill Mall | 2000 Rte. 38 (Haddonfield Rd.) | 856-317-8317 | www.bahamabreeze.com

To its fans, this "festive" Caribbean canister in Cherry Hill (and other U.S. outposts) delivers "island" decor, "gargantuan" portions of "good", "reasonably" priced food and "marvelous" cocktails; still, detractors don't like "average" fare, "long waits" ("have *War and Peace* ready") and "slow" service that makes some want to "breeze on out."

Bahrs Landing *Seafood*
FOOD	DECOR	SERVICE	COST
15	14	16	$37

Highlands | 2 Bay Ave. (bet. Hillside Ave. & South St.) | 732-872-1245 | www.bahrs.com

This very "New England" 90-year-old Highlands seafooder offers some "excellent" scenery, in this case a "great" view of Sandy Hook Bay thanks to its location right on the water; the "typical", "fried-and-broiled" fare may not win awards, and though the place "looks like it's about to fall into the water", some say "that's part of its charm."

Baja *Mexican*
FOOD	DECOR	SERVICE	COST
20	16	18	$27

Hoboken | 104 14th St. (Washington St.) | 201-653-0610
Jersey City | 117 Montgomery St. (bet. Marin Blvd. & Warren St.) | 201-915-0062
www.bajamexicancuisine.com

The "impressive" selection of tequilas fuels the "fun" at this Mexican chips 'n' salsa twosome in Hoboken and Jersey City issuing the "best" margaritas and "solid" "south-of-the-border" fare; it's best to come with patience, since the "staff is fighting the crowds" too.

Bamboo Leaf *Thai/Vietnamese*

FOOD	DECOR	SERVICE	COST
24	19	19	$28

Bradley Beach | 724 Main St. (bet. Lareine & McCabe Aves.) | 732-774-1661 Ⓜ

Howell | Howell Ctr. | 2450 Rte. 9 S. (White Rd.) | 732-761-3939
Transport yourself into "another land" via these Thai-Vietnamese BYOs that guarantee "delightful" dining thanks to "delicious" dishes, "none of which disappoint"; the "pleasing" bamboo-accented decor provides another reason why diners never want to leaf; N.B. post-Survey changes in ownership and chefs at both venues may outdate the above scores; Howell locale closed Tuesdays.

Bangkok Garden *Thai*

FOOD	DECOR	SERVICE	COST
24	15	21	$26

Hackensack | 261 Main St. (bet. Camden & Salem Sts.) | 201-487-2620 | www.bangkokgarden-nj.com
"Excellent" – if not "outstanding" – Thai cooking is guaranteed at this "no-frills" Hackensack "hit", Bergen County's "best bet for a taste of Bangkok", especially in light of "can't-be-beat" tabs; "helpful" service rounds out this overall "superb" operation.

🆕 Bank 34 Ⓜ *Pan-Asian*
(fka Madame S)

FOOD	DECOR	SERVICE	COST
-	-	-	M

Somerville | 34 Division St. (South St.) | 908-722-9995 | www.bank34.com
A hefty savings account needn't be necessary to eat at this new Somerville BYO (formerly known as Madame S) offering a wide range of prices for its Pan-Asian and seafood dishes; there's still plenty of fin fare (even salmon pizza) but you'll also find steaks – and profiteroles; more low-key than its nearby sister, Origin (also helmed by chef-owner Manop Sutipayakul), it suits those seeking quiet conversation.

Bareli's Ⓢ *Italian*

FOOD	DECOR	SERVICE	COST
23	20	23	$56

Secaucus | 219 Rte. 3 E. (Plaza Ct.) | 201-865-0473 | www.barelis.com
"Big spenders" show up at this Secaucus Italian turning out "fine" food, "fabulous" wines, "top-notch" service and lots of folks, whether it's those "on business" at lunch or others in the evening; it's all "boys' club" inside, and some marvel that the place is as "consistent as the expensive cars that are always parked in the lot."

Barnacle Ben's *Seafood*

FOOD	DECOR	SERVICE	COST
19	17	19	$30

Moorestown | Acme Shopping Ctr. | 300 Young Ave. (bet. Marne Hwy. & Marter Ave.) | 856-235-5808 | www.barnaclebens.com
"Generously" doled out portions of "fresh", "reliable" seafood help explain why this Moorestown BYO has stayed in business for over a quarter century; the "friendly" service can be "uneven", but "reasonable" tabs mean you'll pay far less than a Franklin.

Barnacle Bill's ● *Burgers*

FOOD	DECOR	SERVICE	COST
21	16	18	$27

Rumson | 1 First St. (River Rd.) | 732-747-8396
"Eat some peanuts, throw the shells on the floor, then grab a burger and beer" say sage vets of this "nautically" appointed 25-year-old

Rumson American still slinging and serving patties that "can't be beat"; "beautiful" views of the Navesink River top it all off.

Barone's *Italian*   20 | 18 | 19 | $30

Moorestown | 280 Young Ave. (Main St.) | 856-234-7900

Villa Barone *Italian*

Collingswood | 753 Haddon Ave. (bet. Frazer & Washington Aves.) | 856-858-2999
www.baronerestaurants.com

"Don't change a thing!" plead backers of this South Jersey BYO duo whose setting feels "like mom's" and where the "reliably good", "red-gravy" cooking and "friendly" service are hits; overall, it's easy to see how they've "become a favorite" for many.

Barrel's *Italian*   19 | 11 | 17 | $27

Linwood | 199 New Rd. (Central Ave.) | 609-926-9900 ⍉

Margate | 9 S. Granville Ave. (Ventnor Ave.) | 609-823-4400
www.barrelsfoods.com

"Families" who frequent these Shore Italian BYOs come back for their "affordable" menus of "solid" fare, namely the "great" soups; fans also tout takeout as a "good" option.

⚡ Basilico *Italian*   23 | 21 | 21 | $44

Millburn | 324 Millburn Ave. (Main St.) | 973-379-7020 | www.basilicomillburn.com

An "impressive array" of "top-quality" Northern Italian dishes greets guests at this "chic" Millburn BYO, a "good bet for tasty pre-theater" supping near the Paper Mill Playhouse; enthusiasts enjoy a "warm" atmosphere and indoor and outdoor dining options, adding it's "never a disappointment – unless you forget to make a reservation."

Basil T's ◑ *American/Italian*   20 | 18 | 19 | $34

Red Bank | 183 Riverside Ave. (Maple Ave.) | 732-842-5990 | www.basilt.com

The "crowds" converge on this American-Italian "fixture" in Red Bank, a quintessential "meeting place" known as much for its "excellent" microbrews (crafted on-site) as its "lively", "boisterous" bar scene abetted by TVs all around; otherwise, expect "good" pastas and pizzas and "pricey" checks.

⚡ Baumgart's Café *American/Pan-Asian*   19 | 14 | 18 | $26

Edgewater | City Pl. | 59 The Promenade (River Rd.) | 201-313-3889

Englewood | 45 E. Palisade Ave. (bet. Dean St. & Grand Ave.) | 201-569-6267

Livingston | 4175 Town Center Way (Livingston Ave.) | 973-422-0955

Ridgewood | 158 Franklin Ave. (N. Walnut St.) | 201-612-5688
www.baumgartscafe.com

For a "diverse" slate of Traditional American (by day) and Pan-Asian (by night), these "kid-friendly" BYOs are counted on for "superfast" service and "solid" eats, from Chinese and sushi to chicken salad, burgers and "yummy" old-fashioned ice cream; if partisans argue the merits of each location, most report, overall, that these "split-personality" standbys are a winning quartet.

☒ Bay Avenue Trattoria Ⓜ American/Italian | 28 | 11 | 21 | $38 |

Highlands | 122 Bay Ave. (Jackson St.) | 732-872-9800 | www.bayavetrattoria.com

The "fantastic" American-Italian preparations at Joe Romanowski and Maggie Lubcke's "friendly" Highlands BYO (No. 1 for Food on the Shore) are a cause for "rejoicing"; true, you "don't have to get dressed up" given the somewhat "lacking" ambiance, but the "top-quality" cooking trumps any decor issues (and is even worth a "detour").

Bay Head Bistro & Café American | ▽ 21 | 17 | 18 | $46 |

Bay Head | 530 Main Ave. (bet. Howe & Mount Sts.) | 732-714-8881 | www.heatwavecafe.com

Go see "the sunsets" while dining at this Bay Head BYO near the beach offering "good", "something-for-everybody" American food in a "comfortable", "understated" atmosphere "conducive to entertaining"; the "friendly" staff helps make it a "worthwhile" stop in these parts.

Bayou Cafe Ⓜ Cajun/Creole | ▽ 23 | 17 | 22 | $26 |

Manasquan | 209 First Ave. (bet. Brielle Rd. & Main St.) | 732-223-6678 | www.bayoucafe.net

This Manasquan BYO is still the go-to for "wonderfully" spicy Cajun-Creole cookery, the kind that "makes you feel like you're in the heart of the Big Easy"; chef Robert Lumley is kicking up the menu with Caribbean dishes; N.B. also closed Tuesdays.

BayPoint Prime Steak | ▽ 24 | 12 | 17 | $50 |

Point Pleasant Beach | 1805 Ocean Ave. (Rte. 35) | 732-295-5400

Dennis Foy, one of Jersey's "best" chefs, oversees this seasonal Point Pleasant Beach BYO for "excellent" steaks supplemented by seafood; overall, the cooking "lives up to the toque's standards" – just visit between Memorial Day and Labor Day to experience it.

Bazzarelli Italian | 22 | 14 | 18 | $30 |

Moonachie | 117 Moonachie Rd. (Joseph St.) | 201-641-4010 | www.bazzarellirestaurant.com

"Making Meadowlands events much more enjoyable" for over 35 years, this Moonachie mainstay stays "busy" given "fair" pricing and "good-all-around" Italian offerings, even when it's just for a "slice and a coke"; perhaps better yet, the family-owned operation does its best to make you "feel at home."

Bazzini at 28 Oak Street ☒ American | 21 | 16 | 19 | $45 |

Ridgewood | 28 Oak St. (bet. Franklin & Ridgewood Aves.) | 201-689-7313 | www.28oakstreet.com

"Friendly" servers complement the "comfortable" atmosphere at this Ridgewood BYO whose New American preparations generally please; whereas some allow the food is "hit-or-miss", relatively "reasonable" prices – and an early-bird that's a "fantastic" bargain – are pluses.

	FOOD	DECOR	SERVICE	COST

Beau Steak & Seafood *Seafood/Steak*   `22` `22` `22` `$53`

Medford | 128 Taunton Blvd. (2 miles e. of Hwy. 70/73 Circle) |
856-983-1999 | www.beausteak.com

Steaks galore and a new raw bar complement the cuisine (lobster
bisque, beef Wellington) – and a 400-plus-label wine list – at this
"expensive", "special-occasion" Medford eatery entering its 31st
year; the rural scenery outside is a perfect foil for the "lovely",
freshly refurbished Louis XVI–style decor that makes this "old favorite" "worth the trip."

Bella Sogno Ⓜ *Italian*   ▽ `21` `16` `17` `$37`

Bradley Beach | 600 Main St. (Brinley Ave.) | 732-869-0700 |
www.bellasogno.com

Look forward to a "good" Italian meal in a "nice, quiet" setting at this
under-the-radar, wood-appointed Bradley Beach BYO providing a
sound "alternative" to the crowded Shore scene; relatively "inexpensive" tabs are just *bella;* N.B. also closed Tuesdays.

Bell's ⊄ *American/Italian*   `19` `11` `18` `$26`

Lambertville | 183 N. Union St. (bet. Buttonwood & Elm Sts.) |
609-397-2226 | www.bellstavern.com

For a "walk down memory lane" look no farther than this cash-only
Lambertville American-Italian and bona fide "neighborhood classic"
(since 1938) offering "appealing" food and noteworthy pasta
dishes, all at "bargain" prices; "comfortable" quarters draw "longtime regulars" to the "cozy" bar area.

Bell's Mansion Ⓜ *American*   `18` `19` `16` `$40`

Stanhope | 11 Main St. (Rte. 183 S.) | 973-426-9977 |
www.bellsmansion.com

In this "charming" converted 1840 Stanhope home (complete with
uneven wooden flooring), a "large", diverse American menu – from
"pub grub" to more "gourmet" items – awaits clientele who opt for
the taproom or one of the more formal areas; while "ordinary" food
keeps the disenchanted at bay, more say the place offers "good
all-around dining."

Belmont Tavern ⊄ *Italian*   `24` `7` `15` `$29`

Belleville | 12 Bloomfield Ave. (Heckel St.) | 973-759-9609

This "ma-and-pa" Belleville Italian has the "best-ever" chicken
Savoy and other "fabulous" "homestyle" dinners; yes, the digs are
"drab" and the waitresses "yell at you" (it's all "part of the charm"),
but acolytes agree the "cast of characters" that turn up make it all
seem very "*Sopranos*"; N.B. closed Tuesdays.

Belvedere Ⓜ *Italian*   `19` `18` `21` `$38`

Clifton | 247 Piaget Ave. (Main Ave.) | 973-772-5060 |
www.thebelvedererestaurant.com

The menu is "massive" and the parking "minimal" at this "consistently good" and "often overlooked" Clifton venue lauded for its
hearty Italian cooking; it's "nice and old-fashioned", and true believers attest "once you go here, you'll be back."

	FOOD	DECOR	SERVICE	COST

Benihana *Japanese* — | — | — | M

Short Hills | 840 Morris Tpke. (South Terrace) | 973-467-9550
Edison | 60 Parsonage Rd. (bet. Mason St. & Oakwood Ave.) | 732-744-0660
Pennsauken | 5255 Marlton Pike (Lexington Ave.) | 856-665-6320
www.benihana.com

The pioneering Japanese chain, with locations in Edison and Short Hills, has reopened its Philly-area outpost (in Pennsauken, NJ) with a striking renovation including fieldstone walls and sleek metals; though sushi adherents can groove on a fair variety from the mid-priced menu, most seek out the teppanyaki show with a group.

Benito's Ⓜ *Italian* 24 | 21 | 25 | $41

Chester | 44 Main St. (bet. Hedges Rd. & Warren St.) | 908-879-1887 | www.benitostrattoria.com

This "quaint", "romantic" BYO in Chester is where the "locals go" for "excellent" "homestyle" Northern Italian brought by staffers who make you feel like "family" and ultimately help "guarantee a loyal following"; naturally, it can get "noisy", but that comes with the territory of a "real find."

Benny Tudino's ●⇄ *Pizza* 21 | 7 | 14 | $11

Hoboken | 622 Washington St. (bet. 6th & 7th Sts.) | 201-792-4132

"Bigger is better" they say about the "XL"-size slices doled out at this pizza "institution" that's still the place to go when you've had "too many" at one of Washington Street's bars; true, the digs are "dumpy", but at $2.50 a slice, the Hoboken hordes don't mind.

Berkeley Restaurant &
Fish Market *Seafood* 18 | 12 | 17 | $28

South Seaside Park | Central & 24th Aves. (J St.) | 732-793-0400

Sure, the "decor is unimpressive", but this ramshackle, 60-plus-year-old South Seaside Parker is still a "real catch" for its "pretty" views of Island Beach State Park and "affordable" seafood, for some, the "freshest you'll find in the area"; N.B. the restaurant and adjoining fish market are seasonal; the raw bar is open year-round.

Ⓩ Bernards Inn *American* 26 | 25 | 25 | $65

Bernardsville | 27 Mine Brook Rd. (Quimby Ln.) | 908-766-0002 | www.bernardsinn.com

It's "high class all the way" at this "romantic", expense-account Bernardsville New American that keeps delivering "consistent excellence" from the kitchen of chef Corey Heyer; an "incredible" 750-label wine list, "professional" service and "wonderfully" refurbished interior are equally "impressive"; N.B. jacket suggested.

Berta's Chateau *Italian* 22 | 17 | 19 | $48

Wanaque | 7 Grove St. (Prospect St.) | 973-835-0992 | www.bertaschateau.com

The "faithful" return to this "venerable" site in Wanaque for "plenty" of "delightful" Northern Italian and "good" wines (from an extensive Italian list) in a country homestyle setting; "nothing's changed in

years – and that's a compliment" – laud fans of this "old-timer"
that's been "part of the North Jersey fabric" for eight decades.

Beyti Kebab *Turkish*   24 | 10 | 16 | $26

Union City | 4105 Park Ave. (41st St.) | 201-865-6281 |
www.beytikebab.com

For a taste of Istanbul, meat mavens head to this Union City Turk ("a
lamb lover's delight") also esteemed for "excellent" meze and salads; the decor may be "lacking" but the price – "cheap" – is right, the
staff "friendly" and "they bring on the belly dancing" on weekends;
N.B. there's an on-premises halal butcher shop.

Bienvenue Ⓜ *French*   24 | 19 | 21 | $50

Red Bank | 7 E. Front St. (Wharf Ave.) | 732-936-0640 |
www.bienvenuerestaurant.com

This "delicious" Red Bank BYO bistro emits French "country charm"
in its convincingly "cozy" quarters, where "wonderful" classics
(among them cassoulet, crème brûlée and foie gras) are served;
that and a $65 five-course tasting menu "comes cheaper than flying
to Paris" to taste "Gallic romance at its best."

Big Ed's BBQ *BBQ*   17 | 10 | 16 | $24

Old Bridge | 305 Rte. 34 N. (Amboy Rd.) | 732-583-2626 |
www.bigedsbbq.com

It's "hog heaven" at this barbecue joint, a "meat-eater's paradise"
where "lots of food for the money" means "the whole family" can
feast on the "best" babyback ribs, chicken and steaks delivered by
"friendly" staffers; "laughable" decor makes takeout sensible.

Bistro at Red Bank, The *Eclectic*   21 | 18 | 18 | $36

Red Bank | 14 Broad St. (bet. Front & Mechanic Sts.) | 732-530-5553 |
www.thebistroatredbank.com

A "casual", "attractive" brick-walled interior syncs up nicely with
the "diverse", "interesting" menu at this Red Bank Eclectic that
seems to be "buzzing" all the time; the outdoor dining is so "perfect", it may even be able to trump the somewhat "inattentive service"; N.B. for alcohol, only NJ wines are served.

Bistro En Ⓜ *French*   22 | 16 | 17 | $34

Teaneck | 252 Degraw Ave. (Queen Anne Rd.) | 201-692-0700 |
www.bistro-en.com

"Japanese meets French bistro" at this Teaneck spot knitting East and
West items (think hanger steak and shrimp tempura); the "good"
menu is "reasonably" priced, but it's the prix fixe lunch and dinners
that really add up to a "bargain" at this "citified" newcomer.

Bistro 44 Ⓢ Ⓜ *American/French*   ∇ 25 | 17 | 23 | $37

Toms River | 44 Washington St. (bet. Hooper Ave. & Main St.) |
732-818-7644 | www.bistro-44.com

Those who've made their way to this Toms River BYO in an unlikely
location (an office building) are "so glad they did", since the French-
American slate is "excellent" and the "attentive" service a delight; up
for applause is the twilight menu, a steal of a "superb" deal at $15.95.

	FOOD	DECOR	SERVICE	COST

☑ Bistro Olé *Portuguese/Spanish*

| 25 | 18 | 23 | $39 |

Asbury Park | 230 Main St. (bet. Cookman & Mattison Aves.) |
732-897-0048 | www.bistroole.com

"Why go to Newark?" when you can step into this Asbury Park
Iberian and experience "consistently delicious" cooking, not to mention "friendly" service and the "ebullience" of owner Rico Rivera,
who showers diners with his well-known hospitality; BYO red wine,
and watch it turn into "tasty" sangria (excluding Mondays and
Tuesdays during the winter, when the place is shuttered); N.B. the
addition of a new chef may outdate the above Food score.

🆕 Blackbird Dining Establishment Ⓜ *American*

| - | - | - | E |

Collingswood | 619 Collings Ave. (White Horse Pike) | 856-854-3444 |
www.blackbirdnj.com

A chef reared in acclaimed Central Jersey restaurants is behind this
Collingswood BYO, where French, Italian and Asian influences run
through the pricey New American menu; though occupying a former
hardware store it sports a bright and cheery look.

☑ Black Duck on Sunset *Eclectic*

| 26 | 22 | 24 | $45 |

West Cape May | 1 Sunset Blvd. (Broadway) | 609-898-0100 |
www.blackducksunset.com

At the sunset end of the West Cape May dining strip dwells this
"thoroughly enjoyable" Victorian BYO where you're bound to "eat
well" in light of the "excellent" Eclectic fare; black-and-white photos
give the place its "low-key" charm.

Black Forest Ⓜ *German*

| ∇ 19 | 15 | 19 | $34 |

Allentown | 42 S. Main St. (Lakeview Dr.) | 609-259-3197 |
www.blackforestallentownnj.com

Munich comes to Allentown via this Central Jersey Teutonic, one of
the area's only spots for those looking for "good home-cooked"
German meals and a "homey" ambiance to go with them; N.B. the
restaurant is BYO, so bring your best lager.

☑ Black Forest Inn *Continental/German*

| 23 | 21 | 21 | $46 |

Stanhope | 249 Rte. 206 N. (I-80, exit 25) | 973-347-3344 |
www.blackforestinn.com

If you dig "dumplings and spaetzle", this rustic Stanhope
Continental-German with its "stick-to-your-ribs" fare and "excellent" wines fits the bill; some see the atmosphere as "kitschy", others as "quaint", but the majority maintains this Bavarian has been a
"landmark for years" for good reason; N.B. closed Tuesdays.

Black Horse Tavern & Pub *Pub Food*

| 19 | 19 | 19 | $36 |

Mendham | 1 W. Main St. (Hilltop Rd.) | 973-543-7300 |
www.blackhorsenj.com

A real "local haunt", this "perpetually crowded" American (in a converted 1742 farmhouse) in "quaint" Mendham is perfect for a "burger
and beer" in the "lively" pub, the scene of "all the action"; P.S. for a
"more formal" meal, try the tavern (except Mondays – it's closed).

	FOOD	DECOR	SERVICE	COST

Black Trumpet *American* 23 | 17 | 22 | $49

Spring Lake | The Sandpiper Inn | 7 Atlantic Ave. (Ocean Ave.) |
732-449-4700 | www.theblacktrumpet.com

Chefs Mark Mikolajczyk and Dave McCleery (both alums of
Whispers) try for the 'inn' crowd with this "romantic" New
American BYO whose "unfailingly polite" staff serves "exceptional"
dishes just steps from the beach in Spring Lake's Sandpiper Inn;
N.B. live piano can be heard every weekend.

Blu ⓜ *American* 25 | 17 | 20 | $42

Montclair | 554 Bloomfield Ave. (bet. Maple Pl. & Park St.) |
973-509-2202 | www.restaurantblu.com

The plate is a "palette" in the hands of chef Zod Arifai, whose "inspired", "exciting" preparations of New American fare bring acclaim
to his Montclair BYO storefront, a "small", "narrow" space suited to
its "low-key" service; as for prices, the consensus is it's "a bargain
considering the amazing food"; N.B. his more casual spot, 'Next
Door', recently opened.

Blue *American/Eclectic* 23 | 19 | 21 | $46

Surf City | 1016 Long Beach Blvd. (11th St.) | 609-494-7556 |
www.bluelbi.com

"Upscale yet comfortable", this seasonal Surf City BYO "oasis" is
"not-your-average" LBI restaurant, with a "unique" Eclectic–New
American menu that stands "several notches above" its competitors; the "minimalist", albeit "warm" decor seems an ideal partner
for the food here.

ⓩ Blue Bottle Café ⓢⓜ *American* 27 | 18 | 22 | $43

Hopewell | 101 E. Broad St. (Elm St.) | 609-333-1710 |
www.thebluebottlecafe.com

"Super-talented" husband-and-wife team Aaron and Rory Philipson
(chef and pastry chef, respectively) join forces at this "rural"
Hopewell BYO "home run" serving "fantastic" New American cuisine in a "nondescript" building decked out in blue bottles; just be
sure to reserve early, as it's "almost impossible" to get in.

Blue Danube ⓜ *E European* ▽ 22 | 14 | 17 | $25

Trenton | 538 Adeline St. (Elm St.) | 609-393-6133 |
www.bluedanuberestaurant.com

"Abundant" helpings of "comforting", "old-world" Eastern European
(Polish, Hungarian, German) is the allure at this "sweet" Trenton spot;
the service is "slow" but "always nice", and locals like the idea of
supping on something "different" in this mecca of Italian restaurants.

Blue Eyes *Steak* 20 | 22 | 18 | $42

Sewell | 139 Egg Harbor Rd. (County House Rd.) | 856-227-5656 |
www.blueeyesrestaurant.com

"Wonderful martinis start things off" for Sinatra-ites who've dined
at this paean to the Rat Pack in Sewell selling "good" steaks and such
along with a "swanky", loungey ambiance abetted by live singing;
some say the alfresco option helps take the "after-work" edge off.

	FOOD	DECOR	SERVICE	COST

Blue Fish Grill ⓜ *Seafood*
▽ 20 | 12 | 13 | $24

Flemington | 9 Central Ave. (Mine St.) | 908-237-4528 |
www.thebluefishgrill.com

For a "little bit of New England" in Flemington, this "lively", "no-frills" BYO seafooder is quite the catch for "tasty", "well-prepared fish" cooked on a wood-fire grill; it's family-friendly and ideal "for casual outdoor get-togethers", plus it's so "inexpensive", "you'll have money left over for shopping" at the nearby outlet stores.

Blue Pig Tavern *American*
20 | 19 | 19 | $38

Cape May | Congress Hall Hotel | 251 Beach Ave. (bet. Congress & Perry Sts.) | 609-884-8421 | www.congresshall.com

While you "shouldn't expect anything too inventive", there's still "solidly consistent" cooking that emerges from the kitchen at this Cape May American tavern tucked into the "wonderfully restored" Congress Hall Hotel; "sit outside if you can", though in colder months, "ask for a table near the fireplace" in one of the adjacent rooms.

☒ Blue Point Grill *Seafood*
25 | 16 | 21 | $37

Princeton | 258 Nassau St. (Pine St.) | 609-921-1211 |
www.bluepointgrill.com

It's all about the gills – not necessarily the frills – at this Princeton BYO seafooder serving a menu of the "finest", "freshest", "perfectly" cooked fish in a "casual" space; a "knowledgeable" staff is on hand to help you wade through the "multiple" choices.

Bobby Chez ⓜ *Seafood*
25 | 10 | 16 | $22

Margate | 8007 Ventnor Ave. (S. Gladstone Ave.) | 609-487-1922
Cherry Hill | Village Walk Shopping Ctr. | 1990 Rte. 70 E. (Old Orchard Rd.) | 856-751-7575 ⑤
Collingswood | 33 W. Collings Ave. (bet. Cove Rd. & Norwood Ave.) | 856-869-8000 ⑤
Mount Laurel | Centerton Sq. | Marter Ave. & Rte. 38 (bet. Centeron Rd. & New Jersey Tpke. N.) | 856-234-4146
Sewell | 100 Hurffville Cross Keys Rd. (Tuckahoe Rd.) | 856-262-1001
Voorhees | Southgate Plaza | 1225 Haddonfield-Berlin Rd. (South Gate Dr.) | 856-768-6660 ⑤
www.bobbychezcrabcakes.com

"They have no equal" conclude cognoscenti about the "best" crab cakes "bar none" dispensed from these South Jersey specialists, where followers far and wide "stand in line" for the "legendary" signatures; note that the goods aren't necessarily a bargain, and it's not surprising that the quintet is touted for "takeout" (you can always "cook 'em up at home") given the "basic" decor.

Bobby Flay Steak *Steak*
24 | 25 | 22 | $66

Atlantic City | Borgata Hotel, Casino & Spa | 1 Borgata Way (Atlantic City Expwy., exit 1) | 609-317-1000 | www.bobbyflaysteak.com

"Even if you don't win at the casino tables", you'll still come out on top at Bobby Flay's "winner" in AC's Borgata serving "so-good" steaks (enhanced by the TV toque's "wonderful" Southwest-influenced rubs) amid a "spectacular" leather, wood and glass David

Rockwell design; bring extra cash – "all this flavor and beef doesn't come cheap."

Bombay Curry & Grill   *Indian*

FOOD	DECOR	SERVICE	COST
-	-	-	M

Basking Ridge | Lyons Mall | 973 S. Finley Ave. (Stonehouse Rd.) | 908-953-9400 | www.bombaycurryandgrill.com

Warmth from the setting, service and Indian fare makes this Basking Ridge BYO a favorite among locals looking for something other than the usual edible suspects; the lunch buffet's single-digit tabs are alone cause for celebrating.

Bombay Gardens   Ⓜ *Indian*

FOOD	DECOR	SERVICE	COST
22	13	20	$23

East Brunswick | Center 18 Mall | 1020 Rte. 18 N. (bet. Gunia St. & Hillsdale Rd.) | 732-613-9500 | www.bombaygardens.com

"The most helpful servers" ferry "truly delicious", "reasonably" priced Indian dishes at this East Brunswick strip-mall BYO whose food draws "oohs and aahs"; in a county "bursting with similar" restaurants, some say this one stands out among the "best."

Bosphorus   *Turkish*

FOOD	DECOR	SERVICE	COST
∇ 22	8	17	$21

Lake Hiawatha | 32 N. Beverwyck Rd. (bet. Lakeshore Dr. & Vail Rd.) | 973-335-9690

Ok, "don't look for any atmosphere" here, but if you want "great" food "cooked with love", you can't go wrong at this Lake Hiawatha Middle Eastern BYO, the place for "authentic" Turkish offerings; portions are "plentiful", and fans tout takeout too.

Boulevard Grille   *American*

FOOD	DECOR	SERVICE	COST
18	15	16	$35

Mahwah | 1033 MacArthur Blvd. (bet. Corporate Dr. & Ridge Rd.) | 201-760-9400 | www.thewould.com

Vending "appealing" lunches on its "diverse" menu, this BYO New American in a Mahwah strip mall also offers a "pleasant" setting and affordable tabs; though cons criticize "inconsistent service", most prefer to say meals here are "better than you'd expect"; N.B. closed Saturdays and Sundays.

Braddock's Tavern   *American*

FOOD	DECOR	SERVICE	COST
22	23	22	$41

Medford | 39 S. Main St. (Coates St.) | 609-654-1604 | www.braddocks.com

Its menu's been tweaked slightly (some dishes now have a more modern edge), and most applaud the "surprising" quality of the fare at this Medford Traditional American still supplying a "Colonial", "quaint-Americana" setting; as for the ambiance, some say "it's the only place where grandparents and 20-year-olds can eat in harmony"; N.B. it's in the process of being sold.

Brandl.   Ⓜ *American*

FOOD	DECOR	SERVICE	COST
24	17	19	$53

Belmar | 703 Belmar Plaza (bet. Main St. & 9th Ave.) | 732-280-7501 | www.brandlrestaurant.com

"Worthy of Manhattan", this storefront Belmar BYO is viewed as an "incredible find" for the Jersey Shore, staying "on top of things" with its "terrific" New American preparations; for those stung by "sticker shock", there's always the weekday three-course prix fixe.

	FOOD	DECOR	SERVICE	COST

Brasilia Grill *Brazilian*   23 | 15 | 21 | $32

Newark | 99 Monroe St. (bet. Ferry & Lafayette Sts.) | 973-589-8682

Brasilia Restaurant *Brazilian*

Newark | 132 Ferry St. (bet. Madison & Monroe Sts.) | 973-465-1227
www.brasiliagrill.com

"Come hungry and leave stuffed" at these "festive", roomy Ironbound Brazilians where "quality and quantity" come together; it's an all-you-can-eat "beef orgy", and the salad bar is worth "checking out", as are the prix fixe lunch and dinner specials; N.B. the original BYO Ferry Street locale, shuttered due to a fire, reopened post-Survey.

Brass Rail, The *American*   19 | 19 | 18 | $40

Hoboken | 135 Washington St. (2nd St.) | 201-659-7074 |
www.thebrassrailnj.com

Although some wish this New American "mainstay" in Hoboken would "figure out" if it's "a sports bar or a restaurant", most like it for a bi-level setup where you can "casually" chow down in the "terrific" ground-floor bar area or head "away from the noise" to the "upscale", "romantic upstairs dining room."

Brennen's Steakhouse *Steak*   22 | 20 | 22 | $48

Neptune City | 62 W. Sylvania Ave. (Morris Ave.) | 732-774-5040 |
www.brennenssteakhouse.com

They've got the chops to pull off consistently "solid" steaks at this Neptune City carnivorium that feels like one you'd find in "Midtown Manhattan"; the "plus" of a partition between the bar and dining area is a welcome relief for meat eaters distracted by "noise."

Brickwall Tavern &   ∇ 19 | 23 | 20 | $25
Dining Room ❷ *American*

Asbury Park | 522 Cookman Ave. (Bangs Ave.) | 732-774-1264 |
www.brickwalltavern.com

"Catch up with friends and have a bite" at this Asbury Park "hangout" that attracts with "above-average" Americana (think mac 'n' cheese and chicken pot pie) and with its *"Cheers"*-like atmosphere, the latter bolstered by occasional live music.

Brioso *Italian*   23 | 18 | 17 | $37

Marlboro | Willow Pointe Shopping Ctr. | 184 Hwy. 9 (Union Hill Rd.) |
732-617-1700 | www.briosoristorante.com

Fans "love" this Marlboro BYO, and it's easy to see why on account of the "excellent" cooking that seems like what an "Italian grandma" would offer "for Sunday dinner"; alas, a noticeably "cold attitude" from the staff sends a chill through "commoners" ("if you're not a regular, you'll be ignored").

NEW Brio Tuscan Grille *Italian*   - | - | - | M

Cherry Hill | Town Place at Garden State | 901 Haddonfield Rd.
(Chapel Ave.) | 856-910-8166 | www.brioitalian.com

With plenty of brio at work (including its peppy staff), this upmarket Tuscan steakhouse chain hailing from Columbus, Ohio, has set up chop in Cherry Hill; besides meat, specialties include flatbreads grilled in the wood oven and Bellini brunches.

Brix 67 *Eclectic/Japanese*

| 18 | 20 | 16 | $41 |

Summit | 67 Union Pl. (Summit Ave.) | 908-273-4448 | www.brix-67.com

This "'in' place in Summit" attracts a "hip crowd" with its "trendy" milieu and an "extensive" Eclectic menu that ranges from "fresh sushi" to pastas to brick-oven pizzas – with "results that are just as eclectic" as the eats; the service can be "hit-or-miss" here, but the "cool", "clubby feel" keeps it "well-trafficked"; P.S. "they serve NJ wines", but you can also BYO.

Brooklyn's Coal-Burning Brick-Oven Pizzeria ⊅ *Pizza*

| 22 | 11 | 15 | $18 |

Edgewater | Edgewater Commons Shopping Ctr. | 443 River Rd. (Hudson River Rd.) | 201-945-9096
Hackensack | 161 Hackensack Ave. (Rte. 4) | 201-342-2727
Ridgewood | 15 Oak St. (Ridgewood Ave.) | 201-493-7600

"It ain't Brooklyn", but this "no-frills", "cash-only" Bergen County trio turns out some of the "best pies this side of the Hudson": "tasty, crispy", brick-oven rounds topped with "fresh mozzarella" and "flavorful sauce"; there are "no slices", but surveyors insist "you'll want the whole pie anyway"; P.S. "you can BYO" at the Edgewater and Ridgewood locations, but "Hackensack serves beer and wine."

Brothers Moon ⓜ *French*

| 22 | 18 | 20 | $41 |

Hopewell | 7 W. Broad St. (Greenwood Ave.) | 609-333-1330 | www.brothersmoon.com

"An oasis in charming Hopewell", this New French BYO "favorite" receives accolades for chef-owner Will Mooney's "always fresh and interesting menu" that "strives to incorporate local", seasonal and "organic" ingredients; though a few fret it's been "hit-or-miss recently", most focus on the "professional staff" and "comfortable ambiance"; N.B. there's an on-site retail and take-out shop.

Buddakan *Pan-Asian*

| - | - | - | E |

Atlantic City | Pier at Caesars | 1 Atlantic Ocean (Arkansas Ave.) | 609-674-0100 | www.buddakanac.com

The Pier at Caesars hosts version 3.0 of Stephen Starr's chic Pan-Asian, modeled loosely after his original in Philadelphia and the follow-up hit in NYC; eager servers whisk about with plates of dumplings and oversized drinks, and though the locale is nautical, the atmosphere here is dimly lit and anything but tranquil, despite the mammoth Buddha.

Busch's Seafood ⓜ *Seafood*

| 19 | 16 | 17 | $38 |

Sea Isle City | 8700 Landis Ave. (87th St.) | 609-263-8626 | www.buschsseafood.com

In the same family for 124 years, this durable, "old-school" Sea Isle City roadhouse is still "worth the trip for the she-crab soup alone", although the other "classic" fish fare comes up for praise too; crabs consider the seafood "fresher" than the "dark 'n' dingy" digs.

	FOOD	DECOR	SERVICE	COST

Buttonwood Manor · *American* ▽ 18 | 18 | 18 | $36

Matawan | 845 Rte. 34 (Edgewater Dr.) | 732-566-6220 |
www.buttonwoodmanor.net

Tablecloths and flowers complete the very Victorian setting at this
"stable" Matawan American dishing a "standard" "steak-and-
seafood"-oriented slate; there's a "great" view of Lake Lefferts, and
a scene that's mostly "senior citizen."

Cabin, The *American* 18 | 17 | 18 | $24

Howell | 984 Rte. 33 E. (Fairfield Rd.) | 732-462-3090 |
www.thecabinrestaurant.net

"Big" portions and "real" American food add up to "happy people"
at this "popular" Monmouth County "roadhouse" doling out "very
good" bar food amid "woodsy" quarters; the "pickup truck" vibe is
so authentic here, some dub the place "Howell, Alabama."

Cafe Arugula Ⓜ *Italian* 20 | 16 | 19 | $38

South Orange | 59 S. Orange Ave. (Scotland Rd.) | 973-378-9099 |
www.cafearugula.net

For "generous quantities" of "creative, consistent" Italian fare, head
to this "comfortable, cozy neighborhood" "standby" in South
Orange where the menu is topped off with an extensive list of
"nightly specials" and "wonderful" homemade gelato; though a few
feel this "bang-for-your-buck" BYO "needs a face-lift", most agree
it's a "reliable" "place to take the family."

Cafe at Rosemont, The Ⓜ *American* 22 | 18 | 22 | $32

Rosemont | 88 Kingwood-Stockton Rd. (Rte. 519) | 609-397-4097 |
www.cafeatrosemont.com

"Worth the scenic drive" to Rosemont, this "quaint country cafe" "in
an old general store" (circa 1865) offers "wonderful" New American
fare served by a "warm", "efficient" staff; although there's a "fantastic weekend brunch", your "best bet" is on Wednesday night, when
a three-course, $22 prix fixe menu "highlights a different [global]
cuisine each week"; P.S. "the BYO policy is a plus."

Café Azzurro *Italian* - | - | - | M

Peapack | 141 Main St. (bet. Todd & Willow Aves.) | 908-470-1470 |
www.cafeazzurroonline.com

There's rarely an empty table at this Peapack BYO Northern Italian –
no surprise, given the kitchen's fluency with standards (osso buco)
and creative signatures (veal with chopped shrimp and asparagus)
at reasonable prices; seating options include the comfortable,
white-tablecloth dining room and the seasonal patio.

Café Coloré Ⓜ *Italian* 21 | 18 | 21 | $32

Freehold Township | Chadwick Sq. | 3333 Rte. 9 N. (Jackson Mills Rd.) |
732-462-2233 | www.cafecolorefreehold.com

The strip mall is just part of the "disguise" of this Freehold Township
BYO, where you're bound to leave "well fed" on a variety of "quality"
Italian preparations offered by "friendly" servers; the "comfort-
able", "inviting" environs are even good for "dates."

	FOOD	DECOR	SERVICE	COST

Cafe Cucina ⑤ *Italian*
23 | **18** | **22** | **$39**

Branchburg | 3366 Rte. 22 W. (bet. County Line & Readington Rds.) | 908-526-4907 | www.cafecucina.com

Supping on "delicious" Italian fare on the dining room's balcony is a "romantic" touch at this "wonderful" Branchburg restaurant that's "a hit" "for special occasions, celebrations" or "executive lunches"; plus, the "fabulous food" and killer martinis are served by a "courteous" staff; N.B. weekend entertainment is in the offing.

Cafe Emilia *Italian*
22 | **21** | **22** | **$42**

Bridgewater | 705 Rte. 202 N. (Charlotte Dr.) | 908-429-1410 | www.cafeemilia.com

They turn out the "charm" at this Bridgewater Italian where clients "return" on account of the ambiance (you'll "feel like a part of their family") and "well-prepared" food; P.S. it's "the place to go" when you want to fill up "before a movie at Bridgewater Commons."

Café Gallery *Continental*
21 | **22** | **22** | **$38**

Burlington | 219 High St. (Pearl St.) | 609-386-6150 | www.cafegalleryburlington.com

"Peaceful" views of the Delaware River are just one factor in the "lovely" setting at this bi-level Burlington Continental, since the works of local art (displayed in the dining room and upstairs gallery) lend their own "charm"; while the food's "not mind-blowing", it's still "reliably" good, and most tout the "Sunday brunch as your best bet."

Cafe Graziella *Italian*
22 | **15** | **19** | **$31**

Hillsborough | Cost Cutters Shopping Ctr. | 390 Rte. 206 (Andria Ave.) | 908-281-0700 | www.cafegraziella.com

"Sshh . . . don't tell anyone" about this "solid" BYO Italian "surprise" that "doesn't look like much from the outside" (it's "hidden" in a Hillsborough strip mall) but offers "delicious", "dependable food" brought by "a personable staff"; "friendly owners" and a "nice atmosphere" "make for a relaxing evening."

Cafe Italiano *Italian*
18 | **16** | **18** | **$40**

Englewood Cliffs | 14 Sylvan Ave. (Irving Ave.) | 201-461-5041 | www.cafeitaliano.net

For "old-world style" and an "up-to-date" Italian menu, locals "just love" this "cheery" Englewood Cliffs cafe that's a "solid standby" for "decent food" ferried by an "amicable" staff; it now serves wine and liquor too (it's no longer BYO), which may "up the ante" pricewise, but doesn't diminish the value of the "great early-bird deal" and "relaxing" outside seating.

Cafe Loren Ⓜ *American*
▽ **25** | **20** | **26** | **$40**

Avalon | 2288 Dune Dr. (23rd St.) | 609-967-8228 | www.cafeloren.com

This seasonal BYO Avalon American, the doyenne of the local fine-dining scene for nearly 30 years, keeps turning out "first-class" fare accompanied by "attentive" service; once again, the only lament is that fans "wish it were open all year."

	FOOD	DECOR	SERVICE	COST

☑ Cafe Matisse *Eclectic*

| | 27 | 25 | 26 | $66 |

Rutherford | 167 Park Ave. (bet. E. Park Pl. & Highland Cross) | 201-935-2995 | www.cafematisse.com

This "artful find" in Rutherford is "as good as it gets" for "outstanding", "beautifully presented" Eclectic cuisine (with early-bird and prix fixe options) from "creative" chef-owner Peter Loria; though "pricey", this "special-occasion" experience comes complete with "superior service" and an "exceptional ambiance" that includes an "elegant dining room" with hand-blown glass chandeliers and "romantic" garden seating; P.S. it's BYO with a "lovely wine shop up front."

Cafe Metro *Eclectic*

| | 21 | 17 | 20 | $27 |

Denville | 60 Diamond Spring Rd. (bet. 1st Ave. & Orchard St.) | 973-625-1055 | www.thecafemetro.com

"Those looking to eat healthy" "have a range of options" at this veggie-centric Eclectic that's a "casual" stop for lunch or "a light meal" with its "interesting menu" of fish, chicken, pasta and "vegan choices too", all "appealingly presented" in a "cute converted house" in Denville; although it remains BYO in the dining room, the upstairs wine bar serves local vino along with small plates.

☑ Cafe Panache ☒ *Eclectic*

| | 28 | 21 | 26 | $55 |

Ramsey | 130 E. Main St. (Franklin Tpke.) | 201-934-0030 | www.cafepanachenj.com

"From the minute you walk in until you leave", expect a "quality dining experience" at chef-owner Kevin Kohler's "gift to the palate"; this "first-rate" "shining star" in Ramsey where an "always wonderful", "always changing" Eclectic menu is served by a "friendly", "knowledgeable" staff in a "charming" if "small" space; it's "expensive", but the BYO policy can "bring costs down"; P.S. be sure to make your reservation "well in advance."

Caffe Aldo Lamberti *Italian*

| | 23 | 21 | 22 | $41 |

Cherry Hill | 2011 Rte. 70 W. (Haddonfield Rd.) | 856-663-1747 | www.lambertis.com

At the "high end" of a prominent restaurant group (with outposts in Delaware and Pennsylvania), this "special-occasion" Cherry Hill Italian "never disappoints" its fans given the consistently "excellent" cuisine and service, and "very good" wine list; P.S. bring good credit – the tabs are "pricey."

California Grill *Eclectic*

| | 20 | 13 | 17 | $26 |

Flemington | Kitchen Expo Plaza | 1 Rte. 31 (US Hwy. 202) | 908-806-7141 | www.californiagrillnj.com

For "the biggest and best salads you've ever seen" "piled high" with "unique" ingredients plus "fabulous" soups, "thin-crust pizzas" and weekend breakfasts, hit this strip-mall Eclectic in Flemington that's a "surprisingly good", "veg-friendly" option for a BYO "lunch or dinner"; although a few find the staff "preoccupied" and the ambiance "a turnoff", most consider it to be a "healthy", "easy" stop after shopping the nearby outlets; N.B. also serves NJ wines.

	FOOD	DECOR	SERVICE	COST

Caneel Bay Caribbean Grill *Caribbean* ∇ 17 | 15 | 18 | $37
(aka CBCG's)
Harvey Cedars | 7601 Long Beach Blvd. (76th St.) | 609-361-6490 |
www.caneelbaycaribbeangrill.com
This north-end LBI Caribbean specialist in Harvey Cedars purveys
Island food that tastes "authentic" in "small", blue-and-green digs;
its fans want it to "stay around", but not before detractors cite cooking that "falls short of the mark."

Capriccio *Italian* 25 | 23 | 25 | $58
Atlantic City | Resorts Atlantic City Casino & Hotel | 1133 Boardwalk
(North Carolina Ave.) | 609-340-6789 | www.resortsac.com
"Splendid dining experiences" are not uncommon at this long-
running (since 1979) Italian in the Resorts Casino & Hotel whose
"elegant" decor pairs nicely with the "top-notch" menu; slot players
pronounce it's even "worth spending part of your jackpot here."

Capt'n Ed's Place *Seafood/Steak* 19 | 15 | 17 | $33
Point Pleasant | 1001 Arnold Ave. (Pine Bluff Ave.) | 732-892-4121 |
www.captainedsplace.com
"Sizzling" surf 'n' turf that you cook on "hot stones" is the hook (or
"gimmick") at this Point Pleasant BYO, the catalyst for "interesting"
conversations, especially if you're on a "first date"; in fact, some are
so focused on DIY cooking that they take the "friendly" staff for
granite; N.B. local wines are available.

Carmine's ● *Italian* 20 | 19 | 19 | $38
Atlantic City | The Quarter at the Tropicana | 2801 Pacific Ave.
(S. Iowa Ave.) | 609-572-9300 | www.carminesnyc.com
"Lotsa pasta" "busts" lotsa guts at this AC Italian in the Quarter (a
spin-off of the famed NYC eatery) where bringing "friends and families" is the only way to polish off the "red-sauce" specialties doled
out in "daunting" servings amid a "madhouse" of a setting.

Carmine's Asbury Park Ⓜ *Italian* - | - | - | M
Asbury Park | 162 Main St. (bet. Cookman & Lake Aves.) | 732-774-2222 |
www.carminesnj.com
Mangia in style at this Asbury Park Southern Italian serving moderately priced chef-owner signatures (e.g. bone-in veal parm) and
pizza from a wood-burning oven; the inviting digs – exposed-brick
walls, an open kitchen and a 100-year-old oak bar (sporting flat-
screen TVs) – are housed in a refurbished 19th-century building.

Casa Dante *Italian* 22 | 18 | 21 | $46
Jersey City | 737 Newark Ave. (bet. Kennedy Blvd. & Summit Ave.) |
201-795-2750 | www.casadante.com
Despite a 2005 ownership and menu change, this 35-plus-year-old
Jersey City "legend" still pulls down praise for "well-prepared"
Traditional Italian "served with care" by a "capable staff" in a
"friendly atmosphere"; though regulars are pleased it's been "given
a fresh look", those who feel it's "not what it used to be" urge management to "bring back the old menu."

	FOOD	DECOR	SERVICE	COST

Casa Giuseppe ⓜ *Italian* — 24 | 18 | 23 | $41

Iselin | 487 Rte. 27/Lincoln Hwy. (Oaktree Rd.) | 732-283-9111 |
www.casagiuseppe.com

A "surprise find" that "belies its location" among the offices of
Metropark, this Iselin Northern Italian is "a cut above" considering
its "varied menu", "friendly", "attentive service" and "homey atmosphere"; it's "a little pricey" "for the area", however, so keep it in
mind "for a business lunch" or "to celebrate a special occasion."

Casa Maya *Mexican* — 20 | 16 | 19 | $26

Meyersville | 615 Meyersville Rd. (Hickory Tavern Rd.) | 908-580-0799
High Bridge | 1 Main St. (W. Main St.) | 908-638-4032 ⓜ
www.casamayamexican.com

For "*delicioso*" Mexican, aficionados affirm these "charming,
kitschy" BYO cantinas are just the ticket for "abundant" portions of
"reasonably priced" Sonoran-style (i.e. mildly spiced) fare; although they "can get extremely crowded" (there are "no reservations"), "super-friendly" service atones for it.

Casa Solar ⓜ *Pan-Latin* — 25 | 19 | 16 | $40

Belmar | 1104 Main St. (bet. 11th & 12th Sts.) | 732-556-1144 |
www.casasolarbelmar.com

The kitchen sends out "memorable" meals at this "tightly
spaced" and frequently "busy" Pan-Latin Belmar BYO that's open
year-round; some stung by "slow service" and "excessive wait
times" for food advise you bring "lots of wine" to pass the time;
N.B. also closed Tuesdays.

Casa Vasca *Spanish* — 24 | 14 | 22 | $33

Newark | 141 Elm St. (Prospect St.) | 973-465-1350

This 31-year-old Ironbound institution is "always crowded for a
good reason": "huge portions" of "consistently delicious" Basque
cuisine that has an equally "big taste" and is served by a "friendly"
staff; it may have "tired decor" and "long waits" (even with reservations), but its "free parking lot" and convenient location near the NJ-
PAC make it a "favorite."

Casona ⓜ *Cuban* — 24 | 22 | 21 | $34

Collingswood | 563 Haddon Ave. (Knight Ave.) | 856-854-5555 |
www.mycasona.com

"Modernized" Cuban dishes are "well prepared" and the mojitos are
the "best" (bring rum) at this Collingswood BYO operating in an old
Victorian; while the "inviting" dining room attracts, some prefer to
"hold out for warm weather" to dine on the "great" wraparound porch.

Catelli *Italian* — 24 | 24 | 22 | $50

Voorhees | The Plaza | 1000 Main St. (bet. Evesham & Kresson Rds.) |
856-751-6069 | www.catellirestaurant.com

"Very good" meals are assured at this "elegant" Voorhees Italian, a
welcome "oasis in hoagieland" frequented by South Jersey pols and
other bigwigs; it's "special-occasion" central, evidenced by the
"expense"-account pricing (though "it's money well spent").

	FOOD	DECOR	SERVICE	COST

Cathay 22 *Chinese*
23 | **16** | **20** | **$33**

Springfield | 124 Rte. 22 W. (Hillside Ave.) | 973-467-8688 |
www.cathay22.com

"If you like spicy food, this place is for you" aver acolytes of this "terrific, upscale" Sichuan in Springfield, where the "stark interior should not deter you" from ordering one of the "authentic, delicious" dishes that are "nicely presented" and "elegantly served"; though "expensive", its "fully stocked bar" and "friendly faces" make this Asian "worth every penny."

Ⓩ Catherine Lombardi *Italian*
21 | **26** | **21** | **$54**

New Brunswick | 3 Livingston Ave. (George St.) | 732-296-9463 |
www.catherinelombardi.com

"What a beautiful place!" rave respondents about this dinner-only New Brunswick "upscale Italian" – complete with "glowing faux fireplaces [to] add to the ambiance" – from the group behind downstairs sibling Stage Left; it's named after co-owner Mark Pascal's grandmother, so expect "generous portions" of "yummy" dishes; those who find it "pricey" can "head for the bar" to sample from the 1,000-label wine list and "fantastic cocktail menu."

Cenzino Ⓢ *Italian*
24 | **21** | **25** | **$46**

Oakland | 589 Ramapo Valley Rd. (Franklin Ave.) | 201-337-6693 |
www.cenzinos.com

The "affable" "owner is there to greet you" at the door and his "extremely professional", "tuxedoed" staff will "see to every detail to make your evening enjoyable" at this classy Oakland Italian restaurant offering "consistent", "terrific" entrees and "creative, tasty specials"; pampered patrons should prepare for a "fabulous dining experience" that may be a "little pricey" but is "first-class" all the way.

Ⓩ Chakra *American*
21 | **27** | **18** | **$52**

Paramus | 144 W. Rte. 4 E. (Arcadian Way) | 201-556-1530 |
www.chakrarestaurant.com

"Let loose your inner om" at this "exotic" "oasis" within "the concrete jungle of Bergen County", an "upscale" New American "scene" where the "amazing atmosphere" ("romantic candles, pillows and drapes" plus a "cascading" water wall) "stimulates the senses as much as" the "fresh, unique" food; all in all, it's "out of this world", but expect the "loud" environs and "expensive" tabs to bring you back to earth.

Chand Palace *Indian*
22 | **12** | **18** | **$24**

Parsippany | 257 Littleton Rd. (Parsippany Rd.) | 973-334-5444
NEW **Piscataway** | 1296 Centennial Ave. (bet. Stelton Rd. &
Washington Ave.) | 732-465-1474 Ⓢ Ⓜ
www.chandpalace.com

If you like "tingling taste buds", you'll find "the spice is right" at these North and Central Jersey siblings where the "fresh, quality" Indian items include a "variety of vegetarian dishes" that ensure "you'll never miss the meat"; a "pleasant" staff and "wonderful lunch buffet" make them a "steal"; N.B. closed Tuesdays.

	FOOD	DECOR	SERVICE	COST

Chao Phaya *Thai* — 23 | 14 | 20 | $24

Somerset | Somerset Village Shopping Ctr. | 900 Easton Ave. (Foxwood Dr.) | 732-249-0110
Somerville | 9 Davenport St. (W. Main St.) | 908-231-0655
www.chaophaya.com

Although the decor is "casual" at these "no-frills Thais", the "delicious" food is "prepared with a touch of mystery" that proves "authentically hot" but can be adjusted "to your tolerance level for spice"; "BYO" and "quick and courteous" service are welcome pluses.

Charley's Ocean Grill *American* — 19 | 12 | 19 | $34

Long Branch | 29 Avenel Blvd. (Ocean Ave.) | 732-222-4499
This recently renovated Long Branch "hangout" is a "favorite" for those looking for a "quick bite", "good" American chow and a "great" value; hence, it's no surprise that the joint is "always crowded."

Charrito's *Mexican* — 24 | 18 | 18 | $25

Hoboken | 1024 Washington St. (bet. 10th & 11th Sts.) | 201-659-2800
Hoboken | 121 Washington St. (bet. 1st & 2nd Sts.) | 201-418-8600
Jersey City | 395 Central Ave. (bet. Bowers St. & Paterson Plank Rd.) | 201-963-4312
Union City | 4900 Bergenline Ave. (49th St.) | 201-863-0345
www.loscharritos.com

"They're tight, but the goods are worth every bite" is the word on these popular family-run BYO Mexicans, sources for "excellent" Oaxacan specialties including the "best" tableside guacamole and "accommodating" service; N.B. a fifth location with three floors and a liquor license is scheduled to open in Weehawken in summer 2008.

⦿ Chart House *American/Seafood* — 20 | 25 | 20 | $49

Weehawken | Lincoln Harbor | Pier D-T (Harbor Blvd.) | 201-348-6628 | www.chart-house.com

With its floor-to-ceiling windows, you can't ignore the "stunning" views of NYC that keep the "all-time-favorite" standing in tact of this roomy Weehawken American seafooder, the perfect ticket for guaranteed "romantic" dining; though it's given second-stage status, most consider the food "first-rate, especially for a chain."

⦿ Cheesecake Factory *American* — 19 | 19 | 17 | $28

Hackensack | Riverside Square Mall | 197 Riverside Sq. (Hackensack Ave.) | 201-488-0330 ☽
Wayne | Willowbrook Mall | 1700 Willowbrook Blvd. (Rte. 46) | 973-890-1400
Edison | Menlo Park Mall | 455 Menlo Park Dr. (Rte. 1) | 732-494-7000
Freehold | Freehold Raceway Mall | 3710 Rte. 9 S. (Raceway Mall Dr.) | 732-462-2872
Cherry Hill | Marketplace at Garden State Park | 931 Haddonfield Rd. (bet. Graham & Severn Aves.) | 856-665-7550
www.thecheesecakefactory.com

"There should be more of these places around" to feed the throngs marvel fans of these "overcrowded" Traditional American chain outlets famed for their "oversized" portions, "majestically" long menus and "dependably" good fare, not to mention "great" cheesecakes (with over 30 varieties); despite "crazy" waits, most leave these "cholesterol factories" "happy and well fed."

☑ Chef's Table Ⓜ *French*

| | 28 | 18 | 25 | $49 |

Franklin Lakes | Franklin Square Shopping Ctr. | 754 Franklin Ave. (Pulis Ave.) | 201-891-6644

Everything that comes out of the kitchen is *"extraordinaire"* at this "fabulous" Classic French BYO in Franklin Lakes (the bailiwick of "pro" chef Claude Baills), a "little jewel" shoehorned into a "dowdy" strip mall; the setting's warmed by "knowledgeable" service, and regulars advise to just "sit back and let it all enchant you."

Chef Vola's Ⓜ🚭 *Italian*

| | 26 | 10 | 23 | $49 |

Atlantic City | 111 S. Albion Pl. (Pacific Ave.) | 609-345-2022

Although you "take one look and stare in disbelief" at the decor, when the Italian "food comes out you'll understand" why this cash-only, 87-year-old Atlantic City BYO in a basement is a "cult" classic for so many admirers; true, it may not be the "best-kept secret it once was", but you still have to "know someone" to get a reservation.

Chengdu 46 Ⓜ *Chinese*

| | 24 | 18 | 21 | $42 |

Clifton | 1105 Rte. 46 E. (Rock Hill Rd.) | 973-777-8855 | www.chengdu46.com

This "consistent" Clifton performer makes for "memorable" Chinese meals presented by "attentive" servers within an "elegant" space that looks like it hasn't changed in years; for fine dining, this "tried-and-true" institution is still "worth getting dressed up for"; P.S. oenophiles appreciate the "great" wine list.

☑ Chez Catherine ⓈⓂ *French*

| | 27 | 21 | 25 | $64 |

Westfield | 431 North Ave. W. (bet. E. Broad & Prospect Sts.) | 908-654-4011 | www.chezcatherine.com

For a "top-drawer" experience, be sure to visit this "pretty" Provençal Westfield bistro where the French cuisine is "delectably" "expert", backed by "excellent" wines and "polished" service, all presided over by proprietors Didier and Edith Jouvenet; try to imagine a "slice of France" to shake off any thoughts about "steep prices"; N.B. the presence of a new chef may not be reflected in the above Food score.

Chez Elena Wu *Asian/French*

| | 24 | 19 | 22 | $33 |

Voorhees | Ritz Shopping Ctr. | 910 Haddonfield-Berlin Rd. (Voorhees Dr.) | 856-566-3222 | www.chezelenawu.com

"First-class" dining, namely "terrific", "beautiful" Asian-French cooking, "attentive", "eager-to-please" service and an upscale setting support the well-deserved popularity of this Voorhees BYO under the stewardship of the "gracious" Elena Wu and family; overall, it's a "great alternative" to the neighborhood's other eateries.

Chilangos Ⓜ *Mexican*

| | ▽ 21 | 16 | 19 | $24 |

Highlands | 272 Bay Ave. (Sea Drift Ave.) | 732-708-0505 | www.chilangosnj.com

The food "never fails" followers of this "cute" Highlands Mexican whose menu is priced "reasonably" and where the service is "pleasant"; the spot's stature is enhanced by the "best" selection of tequilas, with over 150 varieties to choose from.

China Palace *Taiwanese*

| - | - | - | I |

Middletown | Harmony Bowl | 1815 Rte. 35 (Old Country Rd.) | 732-957-0554

Tucked inside Harmony Bowl, this authentic Taiwanese specialist (known mostly to local Chinese residents) proffers hearty fare in modest digs; the homey plates warm purists' palates, as do the bargain checks.

Chophouse, The *Seafood/Steak*

| 23 | 22 | 21 | $54 |

Gibbsboro | 4 Lakeview Dr. S./Rte. 561 (E. Clementon Rd.) | 856-566-7300 | www.thechophouse.us

There's an ambiance that's pure "high-end" (read: mahogany, leather booths and white tablecloths) at this lively steakhouse in out-of-the-way Gibbsboro that "excels" at steak and seafood; from the sight of things, folks are having "fun", since the noise levels are high and the bar is "yuppie-pickup" paradise.

Chowpatty Ⓜ *Indian*

| - | - | - | I |

Iselin | Little India | 1349 Oak Tree Rd. (Marconi Ave.) | 732-283-9020 | www.chowpattyfoods.com

Serving a massive menu of Indian foods, including Gujarati selections along with items from the southern and northern parts of India, this Iselin BYO landmark is widely known for not only its fare but also for its catering and mail-order business; take-out fans can stop in the adjacent market, which vends sweets, snacks and the like.

Christie's Italian Seafood Grill *Italian*

| 24 | 18 | 20 | $37 |

Howell | Howell Ctr. | 2420 Rte. 9 S. (White Rd.) | 732-780-8310 | www.christiesrestaurant.us

The menu is "wonderful" and the setting "charms" at this strip-center Howell BYO made for those with "big appetites" who savor the "large" portions of "excellent" Italian dishes; "good" specials and "attentive" service are part of the package.

Christopher's Cafe Ⓜ *American*

| 21 | 13 | 16 | $26 |

Colts Neck | 41 Rte. 34 (Rte. 537) | 732-308-3668 | www.christopherscafe.com

For the "best breakfast around" diners are drawn to this Colts Neck American BYO that also offers "interesting" selections for lunch and dinner; the "cozy" setting counterbalances the occasionally "slow service."

Cinque Figlie Ⓢ *Italian*

| 21 | 19 | 21 | $46 |

Whippany | 302 Whippany Rd. (Park Ave.) | 973-560-0545 | www.fivedaughters.com

It's "not unusual" to have one of the owner's eponymous, "eager-to-please" *cinque figlie* (five daughters) serve you at this "charming", "family-operated" Whippany Italian where the "delicious" vittles are "carefully prepared" "in a "quaint restored house"; P.S. the bar/seating area is ideal to "grab a drink if you have to wait."

	FOOD	DECOR	SERVICE	COST

Circa *French*

▽ 20 | 21 | 20 | $46

High Bridge | 37 Main St. (McDonald St.) | 908-638-5560 |
www.circarestaurant.com

Bringing some "SoHo" (think Balthazar) to "small-town" High
Bridge, this "hit" of a French brasserie comes equipped with
pressed-tin ceiling, mirrors and banquettes to highlight the food,
along with wines and a "top-flight" raw bar; "who'd have thought"
this "favorite" would be in the neighborhood?; N.B. the presence of
a new chef may outdate the above Food score.

City Bistro *American*

19 | 19 | 19 | $34

Hoboken | 56-58 14th St. (bet. Hudson & Washington Sts.) |
201-963-8200 | www.citybistrohoboken.com

"Young" Hobokenites descend upon this "always-busy" split-level
New American brownstone for its "phenomenal" rooftop views of
NYC and equally phenomenal scene sparked by "great" drink specials; with all the "socializing" going on, it may be "hard to remember what you ate" – namely solidly "good" food – especially once the
venue morphs into a "meat market."

Clark's Landing *American*

17 | 19 | 17 | $35

Point Pleasant | 847 Arnold Ave. (bet. Lincoln & Trenton Aves.) |
732-899-1111 | www.clarksbarandgrill.com

"Watching the sunset" over the Manasquan River is what it's all
about for a "mature" crowd that convenes at this seasonal Point
Pleasant American with "great" bars inside and outside on the deck;
indeed, the "gorgeous" views help neutralize any negatives about
the "ok" vittles.

Claude's *French*

▽ 25 | 20 | 22 | $48

North Wildwood | 100 Olde New Jersey Ave. (1st Ave.) | 609-522-0400 |
www.claudesrestaurant.com

Gallic to its core, this warm-weather white-tablecloth BYO bistro offers an alternative to North Wildwood's bars in large part to a "very
good" French roster (bouillabaisse and the like); "quaint" decor
completes the *très français* picture.

Clydz ◑ *American*

23 | 19 | 21 | $42

New Brunswick | 55 Paterson St. (Spring St.) | 732-846-6521 |
www.clydz.com

Squeeze into the "so-crowded" quarters for the "longest" list of the
"best" martinis at this "dark" "speakeasy" of a New Brunswick New
American bar/eatery, where the "amazing" cocktail specialties
overshadow the "consistently good", "adventurous" kitchen; no
doubt, it's a "loud", sometimes "rowdy" scene, but the "fireplace in
the bar is a nice homey touch."

⊠ CoccoLa *American/Italian*

22 | 26 | 19 | $46

Hillsborough | 150 Rte. 206 S. (bet. Brooks Blvd. & Camplain Rd.) |
908-704-1160 | www.coccolarestaurant.com

You "won't feel like you're in Hillsborough" when you show up at this
roomy New American–Italian, whose "beautiful" "mod" decor (fea-

turing purple, semicircular banquettes and a raw bar) frames the "delicious" food paired with an eclectic list of wines (try to secure a table "near the open kitchen"); N.B. entertainment is offered every Friday night and on the first Thursday of each month.

Coconut Bay Asian Cuisine 🅼 *Asian* | 21 | 18 | 20 | $23 |

Voorhees | Echelon Village Plaza | 1120 White Horse Rd. (Berlin Rd.) | 856-783-8878 | www.coconutbayasiancuisine.com
Red hues and low lighting set an "exotic" mood at this Voorhees BYO whose Asian menu incorporates Chinese, Japanese and Thai influences and yields "dependably good" dishes; fans forget the strip-mall location once they notice "attentive" service and "inexpensive" tabs.

Columbia Inn 🅼 *Pizza* | 20 | 12 | 17 | $34 |

Montville | 29 Main Rd./Rte. 202 (Morris Ave.) | 973-263-1300 | www.thecolumbianinn.com
Although this Montville Italian does a "brisk business" with its "thin-crust" brick-oven pizzas, the "honest", "reliable" cooking extends to the other offerings that include "imaginative" daily specials; "bargain" bills ally with the food to help overcome "not-five-star" decor.

Conte's *Pizza* | - | - | - | I |

Princeton | 339 Witherspoon St. (Guyot Ave.) | 609-921-8041
In Princeton, pizza means this congenial Italian spot in the Downtown district where collegians and families convene over the thin-crust pies; though the menu ventures beyond 'zas, most look no further for a slice and a Coke.

Continental *American* | - | - | - | M |

Atlantic City | Pier at Caesars | 1 Atlantic Ocean (Arkansas Ave.) | 609-674-8300 | www.continentalac.com
With its menu of upscale comfort food (and seating areas including one modeled after a '60s-style coffee shop), Stephen Starr's swank diner adds a postmodernist twist to the Pier at Caesars; there's something pleasantly retro about digging into a big bowl of lobster-mashed potatoes amid all the glitz of Atlantic City.

Copeland Restaurant *American* | 25 | 25 | 23 | $58 |

Morristown | Westin Governor Morris | 2 Whippany Rd. (Lyndsey Dr.) | 973-451-2619 | www.copelandrestaurant.com
For "NY style in NJ", those in-the-know go to this "outstanding" New American tucked inside Morristown's Westin Governor Morris to "marvel" at "talented" chef Thomas Ciszak's "truly distinguished" fare delivered by an "attentive" staff in a "luxurious", "tiered" setting; although it's "pricey", it'll be "the best money you've spent in a while"; P.S. spot cocktail connoisseurs at the "sophisticated" martini bar.

Copper Canyon 🆉 *Southwestern* | 25 | 23 | 18 | $45 |

Atlantic Highlands | Blue Bay Inn | 51 First Ave. (bet. Center Ave. & Ocean Blvd.) | 732-291-8444 | www.thecoppercanyon.com
"Superlative" margaritas are crafted from the "enormous" (over 150 kinds) tequila list at this "hip" purveyor of "impressive" Southwestern

food in Atlantic Highlands featuring a "fun" bar scene; the place is stocked with "beautiful" people, some of whom don't seem too bothered by the "high noise levels" or occasionally "arrogant" service.

Copper Fish *American/Seafood* ▽ 20 | 19 | 19 | $40

Cape May | 1246 Rte. 109 S. (3rd Ave.) | 609-898-0354
Seafood turns up in eclectic ways at this "out-of-the-way" Cape May New American, where patrons can choose from a "good" selection of dishes and local wine list; the "snazzy" decor and "nice" staff also add appeal; N.B. open Thursdays–Sundays, with chef demos on Wednesday evenings.

Cork *American* 21 | 21 | 20 | $35

Westmont | 90 Haddon Ave. (bet. Cooper St. & Cuthbert Blvd.) | 856-833-9800 | www.corknj.com
"Urban sophistication" are the buzzwords on restaurateur Kevin Meeker's Westmont New American "lively" destination serving "well-prepared", "upscale" food; "inconsistent" service is all forgotten once you check out the happy hour and "fabulous" bar; N.B. the arrival of a new chef may outdate the above Food score.

Corky's Ribs & BBQ *BBQ* 16 | 12 | 17 | $25

Atlantic City | Mktpl. at the Tropicana Casino | 2831 Boardwalk (Brighton Ave.) | 609-345-4100 | www.corkysbbq.com
Some "Tennessee" turns up in the Tropicana with this Memphis-based rib chain dishing up "cheap, plentiful" 'cue; it's worth it when "you're hungry" or "with the guys", but foes find it a "tough sell", citing "unimpressive" chow and a setting that "could use some ambiance."

Corso 98 Ⓜ *Italian* 21 | 18 | 21 | $41

Montclair | 98 Walnut St. (Willow St.) | 973-746-0789 | www.corso98.com
"Off the beaten path" in Montclair, this dinner-only Italian "charmer" stays the course with its "inventive menu" of "delicious", "hearty fare served with gusto" by a "friendly, prompt" staff; its "warm, cozy decor" and BYO policy are just two more reasons admirers agree this "hideaway" "doesn't get the raves it deserves."

Country Pancake House ⊘ *American* 19 | 9 | 15 | $17

Ridgewood | 140 E. Ridgewood Ave. (Walnut St.) | 201-444-8395
For "pancakes the size of pizzas" in "every flavor imaginable", Ridgewood residents head to this "kid-friendly" "institution" that dishes out the "best breakfast in Bergen County" as well as "simple" American lunches and dinners; sure, the staff gets "frazzled" and there's a "long wait on weekends", but "it's worth it" – as long as you're "ready to be rolled out of the restaurant"; N.B. cash-only.

Court Street *Continental* 21 | 18 | 20 | $32

Hoboken | 61 Sixth St. (bet. Hudson & Washington Sts.) | 201-795-4515 | www.courtstreet.com
The cobblestone street nearby lends charm to this Hoboken "hideaway" serving "excellent" wines and "consistent" Continental cuisine that "satisfies any palate"; Casanovas consider it a "romantic"

retreat from the town's other offerings, and bargain-hunters tout the "great" early-bird.

Crab's Claw Inn, The Seafood
17 | 13 | 18 | $32

Lavallette | 601 Grand Central Ave. (President Ave.) | 732-793-4447 | www.thecrabsclaw.com

Claw through the summer crowds for some seafood at this "typical-Shore", Lavallette "fixture" whose goods attract locals and seasonals on the basis of "price and quantity"; the bar, along with "good" live entertainment, please too.

Crab Trap Seafood
21 | 16 | 19 | $34

Somers Point | 2 Broadway (Somers Point Circle) | 609-927-7377 | www.thecrabtrap.com

Offering "nostalgia" and an "old-fashioned" ambiance for its advocates, this Somers Point seafooder is a "landmark" on the Shore thanks to its "consistent, quality" fish dishes, "superb" views of the bay, "fun" bar and seven-days-a-week live music (summers); P.S. some sing the praises of the "value" early-bird.

Cranbury Inn American
17 | 19 | 19 | $33

Cranbury | 21 S. Main St. (Cranbury Station Rd.) | 609-655-5595 | www.thecranburyinn.com

A "fantastic" pre-Revolutionary ambiance, including an added-on high-ceilinged room seating 220, is the main attraction of this 250-plus-year-old Cranbury American; the food elicits little excitement, though, with surveyors citing "ok" if "boring" preparations.

Creole Cafe Ⓜ Cajun/Creole
▽ 27 | 20 | 23 | $31

Sewell | Harbor Pl. | 288 Egg Harbor Rd. (Huffville Grenloch Rd.) | 856-582-7222 | www.creole-cafe.com

Perhaps "South Jersey's best-kept secret", this "authentic" N'Awlins Sewell BYO prepares Cajun-Creole specialties, all of them "superb" and many of them featuring "to-die-for" sauces; in sum, it's a "favorite" in an "out-of-the-way" location that devotees are willing to trek to.

Crown Palace Chinese
22 | 20 | 19 | $28

Marlboro | 8 N. Main St. (School Rd.) | 732-780-8882
Middletown | 1283 Hwy. 35 (Kings Hwy.) | 732-615-9888

The "extremely popular" weekend dim sum is an "absolute hit" at this duo hosting "capacity crowds" that savor other Chinese offerings, including the "great buy" of a dinner prix fixe; in light of the "upscale" decor, acolytes appreciate that the settings come "without a take-out vibe."

Cuba Libre Cuban
21 | 24 | 19 | $41

Atlantic City | The Quarter at the Tropicana | 2801 Pacific Ave. (S. Iowa Ave.) | 609-348-6700 | www.cubalibrerestaurant.com

"Fabulous" decor meant to evoke 1940s Havana sets the "lively" tone at this casino-city spin-off of the Philly original, a "truly transporting" Cuban in the Quarter serving "good" fare and mojitos that'll make you "forget you're just steps away from losing large sums of cash"; N.B. night owls opt for the weekend late-night menu.

	FOOD	DECOR	SERVICE	COST

Cuban Pete's ● *Cuban* 17 | 21 | 14 | $29

Montclair | 428 Bloomfield Ave. (S. Fullerton Ave.) | 973-746-1100
Experience "a night in Old Havana" via this "packed" Montclair Cuban BYO serving a "modestly" priced menu in either a "fabulous" indoor setting or in the "beautiful" palm tree–lined patio; still, "inconsistent food" and "spacey service" are letdowns; N.B. bring wine to spike the sangrias.

Cubby's BBQ Restaurant *BBQ* 17 | 7 | 12 | $18

Hackensack | 249 S. River St. (bet. E. Kennedy & Water Sts.) | 201-488-9389 | www.cubbysbarbeque.com
"Bring your favorite carnivore" to this "no-frills" "cafeteria-style" Hackensack BBQ featuring a "patriotic owner" along with "generous" portions of "finger-lickin' good" 'cue (especially "tender 'n' tasty" ribs) that, for believers, is "right up there with the best."

☑ Cucharamama Ⓜ *S American* 26 | 23 | 20 | $43

Hoboken | 233 Clinton St. (3rd St.) | 201-420-1700 | www.cucharamama.com
"Unique", "extraordinary" South American fare, a "beautiful" setting to match and "fantastic" drinks add up to "the best of what Hoboken has to offer", celeb-chef Maricel Presilla's venue situated a block away from its counterpart, Zafra; insiders tout bar dining, which offers a perfect vantage point to "watch food being prepared in the wood-burning oven"; N.B. open for Sunday brunch.

Cucina Rosa *Italian* 23 | 18 | 21 | $33

Cape May | Washington Street Mall | 301 Washington St. (bet. Jackson & Perry Sts.) | 609-898-9800 | www.cucinarosa.com
A "family-friendly" vibe and "bargain" pricing drives fans to this seasonal Cape May Italian also recommended for its "very good" cooking and "people-watching", the latter thanks to its "convenient" location in a mall; N.B. though BYO, NJ wines are available.

☑ CulinAriane ⓏⓂ *American* 27 | 18 | 22 | $50

Montclair | 33 Walnut St. (Pine St.) | 973-744-0533 | www.culinariane.com
It's "foodie heaven" at this modern New American BYO, a boon to Montclair's dining scene thanks to the "stellar", "adventurous" cooking of husband-and-wife-team Michael and Ariane Duarte (pastry chef and executive chef, respectively), both ably backed by a "pleasant" staff; though it's hard to ignore the "tiny size and no waiting area", sidewalk seating almost doubles the capacity; N.B. also closed Tuesdays.

Cup Joint Ⓜ *American* ▽ 20 | 12 | 25 | $17

Hoboken | 732 Jefferson St. (8th St.) | 201-222-2660 | www.thecupjoint.com
"Comforting, aim-to-please" service and "simple, but delicious" chow (think "amazing" breakfasts) are what keep this "friendly" Hoboken coffee shop/diner joint popular; correspondents concur "cheap" tabs are what's great here, though the "life-altering" pretzel bread may not be far behind.

	FOOD	DECOR	SERVICE	COST

DabbaWalla Ⓜ *Indian*
`19` `19` `18` `$33`

Summit | 427 Springfield Ave. (Summit Ave.) | 908-918-0330 | www.dabbawalla.com

A "funky" design and "interesting concept" define this new Summit Indian, whose name (which means 'lunch box man') describes the premise: the fare is served in lunch boxes in a communal seating arrangement (this may change in the future); food disputes aside ("flavorful" vs. "bland"), fans applaud it as an "alternative to the usual."

daddy O *American*
`18` `20` `17` `$46`

Long Beach Township | daddy O | 4401 Long Beach Blvd. (44th St.) | 609-494-1300 | www.daddyorestaurant.com

"Dress to be seen" at this "sharp-looking", retro Long Beach New American (in the eponymous boutique hotel) bringing "a little NYC to LBI" while drawing "hip" patrons; the "average" eats seem secondary to the main show here, namely the "fun" bar scene.

da Filippo Autentica
`24` `17` `23` `$40`
Cucina Italiana Ⓢ *Italian/Seafood*

Somerville | 132 E. Main St. (Meadow St.) | 908-218-0110 | www.dafilippos.com

The background "piano" music gets a lot of attention at "wonderful" chef-owner Filippo Russo's "convivial" Somerville BYO, but the real show may be the food, in this case "superb", "authentic" Italian-style seafood; what's more, the staff seems to treat everyone "like a long-lost relative."

Dai-Kichi *Japanese*
`22` `14` `20` `$28`

Upper Montclair | 608 Valley Rd. (Bellevue Ave.) | 973-744-2954

Surveyors are hooked on this "neighborhood" sushi bar in Upper Montclair; the BYO's "basic" digs take a back seat to the "consistently fresh", "quality" (and "reasonably" priced) fish served by a "wonderful" staff.

NEW D & L Barbecue *BBQ/Southern*
`-` `-` `-` `I`

Asbury Park | 1206 Main St. (bet. 4th & 5th Aves.) | 732-722-7488 | www.dlbbq.com

This low-key, off-the-beaten-path Asbury Park BYO newcomer dishes up low-cost traditional Southern grub (fruit wood-smoked ribs, fried catfish) in cozy, warm-hued surroundings; the welcoming staff and daily specials are the brandied syrup on the bread pudding.

Danny's Steakhouse & Sushi Bar *Steak*
`-` `-` `-` `M`

Red Bank | 11 S. Bridge Ave. (bet. Front & Monmouth Sts.) | 732-741-6900 | www.dannyssteakhouse.com

It's all about the scene at this 41-year-old steakhouse institution in Red Bank, where the victuals – dry-aged beef, seafood, sushi – are almost beside the point; locals looking to schmooze at the bar can also retire to the minimalist dining room for a laid-back, midpriced meal, all overseen by owner Danny Murphy; N.B. in season, the French doors open to outside seating.

	FOOD	DECOR	SERVICE	COST

Dante's Ristorante *Italian* | 21 | 17 | 21 | $36 |

Mendham | 100 E. Main St. (Cold Hill Rd.) | 973-543-5401 |
www.dantanj.com

"Attentive" service, "excellent" pizzas and "substantial" portions of
"good" homestyle cooking sit well with "families" at this Mendham
Italian BYO standby; devotees tout takeout as your best option, especially when the conditions start to look "a little overcrowded."

NEW Daryl Wine Bar *American* | - | - | - | E |

New Brunswick | 302 George St. (New St.) | 732-253-7780 |
www.darylwinebar.com

Contemporary New American cuisine and creative concept converge
at celebrity chef David Drake's (Restaurant David Drake, Rahway) distinctive addition to the New Brunswick dining scene, where dishes like
apple lasagna come on small or large plates (mix 'n' match, share – or
eat it all by yourself) to pair with wine or beer; the digs are fine-dining-
chic, with striking high-back chairs, chandeliers and couches by the
bar and while it'll cost you, high style doesn't come cheaply; N.B. a
late-night menu is served 10 PM–1 AM Fridays–Saturdays.

Z David Burke Fromagerie M *American* | 26 | 25 | 24 | $67 |

Rumson | 26 Ridge Rd. (Ave. of Two Rivers) | 732-842-8088 |
www.fromagerierestaurant.com

Culinary icon David Burke (of NYC renown) has "ratcheted things
up" at this "great reincarnation" of a Rumson landmark that sports
updated decor and, more importantly, "exciting", "unique presentations" of New American fare (like cheesecake lollipops) on which
the toque's fame rests; "attentive" service rounds out an experience
at "one of New Jersey's finest" – and priciest – restaurants.

Z David Drake, Restaurant *American* | 27 | 24 | 26 | $66 |

Rahway | 1449 Irving St. (Cherry St.) | 732-388-6677 |
www.daviddrakes.com

A bona fide "destination for gourmets", David Drake's eponymous
Rahway New American townhouse eatery is a "brilliant" "symphony of
food, decor and service", with "fantastic" $58 three-course prix fixe
meals and tasting menus ("order anything and be satisfied") and
"attentive" servers who maneuver through "intimate", "jewel"-like
rooms; yes, it's "very expensive", but that's the price of "perfection."

Dayi'nin Yeri *Turkish* | - | - | - | I |

Cliffside Park | 333 Palisade Ave. (Cliff St.) | 201-840-1770 |
www.dayininyeri.com

Turkish pizza might not be common in NJ, but it is at this Cliffside Park
BYO where the toppings (feta, lamb, spinach) give away the cuisine,
served in a modest but appealing space.

De Anna's M *Italian* | - | - | - | M |

Lambertville | 54 N. Franklin St. (bet. Church & Coryell Sts.) |
609-397-8957 | www.deannasrestaurant.com

Lambertville locals looking for midpriced, homestyle Italian turn to this
warm, trendy trattoria for handmade pastas (ravioli), entrees

(Sicilian-style meatloaf) and desserts (ricotta cheesecake); there's also live music Thursdays–Fridays and a patio; N.B. dinner only, Tuesdays–Saturdays, with a $30 prix fixe, Tuesdays–Wednesdays.

☑ DeLorenzo's Tomato Pies Ⓜ *Pizza* | 28 | 8 | 17 | $14 |

NEW **Robbinsville** | Washington Town Ctr. | 2350 Rte. 33 (Commerce Sq.) | 609-341-8480
Trenton | 530 Hudson St. (bet. Mott & Swann Sts.) | 609-695-9534 ⊐ www.delorenzostomatopies.com

"No salads, no appetizers, no ambiance", just "amazingly delicious" pizzas are served at this always-crowded state "classic" in Trenton, the "best of the best", where "house rules" are to be obeyed; all agree it's "worth the hype", "waits" and discomfort – there are no bathrooms, "so plan accordingly"; N.B. the new, upscale Robbinsville branch that opened post-Survey has waiters in ties, antipasti – and two restrooms.

Delta's Ⓜ *Southern* | 22 | 22 | 20 | $36 |

New Brunswick | 19 Dennis St. (bet. Hiram Sq. & Richmond St.) | 732-249-1551 | www.deltasrestaurant.com

"When you want to clog your arteries, Southern-style", this "busy" New Brunswick soul fooder has "all the fat and sass you need"; a "party atmosphere" prevails since there's a "great" bar scene, Saturday-night jazz and "loungey" decor; N.B. there's valet parking (at an extra cost).

Dim Sum Dynasty *Chinese* | 21 | 18 | 19 | $26 |

Ridgewood | 75 Franklin Ave. (Oak St.) | 201-652-0686 | www.dimsumdynastynj.com

"Excellence in dim sum" should be awarded to this Ridgewood BYO, which some say is the "best Chinese for miles around" and is "raising the bar" with "consistently good" cooking and service; in contrast to the regal, gold-toned setting, prices here are relatively "inexpensive."

Dish Ⓜ *American* | 22 | 15 | 18 | $39 |

Red Bank | 13 White St. (Broad St.) | 732-345-7070 | www.dishredbank.com

"Well-prepared" New Americana served in a "small" space with "pleasant" if "minimal" decor is the dish on this "cozy" Red Bank BYO; the "hospitable" staff adds to the "no-pretense" ambiance.

NEW Divino *Italian* | – | – | – | E |
(fka Domaine Laurino)

Berkeley Heights | 538 Springfield Ave. (bet. Plainfield & Sherman Aves.) | 908-898-1444 | www.divino538.com

The ownership hasn't changed at this pricey Berkeley Heights Italian, but the name (formerly Domaine Laurino) and concept (unfussy dishes) have; a selection of scotches and wines also appeal.

NEW Dockhoppers | – | – | – | M |
Seafood House Ⓜ *Seafood*

Collingswood | 124 Haddon Ave. (E. Crescent Blvd.) | 856-869-4600 | www.pjwrestaurantgroup.com

There's nothing fancy going on at this South Jersey seafooder – just fried fish, fries, housemade chowder and a simple raw bar;

its charmingly retro 1950s setting fits right into the old-time Haddon Avenue strip.

Dock's Oyster House *Seafood*   26 | 20 | 23 | $49

Atlantic City | 2405 Atlantic Ave. (Georgia Ave.) | 609-345-0092 | www.docksoysterhouse.com

Since 1897, this "venerable" Atlantic City seafood house has been a picture of "consistency", still turning out "fantastic" fare from its "impeccably fresh" fish that includes the "best" oysters, all in a "wonderful", wood-filled room; P.S. the extensive selection at the raw bar is "everything you could ask for."

Don Pepe *Portuguese/Spanish*   21 | 15 | 19 | $37

Newark | 844 McCarter Hwy. (Raymond Blvd.) | 973-623-4662 | www.donpepeii.com
Pine Brook | 18 Old Bloomfield Ave. (Changebridge Rd.) | 973-882-6757 | www.donpeperestaurant.com

"Overeating is easy" at these "busy" Iberians where "abundant" amounts of garlicky surf 'n' turf specialties and "amazing" sangria are delivered by "friendly", "quick servers"; if the "tired" settings need pepping up, "reasonable" prices – especially in light of the quantity – present an offer you "can't refuse."

Don Pepe's Steakhouse *Steak*   22 | 17 | 20 | $42

Pine Brook | 58 Rte. 46 W. (Old Bloomfield Ave.) | 973-808-5533 | www.donpepesteakhouse.com

"Serious meat eaters" (and lobster lovers) don't mind the "absence of decor" at this Pine Brook chophouse (an offshoot of the Newark original) where mammoth steaks, colossal crustaceans and "fantastic" sangria take center stage; "friendly" service and "fair" prices come with the turf.

Doo Rae Myun Ok *Korean*   ▽ 21 | 12 | 17 | $23

Fort Lee | 166 Main St. (Palisade Ave.) | 201-346-1331

Check out this Korean BYO, one of Fort Lee's "gems" that vends "spicy", "satisfying" delights backed by "reliable" service; proponents pick it as their "favorite", and it doesn't hurt that it's an "excellent" value.

Doris & Ed's Ⓜ *American/Seafood*   25 | 19 | 22 | $58

Highlands | 348 Shore Dr. (bet. King & Matthews Sts.) | 732-872-1565 | www.dorisandeds.com

"Every which way but plain" describes the "delightful" seafood and American menus (one traditional, the other more modern) that turn up in this "civilized" Highlands venue with a "well-deserved reputation" that also includes a "marvelous" wine list; N.B. the recently spruced-up interior may outdate the above Decor score.

NEW Dream Cuisine Café Ⓜ *French*   – | – | – | M

Cherry Hill | Village Walk Shopping Ctr. | 1990 Rte. 70 E. (Old Orchard Rd.) | 856-751-2800 | www.dreamcuisinecafe.net

This simple Modern French BYO, reminiscent of a European cafe, is the vision of Vincent Fanari (chef at Philly's The Plough & the Stars);

the menu, based on dishes from his native Nice, is a nice departure from Cherry Hill's usual New American or Italian bents.

Drew's Bayshore Bistro Ⓜ *American* ▽ 28 | 16 | 24 | $34

Keyport | 58 Broad St. (W. Front St.) | 732-739-9219 | www.bayshorebistro.com

Cajun-Creole influences inform the "original", "excellent" New American cuisine at this "quaint" BYO a few blocks off Keyport's waterfront; the "loveliest" staff supplements the "friendly" ambiance while keeping up with the "increasing number of clientele."

🆕 Due Terre Enoteca *Italian* - | - | - | E

Bernardsville | 107 Morristown Rd. (Finley Ave.) | 908-221-0040 | www.dueterre.com

Impeccable credentials (namely consulting chef and partner Michael White, who's now leading the kitchens of NYC's Alto and L'Impero, and executive chef Bill Dorrler (ex Ciao in Basking Ridge), are behind this upscale Bernardsville enterprise serving a modern Italian menu and wines covering various price points; leather chairs and Craftsman touches are part of the decor's luxe profile.

Dune Restaurant *Seafood* - | - | - | M

Margate | 9510 Ventnor Ave. (bet. Jefferson & Madison Aves.) | 609-487-7450 | www.dunerestaurant.com

Foodies jam this Margate storefront BYO American seafooder with a cheery, shabby-chic Key West feel for the chef's whimsical, adventurous, what-will-it-be-this-week? midpriced menu; count on items like walu (aka butterfish), dorade, hamachi or mussels and fries in a champagne broth – if you're baffled by the unusual options, that's part of the adventure.

E & V Ⓜ⇗ *Italian* 24 | 11 | 21 | $32

Paterson | 320 Chamberlain Ave. (bet. Preakness & Redwood Aves.) | 973-942-8080 | www.evrestaurant.com

"Down-home" "red-sauce" Italiana keeps fans flocking to this Paterson establishment, where the decor "doesn't impress" but the "delicious", "on-the-money" cooking does; the seating is "cramped" and the "lines long", but "it's worth the wait" since "huge" portions mean you "eat for days on leftovers."

East *Japanese* 18 | 14 | 15 | $27

Teaneck | 1405 Teaneck Rd. (bet. Rte. 4 & Tryon Ave.) | 201-837-1260

"Pick your pieces" from the "varied" selection traveling via "conveyor belt" at this "busy" Teaneck Japanese sushi house catering to fans of all ages; though "not five star" and perhaps "unremarkable", the fish still "satisfies", especially when you consider the "bang for the buck"; P.S. some say it "could use a makeover."

⧉ Ebbitt Room *American* 27 | 24 | 26 | $60

Cape May | Virginia Hotel | 25 Jackson St. (bet. Beach Dr. & Carpenter Ln.) | 609-884-5700 | www.virginiahotel.com

"Elegant, refined" atmosphere syncs up nicely with the "wonderful" food at this "romantic" Cape May New American (which resides in the Virginia Hotel), the epitome of "gourmet dining at its finest" thanks in no small part to the "great" service; a "charming" nightly jazz trio caps the "beautiful", "classy" scene.

Eccola Italian Bistro *Italian*   23 | 18 | 19 | $39

Parsippany | 1082 Rte. 46 W. (N. Beverwyck Rd.) | 973-334-8211 | www.eccolarestaurant.com

"The vibe is electric" (as in, the setting is "loud") at this "established" Parsippany strip-mall Italian dealing in "delicious" dishes (including "wonderful" specials for lunch and dinner), many from the wood-burning oven; N.B. reservations are accepted for lunch and for five or more for dinner.

Echo ⊠ *Eclectic*   ▽ 19 | 18 | 18 | $35

Red Bank | 79 Monmouth St. (Maple Ave.) | 732-747-8050 | www.echo-redbank.com

"More watering hole than restaurant", this dimly lit Red Bank venue features crowds that congregate over drinks at the bar, where "ogling is sport"; the "ok" Eclectic small plates don't provide much of a match for the "hipster"-central scene – but the new weekend entertainment should.

Edo Sushi *Chinese/Japanese*   20 | 11 | 17 | $27

Pennington | Pennington Shopping Ctr. | 25 Rte. 31 S. (bet. Delaware & Franklin Aves.) | 609-737-1190

"Somehow, it works" say supporters of this Pennington Chinese-Japanese strip-mall BYO proffering a combination of "good" sushi and "pretty good Chinese"; it's "friendly" and "familial", though the setting doesn't score when it comes to decor.

Egan & Sons *Irish*   17 | 20 | 18 | $28

Montclair | 118 Walnut St. (Forest St.) | 973-744-1413 | www.eganandsons.com

For a "bit of Dublin in New Jersey", try this "congenial" consistently "crowded" Montclair Irish restaurant/brewery specializing in "comforting" gastropub fare that's usually very "solid"; furnishings and artwork from the mother country complete the vibe, as does the "off-the-charts noise levels" (which may have abated since a recent expansion); N.B. a pricier, adjacent relation is planned for summer 2008.

El Azteca *Mexican*   17 | 9 | 16 | $18

Mount Laurel | Ramblewood Shopping Ctr. | 1155 Rte. 73 N. (Church Rd.) | 856-914-9302

You'll find "straightforward" Mexican at this hard-to-top Mount Laurel BYO cantina, serving "overflowing" helpings of "heavy-on-the-cheese" *comidas*; the decor isn't much but the eats are "cheap."

El Cid *Spanish*   21 | 15 | 19 | $41

Paramus | 205 Paramus Rd. (bet. Century Rd. & Rte. 4 W.) | 201-843-0123

Be prepared to "loosen your belt a notch" at this Paramus Iberian, "home of the dinosaur prime rib" and other "obscenely large portions" of "good" Spanish surf 'n' turf; though some respondents give fewer *olé*'s for the "run-down" digs, most don't seem to mind.

Elements Asia *Pan-Asian*

23 | 20 | 19 | $28

Lawrenceville | Village Commons | 4110 Quakerbridge Rd. (Village Rd.) | 609-275-4988 | www.elementsasia.com

"Inspired" fusion that's "beautifully presented" is what pleased partisans prefer about this strip-mall Lawrenceville BYO Pan-Asian also prized for its "on-point", "accommodating" service; all seem elementally enthralled with a dining room that's "photo-shoot" "lovely."

Elements Café 🛒 Ⓜ *American*

21 | 15 | 19 | $35

Haddon Heights | 517 Station Ave. (White Horse Pike) | 856-546-8840 | www.elementscafe.com

"Tantalizing" tapas is just the element needed to draw diners to this Haddon Heights New American BYO "proffering" an "assortment" of small plates that quickly add up to "satisfying" meals; overall, regulars recommend this "unique" experience.

Elephant & Castle ● *Pub Food*

10 | 11 | 12 | $24

Cherry Hill | Clarion Hotel | 1450 Rte. 70 E. (I-295) | 856-427-0427 | www.elephantcastle.com

"Think London 1972 and the rest will make sense" at these Philly and Jersey links in a "faux" "English Empire"–themed chain; charitable blokes find the fish 'n' chips "acceptable" and the beer list "large", but many are "unimpressed" with "stale" decor, "spotty" service and "mediocre" grub ("don't just send it back to the kitchen, send it back to England!"); N.B. the addition of weekend comedy shows might spice things up.

El Familiar *Colombian/Mexican*

- | - | - | M

Freehold | 3 W. Main St. (Court St.) | 732-303-9400 🛒 Ⓜ
Toms River Township | Stella Towne Ctr. | 1246 Rte. 166 (Hilltop Rd.) | 732-240-6613
www.jerseyshorefood.com

Colombian cooking pairs up with Mexican specialties at these separately owned, South Jersey BYOs, uncommon alternatives to the area's familiar eateries; the modest decor is handily offset by the interesting – and modestly priced – homestyle fare; N.B. the new Freehold locale offers breakfast in addition to lunch and dinner.

ⓩ El Meson Cafe *Mexican*

24 | 14 | 20 | $23

Freehold | 40 W. Main St. (Court St.) | 732-308-9494

"As close to south of the border" as it gets in Central Jersey, this BYO dishes out "huge" portions of the "very best" Mexican that ultimately "generates crowds"; "friendly" service and "attractive" prices are pluses, as is the attached market that's perfect for bodega browsing.

Elysian Cafe *French*

21 | 22 | 20 | $33

Hoboken | 1001 Washington St. (10th St.) | 201-798-5898 | www.elysiancafe.com

All the neighborhood seems to turn up for the "good" food and the "great" bar at this "lovingly restored" and "beautifully detailed" Hoboken French bistro (owned by the proprietors of Amanda's);

P.S. as far as "people-watching", insiders know all about the patio, considered the "best in town."

NEW Embers Wood Fired Grill *American* | – | – | – | M |

Cherry Hill | Crowne Plaza Cherry Hill | 2349 W. Marlton Pike (Cuthbert Blvd.) | 856-665-6666 | www.cherryhillcrowne.com

The look is all cherry wood and fieldstone at the Crowne Plaza Cherry Hill's main dining room, a New American specializing in moderately priced meat and fish prepared on a wood-fired grill; everything on the wine list (which has some interesting choices) is available by the glass – and can also be enjoyed in the cocktail lounge.

Epernay M *French* | 21 | 18 | 18 | $41 |

Montclair | 6 Park St. (Bloomfield Ave.) | 973-783-0447 | www.epernaynj.com

Montclair's Gallic-loving gourmands say *oui* to this "traditional" bi-level BYO French bistro proffering "plentiful" portions of "fabulous" steak frites and assorted "standout" "comfort" foods; the jury's still out on service ("brusque" vs. "friendly"), but most avow it's worth your time if just to "feel transported" to the Left Bank.

Eppes Essen *Deli* | 18 | 9 | 12 | $21 |

Livingston | 105 E. Mt. Pleasant Ave. (S. Livingston Ave.) | 973-994-1120 | www.eppesessen.com

"What's not to like?" at this classic (51 years and counting) Livingston kosher-style deli serving "freakishly huge", "top-quality" corned beef and pastrami sandwiches; it's true, the place may "not be pretty", but overall, the current management has "vastly improved this old standby."

NEW Equus *American* | – | – | – | VE |

Bernardsville | 1 Mill St. (Anderson Rd.) | 908-766-3737 | www.equustavern.com

The local gentry meets at this bi-level, Bernardsville New American newcomer, an atmosphere-laden renovation of the 19th-century Stone Tavern landmark; the food (including aged steaks) and drinks (best enjoyed in the stunning bar) are added draws at this pricey hot spot; N.B. some may find the outdoor terrace a more tranquil option during prime time.

Espo's Ø *Italian* | 21 | 9 | 18 | $24 |

Raritan | 10 Second St. (bet. Anderson & Thompson Sts.) | 908-685-9552

"Thriving for decades", this Raritan "diamond-in-the-rough" is known for "huge" portions (expect "doggy bags") of "great", "rib-stickin'" red-sauce Southern Italian brought to the table by a "friendly" staff; as for the "basic" bar decor, that's "part of the charm" too.

Esty Street 🗷 *American* | 23 | 18 | 21 | $51 |

Park Ridge | 86 Spring Valley Rd. (Fremont Ave.) | 201-307-1515 | www.estystreet.com

"Dining with family and friends" is a joy at this "pricey" Park Ridge New American that is also known to be "great for business lunches";

a "prompt" staff and a "good" all-American wine list place it a "cut above"; N.B. the Decor score may not reflect a recent redo.

Eurasian Eatery ⓜ *Eclectic*
20	11	20	$21

Red Bank | 110 Monmouth St. (bet. Maple Ave. & Pearl St.) | 732-741-7071 | www.eurasianeatery.com

The "variety" is as large as the portions served at this BYO opposite Red Bank's Count Basie Theater; while the "not-much-atmosphere" decor may not please everyone, most applaud the "different", "well-prepared" Eclectic eats offered at a "low cost."

Europa at Monroe ⓜ *Mediterranean*
–	–	–	E

Monroe Township | 146 Applegarth Rd. (Old Church Rd.) | 609-490-9500 | www.europanj.com

Channeling Italy and Spain through its cuisine, this Monroe Med turns out pastas, paellas and other local fare, along with a separate slate of tapas, the latter enjoyed at the bar; within the main dining room is a stone fireplace and wine display, both ably underscoring the inviting ambiance.

Europa South ⓜ *Portuguese/Spanish*
20	15	19	$38

Point Pleasant Beach | 521 Arnold Ave. (Rte. 35 S.) | 732-295-1500 | www.europasouth.com

One helping can "feed two" at this Point Pleasant Beach outpost specializing in "authentic" Portuguese and Spanish cooking backed by "energetic" waiters; though it's "been around a long time" – and it shows in the "drab" decor – the deal for devotees is that the goods served here are "reliable."

ⓩ Far East Taste *Chinese/Thai*
26	7	22	$21

Eatontown | 19 Main St. (Broad St.) | 732-389-9866

"Masterpieces" are turned out at this Eatontown Chinese-Thai BYO helmed by Frank Qui (nephew of retired top toque Richard Wang), who inherited a knack for cooking "fantastic" fish dishes; sure, it "defines hole-in-the-wall", but the decor is easy to overlook considering the quality – and low prices – offered here.

Farnsworth House, The *Continental*
21	16	19	$36

Bordentown | 135 Farnsworth Ave. (Railroad Ave.) | 609-291-9232 | www.thefarnsworthhouse.com

Perfectly "suited to romantic evenings" given its "charming", "historic" (circa 1682) house setting, this Bordentown Continental delights diners with "surprisingly good" preparations; casual comers endorse the downstairs bar dining, while others opt for upstairs, which provides more of a "treat" for the eyes.

ⓩ Fascino Ⓢ *Italian*
26	21	24	$52

Montclair | 331 Bloomfield Ave. (bet. Grove & Willow Sts.) | 973-233-0350 | www.fascinorestaurant.com

"Fascinating" and "fantastic" are some of the superlatives used to describe this BYO "star" in Montclair, the home of the "incredible" DePersio family, and to the "superb" modern Italian cuisine of chef Ryan (and of "mom" Cynthia's "amazing" desserts); to get into the "place that has it all", fans are deterred by neither the "tough reservation" nor "pricey" tabs.

Federici's ⊄ *Pizza*

21 | 10 | 18 | $22

Freehold | 14 E. Main St. (South St.) | 732-462-1312 | www.federicis.com

"What would we do without the Fed's?" wonder groupies of this 87-year-old Italian stronghold in "Boss-loving" Freehold, a "staple" for "terrific" thin-crust pizza; pros point out it's best to stick with the pies and avoid the rest of the "so-so", "serviceable" menu.

Fedora Cafe Ⓜ *Eclectic*

19 | 19 | 16 | $19

Lawrenceville | 2633 Main St. (bet. Craven Ln. & Phillips Ave.) | 609-895-0844

The setting seems lifted from an "episode of *Friends*" say followers attracted to this "quirky", "funky" Lawrenceville BYO hosting "trendy young" patrons who sit on "comfy couches" to sip coffee or nosh on "comforting" Eclectic vittles; "spacey" service completes the "relaxed" scene.

ⓏFernandes Steakhouse II *Steak*

26 | 20 | 24 | $34

Newark | 152-158 Fleming Ave. (Chapel St.) | 973-589-4099 | www.fernandessteakhouse.com

Be sure to "take a double dose of your cholesterol" meds before you load up on the "enormous" portions of "terrific", "melt-in-your-mouth" reef 'n' grilled beef delivered by an "attentive" staff at this "excellent" Ironbound Iberian-Brazilian steakhouse; carnivores like that for $24.50, you can "eat all you can."

Ferrari's Ocean Grill Ⓜ *Italian*

22 | 17 | 21 | $34

Freehold Township | A & M Plaza | 3475 Rte. 9 N. (Three Brooks Rd.) | 732-294-7400 | www.ferrarisrestaurantnj.com

"Enthusiastic" servers make meals here "feel like you're eating at home" at this Freehold Township shopping-center BYO, where the "good" Italian food pleases; P.S. some suggest the "seafood is the best in town."

ⓏFerry House, The *American/French*

25 | 20 | 22 | $48

Princeton | 32 Witherspoon St. (Spring St.) | 609-924-2488 | www.theferryhouse.com

"Too many fabulous dishes to choose from" is a common refrain at Bobby Trigg's BYO "winner", one of the only "special-event" venues in Princeton whose French–New American cooking excels even more with backup from a staff that "shows the right amount of attentiveness"; as expected, it's not cheap, but it's near unanimous that the operation is "first-rate."

NEW 55 Main Ⓢ *American*

- | - | - | M

Flemington | 55 Main St. (Bloomfield Ave.) | 908-284-1551 | www.55main.com

Take a break from shopping the nearby Flemington outlets at this sophisticated BYO New American newcomer distinguished by the reasonably priced, globally influenced dishes (ranging from short rib ravioli to grilled Thai sweet chile shrimp) of well-known area chef

Jonas Gold (ex Fox and Hound Tavern); a seat in the serene powder-blue dining room or on the seasonal sidewalk patio should suit.

Filomena Cucina Italiana *Italian*

| 20 | 20 | 18 | $36 |

Clementon | 1380 Blackwood-Clementon Rd. (Millbridge Rd.) | 856-784-6166 | www.filomenascucina.com

Filomena Cucina Rustica *Italian*

Berlin | 13 Milford Cross Keys Rd. (White Horse Pike) | 856-753-3540 | www.filomenasberlin.com

Filomena Lakeview *Italian*

Deptford | 1738 Cooper St. (Almonesson Rd.) | 856-228-4235 | www.filomenalakeview.com

"Italian as it should be" sums up this "affordable", separately owned South Jersey trio that is likely to "never let you down"; N.B. the Berlin branch was recently renovated, and all outposts showcase "great" evening entertainment.

Fiorino ⑤ *Italian*

| 23 | 20 | 21 | $49 |

Summit | 38 Maple St. (Springfield Ave.) | 908-277-1900 | www.fiorinoristorante.com

Those out for "special occasions" hardly do wrong when dining at this Summit Northern Italian "mainstay" hitting high notes with "delicious" meals "every time" and offering lots of libations at the "active bar"; the cream on the tiramisu, though, is a seat in the wine cellar for a "true food and drink experience."

Five Guys Famous Burgers & Fries *Burgers*

| - | - | - | I |

NEW **Hackensack** | Home Depot Shopping Ctr. | 450 Hackensack Ave. (Grand Ave.) | 201-343-5489 ✆

NEW **Millburn** | Milburn Mall | 2933 Vauxhall Rd. (Valley St.) | 908-688-8877

NEW **Edison** | Wick Shopping Plaza | 561 Rte. 1 (bet. Dey Pl. & Fulton St.) | 732-985-5977

NEW **Parsippany** | Troy Hills Shopping Ctr. | 1105 Rte. 46 (Beverwyck Rd.) | 973-335-5454

NEW **Watchung** | Blue Star Shopping Ctr. | 1701 Rte. 22 (Terrill Rd.) | 908-490-0370

NEW **Woodbridge** | Woodbridge Mall | 344 Woodbridge Center Dr. (Rte. 1) | 732-636-1377

Brick | Habitat Plaza | 588 Rte. 70 (Cedar Bridge Ave.) | 732-262-4040 ⑤Ⓜ

NEW **Toms River** | Orchards at Dover | 1311 Rte. 37 W. (bet. Bimini Rd. & St. Catherine Blvd.) | 732-349-3600

Cherry Hill | 1650 Kings Hwy. N. (Hwy. 70) | 856-795-1455

Mount Ephraim | 130 Black Horse Pike (White Horse Pike) | 856-672-0442 www.fiveguys.com

Additional locations throughout New Jersey

Bang-for-the-buck burgers – handmade daily from fresh ground beef, grilled to order, placed on buns and smothered in free toppings – are the hallmark of these popular quick-bite NJ links of a national chain; the short 'n' sweet menu also offers hot dogs, grilled cheese and hand-cut fries (plain or Cajun-style).

	FOOD	DECOR	SERVICE	COST

503 Park ⊠ *Eclectic* ▽ 20 | 15 | 16 | $36

Scotch Plains | 503 Park Ave. (Westfield Ave.) | 908-322-5880 | www.503park.com

This "informal" neighborhood BYO bistro in Scotch Plains has fans delighted with the "good" Eclectic menu priced at a "bargain"; while some say things here "are getting better", "unseasoned service" doesn't measure up to the "well-prepared" food.

Fleming's Prime Steakhouse *Steak* 22 | 23 | 22 | $57

Edgewater | City Pl. | 90 The Promenade (River Rd.) | 201-313-9463 | www.flemingssteakhouse.com

"What a lovely way to blow your cholesterol count" quip carnivores at this upscale Edgewater chain chophouse, the "pricey" cousin of the Outback Steakhouse proffering "nicely prepared" steaks and sides; now, if only the "great" view of NYC was visible from your seats ("lower the windows!").

Food for Thought *American* 24 | 24 | 22 | $40

Marlton | Marlton Crossing Shopping Ctr. | 129 Marlton Crossing (Rte. 70) | 856-797-1126 | www.foodforthoughtnj.com

Although slotted away in the corner of Marlton Crossing, this strip-mall BYO "pearl" isn't an afterthought for those who endorse its "well-prepared" New American savories, "good" desserts and "warm" service; the "less than glamorous" setting belies the "romantic" possibilities at this overall "impressive" operation.

☒ Fornos of Spain *Spanish* 23 | 17 | 20 | $39

Newark | 47 Ferry St. (Union St.) | 973-589-4767 | www.fornosrestaurant.com

Considered by many the "king of the Ironbound", this "large" Newark "institution" is synonymous with "abundant" portions, "reasonable" prices and Spanish fare that's bound to "leave you satisfied"; expect a "busy", "crowded" scene, but it's "worth the wait" – the food is "great" and the "parking lot is a plus."

☒ 410 Bank Street *Creole* 27 | 21 | 24 | $51

Cape May | 410 Bank St. (bet. Broad St. & Lafayette Ave.) | 609-884-2127

"Intoxicating", "complex" Creole cooking is the 411 on this Cape May mainstay whose combination of "culinary razzle-dazzle" (the work of chef Henry Sing Cheng) and "cozy" Victorian atmosphere like "Key West" makes a visit here "better than a week in New Orleans"; if the "waits" grate, "engaging" servers help ease the pain; N.B. although BYO, the restaurant offers a short list of NJ wines.

Frankie & Johnnie's *Steak* 23 | 20 | 21 | $51

Hoboken | 163 14th St. (Garden St.) | 201-659-6202 | www.frankieandjohnnies.com

Yes, this Uptown Hoboken steakhouse may be somewhat "pricey", but that's no problem for fans who describe "cooked-to-perfection" beef and other chophouse favorites, an "excellent" bar and "charming" late-19th-century ambiance; P.S. they offer validated parking, a "priceless" commodity in this town.

	FOOD	DECOR	SERVICE	COST

Frankie Fed's Ⓜ *Italian*
20	10	17	$22

Freehold Township | 831 Rte. 33 E. (Weaverville Rd.) | 732-294-1333 |
www.frankiefeds.com

The thin-crust pizzas may even "equal those of big brother Federici's" argue backers of this "busy", "friendly" Freehold Township Italian, who some say has a "nicer atmosphere" than its famous relative; plus, there's no need to bring cash since "they take plastic."

Frenchtown Inn, The Ⓜ *Eclectic/French*
23	22	21	$52

Frenchtown | 7 Bridge St. (Rte. 29) | 908-996-3300 |
www.frenchtowninn.com

Right alongside the Delaware River in "bucolic" Frenchtown, this "country" inn "treasure" is "a pleasure" for "wonderful" meals given the Eclectic-French menu and "classy", "romantic" rooms; N.B. the adjacent grill room is an alternative for more dress-down dining.

Frescos *Italian/Mediterranean*
24	20	22	$42

Cape May | 412 Bank St. (Lafayette Ave.) | 609-884-0366

A "distinctive" menu of Italian-Mediterranean specialties delivered in "warm" environs makes some ask "why go to Italy?" when there's this "Tuscan"-inspired, BYO-friendly Cape May trattoria hitched to its relative, 410 Bank Street; P.S. seafood that's "fresher than fresh" steals the show.

Fresco Steak & Seafood Grill *Seafood/Steak*
23	19	19	$37

Milltown | Heritage Shopping Plaza | 210 Ryders Ln. (Blueberry Dr.) |
732-246-7616 | www.restaurantfresco.com

Most agree the fare really "is that good" at this Milltown reef 'n' beef BYO that relies on its offerings to override the strip-mall surroundings; it seems always "busy" – maybe it's because here, you get the "most food for your money."

🅩 Frog and the Peach *American*
26	23	24	$57

New Brunswick | 29 Dennis St. (Hiram Sq.) | 732-846-3216 |
www.frogandpeach.com

"Amazing in every respect", this multilevel New Brunswick New American "gastronomic paradise" is the home of Bruce Lefebvre's "flawless" cooking (with new lunch and dinner prix fixe options), "top-notch" service and wines, and an "extraordinary", "modern" ambiance reflecting the building's industrial history; you may have to "mortgage a friend" for the experience, but then, what are friends for?

NEW Fuji Ⓜ *Japanese*
-	-	-	M

Haddonfield | Shops at 116 | 116 E. Kings Hwy. (Tanner St.) |
856-354-8200 | www.fujirestaurant.com

Matt Ito, who drew sushionados from all over the area to his BYO in a ramshackle Cinnaminson strip mall, offers fresh fish followers fancier quarters in Downtown Haddonfield; it's almost a sport to see who can land a seat at the sushi bar.

	FOOD	DECOR	SERVICE	COST

Full Moon *Eclectic*

| 17 | 13 | 16 | $21 |

Lambertville | 23 Bridge St. (Union St.) | 609-397-1096 |
www.cafefullmoon.com

The name says it all at this "quirky" BYO Eclectic in Lambertville
that's "only open for dinner during a full moon" but nevertheless
draws raves for a "well-executed menu" served by a "friendly staff";
at other times of the month, you can settle in for "big breakfasts",
"really good" lunches and brunches that last "until 4 PM on weekends"; N.B. closed Tuesdays.

NEW Fusion 🅢 *Asian Fusion*

| - | - | - | M |

Flemington | 123 Main St. (Mine St.) | 908-788-7772 |
www.fusiononmain.com

Adventurous eaters at this new BYO Asian fusion in Downtown
Flemington have numerous offerings from which to choose (including food from the tandoor, wild boar, venison and Kuril salmon), all
at moderate prices; the dramatic, antiques-laden dining room is as
striking as the cuisine, though during peak hours some might prefer
the more peaceful porch.

🅩 Gables, The *Eclectic*

| 26 | 25 | 22 | $63 |

Beach Haven | Green Gables Inn | 212 Centre St. (bet. Bay & Beach Aves.) |
609-492-3553 | www.gableslbi.com

This Eclectic "oasis of elegance" and "fine dining" is an LBI "standard" that retains its high status and still "oozes romance in every
corner"; kudos to the BYO's "great" B&B setting and "charming"
porch, the latter the site of "delightful" afternoon teas; N.B. new
owners recently came on board.

Gaetano's *Italian*

| 19 | 15 | 16 | $33 |

Red Bank | 10 Wallace St. (Broad St.) | 732-741-1321 |
www.gaetanosredbank.com

More "steady Eddie than special night out", but this "dependable"
BYO (with only NJ wines sold) Italian is nonetheless a "good every-
day" alternative thanks in part to a "relaxed" atmosphere that's a
change from the hip Red Bank scene; "routinely inattentive service",
however, is a shortcoming for some.

Gagan Bistro 🅜 *Indian*

| - | - | - | M |

Marlton | 150 Rte. 73 N. (Rte. 70) | 856-988-8751 |
www.gaganindianbistro.com

Settling into Burlington County is this low-key Marlton Indian BYO that
features all the staples sought by locals who crave curries, tandoor-
baked breads and an extensive list of vegetarian goods; at $8.95
($9.95 weekends), the lunch buffet is a magnet for budget hounds.

Gallagher's Steak House *Steak*

| 22 | 23 | 21 | $57 |

Atlantic City | Resorts Atlantic City Casino & Hotel | 1133 Boardwalk
(North Carolina Ave.) | 609-340-6555 | www.resortsac.com

"Cholesterol here I come" say brave-hearted fans more than willing
to indulge in "great" beef served at this "sleeper", an Atlantic City
offshoot (of the NYC original) tucked away in the Resorts Casino

Hotel and looking like "an old steakhouse should" – and costing as much (you'll need a "thick bankroll").

Garlic Rose Bistro *Eclectic*   21 | 15 | 20 | $35

Cranford | 28 North Ave. W. (N. Union Ave.) | 908-276-5749
Madison | 41 Main St. (bet. Green Village Rd. & Waverly Pl.) |
973-822-1178
www.garlicrose.com

These Eclectics in Madison (BYO) and Cranford (serving alcohol) stay true to their name, with garlic-infused offerings that are "satisfying" and "unexpectedly interesting"; the settings are "casual", all the better so you can focus on meals that "help maintain clear blood vessels."

Gaslight *American/Italian*   20 | 16 | 21 | $30

Hoboken | 400 Adams St. (4th St.) | 201-217-1400 | www.gaslightnj.com
"Off the beaten path" in Hoboken, this "comfortable" bar/restaurant has something for everyone, including a "hopping" front bar with an "extensive martini menu" and a "lovely back room" for dining on "unexpectedly" "decent" American comfort food and Italian eats; it may "get a little noisy" but the polished service ("one of its best assets") keeps things humming.

Gazelle Café & Grille ⊠ *American*   - | - | - | E

Ridgewood | 11 Godwin Ave. (Franklin Ave.) | 201-689-9689 |
www.gazellecafe.com

At this Ridgewood New American BYO near Whole Foods, the open kitchen of chefs Jim Miceli and Ron Norrell invites diners to watch the toques turn out health-conscious dishes; decorwise, the small, low-lit room is graced by figurines of the namesake.

Gianna's Ⓜ *Italian*   ▽ 25 | 19 | 23 | $42

Atlantic Highlands | 42 First Ave. (Bay Ave.) | 732-872-3309 |
www.giannasnj.com

A "treasure" in tiny Atlantic Highlands, this BYO "find" of an Italian storefront distinguishes itself with truly "delicious" cooking supported by an "accommodating" staff; despite "tight" quarters, the air of "intimacy" prevails here.

Ginger & Spice *Asian*   - | - | - | M

Ramsey | Kohl's Shopping Ctr. | 1300 Rte. 17 N. (Spring St.) |
201-934-8900 | www.gingerandspice.com

Asian fusion cuisine with a Thai bent kicks this Ramsey BYO into high gear nightly, as adventurers arrive for dishes such as squid with chiles and aïoli, and whole fishes; perfectly appropriate is the name, which sums up both the edgy cuisine and scene.

Ginger Thai *Thai*   ▽ 15 | 14 | 15 | $29

Freehold Township | A & M Plaza | 3475 Rte. 9 N. (Three Brooks Rd.) |
732-761-2900

This Freehold Township BYO Thai is applauded for "reasonable" prices and a "comfortable" dining area; but "disappointing" fare upends the experience, so some say try ordering items from the "Indian menu" offered at adjacent sister-storefront Aangan.

	FOOD	DECOR	SERVICE	COST

Girasole *Italian* — 25 | 22 | 21 | $53

Atlantic City | Ocean Club Condos | 3108 Pacific Ave. (bet. Chelsea & Montpelier Aves.) | 609-345-5554 | www.girasoleac.com

"In a word – *magnifico!*" is this "chic"-but-casual Southern Italian near the Tropicana sporting a "beautiful" blue-black-yellow Versace design and boasting "delicious" dishes, particularly "great" seafood; one look at the celeb- and power-crowd-filled room and you'll know it's the "place to be" in AC.

Girasole *Italian* — 25 | 19 | 24 | $39

Bound Brook | 502 W. Union Ave. (Thompson Ave.) | 732-469-1080 | www.girasoleboundbrook.com

"Superb" Italian food (from "bruschettas to desserts") isn't the sole reason why this "so-popular" Bound Brook BYO is a "tough reservation", since there's also "excellent", "welcoming" service and prices "low" for the quality of the fare; it's been around for over a decade, so it's no shock that it's a "well-oiled machine"; N.B. a recent remodeling may outdate the above Decor score.

Giumarello's ⑤ *Italian* — 25 | 24 | 24 | $46

Westmont | 329 Haddon Ave. (bet. Cuthbert Blvd. & Kings Hwy.) | 856-858-9400 | www.giumarellos.com

The "best" martinis help keep turnout high for this "all-time area favorite" in Westmont, a "friendly" family-run Northern Italian prized for consistently "wonderful" food, "lively" quarters and "great" bar, where "single diners" feel at home; no, it's "not cheap", but fans who chirp about the early-bird "couldn't be happier."

Gladstone Tavern *American* — - | - | - | M

Gladstone | 273 Main St. (Pottersville Rd.) | 908-234-9055 | www.gladstonetavern.com

A life-size horse statue on the sweeping front porch of this stylish Gladstone American welcomes families from hunt country and beyond for a solid selection of midpriced signatures like crispy crab 'tots' and short ribs; on weekends, the bar is a popular spot.

GoodFellas Ristorante ⑤ *Italian* — - | - | - | E

Garfield | 661 Midland Ave. (Plauderville Ave.) | 973-478-4000 | www.goodfellasnj.com

All the classic Italian bases are covered at this airy Garfield eatery serving a deep savory lineup including veal scaloppine and shrimp scampi; hand-painted walls and cherry wainscoting attract, as does the private party potential, since the restaurant can accommodate up to 100 people.

❷ Grand Cafe, The ⑤ *French* — 25 | 25 | 26 | $62

Morristown | 42 Washington St. (Rte. 24 W.) | 973-540-9444 | www.thegrandcafe.com

Embodying "elegance" to the hilt, this "formal" Morristown French set in a townhouse is surely "pricey", but the "wonderful" cuisine and "top-notch" "veterans" for servers more than compensate; "what can you say?", for it's "one of the last bastions of fine dining around."

| | FOOD | DECOR | SERVICE | COST |

Grand Colonial, The Ⓜ *Eclectic* `25` `23` `20` `$49`
Union Township | 86 Hwy. 173 W. (Rte. 78, exit 12) | 908-735-7889 | www.grandcolonialnj.com
"Wow!" gush gastronomes about the "inventive, delicious" Eclectic dinners (and brunch-only Sundays) – including "fun small plates" and a Friday night raw bar – at this "spectacular" establishment situated in a "beautifully" remodeled Colonial building in Hunterdon County; although some squawk about "hit-or-miss" service, most consider it "a pleasure" given its "warm, tasteful ambiance", "large wine selection" and "fantastic" cheese cave; N.B. the recently launched Grand Ballroom accommodates up to 300 for private parties.

Grand Shanghai *Pan-Asian* `21` `16` `15` `$23`
Edison | 700 US Hwy. 1 (Old Post Rd.) | 732-819-8830
For "dishes you don't see everywhere" else, try this clubby Pan-Asian in Edison that seats 200 and offers "interesting", "inventive cuisine" like braised sea cucumber as well as more familiar fare (e.g. "don't-miss pork buns" and sushi); a few find the service "gruff", so go here "for a fast meal" or, better yet, opt for takeout.

Grenville, The Ⓜ *American* `21` `22` `19` `$44`
Bay Head | Grenville Hotel | 345 Main Ave. (bet. Harris & Karge Sts.) | 732-892-3100 | www.thegrenville.com
The "lovely" Grenville Hotel complements the "delightful" repasts for patrons who check in to this "special-occasion" New American in Bay Head, the standby for "elegant" Victorian dining; some swear brunch on Sunday "couldn't be more perfect"; N.B. the presence of a new chef may outdate the above Food score.

Grill 73 Ⓜ *American* `22` `15` `20` `$39`
Bernardsville | 73 Mine Brook Rd. (Woodland Rd.) | 908-630-0700 | www.grill73.com
Adding "upscale" touches to "casual" chow helps keep things "tasty" at this "lively" New American Bernardsville BYO where you get "quality treatment"; some say the "trendy" retro "luncheonette" look is part of the perfect union of food and decor.

Grimaldi's Pizza *Pizza* `25` `13` `17` `$19`
Hoboken | 133 Clinton St. (2nd St.) | 201-792-0800 | www.grimaldis.com
It's the "one you want" counsel pros who've hit this Downtown Hoboken Italian pizza parlor slinging "tantalizing" thin-crust pies topped with "real mozz" and other "fresh" ingredients; it's obviously "a damn fine choice", but remember: no slices here.

Grissini Restaurant *Italian* `22` `20` `19` `$51`
Englewood Cliffs | 484 Sylvan Ave. (Palisade Ave.) | 201-568-3535 | www.grissinirestaurant.com
It may be "showy", but that's the point of this "fashionable" Englewood Cliffs Italian where the "beautiful people" meet to "see and be seen"; the open kitchen's food is "always good", there's a "great" wine list that goes with the "great" vibe at the bar and the service is "attentive", so all in all, it's "*bella.*"

GRUB Hut BBQ

| - | - | - | I |

Manville | 307 N. Main St. (Knopf St.) | 908-203-8003 |
www.grubhutbbq.com

Although this Manville BYO had to rename itself, nothing about the unique BBQ-Southwestern grub has changed – and pork partisans are spreading the word of the pit-inspired fare on offer.

Gusto Grill *American*

| - | - | - | M |

East Brunswick | 1050 Rte. 18 N. (Rues Ln.) | 732-651-2737 |
www.gustogrill.com

Open late-night and clubbier with each passing hour, this East Brunswick American boasts a vast martini list and a bounty of brews on tap, all the more to fuel the goings on; the casual vittles – burgers, sandwiches and pizzas – are perfect for a little stomach lining.

Habana Latin *Cuban/Mexican*

| - | - | - | M |

Ridgefield Park | 206 Main St. (bet. Grove & Mt. Vernon Sts.) |
201-641-5588 | www.habanalatin.com

Mexican and Cuban merge at this popular Ridgefield Park Latin BYO that manages to straddle not only two culinary worlds, but both standard and inventive styles of cooking; candles and tropical plants add some spice to the modest quarters.

NEW Hale & Hearty Soups *Sandwiches/Soup*

| - | - | - | I |

Livingston | 464 W. Mount Pleasant Ave. (Old Rd.) | 973-597-0200 |
www.haleandhearty.com

Hail to the NY-based soup/salad/sandwich chain's Livingston outpost (the first outside the Big Apple) where locals have their pick of potage (some 20 daily) without the commute; the family-friendly spot offers dessert, a kids' menu (PB & J, grilled cheese) and free WiFi service too; N.B. a second NJ H & H is scheduled to open in Jersey City in summer 2008.

Hamilton's Grill Room *Mediterranean*

| 24 | 20 | 21 | $46 |

Lambertville | 8 Coryell St. (N. Union St.) | 609-397-4343 |
www.hamiltonsgrillroom.com

"There's a reason why it's hard to nab a reservation" at this Med BYO that "sets the standard" for Lambertville with chef Mark Miller's "amazing" grill work (the result is "excellent" fish and seafood); the courtyard setting near the Delaware Canal only "adds to the wonderful ambiance."

Hard Grove Cafe ☾ *American/Cuban*

| 14 | 12 | 13 | $19 |

Jersey City | 319 Grove St. (Christopher Columbus Dr.) | 201-451-1853 |
www.hardgrovecafe.com

The verdict is mixed on this diner "institution" in Jersey City: while diehards dig its "kitschy", "fun" decor and "consistent" Cuban-American "favorites", detractors dis it for having a "tacky ambiance" and "slow" service; nevertheless, a "location opposite the PATH station" ensures this joint's "always bustling" with "a diverse clientele."

Harrison, The *American*   ∇ 24 | - | 19 | $41

Asbury Park | 716 Cookman Ave. (Bond St.) | 732-774-2200

A relocation to bigger, fancier digs (a brick facade, dark woods, white linens) on Asbury Park's Restaurant Row gives this New American's loyal following a more suitable backdrop in which to dine on "interesting", "well-prepared" dishes and "great" drinks – and may also outdate the above Decor score.

Harry's Lobster House *Seafood*   ∇ 22 | 11 | 17 | $57

Sea Bright | 1124 Ocean Ave. (New St.) | 732-842-0205

Sea Bright's seafood standby (since 1933) still shows what the "best" stuffed lobsters are all about, even if the "expensive" tabs that accompany them are daunting to some; "accommodating" service helps counterbalance any issues with the "plain", "vanilla" setting; N.B. closed Tuesdays.

Harvest Bistro Ⓜ *French*   22 | 25 | 20 | $52

Closter | 252 Schraalenburgh Rd. (Bergenline Ave.) | 201-750-9966 | www.harvestbistro.com

In the small town of Closter, this French bistro is fertile ground for folks who like the "gorgeous" decor (featuring copper, stone and wood), "loungey" vibe and "busy" bar scene, all abetted by "good" (although "pricey") food; no, "hearing aids aren't necessary", but that's just the sound of fans happy to have something "right out of NYC" in town.

Harvest Moon Inn Ⓜ *American*   24 | 22 | 22 | $51

Ringoes | 1039 Old York Rd. (Rte. 202) | 908-806-6020 | www.harvestmooninn.com

"They put the 'excel' in 'excellent'" at this "wonderful" New American nestled in a "lovely" stone house in Ringoes; whether you're enjoying "outstanding gourmet fare" in the "romantic" dining room or chowing down on "pub-style dinners" in the tavern, it's "never a bad decision to spend the evening" at this "all-round favorite", especially given its "cozy" fireplaces and "deep wine list."

Harvey Cedars Shellfish Co. ⊅ *Seafood*   22 | 10 | 18 | $30

Beach Haven | 506 Centre St. (Pennsylvania Ave.) | 609-492-2459
Harvey Cedars | 7904 Long Beach Blvd. (bet. 79th & 80th Sts.) | 609-494-7112
www.harveycedarsshellfishco.com

"Any real LBIer" considers this cash-only BYO seafood duo a "staple" for its "relaxed" vibe and "simple", "fresh" affordable fish; note that to enjoy the "essence of beachiness" at these "true summer dining experiences", expect "long lines" and "crowds."

🆕 Havana *Cuban*   - | - | - | I

Highlands | 409 Bay Ave. (Shore Dr.) | 732-708-0000 | www.havanatropicalcafe.com

For traditional Cuban fare at inexpensive prices in restaurant-rich Highlands, this colorful new spot should suit; sip a mojito along with your skirt steak or paella amid palm trees and murals of the old country, or in season, on the outdoor patio.

	FOOD	DECOR	SERVICE	COST

☑ Highlawn Pavilion *American*
24 | 27 | 23 | $61

West Orange | Eagle Rock Reservation | Eagle Rock Ave. (Prospect Ave.) | 973-731-3463 | www.highlawn.com

"Astonishing NYC views" aren't the only draw at this "stunning" "occasion" New American housed in a grand, late-19th-century building atop an overlook in West Orange, since the food is "to die for" ("no wonder the place is so close to heaven!"); plus, the staff makes "your every wish their command", so acolytes aver it's all "well worth the $$$"; N.B. the large wine cellar is reserved for private parties.

High Street Grill *American*
▽ 23 | 18 | 22 | $36

Mount Holly | 64 High St. (bet. Brainerd & Garden Sts.) | 609-265-9199 | www.highstreetgrill.net

"Good" New Americana is on offer at this spot brightening up Downtown Mount Holly; the hosts (or the new owner) "meet and greet" diners in a space divided by a recently refurbished upstairs and a tavernlike downstairs, where lunch and dinner are served every day.

Ho-Ho-Kus Inn, The *Continental/Italian*
21 | 21 | 21 | $50

Ho-Ho-Kus | Ho-Ho-Kus Inn | 1 E. Franklin Tpke. (Sheridan Ave.) | 201-445-4115 | www.hohokusinn.com

You'll "step back in time" when you enter this Ho-Ho-Kus mainstay (housed in an 18th-century Dutch Colonial) offering Continental-Italian meals and "excellent" service; food issues aside ("up and down" to "wonderful"), dedicated diners laud the "romantic" setting.

Holsten's ● *American*
- | - | - | I

Bloomfield | 1063 Broad St. (Watchung Ave.) | 973-338-7091 | www.holstens.com

Even if its fame as the setting for *The Sopranos* finale lasts only the proverbial 15 minutes, this vintage Bloomfield ice cream parlor/coffee shop will no doubt carry on as it has for decades, dishing up homemade scoops and sundaes plus burgers, onion rings and more in surroundings that are as authentically retro as the prices; P.S. the candy counter in front also sells 'final episode' T-shirts.

Homestead Inn ⊅ *Italian*
▽ 23 | 9 | 19 | $47

Trenton | 800 Kuser Rd. (bet. Hamilton & Whitehorse Aves.) | 609-890-9851

Known as Chick & Nello's to insiders, this family-run Trenton institution (since 1939) dishes up "old-school", "no-nonsense" Italiana and "no printed menus" (the waiters tell you what's on offer); "minimal" decor and "sketchy service" (unless "you're a regular") is somehow part of the appeal; N.B. closed Tuesdays.

NEW Hotoke *Pan-Asian*
- | - | - | E

New Brunswick | 350 George St. (Bayard St.) | 732-246-8999 | www.hotokerestaurant.com

Striking surroundings, including a giant golden Buddha, high ceilings and lava stone countertops, provide a dramatic backdrop for new chef Convoy Arnold's Pan-Asian fare at this New Brunswick addition; prices are high-end, but $15 prix fixe lunches are an affordable way to go.

	FOOD	DECOR	SERVICE	COST

House of Blues ● *Southern* | 16 | 19 | 17 | $31 |

Atlantic City | Showboat Casino | 801 Boardwalk (Pacific Ave.) |
609-236-2583 | www.hob.com

Thanks to the "to-die-for" Sunday gospel brunch, "great" music and
"good" drinks, there's "a better return on your money" than playing
at the casino reason backers of this Showboat Southerner in Atlantic
City; still, "dark" digs detract, and some say the "food may give
you the blues."

Hunan Chinese Room *Chinese* | 23 | 19 | 21 | $25 |

Morris Plains | 255 Speedwell Ave. (W. Hanover Ave.) |
973-285-1117

The "cool" decor is "eye catching" at this Morris Plains Chinese also
setting itself apart with its array of "top-notch" Cantonese, Hunan
and Sichuan specialties; the especially "attractive" bar is a dispen-
sary for some seriously "potent" potables.

Hunan Spring *Chinese* | 19 | 10 | 16 | $22 |

Springfield | 288 Morris Ave. (Caldwell Pl.) | 973-379-4994

"Basic" and "efficiently" run, this Springfield Chinese BYO (relative
of Morris Plains' Hunan Chinese Room) is considered a "standby"
for "solid" "albeit not very imaginative" cooking; the "no-frills"
digs "could use an update", but most insist the place "sates" any
hot 'n' sour cravings.

Hunan Taste *Chinese* | 23 | 24 | 21 | $31 |

Denville | 67 Bloomfield Ave. (Broadway) | 973-625-2782 |
www.hunantaste.com

"Great", "gracious" service plus "delicious" food equals success at
this Denville Chinese that's the talk of the town not only for its fare,
but for the "elaborate" "over-the-top" decor featuring a number of
fish tanks, especially the 20-ft. one near the bar; the quasi "formal-
ity" here may help explain tabs on the slightly "expensive side."

Hunt Club Grill *Seafood/Steak* | 20 | 20 | 20 | $45 |

Summit | Grand Summit Hotel | 570 Springfield Ave. (Morris Ave.) |
908-273-7656 | www.grandsummit.com

This "clubby", American Summit surf 'n' turf hotel "standby"
(debuted in 1929) keeps its audience partly thanks to servers who
"go out of their way to please"; while sometimes "good",
sometimes "bland" sums up the food for some, optimists say that
though the setting's "not lively at all", at least "you're able to talk
with your companions."

☑ Huntley Taverne *American* | 22 | 24 | 19 | $47 |

Summit | 3 Morris Ave. (bet. Broad St. & Springfield Ave.) |
908-273-3166 | www.harvestrestaurants.com

With its "ski-lodge" decor, this "handsome", "pricey" Summit New
American warms its clientele with a "cozy" high-ceilinged setting
replete with fireplaces (it feels like "you're in a remote lodge") and
with food that "shines"; the "porch is the place to be" in summers,
and the "lively" bar is the place to be seen year-round.

		FOOD	DECOR	SERVICE	COST

Iberia Peninsula ⏺ *Portuguese/Spanish*   21 | 16 | 19 | $35

Newark | 63-69 Ferry St. (bet. Prospect & Union Sts.) | 973-344-5611

Iberia Tavern ⏺Ⓜ *Portuguese/Spanish*

Newark | 80-84 Ferry St. (bet. Congress & Prospect Sts.) | 973-344-7603
www.iberiarestaurants.com

They may be "busy", "noisy" and "need updated decor", but these Ironbound Iberians keep the crowds "coming back" with their "mounds of paella", "best-buy lobster specials" and "plentiful" portions of "delicious meat" ("one word: rodizio"); given "fun people-watching" and a "carnival atmosphere", "don't skip the sangria" – it's "homemade and very potent!"

I Cavallini *Italian*   25 | 22 | 21 | $51

Colts Neck | 29 S. Rte. 34 (Hwy. 537) | 732-431-2934

"Superior" Italian dishes emerge from the kitchen at this destination for upscale dining, a "rustic" yet elegant eatery in Colts Neck; thanks to the combination of food, setting and service, it's no shock this site is among the "very best" Monmouth County has to offer.

Ichiban *Japanese*   17 | 12 | 17 | $28

Princeton | 66 Witherspoon St. (bet. Hulfish St. & Paul Robeson Pl.) | 609-683-8323

This "simple storefront Japanese tries to please" Princeton natives with "standard sushi" and "quick lunch boxes" "at an affordable price"; "they have all the basics, but not much more", with picky patrons pointing to its "bare-bones setting" and minimal service – "don't expect to finish your conversation" at dinner, as "they turn the tables quickly"; N.B. it's BYO.

Ikko *Japanese*   ∇ 22 | 17 | 21 | $26

Brick | Brick Plaza Mall | 107 Brick Plaza (Chambers Bridge Ave.) | 732-477-6077 | www.ikkosteakhouse.com

"One of Brick's better choices" is the word on this Japanese BYO proffering a large menu including sushi, tempura and the like; if you're "looking for excitement", bring the "family" with you – the hibachi chefs put on a "show."

Il Capriccio Ⓩ *Italian*   26 | 25 | 25 | $63

Whippany | 633 Rte. 10 (Whippany Rd.) | 973-884-9175 | www.ilcapriccio.com

A "high-class", "dressed-up" ambiance infuses this Whippany Italian winner for "food beyond compare" accompanied by "extensive" wines and a staff that knows "when you want to be fawned over, or left alone"; in sum, "everything you're looking for in fine dining is here" – "as long as you can afford it."

Il Michelangelo *Italian*   21 | 19 | 20 | $39

Boonton | 91 Elcock Ave. (Powerville Rd.) | 973-316-1111 | www.ilmichelangelo.com

"Tucked away" in Boonton Township, this "old-world" ristorante residing in a restored 1856 stagecoach inn is welcomed for its "large" portions of "homestyle" Italian fare and "warm, cozy" vibe; if the fare's a touch "inconsistent" at times, most note it's "worth the trip", and "sitting out on the porch" is certainly "a nice touch."

☑ Il Mondo Vecchio ⓈI *Italian* — 25 | 20 | 21 | $48

Madison | 72 Main St. (Central Ave.) | 973-301-0024 | www.ilmondovecchio.com

Michael Cetrulo's Madison storefront (the slightly dressed-down alternative to Scalini Fedeli) serves "consistently excellent" Italian fare that some say is on par with the Chatham flagship; the "warm" storefront invites, BYO keeps prices to a relative "bargain", and thanks to the "crowds" and "tin ceiling", expect a healthy amount of "noise."

Il Villaggio ⓈI *Italian* — 23 | 16 | 24 | $50

Carlstadt | 651 Rte. 17 N. (Passaic Ave.) | 201-935-7733 | www.ilvillaggio.com

"A diamond in the shadow of the Meadowlands", this "incredible" Carlstadt Italian is "the place to go before or after the game" for "old-style cuisine that never disappoints" served by an "attentive" staff; it's all set in "dated but comfortable" digs that have recently been renovated, a change that may outdate the above Decor score.

India on the Hudson *Indian* — 19 | 13 | 16 | $26

Hoboken | 1210 Washington St. (bet. 12th & 13th Sts.) | 201-222-0101 | www.indiaonthehudson.com

For "a taste of India" in Hoboken, try this "reliable" choice for "standard" subcontinental cuisine that includes a "can't-beat" lunch buffet; given "average service" and decor that "could use a redo", "you may want to [opt for] takeout", especially since delivery can be so "slow", you'll wonder if they "had to go to Bombay, grow the vegetables and bring them back."

NEW Indigo Restaurant & Bar *Indian* — - | - | - | M

North Brunswick | Ramada Inn | 999 Rte. 1 S. (off Weymouth Rd.) | 732-247-8500 | www.indigorestaurantbar.com

This upscale North Brunswick Indian newcomer comes complete with a liveried doorman and a waterfall behind the bar; the mid-priced, sophisticated food (e.g. lamb chops marinated in mustard and ginger) clicks for an appreciative crowd.

Indigo Smoke *BBQ* — 22 | 17 | 17 | $29

Montclair | 387 Bloomfield Ave. (Willow St.) | 973-744-3440 | www.indigosmoke.com

"Loosen your belt and leave your diet at the door" before entering this Montclair BYO dishing out "to-die-for" Kansas City BBQ ("great" babybacks) and Southern soul food ("delish" fried chicken, mac 'n' cheese, etc.); the "funky", recently expanded space allows room for all the extra "pounds you may put on"; N.B. closed Tuesdays.

NEW Inlet, The *American* — - | - | - | M

Somers Point | 998 Bay Ave. (Goll Ave.) | 609-926-9611 | www.inletrestaurantnj.com

The Somers Point 'in' crowd drops anchor at this sprawling New American newcomer on Great Harbor Bay for updated (wasabi-crusted sea bass) and old-time (crab-stuffed flounder) seafood; the spectacular views from numerous decks and dining rooms are another draw; N.B. a jazz brunch is offered year-round, and live bands perform nightly during the summer.

Inlet Café *Seafood*

19	15	17	$35

Highlands | 3 Cornwall St. (Shrewsbury Ave.) | 732-872-9764 | www.inletcafe.com

"What could be better on a summer day" than a "bite and a beer"? at this "casual" seafooder overlooking Sandy Hook Bay and offering "gorgeous" views; the "good" fare and "friendly" service also please.

Inn at Millrace Pond *American/Continental*

21	25	20	$46

Hope | 313 Johnsonburg Rd. (Rte. 611) | 908-459-4884 | www.innatmillracepond.com

The building alone – a "charming", converted 18th-century mill in "lovely" Hope – "is reason enough to visit" this "romantic" American-Continental supplying "sophistication in spades"; although the food is "generally very good" and the service is "correct", there are "no bells and whistles", "just straightforward" "grace and style in the woods"; N.B. under new management.

Inn at Sugar Hill Ⓜ *American*

-	-	-	M

Mays Landing | 5704 Mays Landing-Summers Point Rd. (River Rd.) | 609-625-2226 | www.innatsugarhill.com

A Traditional American eatery resides within this historic Mays Landing mansion, blending history and a menu of small and large plates; on summer weekends, a tented Dockside Grill proffers fresh seafood, live music and river views; N.B. there's a $19.95 three-course prix fixe dinner on Wednesdays, Thursdays and Sundays.

Inn of the Hawke *American*

18	17	18	$28

Lambertville | 74 S. Union St. (Mount Hope St.) | 609-397-9555

An "easygoing" "local spot" with the aura of an old English pub, this "lovely" Lambertville bar/restaurant proffers a "fine selection of beers" and an "eclectic" American menu; it's best enjoyed on the "beautiful flagstone garden patio", although the "cozy indoor dining rooms" are winning in winter too.

Irish Pub & Inn ⊘⊟ *Irish*

18	15	19	$16

Atlantic City | 164 St. James Pl. (Pacific Ave.) | 609-344-9063 | www.theirishpub.com

The "cheapest" chow and drinks are on tap at this "dark" AC warhorse still packing the house with the "coldest" beers and "standard" Irish vittles; the place seems like "it's been open every hour since it opened", a godsend to its huge fan base; N.B. credit cards accepted in hotel and gift shop.

Isabella's American Bistro Ⓜ *American*

22	19	20	$36

Westfield | 39 Elm St. (bet. Franklin & Hill Sts.) | 908-233-8830 | www.isabellasbistro.com

"Another winner from the owners of Mojave Grille and Theresa's" is this adjacent BYO storefront in Westfield, offering "delectable spins on old favorites" on its "creative" New American menu; a "comfortable" ambiance adds to the mix, but a few still feel the place "needs to come up to par with area restaurants."

Island Palm Grill Ⓜ American   ▽ 18 | 15 | 19 | $36

Spring Lake | 1321 Third Ave. (bet. Jersey & Washington Aves.) | 732-449-1909 | www.islandpalmgrill.com

"Creative" comestibles are cobbled together at this New American Spring Lake BYO bringing a touch of "Key West" to town (think bamboo, along with reds and blues); some say it's a "find" that still seems to be a "secret."

🄩 It's Greek To Me Greek   18 | 12 | 16 | $22

Cliffside Park | Vitos Plaza | 352 Anderson Ave. (bet. Jersey & Morningside Aves.) | 201-945-5447

Englewood | 36 E. Palisade Ave. (bet. Dean & Engle Sts.) | 201-568-0440

Fort Lee | 1636 Palisade Ave. (Main St.) | 201-947-2050

Hoboken | 538 Washington St. (6th St.) | 201-216-1888

Jersey City | 194 Newark Ave. (Jersey Ave.) | 201-222-0844

Livingston | 6230 Town Center Way (bet. Livingston Ave. & Rte. 10) | 973-992-8999

Ridgewood | 21 E. Ridgewood Ave. (bet. Broad & Chestnut Sts.) | 201-612-2600

Westwood | 487 Broadway (Westwood Ave.) | 201-722-3511

Holmdel | 2128 Hwy. 35 (S. Laurel Ave.) | 732-275-0036

Long Branch | 44 Centennial Dr. (Chelsea Ave.) | 732-571-0222

www.itsgreektome.com

Whether you find the food "passable" or "perfect" or the settings "comfortable" or ready "to be updated", the consensus is this chain-gang of BYO Greek eateries offers "large" helpings of "yummy" Hellenic vittles that often arrive "quickly"; pricewise, the "cheap" tabs are just ouzo special.

Jack Cooper's Celebrity Deli Deli   19 | 9 | 15 | $21

Edison | Tano Mall | 1199 Amboy Ave. (Rte. 1) | 732-549-4580 | www.jackcoopersdeli.com

All the "old faves" are doled out at this "old-fashioned" kosher-style Edison deli selling "high-quality" corned beef and pastrami sandwiches among other items, all served "fast and gruff"; beware of bloat before noshing on all the "wonderful" free pickles.

Jamie's Restaurant Italian   - | - | - | E

Clifton | 915 Bloomfield Ave. (Brighton Rd.) | 973-779-8596 | www.jamiesrestaurant.com

Supplying clientele with an upscale ambiance in Clifton, this licensed Italian cigar bar (yup – smoking tobacco isn't taboo here) serves classic dishes (notably pastas) along with a selection of prime chops (T-bones, porterhouses and filets); given the food and setting, it's not a stretch to expect expense account–style tabs.

Java Moon American   19 | 15 | 16 | $23

Jackson | 1022 Anderson Rd. (Rte. 537) | 732-928-3633

Manalapan | 345 Hwy. 9 S. (Rte. 520) | 732-294-1675

Shrewsbury | 431 Broad St. (Rte. 520) | 732-530-0141

(continued)

Java Moon

Lawrenceville | Avalon Commons Mall | 4110 Quakerbridge Rd.
(Village Rd. W.) | 609-275-7447
www.javamooncafe.com

"Fresh, healthy, tasty" could be the motto for this chain and its "eclectic" Traditional American fare, namely "fancy", "unusual" sandwiches, "giant", "terrific" salads and other items vended in "offbeat" digs; and as always, the "great" coffee surprises no one; N.B. the Jackson location has a no-alcohol policy, whereas the other outposts are BYO.

NEW Javier's ⊠ *American*   - | - | - | E

Haddonfield | 208 Kings Hwy. E. (Haddon Ave.) | 856-428-4220 |
www.javiercontinental.com

The crew from Collingswood's Word of Mouth picked posh Haddonfield for this fittingly upscale New American BYO turned out in rich creams and browns; its subdued vibe appeals to local ladies who lunch as well as to couples out for an evening with a favorite wine or two.

Jerry & Harvey's Noshery *Deli*   18 | 8 | 14 | $19

Marlboro | Marlboro Plaza | 96 Rte. 9 (Rte. 520) | 732-972-1122 |
www.jerryandharveys.com

Devotees deli up for "delectable" goods (chopped liver, corned beef) at this kosher-style Marlboro venue that's "like the old neighborhood" for nostalgists; the "dingy" digs could use some "uplift", but for smoked salmon a-fish-ionados, at least the "countermen cut lox as thin as it gets."

Je's Ⓜ *Soul Food*   ▽ 26 | 13 | 17 | $17

Newark | 34 William St. (Halsey St.) | 973-623-8848

Even Essex County "politicians" speak with one voice and agree they've "never had better" Southern food than what's dished at this Newark soul fooder, a specialist of "delectable" cornbread and mac 'n' cheese; "good" breakfasts – and long "waits" – are both common here.

Jimmy's *Italian*   24 | 14 | 21 | $42

Asbury Park | 1405 Asbury Ave. (Prospect Ave.) | 732-774-5051

The "best" veal chops and other "fantastic" cooking straight "from the old-school" Italian repertoire bring down the house at this "always packed" Asbury Park workhouse, where the fare is "served without bells and whistles"; the authentically "old-time" ambiance makes it seem like "Frank and the Rat Pack" could strut in at any moment; N.B. closed Tuesdays.

Joel's Malibu Kitchen Ⓜ *Eclectic*   - | - | - | M

Ridgewood | 14 Oak St. (bet. E. Ridgewood & Franklin Aves.) |
201-493-9477

Eat under the glow of lava lamps at this Eclectic Ridgewood BYO that proffers a menu that's both original and far-flung; as the name suggests, the vibe is pure paradise for the laid-back.

	FOOD	DECOR	SERVICE	COST

Joe's Peking Duck House Ⓜ⌺ *Chinese* — **23** | **8** | **18** | **$21**

Marlton | Marlton Crossing Shopping Ctr. | 145 Rte. 73 S. (Rte. 70) |
856-985-1551

"Awesome" fare, including the signature ("go nowhere else for
duck", or for soups), is the calling of this affordable Marlton Chinese
BYO; save for "drab", "take-out decor", all agree this spot is "all it's
quacked up to be."

John Henry's Seafood Ⓜ *Seafood* — **21** | **17** | **19** | **$36**

Trenton | 2 Mifflin St. (bet. Franklin & Washington Sts.) | 609-396-3083 |
www.johnhenrysseafood.com

This family-owned "standby" in Trenton "has stood the test of time",
offering "fresh, well-prepared", "inventive" seafood "with an Italian
flair" that's "good enough you can ignore" the drab decor; it's "a favorite" among locals, making "reservations a must on weekends", so
consider a stop at the in-house retail market instead and pick something up for home.

Jose's *Mexican* — ▽ **22** | **7** | **16** | **$17**

Spring Lake Heights | 101 Rte. 71 (Jersey Ave.) | 732-974-8080

"Nothing fancy", just "really good", "homestyle" Mexican is served
up in this "little" Spring Lake Heights BYO also applauded for its
"cheerful" service; if the "hole-in-the-wall" atmosphere "demands
that you take the food home", "great" prices compensate.

Jose's Mexican Cantina *Mexican* — **19** | **16** | **18** | **$25**

New Providence | 24 South St. (Springfield Ave.) | 908-464-4360
Warren | Quail Run Ctr. | 125 Washington Valley Rd. (Morning Glory Rd.) |
732-563-0480
www.josescantina.com

Tuck into *muy* "generous" servings of "home-cooked" Mexican at
these "not-just-another-taco-joint" BYOs, colorfully "kitschy", typi-
cally "tacky" cantinas that tend to get "crowded"; "decent" pricing
is part of the deal here.

Juanito's *Mexican* — **23** | **17** | **19** | **$25**

Howell | 3830 Rte. 9 S. (Aldrich Rd.) | 732-370-1717
Red Bank | 159 Monmouth St. (West St.) | 732-747-9118

"Chain Mexicans can't compare" with these south-of-the-border
BYOs proffering "enormous" portions of "tried-and-true" food, all of
them "well prepared"; "colorful" decor and "competent", "friendly"
service explain why it's consistently "crowded."

NEW Kanji Steakhouse & — **-** | **-** | **-** | **M**
Sushi Bar *Japanese/Steak*

Tinton Falls | 980 Shrewsbury Ave. (Rte. 35) | 732-544-1600 |
www.kanjisteakhouse.com

Local sushi legend Roger Yang (ex SAWA) creates affordable works
of art at his sleek new BYO sushi/hibachi/teriyaki spot in Tinton
Falls; improbable raw fish combos like lobster with mangoes or tuna
with blood oranges are packing in patrons tightly as tuna rolls, but
the staff is up to the task.

	FOOD	DECOR	SERVICE	COST

Kaptan Turkish
Grid & Restaurant Ⓜ *Turkish*
(fka Sultan's Turkish Cuisine)

	-	-	-	M

Hackettstown | 133 Main St. (Liberty St.) | 908-979-9222 |
www.kaptanrestaurant.com

New owners helm this Turkish BYO in Hackettstown (an area not known for ethnic eats), proffering a roster of traditional fare – mezes, shish kebabs, gyros – served in colorful quarters; N.B. a belly dancer on weekends augments the authentic aura.

Karen & Rei's 🏠 *American*

∇ 27	22	24	$45

Clermont | 1882 Rte. 9 N. (1 mi. north of Avalon Blvd.) | 609-624-8205 |
www.karenandrei.com

Deserving of all its accolades is this Clermont New American BYO, the "best fine-dining spot in the area" thanks to chef Karen Nelson's "superb" dishes and the hospitality from the staff, including "gracious" co-owner Rei Prabhakar, who ensures the "super-friendly" service; the consensus: all the above make this a truly "great" restaurant; N.B. closed Tuesdays.

🄯 Karma Kafe *Indian*

25	18	20	$24

Hoboken | 505 Washington St. (bet. 5th & 6th Sts.) | 201-610-0900 |
www.karmakafe.com

You can "feel the karma" from the "incredibly tasty" Indian cooking at this "cute" Downtown Hobokenite (relative of Uptown's India on the Hudson) where the cuisine and "intimate" ambiance translate into "a spicy evening out" "if you can get a seat"; P.S. veterans vouch for the lunch buffet that's the "best $9.95 you'll ever spend."

Kaya's Kitchen Ⓜ *Vegetarian*

-	-	-	M

Belmar | Belmar Mall | 817 Belmar Plaza (bet. 8th & 10th Aves.) |
732-280-1141 | www.kayaskitchennj.com

"Even serious meat eaters" enthuse about this Belmar vegetarian BYO for its "yummy", "healthy" offerings on its "varied" menu; the "great", "earthy" staff supplies the mood.

NEW KC's Chiffafa House 🅱 *Belgian/French*

-	-	-	VE

Mendham | 5 Hilltop Rd. (Main St.) | 973-543-4726

If you're looking to indulge, this new Belgian-French bistro in tony Mendham should suit, proffering $75 three-course prix fixe dinners (supper is served Fridays–Saturdays only, accompanied by a jazz pianist); the casual space also works nicely for the Monday–Saturday breakfast and lunch crowd.

Kibitz Room *Deli*

24	8	13	$17

Cherry Hill | Shoppes at Holly Ravine | 100 Springdale Rd. (Evesham Rd.) |
856-428-7878 | www.thekibitzroom.com

The cholesterol crowd kvells over the "great" Jewish "soul food" at this Cherry Hill deli issuing "really big" corned beef and pastrami sandwiches, matzo ball soup and whatnot; slightly "surly servers" notwithstanding, it's still "the closest thing to the Carnegie in South Jersey."

	FOOD	DECOR	SERVICE	COST

Kinchley's Tavern ●⊅ *Pizza* 21 | 8 | 15 | $20

Ramsey | 586 N. Franklin Tpke. (Spring St.) | 201-934-7777

Although "badly in need of a makeover", most ignore the decor and the other "passable" chow in favor of the "best" thin-crust pizzas purveyed at this "legendary", cash-only 70-year-plus Ramsey Italian tavern; "affordable" tabs even make it worth "the speeding ticket you may get on the way."

Kitchen 233 *American* ∇ 22 | 25 | 20 | $48

Westmont | 233 Haddon Ave. (Ardmore Terr.) | 856-833-9233 | www.kitchen233.com

"Delicious" dining attracts at this American Westmont addition distinguished by a wine bar (abetted by a very solid vino selection) and decor featuring dark woods and banquettes; though "costly", it's nice to "not have to drive all the way to Philadelphia to get this kind of quality"; N.B. there's a new patio.

Klein's Fish Market & Waterside Cafe *Seafood* 20 | 13 | 17 | $32

Belmar | 708 River Rd. (bet. 7th & 8th Aves.) | 732-681-1177 | www.kleinsfish.com

For Jersey Shore "on-the-dock" dining ("watch the boats sail by"), it's hard to pass up this roomy seafooder marketing "fresh" fish and a come-as-you-are atmosphere; there's "not much decor" here, but few care, and even the paper and plastic place settings please; N.B. there are sushi and raw bars on the premises.

K.O.B.E. Ⓜ *Japanese* ∇ 25 | 23 | 18 | $30

Holmdel | The Commons at Holmdel | 2132 Rte. 35 S. (Laurel Ave.) | 732-275-0025 | www.kobecuisine.com

Despite what the name suggests, this Holmdel Japanese BYO's focus is fish, as in "beautiful" presentations of the "best" sushi served in a "modern" space featuring slate and glass; to experience the "terrific" offerings for even less money, check out the "excellent" bento box lunches.

Komegashi *Japanese* 24 | 18 | 21 | $33

Jersey City | 103 Montgomery St. (Warren St.) | 201-433-4567
Jersey City | 99 Pavonia Ave. (Washington Blvd.) | 201-533-8888
www.komegashi.com

These Jersey City Japanese boast unique features: while some prefer the Montgomery Street locale for its more "traditional" eats including "excellent" sushi, others opt for Pavonia's "interesting" selection of fusion-style food and "wonderful" ambiance featuring a waterside "view of NYC and docked yachts"; either way, "quality and consistency" are guaranteed.

Konbu Ⓜ *Japanese* ∇ 25 | 17 | 23 | $29

Manalapan | Design Ctr. | 345 Rte. 9 S. (bet. Gordon's Corner & Taylor Mills Rds.) | 732-462-6886

Though specializing in "fantastic" sushi, chef James Tran also presents "innovative" takes on Japanese at his "friendly" Manalapan shopping-center BYO; the "relaxing" vibe complements a setting featuring private rooms that are "good for families."

Krakus *Polish*

FOOD	DECOR	SERVICE	COST
-	-	-	M

Wallington | 208 Main Ave. (Alden St.) | 973-779-1922
From borscht to kielbasa, pierogi to potato pancakes, this Wallington spot doles out homey Polish classics from the indigenous inventory; it's all gutsy, filling and robust and served in a humble dining space draped in thick, gold curtains and outfitted with sturdy wood appointments; the addition of a liquor license should complement the cuisine.

Krave Café ☒ *American*

FOOD	DECOR	SERVICE	COST
-	-	-	M

Newton | 15 E. Clinton St. (Water St.) | 973-383-2600
If you crave reasonably priced, eclectic American cuisine (from duck quesadillas to Caribbean shrimp) check out this Newton strip-mall BYO; the easygoing environment is a suitable foil for the vivacious vittles.

Kunkel's Seafood & Steakhouse Ⓜ *Seafood/Steak*

FOOD	DECOR	SERVICE	COST
▽ 20	24	22	$38

Haddon Heights | 920 W. Kings Hwy. (bet. Black Horse & White Horse Pikes) | 856-547-1225 | www.kunkelsrestaurant.com
Something you may find "in Manhattan", this Haddon Heights chophouse purveys "good" beef and seafood that's enhanced by the banqueted, mahogany adorned space; if "just another steakhouse" to foes, fans think the place "charms."

Kuzina by Sofia *Greek*

FOOD	DECOR	SERVICE	COST
-	-	-	M

Cherry Hill | Sawmill Vill. | 404 Rte. 70 W. (Vermont Ave.) | 856-429-1061 | www.kuzinabysofia.com
This Cherry Hill BYO's midpriced Greek menu is Homeric in both size and scope, covering everything from salads, souvlaki and gyros to grilled meats; the simple room (think peach walls and white tablecloths under glass) can get loud with those who think it's worth a Troy.

Labrador Lounge *Eclectic*

FOOD	DECOR	SERVICE	COST
23	17	20	$35

Normandy Beach | 3581 Rte. 35 N. (Peterson Ln.) | 732-830-5770 | www.kitschens.com
"Offbeat" for the Shore, this "funky" Normandy Beach BYO offers something other than the area's standard eats, with a "tasty" Eclectic slate including sushi (there's "not one dog" on the menu) served by a "good" staff; P.S. it's even more "worthwhile if you sit outside."

La Campagna *Italian*

FOOD	DECOR	SERVICE	COST
24	18	20	$44

Millburn | 194 Essex St. (Main St.) | 973-379-8989
Morristown | 5 Elm St. (South St.) | 973-644-4943
www.lacampagnaristorante.com
"Superlative", "comforting" Italian preparations bring plaudits to this "consistent" Morristown BYO whose floor is guided by "efficient" servers who work a "tight" space; just about everybody "likes it here", plus, the newer Millburn spin-off is "wonderful."

	FOOD	DECOR	SERVICE	COST

La Campagne ⓜ *French*
24 | 21 | 20 | $51

Cherry Hill | 312 Kresson Rd. (bet. Brace & Marlkress Rds.) | 856-429-7647 | www.lacampagne.com

Cherry Hill's "elegant", "country" French "farmhouse" BYO "never disappoints" given the "adorable" setting and "flavorful" fare that brings diners close to France; indeed, the food and decor help counterbalance "uneven service."

Laceno Italian Grill *Italian/Seafood*
25 | 17 | 20 | $40

Voorhees | Echelon Village Plaza | 1118 White Horse Rd. (Rte. 561) | 856-627-3700

"Hello, Tuscany" say acolytes who tip their hats to this Voorhees mall BYO specializing in the "best", "freshest" seafood on its "great" menu that's "worthy of a nice bottle of wine"; the "very busy" scene attests to the consensus: "Italian doesn't get any better."

La Cipollina ⓜ *Italian*
23 | 20 | 21 | $41

Freehold | 16A W. Main St. (South St.) | 732-308-3830 | www.lacipollina.com

Holding on to its "special-occasion" appeal, this Freehold Italian BYO is a go-to for "leisurely, upscale" dining accompanied by "eager-to-please" service and "excellent" cooking; while "on the pricey side", there's high regard for the "value" prix fixes.

La Esperanza ⓜ *Mexican*
∇ 24 | 13 | 20 | $23

Lindenwold | 40 E. Gibbsboro Rd. (Arthur Ave.) | 856-782-7114 | www.mexicanhope.com

"Hummers and work trucks" in the lot give away the diverse crowd that frequents this Lindenwold Mexican where a visit is "like a quick trip over the border" when you factor in the "real-deal" cooking; tequila fans tout the selection, deeming it "impressive for the 'burbs."

La Focaccia *Italian*
24 | 18 | 22 | $41

Summit | 523 Morris Ave. (Aubrey St.) | 908-277-4006 | www.lafocaccianj.com

Much is "*buono*" about this "busy" BYO in Summit and its Italian offerings, "tried-and-true" specialties that are "well prepared" and brought to table by a "humorous", "veteran" staff; P.S. the "attractive" expansion may even help ease the "squeeze."

Laguna Grill *American/Eclectic*
∇ 22 | 19 | 21 | $39

Brigantine | 1400 Ocean Ave. (14th St.) | 609-266-8367 | www.lagunagrill.com

"The best view going" – the "beach and ocean provide the ultimate" decor – gives this Brigantine American-Eclectic near the Borgata a leg up, though the food is "good" too; the "friendly" bar area baits fans, thanks partly to the "great" martinis.

Lahiere's ⓩ *Continental/French*
21 | 19 | 20 | $54

Princeton | 11 Witherspoon St. (Nassau St.) | 609-921-2798 | www.lahieres.com

Princeton's "old reliable" (since 1919) New American has gone Continental-French, with menu changes that may "make it better", but still hosts "graduation-day" affairs and "tweedy professor types" who come for the "tradition" and perhaps a bit of that "worn decor"; N.B. the change in cuisine may outdate the above Food score.

ⓩ La Isla *Cuban* | 26 | 10 | 19 | $21 |

Hoboken | 104 Washington St. (bet. 1st & 2nd Sts.) | 201-659-8197 | www.laislarestaurant.com

It resembles a "cafeteria", but for "amazing" Cuban *comidas*, this "tiny" Hoboken all-day BYO delivers what many consider the "best" fare of its kind – and "cheap" at that; it's perpetually "too crowded", so veterans advise you prepare for a "long wait."

Lalezar *Turkish* | - | - | - | M |

Montclair | 720 Bloomfield Ave. (St. Luke's Pl.) | 973-233-1984 | www.lalezarcuisine.com

Sisters Melinda Basaran and Heidi Birson bring a taste of their homeland to Montclair at this chic BYO Turkish (the name means 'tulip garden') featuring char-grilled kebabs supplemented by a variety of vegetarian selections; belly dancers on Friday and Saturday nights should seal the deal.

Lambertville Station *American* | 17 | 20 | 19 | $36 |

Lambertville | 11 Bridge St. (Delaware River) | 609-397-8300 | www.lambertvillestation.com

"Don't dismiss it as a tourist trap" plead supporters who are "never disappointed" by the "lovely views" of the Delaware River afforded from this brass, glass and oak-filled Lambertville Traditional American set in a former train station; some find "better food in town", but most agree it's a "fine" pit stop.

La Nonna Piancone's *Italian* | 18 | 16 | 17 | $35 |

Bradley Beach | 800 Main St. (McCabe Ave.) | 732-775-0906 | www.piancone.com

If "old-fashioned" Italian is the craving, fill up at this trattoria dispensing "lotsa food" for "reasonable" prices; "hefty eaters" are pleased, but for those citing "heavy" eats that are "short on taste", an adjacent bakery should satisfy the sweet tooth; N.B. the Brielle outpost has closed and the Bradley Beach original has new owners.

La Pastaria *Italian* | 19 | 17 | 18 | $30 |

Summit | 327 Springfield Ave. (Summit Ave.) | 908-522-9088
Red Bank | 30 Linden Pl. (Broad St.) | 732-224-8699
www.lapastaria.com

"Hearty appetites" are welcome at these "crowded" BYO Red Bank and Summit sisters serving up "reliably" satisfying "homestyle" Italian; feeding "families" is a deal here – prices are as small as the "portions are large."

La Scala Ⓜ *Italian* | 22 | 15 | 20 | $39 |

Somerville | 117 N. Gaston Ave. (bet. Bartine & William Sts.) | 908-218-9300 | www.lascalafineitalian.com

For a "very ambitious" menu of Northern Italian cuisine that features "exotic meats like ostrich and buffalo", head to chef-owner

Omar Aly's BYO in Somerville; "the decor doesn't do the restaurant justice" (though a seat on the patio makes for a "pleasant evening"), but surveyors suggest you "get past it and enjoy the food" as well as the "polished", "easygoing service"; N.B. there are plans to remodel.

La Spiaggia *Italian*   ▽ 26 | 20 | 27 | $48

Ship Bottom | 357 W. Eighth St. (Barnegat Ave.) | 609-494-4343 | www.laspiaggialbi.com

The "place to go when you want more than beach food", this "elegant", softly lit Ship Bottom Italian BYO is staffed with "professional" servers who deliver straight-up "fabulous" preparations; few question, then, just why this winning venue is still "raising the bar on LBI dining."

La Strada Ⓜ *Italian*   22 | 19 | 21 | $42

Randolph | 1105 Rte. 10 E. (bet. Canfield & Eyland Aves.) | 973-584-4607 | www.lastradarestaurant.com

With an "extensive" menu of "very good, traditional Italian" fare and "a staff that treats you like family, why go anywhere else?" ask admirers of this "upscale", "old-world restaurant" in Randolph; even better, the "wonderful evening" includes "an elegant atmosphere" highlighted by "piano player that entertains on weekends."

La Tapatia *Mexican*   - | - | - | I

Asbury Park | 707 Main St. (Sewall Ave.) | 732-776-7826

You won't find cheese slathered over every dish at this Asbury Park Mexican selling truly authentic south-of-the-border cuisine including a range of tacos and tamales washed down by horchatas, creamy beverages made with rice or almonds; the shoebox-size setup doesn't detract from its popularity, nor does the new liquor license.

Latitude 40N Ⓜ *Seafood*   23 | 13 | 20 | $36

Point Pleasant Beach | 816 Arnold Ave. (bet. Lincoln Ave. & Woodland Rd.) | 732-892-8553 | www.latitude40n.com

"All you have to do is sit back and enjoy" the "delicious" dishes that turn up in this "tucked-away" Point Pleasant Beach BYO, where "moderate" pricing is as welcoming as the "fresh" seafood; while the nautical decor is "nondescript", "attentive" service isn't.

Ⓩ Latour Ⓜ *French*   27 | 21 | 25 | $52

Ridgewood | 6 E. Ridgewood Ave. (Broad St.) | 201-445-5056 | www.latourridgewood.com

"Warm greetings" from chef-owner Michael Latour enhance the "first-rate" repasts at his Ridgewood BYO, a standby and "standard-setter" for Classic French cookery, from savories to sweets; once you walk in, you're "instantly delighted to be here", with admirers affirming it's "adorable" – every inch of it; P.S. to "cut the expense", call ahead to check when they offer prix fixes.

Le Fandy ⓏⓂ *French*   26 | 16 | 20 | $46

Fair Haven | 609 River Rd. (Cedar Ave.) | 732-530-3338 | www.lefandybistro.com

Behind a "humble storefront" lies this "great" BYO hideaway, the Fair Haven home of Luke Peter Ong's "impeccable" French bistro preparations abetted by a "sincere", "helpful" staff; overall, the "small" quarters belie the quality, "high-end" food – and "matching prices."

☒ Legal Sea Foods *Seafood*
20 | 17 | 18 | $39

Paramus | Garden State Plaza | 1 Garden State Plaza (Rte. 17) | 201-843-8483
Short Hills | Short Hills Mall | 1200 Morris Tpke. (Rte. 24 W.) | 973-467-0089
www.legalseafoods.com

"Good, fresh" fish is the hook at this nautical twosome in Paramus and The Short Hills Mall that "upholds the chain's reputation", offering a "diverse" seafood selection that's appreciated by hordes of fans, including "kids"; hence, it's easy to fathom the appeal, and while "always crowded", "efficient" service keeps things flowing.

Le Petit Chateau Ⓜ *French*
25 | 22 | 25 | $65

Bernardsville | 121 Claremont Rd. (Rte. 202) | 908-766-4544 | www.greatscottchef.com

"Haute" "country" and innovative French at their "finest" is the signature of "talented" chef-owner Scott Cutaneo's "fabulous" Bernardsville destination also prized for a "wine list to behold"; as "one of Jersey's elite" eateries, you can bet it's "expensive", but for less of an expense, the $65 prix fixe is one "smart" way to go.

☒ Le Rendez-Vous Ⓜ *French*
26 | 18 | 24 | $51

Kenilworth | 520 Boulevard (21st St.) | 908-931-0888 | www.lerendez-vousnj.com

For a "bit of Provence" in the midst of Kenilworth, this BYO "dead-ringer" of a French bistro offers a "total Gallic experience", with a "personable" staff and "cozy" quarters supporting the "outstanding" dishes; the meals are "expensive", but bargain-hunters meet up for the tasting menus, which are "fabulous values" considering the quality.

Liberty House Restaurant Ⓜ *American*
20 | 25 | 19 | $50

Jersey City | Liberty State Park | 76 Audrey Zapp Dr. (Freedom Way) | 201-395-0300 | www.libertyhouserestaurant.com

The food's "good", but it's the "unbeatable, unobstructed" views of NYC and "beautiful" wraparound porch for alfresco dining that are the selling points of this Jersey City Traditional American camped out in Liberty State Park; it's so perfect for "celebrations", the restaurant vaunts Valiant, an 80-ft. yacht docked nearby for parties.

Light Horse Tavern, The *American*
22 | 24 | 21 | $39

Jersey City | 199 Washington St. (Morris St.) | 201-946-2028 | www.lighthorsetavern.com

"A slice of old Greenwich Village on the other side of the Hudson", this "upscale" Jersey City tavern (housed in a circa-1850 brick building) boasts a "beautiful" bar in its "gorgeous" split-level space, all the better to frame the kitchen's "delicious" New American pub food; a "bounty" of microbrews and a "good" wine list help transform the place into a "neighborhood destination."

	FOOD	DECOR	SERVICE	COST

Lilly's on the Canal *Eclectic*
21 | 19 | 19 | $35

Lambertville | 2 Canal St. (Bridge St.) | 609-397-6242 |
www.lillysonthecanal.com

This industrial-chic Lambertville Eclectic proffers "flavorful"
fare within its bi-level digs; whereas some favor the "quiet" upper deck to the "frenetic" but "interesting" first floor and its
open kitchen, the "beautiful" waterside patio is an all-around
crowd-pleaser; it's BYO, but a few local wines are sold on-
premises; N.B. closed Tuesdays.

Limestone Cafe Ⓜ *American*
22 | 18 | 19 | $43

Peapack | 89 Main St. (Holland Ave.) | 908-234-1475

Fans of Traditional American "comfort" cookery consider this
"quaint" eatery in a converted Peapack Victorian "worth a ride out
to horse country"; if the decor "needs a little uplift" and the
"friendly" service is "spotty", the "good" food helps atone for any
shortcomings; N.B. also closed Tuesdays.

Lincroft Inn *Continental*
18 | 17 | 19 | $39

Lincroft | 700 Newman Springs Rd. (Middletown Lincroft Rd.) |
732-747-0890 | www.lincroftinn.com

"Cold winter nights" bring local loyalists to this "warm" 'n' "cozy"
Lincroft Continental in business since 1697; aside from an "excellent" wine list, it's "great for burgers at the bar" or for just "filling"
up, but foes feel that the operation "needs to move into the 21st
century"; N.B. a recent renovation seems a step in that direction –
and may outdate the above Decor score.

Little Café, A ⓈⓂ *Eclectic*
25 | 17 | 23 | $37

Voorhees | Plaza Shoppes | 118 White Horse Rd. E. (Burnt Mill Rd.) |
856-784-3344 | www.alittlecafenj.com

"The cutest, quaintest" setting frames the "gorgeous" food, the
handiwork of Marianne Cuneo Powell, who's "at the top of her craft"
with this Eclectic BYO in a "nondescript" Voorhees strip mall; de-
pending on perspective, you get "cramped" conditions or enough
"intimacy" for "romantic" dinners.

Little Saigon *Vietnamese*
- | - | - | I

Atlantic City | 2801 Arctic Ave. (Iowa Ave.) | 609-347-9119

If you're in need of a guaranteed winner, leave the casino and try
this genial little Atlantic City BYO Vietnamese with low prices,
large portions and inspired fare; those in-the-know show up at
odd hours – the lines get long for the chef's phos, fresh fish and
numerous vegetarian dishes.

Little Tuna, The *Seafood*
20 | 18 | 19 | $36

Haddonfield | 141 Kings Hwy. (S. Haddon Ave.) | 856-795-0888 |
www.thelittletuna.com

This Haddonfield BYO is a "reliable" choice for seafood, with generally "well-prepared" fish on a menu that "pleases"; those who land
in the "deafening downstairs" can always opt for the calmer upstairs
on future visits.

	FOOD	DECOR	SERVICE	COST

Lobster House *Seafood*
20 | 17 | 18 | $36

Cape May | Fisherman's Wharf | 906 Schellenger Landing Rd.
(Rte. 109 S.) | 609-884-8296 | www.thelobsterhouse.com
"A must" for some of "the freshest" catch in Cape May, this spacious
docksider, a "true summer tradition" and "tourist" destination,
proves you "don't need to be cutting-edge to be great"; for diehards,
the "absurd" waits are "worth it", for others, there's always the takeout window; N.B. open year-round.

Lodos ⓜ *Mediterranean/Turkish*
▽ 21 | 18 | 18 | $29

New Milford | 690 River Rd. (Henley Ave.) | 201-265-0004
For "delicious", "consistent" Turkish-Mediterranean "treats" in
New Milford, make sure to check out this "terrific" BYO storefront;
all acknowledge that the prices are "reasonable", especially if you
go for the "great deal" of a dinner, when you "get so much food"
for the money.

Lola's *Spanish*
22 | 23 | 20 | $36

Hoboken | 153 14th St. (Bloomfield St.) | 201-420-6062 |
lolas-tapas-wine-bar-hoboken.com/
"Just what Hoboken needed" is what you're bound to hear about this
bi-level Iberian and its "consistently good" tapas, "moderate" pricing and "great" selection of Spanish wines (the cellar holds some
6,000 bottles); the "old-world" ambiance makes some say it feels
like they're "sitting on a veranda in a Spanish town."

Look See *Chinese*
19 | 14 | 17 | $28

Ramsey | 295 N. Franklin Tpke. (Rte. 17) | 201-327-1515
"One of the better" Chinese restaurants in the area is this BYO servicing Ramsey locals with "tasty" dishes; given the undistinguished,
"nothing-fancy" digs and "grumpy" service, is it any surprise that
"takeout is an excellent" alternative?

ⓩ Lorena's ⓜ *French*
27 | 21 | 25 | $56

Maplewood | 168 Maplewood Ave. (off Valley St.) | 973-763-4460 |
www.restaurantlorena.com
"Good things come in small packages" marvel fans of this super-
"small" Maplewood French BYO where chef-owner Humberto
Campos Jr. (ex Ryland Inn, Nicholas) uses "wonderful" ingredients
to showcase his "stunning" preparations while his partner, Lorena
Perez, presides over the "attentive" staff; the consensus: it's the
town's "crown jewel."

Los Amigos *Mexican/Southwestern*
23 | 18 | 20 | $27

Atlantic City | 1926 Atlantic Ave. (bet. Michigan & Ohio Aves.) |
609-344-2293
West Berlin | 461 Rte. 73 N. (Franklin Ave.) | 856-767-5216 ⓜ
www.losamigosrest.com
The "best" "down 'n' dirty" Mexican-Southwestern fare makes this
twosome (in Atlantic City and West Berlin) an obvious choice,
though the "ultimate" margaritas are a draw themselves; a "friendly"
vibe and the "right" prices set the duo up for several "*olés!*"

	FOOD	DECOR	SERVICE	COST

Lotus Cafe *Chinese*   24 | 12 | 18 | $24

Hackensack | Home Depot Shopping Ctr. | 450 Hackensack Ave. (Grand Ave.) | 201-488-7070

This "crowded" BYO Hackensack strip-maller is touted for its "outstanding", "reasonably" priced Chinese cooking, "aim-to-please" service and "fast and friendly" delivery; N.B. for those who called the digs "uninspired", a recent remodeling may outdate the above Decor score.

LouCás *Italian*   24 | 18 | 21 | $38

Edison | Colonial Village Shopping Ctr. | 9 Lincoln Hwy. (Parsonage Rd.) | 732-549-8580 | www.loucasrestaurant.com

"You never leave hungry" – or disappointed – with the "overly generous" portions of consistently "delicious" Italian, seafood and steak offerings in store at this bi-level Edison strip-mall BYO overseen by chef and co-owner Loucás Sofocli; a "warm welcome" is a given, as are "crowds" keen on getting a "great" value.

Lua *Pan-Latin*   22 | 25 | 19 | $48

Hoboken | 1300 Sinatra Dr. N. (14th St.) | 201-876-1900 | www.luarestaurant.com

For what's considered the "best scene" in Hoboken – both inside and outside – hit this huge, "gorgeous" Pan-Latin offering "incredible" views of Manhattan visible from the "fantastic" oval neon bar, the site of "eye candy galore"; as to be expected, though the fare's "tasty", it's more "scene than cuisine" at this "South Beach on the Hudson", where a good credit limit is necessary to cover the (unsurprisingly) "pricey" tabs.

Luchento's Ⓜ *Italian*   20 | 12 | 18 | $36

Millstone | 520 Hwy. 33 W. (Dugans Grove Rd.) | 732-446-8500 | www.luchentos.com

"Generous" helpings of "good", if "basic" Italian is the calling card of this "family-friendly" Millstone BYO that also proffers a handful of Cajun-Creole dishes; "nothing to write home about" describes the decor, not the "reasonable" prices.

Lucky Bones
Backwater Grille ☽ *American*   18 | 14 | 16 | $32

Cape May | 1200 Rte. 109 S. (3rd Ave.) | 609-884-2663 | www.luckybonesrestaurant.com

A popular choice for "casual dining" on Cape May, this American doubles as both a meet-and-greet "scene" for bar fans and as a "family" eatery serving a range of "tasty" offerings; live bands (Wednesdays–Saturdays), good-"value" prices and a recently installed heated porch are added attractions.

Luigi's *Italian*   19 | 15 | 20 | $36

East Hanover | Berkeley Plaza | 434 Ridgedale Ave. (McKinley Ave.) | 973-887-8408 | www.luigisitalianrestaurant.com

This "congenial" East Hanover storefront Italian purveys a "solid" menu and "decent" portions, some of which usually end up in "doggy bags"; no, there's "nothing spectacular" here – just a "pleasant place for a pleasant meal" that's a "great" value.

Luka's ⑤ *Italian* | 22 | 13 | 19 | $32

Ridgefield Park | 238 Main St. (Park St.) | 201-440-2996 |
www.lukasitaliancuisine.com

"Delicious", "high-quality" Italian at "reasonable" prices make this Ridgefield Park BYO "worth seeking out"; perhaps a little "plain", the setting is warmed by both the presence of "charming" Luka Sinishtaj and the "crowds" that visit.

NEW Luke's Kitchen *American* | - | - | - | M

Maplewood | 175 Maplewood Ave. (bet. Baker St. & Highland Pl.) |
973-763-4005 | www.lukeskitchen.com

For a mellow New American meal in Maplewood, locals in-the-know go to this new BYO storefront to linger on the likes of roasted scallops in a black truffle vinaigrette; the comfortable setting is a suitable backdrop for simple dishes prepared precisely, the trademark of this affordable family-friendly bistro.

Lu Nello ⑤ *Italian* | 25 | 18 | 24 | $56

Cedar Grove | 182 Stevens Ave. (Lindsley Rd.) | 973-837-1660 |
www.lunello.com

"Never less than wonderful", this Cedar Grove temple of "soul food" the Italian way is a "gastronome's delight" on account of its "great" cooking and "exceptional" list of specials; it pays to be an insider, though, as some say only "regulars get special treatment."

Madame Claude Cafe Ⓜ⇄ *French* | 23 | 15 | 20 | $26

Jersey City | 364½ Fourth St. (Brunswick St.) | 201-876-8800 |
www.madameclaudecafe.com

"Simple, honest" French bistro fare keeps this "teeny, tiny", "cute" and "quirky" cash-only Jersey City BYO a "delight" for fans of sweet and savory Gallic fare; while the location is unlikely, inside, the "charming", sunny vibe seems pure Left Bank.

Mad Batter *American* | 21 | 19 | 19 | $30

Cape May | Carroll Villa Hotel | 19 Jackson St. (bet. Beach Dr. & Carpenter Ln.) | 609-884-5970 | www.madbatter.com

"Fantastic" breakfasts and lunches including "outrageously" good pancakes and "delicious" omelets are the specialty of this "friendly" venerable American staple set in a Cape May B&B; it's overall an "enjoyable" experience, and "especially if you sit outside" on the porch.

Madeleine's Petit Paris Ⓜ *Continental/French* | 24 | 18 | 23 | $48

Northvale | 416 Tappan Rd. (Paris Ave.) | 201-767-0063 |
www.madeleinespetitparis.com

"Incredible" fare brings Gallic-ing gourmets to this "refined" Northvale French-Continental renowned as much for its "heavenly" soufflés and other dishes (courtesy of chef Gaspard Caloz) as for the "gracious" service of wife Madeleine, a "terrific" hostess; no surprise, this "very special" place is "date" central; N.B. BYO on Tuesdays only.

	FOOD	DECOR	SERVICE	COST

Madison Bar & Grill *American*   `21` `20` `19` `$36`

Hoboken | 1316 Washington St. (14th St.) | 201-386-0300 |
www.madisonbarandgrill.com

Stop in to this "reliable" north "Hoboken classic", as "beyond the
bar" lies a "separate", "nicely appointed dining room that sets the
tone" for the "solid" menu of "well-executed" New American "basics" and "adventurous specials"; "when you'd rather just drink",
however, the "packed bar" provides a "great singles scene", especially on Tuesday's "crazy" half-price martini night.

Magic Pot Ⓜ *Fondue*   `19` `13` `19` `$41`

Edgewater | 934 River Rd. (bet. Dempsey & Hilliard Aves.) | 201-969-8005 |
www.magicpotfondue.com

This Edgewater BYO "hits the spot" for fondue fans who dig "cheesy
goodness" along with "to-die-for" desserts; though some find it
somewhat "pricey considering you're doing all of the cooking", most
maintain it all adds up to a "fun evening."

Mahogany Grille *American*   `23` `23` `21` `$50`

Manasquan | 142 Main St. (Parker Ave.) | 732-292-1300 |
www.themahoganygrille.com

"Excellent" fare accompanied by "professional" service, an "attractive" setting and "nice" wines make this Manasquan New American
so "loved by many"; it's a "comfortable" "class act" and "dependable" option – usually "when cost doesn't matter."

Mahzu *Japanese*   `22` `16` `18` `$31`

Aberdeen | Aberdeen Plaza | 1077 Rte. 34 (Lloyd Rd.) |
732-583-8985

Freehold Township | 430 Mts. Corner Dr. (Rte. 537) |
732-866-9668
www.mahzu.net

It's "hard to choose" between the "wide variety", from "fresh" sushi
to "tasty" hibachi and teppanyaki selections at these BYOs, whose
names suggest "pine tree" in Japanese; the "friendly" service
pleases, even though it tends to be "spotty"; N.B. an East Windsor
location is scheduled to open in summer 2008.

Main Street Bistro Ⓜ *American*   `21` `19` `19` `$39`

Freehold | 30 E. Main St. (Spring St.) | 732-294-1112 |
www.bistro1.com

An "upscale crowd" is attracted to this "noisy" split-level New
American BYO whose reliably "good" food and scene help "spruce
up the dining" situation in Freehold; P.S. some suggest the outdoor
dining qualifies as a "people-watching event."

Main Street Euro-American   `18` `15` `17` `$33`

Bistro & Bar *American/Continental*

Princeton | Princeton Shopping Ctr. | 301 N. Harrison St. (Valley Rd.) |
609-921-2779 | www.mainstreetprinceton.com

Vintage posters lend to the "quaintness" of this seemingly
"always full" yet "comfortable" Princeton shopping-center
American-Continental whose fare is "good" to partisans and "ordi-

| | FOOD | DECOR | SERVICE | COST |

nary" to others; still, all agree the bar is "wonderful" and outdoor seating "pleasant"; N.B. an expanded patio and alfresco bar are slated for summer 2008.

Maize *American* | 21 | 22 | 19 | $43

Newark | Robert Treat Hotel | 50 Park Pl. (bet. Center & E. Park Sts.) | 973-733-2202 | www.maizerestaurant.com

This "pretty", Tony Chi-designed Traditional American in a Downtown Newark hotel opposite NJPAC is a sound alternative to the area's Iberian offerings; not surprisingly, concert nights draw crowds that choose the "great", though "limited" pre-theater option that most consider "the way to go."

Makeda *Ethiopian* | 23 | 23 | 20 | $34

New Brunswick | 338 George St. (bet. Bayard St. & Livingston Ave.) | 732-545-5115

"Be a little adventurous" and try this "unique experience" on New Brunswick's Restaurant Row, where you "use your fingers" (plus "spongy" injera bread) "to scoop up Ethiopian" eats that "burst with flavor"; it's all set in a "beautiful" space, and while the "service can vary greatly, the food" – and "hip" weekend music – "makes up for it."

Malabar House Ⓜ *Indian* | - | - | - | I

Piscataway | 1665 Stelton Rd. (Ethel Rd.) | 732-819-0400

In Piscataway, this BYO is known for its dosas and rare renditions of affordable, authentic Southern Indian classics such as black lentil balls with yogurt; though the strip-mall surroundings may not engage the senses, the fare might.

Manhattan Steakhouse *Steak* | 22 | 19 | 19 | $55

Oakhurst | 2105 Rte. 35 N. (W. Park Ave.) | 732-493-6328 | www.manhattansteakhouse.com

"Easier than going to the city" reason fans of this Oakhurst chophouse dispensing some "good and pricey" "red meat and red wine"; aside from arguments over the manly setting ("terrific" vs. "no atmosphere"), "if you are in the mood for beef, this is the place."

NEW Manna Ⓢ Ⓜ *American* | - | - | - | M

Margate | 8409 Ventnor Ave. (Jerome Ave.) | 609-822-7722 | www.mannaattheshore.com

A peaceful aura pervades this Margate New American BYO newcomer, where a husband-and-wife team turns out moderately priced dishes like vanilla lacquered roasted half-chicken; dine amid candlelight comfortably ensconced on suede sofas or at mahogany tables.

Manon Ⓜ⇄ *French* | 25 | 21 | 23 | $44

Lambertville | 19 N. Union St. (Bridge St.) | 609-397-2596

"Like being transported" to "Provence", this "tiny" BYO "charmer" in Lambertville "remains a favorite" for its "stellar" country French cuisine and "delightful" setting (an "eye-catching" mural of 'Starry Night' blankets the ceiling); even though the tables are "elbow to elbow" and they don't take credit cards, most maintain this is "a real gem" whose facets include a "caring" staff; N.B. dinner only, Wednesdays–Sundays.

🅱 Manor, The Ⓜ *American*   23 | 25 | 24 | $61

West Orange | 111 Prospect Ave. (Woodland Ave.) | 973-731-2360 | www.themanorrestaurant.com

"From the driveway, gardens and fountains" to the "over-the-top" dining room, it's "opulence galore" at this West Orange Traditional American that "rarely disappoints" with "delicious food", "excellent wines" and an "accommodating staff"; if at times "overwhelming", this "local landmark" (in its 51st year) can be "nice when celebrating."

Marco & Pepe Ⓜ *American*   22 | 19 | 19 | $35

Jersey City | 289 Grove St. (Mercer St.) | 201-860-9688 | www.marcoandpepe.com

"A hip place for dinner" or brunch (Tuesdays–Sundays), this "chic" yet "low-key" storefront New American in Jersey City is a destination for small and large plates of deliciously "comforting" New American food; for some, "it doesn't get better", and ex-NYCers ask "who needs Manhattan now?"

Margherita's Ⓜ *Italian*   22 | 12 | 17 | $25

Hoboken | 740 Washington St. (8th St.) | 201-222-2400

"Always a safe bet" for "simple Italian at its best", this "casual" corner BYO in Hoboken serves up "humongous" helpings of "delicious", "homestyle pastas" and other "traditional" dishes plus "can't-beat-pizza"; it's "tiny", so "make sure to get there early" to avoid the "insufferable waits", or better yet, opt to sit outside.

Marie Nicole's ⚫ *American*   ∇ 23 | 21 | 23 | $48

Wildwood | 9510 Pacific Ave. (Richmond Ave.) | 609-522-5425

The few who've ventured to this "classy", "off-the-beaten-track" Wildwood "jewel" near Diamond Beach report a "good" New American menu, "attractive" quarters and a "well-stocked" bar; in short, advocates add the "Shore needs this spot."

Market in the Middle *Eclectic*   23 | 20 | 21 | $34

Asbury Park | 516 Cookman Ave. (Bangs Ave.) | 732-776-8886 | www.kitschens.com

An "interesting" Eclectic menu and equally interesting concept draw applause for this good-vibe Asbury Park place vending "delightful" fare along with its setting – a bistro-like restaurant within a wine shop and a gourmet market offering "unique" items; the "wonderful" bar and "lively" scene prove the place's "popularity"; N.B. closed Mondays during the winter.

Market Roost Ⓜ *Eclectic*   ∇ 22 | 13 | 18 | $21

Flemington | 65 Main St. (Bloomfield Ave.) | 908-788-4949 | www.marketroost.com

"Consistently reliable" sums up this "quaint", long-running Flemington BYO whose Eclectic menu of baked goods, salads and sandwiches are "good" bets for a "quick bite"; N.B. closed Mondays and Tuesdays, and open for breakfast and lunch only.

Marmara Ⓜ Turkish
- | - | - | M

Manalapan | Summerton Plaza | 339 Rte. 9 S. (Union Hill Rd.) | 732-780-9990 | www.marmararestaurant.com

This attractive BYO Turkish newcomer on Manalapan's restaurant-rich Route 9 offers a light touch to traditional Middle Eastern standards, proffering a bounty of seafood and vegetarian options in addition to the usual meat kebabs; the 100-seat, family-friendly spot is SRO on weekends when musicians and belly dancers entertain – so reserve in advance.

Marra's Ⓜ Italian
20 | 15 | 17 | $40

Ridgewood | 16 S. Broad St. (E. Ridgewood Ave.) | 201-444-1332 | www.marrasrestaurant.com

"You get exactly" what you expect at this Ridgewood Italian BYO, namely "good" red-sauce cookery, "warm" service and "long waits even with a reservation"; the convivial scene is confirmed by the "noise" and "elbow-bumping" setup.

Martino's Ⓜ Cuban
21 | 11 | 18 | $25

Somerville | 212 W. Main St. (Doughty Ave.) | 908-722-8602 | www.martinoscubanrestaurant.com

If you're thinking Cuban in Central Jersey, try this "nothing-fancy" Somerville BYO dishing out "heaping" helpings of "tasty" "economical" eats; hence, it's no surprise that locals keep coming back to this "homey" venue that's a "true success story."

Mastoris ◗ Diner
19 | 12 | 19 | $22

Bordentown | 144 Hwy. 130 (Rte. 206) | 609-298-4650 | www.mastoris.com

The menu is "longer than *War and Peace*" and the space is just as "huge" at this "landmark", the "big daddy" of diners in Bordentown catering to patrons who go as much for the "to-die-for" cheese bread as for the "mega" portions; incredible "bargains" keep the "unbelievable" crowds pouring in even at "1 AM, when the parking lot is packed"; N.B. the owners recently debuted the Alstarz Sports Pub, across the parking lot.

Matisse 🅂Ⓜ American
22 | 20 | 20 | $46

Belmar | 1300 Ocean Ave. (13th Ave.) | 732-681-7680 | www.matissecatering.com

"Wonderful" savories and sweets, and ocean views that are even "better" (you "can't get much closer to the Atlantic") paint a picture of success of this Belmar New American BYO that hosts "dates" and is "worth every dollar"; periodic jazz in winter warms the scene; N.B. closed Mondays–Tuesdays off-season.

Mattar's American/Eclectic
24 | 21 | 23 | $52

Allamuchy | 1115 Rte. 517 (Ridge Rd.) | 908-852-2300 | www.mattars.com

A "diamond" in the rough of Warren County, this "middle-of-nowhere" Eclectic–New American provides a bit of "fine dining" to the area with the "best" food around; it "doesn't disappoint", with diehards claiming "it deserves to be in a big city."

Matt's Red Rooster Grill ⓂAmerican   25 | 21 | 23 | $43

Flemington | 22 Bloomfield Ave. (Spring St.) | 908-788-7050 |
www.mattsredroostergrill.com

For a taste of "Manhattan in the middle of Flemington", fans nestle into this "cheery" New American in a restored Victorian for both chef-proprietor Matthew McPherson's "well-executed" food and his "Danny Meyer"–like (think NYC's Union Square Cafe) "hospitality"; though BYO, local wines are offered; N.B. former partner Matt Green is no longer affiliated with the business.

ⓏMcCormick & Schmick's Seafood   20 | 19 | 19 | $39

Hackensack | Riverside Square Mall | 175 Riverside Sq. (Hackensack Ave.) |
201-968-9410
Bridgewater | Bridgewater Commons | 400 Commons Way
(Prince Rodgers Ave.) | 908-707-9996
Cherry Hill | 941 Haddonfield Rd. (Rte. 70) | 856-317-1711   ⓈⓂ
www.mccormickandschmicks.com

The majority just "doesn't care" that these seafood emporiums are part of a chain, adding the items seem "so fresh you have to hold them down"; there's also "reliable" steaks and other turf proffered amid decor that makes you "forget you're in a shopping mall."

McLoone's American   17 | 23 | 18 | $43

Long Branch | 1 Ocean Ave. (Laird St.) | 732-923-1006
Sea Bright | 816 Ocean Ave. (Rumson Rd.) | 732-842-2894
www.mcloones.com

Two "glorious" views (the ocean in Long Branch and the Shrewsbury River in Sea Bright) are what's behind the appeal of these Americans whose fans have "no complaints" with them; detractors decry "amateurish" dishes and "lacking" service, but they're still a "favorite for locals and credit card companies"; N.B. new chefs at both properties may outdate the above Food score.

Mediterra Mediterranean   20 | 22 | 20 | $42

Princeton | 29 Hulfish St. (bet. Chambers & Witherspoon Sts.) |
609-252-9680 | www.terramomo.com

Proponents of this "smart", "sophisticated" Pan-Mediterranean in the heart of Princeton find "fine" food and say the setting is equally suited to "business lunches" or for when "your parents are visiting you at school" (it's particularly "heavenly to sit outside on a hot summer night"); N.B. a sister restaurant, Enoterra, is scheduled to debut summer 2008 in Kingston.

Meemah Ⓜ Chinese/Malaysian   24 | 10 | 19 | $20

Edison | Colonial Village Shopping Ctr. | 9 Lincoln Hwy. (Parsonage Rd.) |
732-906-2223 | www.meemah.com

"Forget the strip mall" and "lack of decor" and just "enjoy the food" say fans of this "yummy" Malaysian-Chinese BYO in Edison, the "greatest little secret in NJ"; the clincher: the "wide variety" of "consistently excellent" Pan-Asian dishes are "cheap and plentiful."

		FOOD	DECOR	SERVICE	COST

Megu Sushi *Japanese* ▽ 22 | 18 | 23 | $31

Cherry Hill | Village Walk Shopping Ctr. | 1990 Rte. 70 E.
(Old Orchard Rd.) | 856-489-6228 | www.megusushi.com

The "colorful" decorations are "intriguing" at this Japanese BYO
working in a Cherry Hill strip mall; it's "no Japan" when it comes to
sushi some say, but most agree the offerings are "consistent", and
likely "as good as you can expect" in the neighborhood.

Mehndi 🅼 *Indian* - | - | - | E

Morristown | 88 Headquarters Plaza (Park Pl.) | 973-871-2323 |
www.mehtanirestaurantgroup.com

This luxe Morristown Indian from the Mehtani Restaurant Group
(Ming, Moghul and Moksha) presents modern fare and specialty
cocktails in a bright, split-level space featuring Murano glass and
hand-painted enlargements of traditional Mehndi art; patrons can
partake in elaborate, temporary henna tattoos on Fridays and
Saturdays provided by an on-site artist; other options under the
same roof include Ming II, a Pan-Asian, and SM23, a posh lounge
serving bar food and drinks.

Meil's 🖗 *American* 23 | 15 | 19 | $29

Stockton | Bridge & Main Sts. (Main St./Rte. 29) | 609-397-0533 |
www.meilsrestaurant.com

For "stick-to-your-ribs" Americana served by a staff that is "a hoot",
this "cute" BYO cafe in Stockton is a "delightfully quirky" find for
"good, filling" breakfasts, brunches, lunches and dinners; just make
sure you bring cash to pay for your "down-home" meil's.

🆉 Mélange Cafe 🅼 *Creole* 26 | 16 | 22 | $35

Cherry Hill | 1601 Chapel Ave. (Woodland Ave.) | 856-663-7339 |
www.melangecafe.com

"Joe Brown is the man!" insist believers about the toque who turns
out étouffée that'll "blow you away" and "incredible" jambalaya
among the "great" menu items (with some Italian and steaks) at this
Cherry Hill BYO, the "real deal" as far as Creole cookery; the setting's "unassuming", but the place is still nice for "celebrations."

Melting Pot *Fondue* 19 | 20 | 19 | $47

NEW Hoboken | 100 Sinatra Dr. (1st St.) | 201-222-1440
Westwood | 250 Center Ave. (Westwood Ave.) | 201-664-8877
Somerville | 190 W. Main St. (Doughty Ave.) | 908-575-8010
Whippany | Pine Plaza Shopping Ctr. | 831 Rte. 10 (N. Jefferson Rd.) |
973-428-5400
Red Bank | The Galleria | 2 Bridge Ave. (W. Front St.) | 732-219-0090
NEW Atlantic City | 2112 Atlantic Ave. (Arkansas Ave.) | 609-441-1100
www.meltingpot.com

It may be a "kitschy chain" but fondue fans and even "jaded foodies"
have a "blast" dipping into "delicious" pots of "cheesy, brothy, choc-
olately goodness" at this Jersey sextet; even though it costs a "small
fortune for the privilege of cooking your own food", regulars say
there's magic in the 'Big Night Out' ($86–$100 per couple), a four-
course prix fixe extravaganza.

	FOOD	DECOR	SERVICE	COST

Memphis Pig Out ≠ *BBQ* — 19 | 11 | 18 | $28

Atlantic Highlands | 67 First Ave. (Center Ave.) | 732-291-5533 |
www.memphispigout.com

At this Atlantic Highlands barbecue joint, you get the "best" baby-backs and other "excellent" 'cue on its "sinner's paradise" of a menu; overall, it's an "excellent" buy, and the "kinda-grimy", pig-motif interior "somehow works."

NEW Merchant House Tavern *American* — - | - | - | M
(fka Aria Ristorante)

Fairfield | 4 Little Falls Rd. (Hwy. 46) | 973-227-6066 |
www.merchanthousetavern.com

This upscale yet affordable Fairfield American tavern (formerly Aria) is geared to families craving babyback ribs and apple pie, or more sophisticated fare (think macadamia-crusted tuna); you can eat in the bustling bar (with TVs, naturally) or in the main dining room; N.B. a guitarist/singer entertains on weeknights.

Merion Inn, The *American* — 20 | 22 | 22 | $44

Cape May | 106 Decatur St. (bet. Columbia & Hughes Aves.) |
609-884-8363 | www.merioninn.com

Diners are "charmed" by this Cape May Traditional American with a nightly piano, "old-fashioned", "unpretentious" ambiance, generally "reliable" eats and "attentive" staff; aficionados affirm it also boasts a "great", "classy" bar reported to be the oldest in town.

Metropolitan Cafe *Asian/Eclectic* — 22 | 21 | 18 | $40

Freehold | 8 E. Main St. (South St.) | 732-780-9400 |
www.greatrestaurantsny.com

"Lower Manhattan in the middle of Jersey" neatly sums up this "dark", "trendy" Freeholder populated by "pretty people" baited by the bar scene, heated patio and "great" cocktails, and perhaps the "good" Asian-Eclectic food; it's a "singles" "meat market", especially on weekends, so couples may want to "plan their romance for weekdays" here.

Metuchen Inn *American* — 22 | 21 | 20 | $51

Metuchen | 424 Middlesex Ave. (Linden Ave.) | 732-494-6444 |
www.themetucheninn.com

A "lovely old-world" ambiance graces this 200-year-old Metuchen inn New American, a "relaxing" option with "reliable" food, "solid" wines and a white-tablecloth setting that "charms"; surveyors are split on the service, though, citing it "always dependable" or "slow."

Mexican Food Factory *Mexican* — 18 | 16 | 17 | $25

Marlton | 601 Rte. 70 W. (Cropwell Rd.) | 856-983-9222

"Consistently consistent", if just a "notch up from typical", is the story of the chow at this 29-year-old Mexican food hall on busy Route 70 in Marlton; no, the "service isn't the greatest" and self portraits of Frida Kahlo "peer at you from every wall", but cronies confess this spot "does the trick."

	FOOD	DECOR	SERVICE	COST

Mexico Lindo 🗿Ⓜ️ *Mexican* ▽ 28 | 15 | 23 | $18

Brick | 1135 Burnt Tavern Rd. (Sage St.) | 732-202-1930
Chicken mole and chiles rellenos help authenticate the menu at this
Brick Township BYO dishing out "excellent" Mexican food for those
"on a budget"; the quality of the cooking more than trumps the
"minimal" decor (which may have improved since a recent redo).

Meyersville Inn, The *American* - | - | - | E

Gillette | 632 Meyersville Rd. (New Vernon Rd.) | 908-647-6302 |
www.meyersvilleinn.com
This cozy, updated former 19th-century country store–turned-tavern
proffers a market-driven, globally influenced New American menu
within three comfortable dining rooms and an inviting bar; perhaps
folks will soon be able to find it in Gillette (not Meyersville).

Mia 🗿Ⓜ️ *Italian* 26 | 23 | 23 | $58

Atlantic City | Caesars on the Boardwalk | 2100 Pacific Ave.
(S. Arkansas Ave.) | 609-441-2345 | www.miaac.com
"Georges Perrier has done it again!" with this Caesars on the
Boardwalk Italian where Philly's most celebrated chef has teamed
up with protégé Chris Scarduzio to create "unbelievable" fare supported by "tip-top" servers in an airy, column-filled setting; thanks
to who's behind this "great" restaurant, the "quality is as you'd expect", as perhaps is the "arm-and-a-leg" pricing.

Michael's Cucina Italia *Italian* 19 | 11 | 16 | $25

Manalapan | Alexander Plaza | 333 Rte. 9 S. (Gordon's Corner) |
732-409-4777
With "huge" portions, it's no surprise this Manalapan BYO attracts;
the "simple", "family-style" Italian cooking pleases, and many con-
fide they'd "return" in spite of atmosphere that "could be improved";
N.B. a recent dining room redo may outdate the above Decor score.

Midori *Japanese* 24 | 14 | 19 | $32

Denville | Denville Commons Mall | 3130 Rte. 10 W. (bet. Franklin &
Hill Rds.) | 973-537-8588 | www.midorirestaurant.com
"If you're a sushi buff, this is the place to be" report raw-fish aficionados of this strip-mall Japanese BYO in Denville, where the "fantastic" selections are so "delicious"; the folks here are "friendly" and
the price is right, so "why go anywhere else?"

Mie Thai *Thai* 25 | 16 | 20 | $24

Woodbridge | 34 Main St. (Berry St.) | 732-596-9400 | www.miethai.com
All that "fabulous" Thai cooking "stands out" at this Woodbridge
BYO whose numerous backers are inspired by all the "spicy" ("mild
is hot!") vittles that come out of the kitchen; the "bargain" lunch
specials ($7.95) are a sweet deal.

Mignon Steakhouse *Steak* 23 | 18 | 20 | $45

Rutherford | 72 Park Ave. (Franklin Pl.) | 201-896-0202 |
www.villagerestaurantgroup.com
"Local carnivores get their kicks" out of this Rutherford chophouse
preparing "perfectly cooked" steaks that some say add up to a "bang

for the buck" given the BYO policy; "great" sides are in the offing, as are "warm" service and a "cozy" wood-and-brick space.

Mikado *Japanese*

FOOD	DECOR	SERVICE	COST
22	16	21	$27

Cherry Hill | 2320 Rte. 70 W. (S. Union Ave.) | 856-665-4411
Maple Shade | 468 S. Lenola Rd. (Kings Hwy.) | 856-638-1801
Marlton | Elmwood Shopping Ctr. | 793 Rte. 70 E. (Troth Rd.) | 856-797-8581
www.mikado-us.com

"Bargain" tabs make it easy for raw-fish lovers to indulge in the "fresh" sushi at this South Jersey Japanese BYO trio fronted by the "nicest" staff; they're ideal for "families", especially at the Marlton and Maple Shade branches, where hibachi is offered.

Milford Oyster House *Seafood*

FOOD	DECOR	SERVICE	COST
-	-	-	M

Milford | 92 Rte. 519 (Water St.) | 908-995-9411 | www.milfordoysterhouse.com

Head for all the oysters offered at this vintage Milford landmark where seafood – and recently added meat and poultry dishes – can be both simply and imaginatively prepared; just a quick skip from the Delaware, it's a day's-end stop for river-rafters and cyclists touring this scenic western area of the state; N.B. closed Tuesdays.

Mill at Spring Lake Heights, The Ⓜ *American*

FOOD	DECOR	SERVICE	COST
20	23	21	$44

Spring Lake Heights | 101 Old Mill Rd. (Ocean Rd.) | 732-449-1800 | www.themillatslh.com

Although the space is known more for "weddings" than for the food, this American steak 'n' seafooder in Spring Lake Heights is now open to the public for Sunday brunch (11 AM–3 PM) and special dinner theater shows (schedule available on website), all proffered amid "beautiful" grounds that include a "lovely" pond where swans glide by.

Ming Ⓜ *Chinese/Indian*

FOOD	DECOR	SERVICE	COST
23	21	18	$35

Edison | Oak Tree Shopping Ctr. | 1655-185 Oak Tree Rd. (bet. Grove & Wood Aves.) | 732-549-5051 | www.mingrestaurants.com

They "don't fool around" with the spices at this Edison BYO Indian-Chinese combo proffering "inspired" food in "upscale" quarters; this "refreshing alternative" in the area is also a little "pricey."

Ming II Ⓜ *Pan-Asian*

FOOD	DECOR	SERVICE	COST
-	-	-	M

Morristown | 88 Headquarters Plaza | 3 Speedwell Ave. (Cattano Ave.) | 973-871-2323 | www.ming2morristown.com

Take a culinary journey via imaginative Pan-Asian cuisine at this glitzy new Morristown spin-off of the popular Edison fixture; the sleek, modern look is a knockout but the prices aren't – the budget-conscious can relax and savor a menu that runs the Far East gamut.

NEW Mirabella Cafe *Italian*

FOOD	DECOR	SERVICE	COST
-	-	-	M

Cherry Hill | 210 Barclay Farms Shopping Ctr. | Rte. 70 E. (Kings Hwy.) | 856-354-1888 | www.mirabellacafe.com

Also known as Joe Palumbo's Mirabella Cafe, the South Jersey restaurant veteran has put his name on this romantic Italian BYO in

Cherry Hill; though the chef-owner's menu appeals to those mindful of healthy dining, his Sunday all-you-can-eat 'Gravy' special brings out folks with big appetites.

NEW Mi Sueño ⓈⓂ *Continental* | - | - | - | M |

Middlesex | 619 Bound Brook Rd./Rte. 28 (Main St.) | 732-529-4830 | www.misueno.org

Though the name denotes 'my dream' in Spanish, this new Middlesex Borough BYO offers a variety of cost-conscious Continental cuisine (Asian fried calamari, duck confit, wood-grilled steaks) with Latin accents (black bean soup); warm, terra-cotta-toned surroundings with well-spaced tables promote privacy – and perhaps romantic reverie.

Moghul Ⓜ *Indian* | 24 | 18 | 20 | $32 |

Edison | Oak Tree Shopping Ctr. | 1655-195 Oak Tree Rd. (bet. Grove & Wood Aves.) | 732-549-5050 | www.moghul.com

"Scintillating aromas" that emanate from this Edison Indian BYO's kitchen "make you crave" the "first-class" curries and "excellent" naan that fans brand the "best in the state"; the "great" lunch buffets are feasts fit for a moghul at pauper's prices ($10.95 weekdays; $12.95 weekends).

☒ Mojave Grille *Southwestern* | 24 | 19 | 20 | $37 |

Westfield | 35 Elm St. (North Ave.) | 908-233-7772 | www.mojavegrille.com

The curved horns are in keeping with the Southwestern motif, and so is the fare at this Westfield BYO "star", a "spicy change of pace" hailed for "consistently terrific" preparations; no doubt, the restaurant is *"magnifico"*, but no surprise: no reservations makes the place a "tough table."

Moksha Ⓜ *Indian* | ▽ 22 | 23 | 22 | $29 |

Edison | Oak Tree Shopping Ctr. | 1655-200 Oak Tree Rd. (bet. Grove & Wood Aves.) | 732-947-3010 | www.moksharestaurants.com

From the group behind Ming and Moghul comes this casual spot in Edison that serves up "simply delicious" South Indian edibles in a "pleasant", "quiet" setting; the "finger-licking-good" cuisine includes many vegetarian options and "excellent meat dishes too", making it "definitely worth a try."

Molly Pitcher Inn *American* | 22 | 25 | 23 | $47 |

Red Bank | Molly Pitcher Inn | 88 Riverside Ave. (W. Front St.) | 732-747-2500 | www.mollypitcher-oysterpoint.com

The "blazer-and-loafer crowd can't get enough" of this hotel Red Bank Traditional American, the place to "have brandy with dad the night before your wedding" (jackets required, naturally) that's still keeping "old-guard" supping alive with "old-world" service and "fine" fare enhanced by "terrific" views of the Navesink River; though a few find it "stodgy", for most, it's what "delightful dining" should be; N.B. the presence of a new chef may outdate the above Food score.

	FOOD	DECOR	SERVICE	COST

Mompou *Spanish* ▽ 20 | 24 | 20 | $32

Newark | 77 Ferry St. (Congress St.) | 973-578-8114 | www.mompoutapas.com

A "hopping place for tapas" and wine "in the heart of the Ironbound", this Ferry Street "find" offers "an upscale take" on Spanish cuisine in a "sophisticated" "lounge atmosphere" that's "like something out of SoHo" with its "exposed-brick walls" and marble-topped bar; the "convivial" vibe extends to live music (Tuesdays-Thursdays), springtime salsa lessons and a "fantastic courtyard."

Monster Sushi *Japanese* 19 | 15 | 18 | $31

Summit | 395 Springfield Ave. (Maple St.) | 908-598-1100 | www.monstersushi.com

"Peter Luger"-size slabs of sushi explain the name and concept behind this "popular" Jersey Japanese (a Summit spin-off sired by the NYC mini-chain) where "kids love" the "fresh" comestibles that include a peanut butter and jelly version, while others indulge in steaks and other cooked items; one thing: those "big portions can be tough to eat"; N.B. outdoor seating available.

Z **Moonstruck** M *American/Mediterranean* 24 | 24 | 22 | $48

Asbury Park | 517 Lake Ave. (bet. Main St. & Ocean Ave.) | 732-988-0123 | www.moonstrucknj.com

"Dinner on one of the terraces is heaven on Earth" dote devotees of this "premier" Asbury Park destination, a supremely "popular", multilevel venue serving "delicious" Mediterranean meals and that's "long on atmosphere" thanks to the "date-worthy", "romantic" space; as always, "no reservations" frustrates, but then again, the "bar is so lovely, so who cares?"

Mo' Pho M *Vietnamese* 24 | 10 | 20 | $25

Fort Lee | 212 Main St. (Lemoine Ave.) | 201-363-8886

Saigon R. M *Vietnamese*

Englewood | 58 W. Palisade Ave. (William St.) | 201-871-4777 www.saigonmopho.com

Fans want nothing mo' than to hit this "no-decor" twosome (Fort Lee's the latest) turning out "terrific" Vietnamese vittles; service is "reliable" and the seating "limited", so expect "cramped" conditions.

Morgan Fishery *Seafood* - | - | - | I

South Amboy | 1812 Rte. 35 N. (Midland Ave.) | 732-721-9100

Local a-fish-ionados applaud this 30-years-and-counting, nautically themed South Amboy BYO seafooder for both its tried-and-true ocean-fresh fare and the updated dishes of most recent chef-owner Joe Resciniti Jr. (ex Renaissance); it's mostly takeout (there are just five tables and a small patio), but the price is right for a quick bite.

Morton's, The Steakhouse *Steak* 24 | 22 | 22 | $63

Hackensack | Riverside Square Mall | 274 Riverside Sq. (Hackensack Ave.) | 201-487-1303 | www.mortons.com

"What you see is what you get" - your server displays the meat you choose to eat - at this "sure bet" of a Hackensack meat emporium

	FOOD	DECOR	SERVICE	COST

that, though part of a chain, still delivers "consistency and quality" when it comes to its steaks and "excellent" sides; if the "great" chops don't, the "costly" tabs may just give you heartburn.

NEW Mr. Bill's *Deli*

`- | - | - | I`

Hammonton | 453 Rte. 73 S. (Winslow Williamstown Rd.) | 609-561-5400

The new owners of this honest-to-goodness Jewish deli in a former hot-dog-and-custard stand in Hammonton on the way to the shore have added Italian-style deli items to the roster of super-size sandwiches, including prepared-on-premises pastrami and corned beef; top it off with freshly made ice cream.

Mr. Chu *Chinese*

`22 | 14 | 18 | $23`

East Hanover | 44 Rte. 10 W. (Ridgedale Ave.) | 973-887-7555

"Dated" decor keeps all eyes on the "delish" dishes at this East Hanover Chinese BYO where the value is "great"; watch out for "crowded" confines, and service is generally "excellent", but when busy, it's so "speedy" (they seem "just as eager getting you in as they are getting you out") that you may not have time to chu.

Mud City Crab House *Seafood*

`21 | 11 | 16 | $29`

Manahawkin | 1185 E. Bay Ave. (Heron St.) | 609-978-3660 | www.mudcitycrabhouse.com

"Quintessential crab house" aptly describes this seasonal Manahawkin BYO marketing "fresh", "great" crustaceans, not its somewhat "shady" digs; for some it's "not worth getting eaten alive" by the mosquitoes, but those willing to abide "long waits" weigh in: the place "can't be beat."

My Little Fat Greek Restaurant *Greek*

`- | - | - | I`

Freehold Township | 3430 Rte. 9 S. (Elton Adelphia Rd.) | 732-683-1304 | www.mylittlefatgreekrestaurant.com

Its catchy name is part of the charm at this agreeable Greek BYO newcomer housed in a renovated rib shack on Freehold's strip-mall-lined Route 9; the skinny-priced traditional fare (moussaka, souvlaki, shish kebab) is prepared and proffered by a family as warm as the basic but homey digs; N.B. there's takeout too.

Nag's Head ⊄ *American*

`∇ 26 | 10 | 19 | $21`

Ocean City | 801 Asbury Ave. (8th St.) | 609-391-9080 | www.nagsheadoc.net

Serving Americana (think Tollhouse pie) in an old bank building, this Ocean Cityite is an "excellent" value in light of "fair" prices and "wonderfully prepared" offerings; one of the Shore's "secrets" is open year-round, but there is no alcohol allowed.

Napa Valley Grille *American*

`22 | 21 | 21 | $43`

Paramus | Garden State Plaza | 1146 Garden State Plaza (Rtes. 4 & 17) | 201-845-5555 | www.napavalleygrille.com

For a "delightful respite" from a Paramus mall "rush" crush, head to this "sophisticated" "California"-esque spot for "good" New American and an "excellent" 500-label West Coast vino selection that's built for "wine lovers"; after all, it's a good place to "splurge after a day splurging in the stores"; N.B. serves brunch and afternoon tea.

☒ Nauvoo Grill Club *American*　16 | 26 | 17 | $40

Fair Haven | 121 Fair Haven Rd. (River Rd.) | 732-747-8777 | www.nauvoogrillclub.zoomshare.com

"Spectacular" Frank Lloyd Wright–inspired, "ski-lodge" looks at this Fair Haven New American are an easy sell for its "hip fortysomething" patrons who also come for the "great" bar scene; as for its other attributes, "unpredictable" fare and "sketchy" service are low points; N.B. the presence of a new executive chef may outdate the above Food score.

Navesink Fishery Ⓜ *Seafood*　24 | 10 | 18 | $34

Navesink | A&P Shopping Ctr. | 1004 Rte. 36 S. (Valley Dr.) | 732-291-8017

"A great steady-Eddie", this "eclectic, quirky" Navesink BYO seafooder "maintains its high standards" with fish that you can't find "any fresher"; if the nautical decor supplies "no atmosphere", there's always takeout – plus a retail market up front.

Neelam *Indian*　18 | 13 | 18 | $25

South Orange | 115 South Orange Ave. (Irvington Ave.) | 973-762-1100
Middletown | Village Mall | 1178 Rte. 35 S. (New Monmouth Rd.) | 732-671-8900 Ⓜ

These separately owned suburban BYOs quell "cravings for Indian food", which most find easy at the lunch buffet, an "incredible" bargain; all told, the vittles are "reliable but lackluster", and some suggest takeout when "dark", "depressing" decor is factored in.

Neil's Original Oyster Ⓜ *American/Seafood*　- | - | - | E

Highlands | 1 Willow St. (Shore Dr.) | 732-872-1450 | www.neilsoriginaloyster.com

Chef Neil West has migrated north to this seasonal Highlands New American-seafood perch on the bay and brought his signature hearty fare that attracts big appetites; the nautical tavern-cum-dining room holds appeal for casual diners.

Nero's Grille *Steak*　17 | 16 | 17 | $44

Livingston | 618 S. Livingston Ave. (Hobart Gap Rd.) | 973-994-1410
This stuccoed "grande dame" (since 1969) of Livingston still has mileage thanks to its "clublike" atmosphere and bar scene that attracts a crowd, and not necessarily on account of decor that looks "like a reupholstered diner"; foodwise, the steakhouse specialties range from "dependable" to "serviceable."

New Main Taste *Thai*　23 | 14 | 18 | $36

Chatham | 225 Main St. (bet. Hillside & S. Passaic Aves.) | 973-635-7333 | www.newmaintaste.dine.com

"Marvelously complex", "high-quality" cooking en-Thai-ces fans at this Chatham Siamese BYO, a "real surprise" for the 'burbs; "helpful", "sweet" yet slow-as-"molasses" service comes with the territory, but most maintain it's "certainly worth the wait."

	FOOD	DECOR	SERVICE	COST

NEW Next Door *American* — - | - | - | I

Montclair | 556 Bloomfield Ave. (bet. Midland Ave. & Park St.) | 973-744-3600

Inventive chef-owner Zod Arifai of Montclair's high-style Blu is doing double-duty with this latest entry adjacent to its celebrated sibling; a family-friendly, dinerlike BYO, it proffers reasonably priced, artfully presented comfort food in spunky pumpkin orange/olive green digs.

Nha Trang Place *Vietnamese* ∇ 24 | 10 | 17 | $18

Jersey City | 249 Newark Ave. (bet. Cole & 2nd Sts.) | 201-239-1988

Go "not for the decor" but for the "excellent" phos and assorted culinary offerings dished out at this Jersey City Vietnamese BYO; the place tends to "fill up" – no shock given the commendably "quick" service and "budget" tabs.

Z Nicholas M *American* 29 | 26 | 28 | $82

Middletown | 160 Rte. 35 S. (bet. Navesink River Rd. & Pine St.) | 732-345-9977 | www.restaurantnicholas.com

Epitomizing "ultrafine" dining, this "modern" (and Most Popular) Middletown New American "utopia of food and wine" near Red Bank is helmed by chef/co-owner (with wife Melissa) Nicholas Harary, whose "extraordinary" cuisine vaults this "amazing" restaurant to the top Food ranking in the state for the fourth straight year; add in "superlative" service (also No. 1), and even the "jaw-dropping" tabs don't deter devotees of NJ's "absolute best"; a new chef's seven-course tasting menu ($150 per person, four guests maximum) on Tuesdays–Fridays at a table in the kitchen and a casual bar/lounge are other eating options.

Niecy's M *Southern* ∇ 20 | 17 | 17 | $30

South Orange | 65B South Orange Ave. (Valley St.) | 973-275-1770

"Down-home" Southern cooking "tastes best when served with a helping of Niecy Hanson's personality" attest admirers of this South Orange BYO whose staff "warms your soul as much as the delicious food"; those who know about this place confess "they'd sell their soul to pay" for the goods; N.B. open for dinner Wednesdays–Sundays.

Nikko *Japanese* 24 | 17 | 21 | $34

Whippany | 881 Rte. 10 E. (Rte. 287) | 973-428-0787 | www.nikkonj.com

"You'd have to go fishing" to get fresher seafood say supporters of this Whippany Japanese featuring a variety of "quality" sushi and an impressive sake selection; the "cheerful" service makes the experience even more "genuinely enjoyable."

NEW 947 Bar & Grille ● M *American* — - | - | - | M

Clementon | 168 White Horse Pike (Brand Ave.) | 856-627-0947 | www.947barandgrille.com

Clementon's venerable Silver Lake Ballroom has dropped its pricey Barons Steakhouse in favor of this bright, comfy New American; local families and business-lunchers pack in for sandwiches and entrees, while happy-hour imbibers and late-nighters gather in the bar around big-screen TVs.

	FOOD	DECOR	SERVICE	COST

Nobi *Japanese*   ▽ 25 | 14 | 20 | $30

Toms River Township | T.J. Maxx Plaza | 1338 Hooper Ave. (Bey Lea Rd.) |
732-244-7888

"Fast", "friendly" service and "excellent" sushi add up at this "traditional" shopping-center Japanese BYO in Toms River; it "never disappoints" its admirers who've noted its success over the last 11 years.

No. 9 Ⓜ *American*   24 | 15 | 21 | $41

Lambertville | 9 Klines Ct. (Bridge St.) | 609-397-6380

The allure of this Lambertville storefront BYO New American lies
quite simply in the "excellent" cuisine prepared by chef-owner
Matthew Kane; N.B. the Decor score may not reflect a makeover
adding warm Tuscan colors and a display of works by local
artists; closed Tuesdays.

Noodle House, The *Asian*   19 | 19 | 17 | $24

North Brunswick | 2313 Rte. 1 S. (bet. Aaron Rd. & Commerce Blvd.) |
732-951-0141

Credit "imaginative", often "tasty" Asian fare and "ultramodern"
decor for the success of this North Brunswick BYO featuring an un-
orthodox ordering policy (you write your order on a notepad) and,
as the name suggests, "lots of noodle dishes"; "slow service" is a
con, but pros propose the "excellent" weekend lunch buffet.

Nori *Pan-Asian*   22 | 15 | 19 | $30

Caldwell | 406 Bloomfield Ave. (Academy Rd.) | 973-403-2400
Montclair | 561 Bloomfield Ave. (Maple Plaza) | 973-655-8805
www.nori-sushi.com

These "consistent" BYO Pan-Asians purvey "fresh, flavorful" fish
and a few "clever" specialty rolls; "reasonable" prices, "neat" decor
(including a tatami room in the Montclair branch) and "good" service keep customers contented.

Norma's Eastern Mediterranean   21 | 13 | 19 | $23
Restaurant *African/Mideastern*

Cherry Hill | Barclay Farms Shopping Ctr. | 132-145 Rte. 70 E. (Kings Hwy.) |
856-795-1373 | www.normasrestaurant.com

"Even less adventurous family members" go for the Middle Eastern
dishes at this Cherry Hill BYO whose weekend belly dancing
supplies as much of its "cult following" as the "very good", "feast-fit-
for-a-king" offerings; the service "charms", and all agree
meals here are "the best deal" going; N.B. the seating area has
recently been expanded.

Nouveau Sushi Ⓜ *Pan-Asian*   25 | 20 | 20 | $48

Montclair | 635 Bloomfield Ave. (Valley Rd.) | 973-746-9608 |
www.nouveausushi.com

Is it the "son of Nobu"? inquire followers who know this Montclair
BYO Japanese-Asian specializing in "truly fresh", "amazingly flavorful" sushi and other "creative" morsels that are "true works of art"
accompanied by sometimes "good", other times "aloof", service;
some say while the decor is "soothing", "sky-high pricing" isn't.

	FOOD	DECOR	SERVICE	COST

Nova Terra *Pan-Latin*
22 | 23 | 20 | $41

New Brunswick | 78 Albany St. (Neilson St.) | 732-296-1600 |
www.terramomo.com

If you're looking for some "salsa" in New Brunswick, slink into this
"stylish" Pan-Latin that has it all – "delicious", "upscale" cuisine and
drinks, "efficient" service and a sultry vibe, thanks to live bands on
weekends; "lots of pretty people" come with the terra-tory, which
may soon include outdoor dining; N.B. the Food score may not
reflect the recent addition of a new chef.

Nunzio Ristorante Rustico *Italian*
23 | 22 | 20 | $39

Collingswood | 706 Haddon Ave. (Collings Ave.) | 856-858-9840 |
www.nunzios.net

With its two-story ceiling and life-sized wall painting surrounding
the dining room, you'll find yourself in "another world" at Nunzio
Patruno's Collingswood BYO Italian cooking up food that's "loved"
along with "loud" acoustics; those put off by the latter try hard not
to let it "detract from savoring the cuisine."

Oasis Grill *Mediterranean/Moroccan*
▽ 25 | 16 | 21 | $24

Cherry Hill | 2431 Church Rd. (Kaighn Ave.) | 856-667-8287 |
www.oasisgrillnj.com

"Affordable" tabs make you want to "try everything" (it's all "addic-
tive") at this unsung Moroccan-Mediterranean BYO in Cherry Hill
purveying an "authentic" menu; the "nice" staff "appreciates" its
customers, whose "hearts belong" to this spot.

Oceanos *Seafood*
- | - | - | E

Fair Lawn | 2-27 Saddle River Rd. (bet. Brookside Ave. & Northern Dr.) |
201-796-0546 | www.oceanosrestaurant.com

Greek goods are proffered at this Fair Lawn Mediterranean
offering an array of mezes, a raw bar and whole fish selections; the
list of wines (including a number of varietals from Greece) is
shipshape for oenophiles.

Octopus's Garden *Seafood*
▽ 22 | 21 | 24 | $36

Stafford | 771 S. Main St./Rte. 9 (Mayetta Landing Rd.) | 609-597-8828

"Well-cooked", "flavorful" fare finds its way into Stafford via this
BYO seafooder a few miles inland from Long Beach Island; its
habitués "highly recommend" it, if not for the food then at least for
its "friendly" service; N.B. open daily June 1–September 15; closed
Mondays off-season.

Oddfellows *Cajun/Creole*
19 | 17 | 18 | $27

Hoboken | 80 River St. (bet. Hudson Pl. & Newark St.) | 201-656-9009 |
www.oddfellowsrest.com

"A piece of N'Awlins" near the PATH is the deal on this Hoboken
Cajun-Creole where work-weary former "frat boys" dig the reliably
"spicy" "happy-hour" scene at the bar that's chased down with
some "satisfying" bayou vittles; some say it's just the right cure for
a jambalaya "fix", especially if you've "never been to Louisiana";
N.B. DJs on weekends add to the friendly vibe.

	FOOD	DECOR	SERVICE	COST

Old Bay Restaurant, The ⊠ *Cajun/Creole* | 17 | 16 | 17 | $32 |

New Brunswick | 61-63 Church St. (Neilson St.) | 732-246-3111 |
www.oldbayrest.com

It's "busy" and "loud", but "what else do you expect, since it's Mardi
Gras every day?" at this New Brunswick Cajun-Creole where the
food is "spicy" and the large selection of brews go down easy; if the
fare is "not exactly at NOLA" level, at least the live entertainment
and outdoor "beer garden" maintain the "festive" feeling.

Old Homestead *Steak* | 25 | 24 | 23 | $68 |

Atlantic City | Borgata Hotel, Casino & Spa | 1 Borgata Way
(Atlantic City Expwy., exit 1) | 609-317-1000 | www.theborgata.com
"Heavy eating" is necessary at this Borgata Hotel, Casino & Spa
chophouse (a satellite of the NYC legend) sending out "some of the
best slabs of beef you've ever seen" into a "beautiful" space; it's pricey,
but thanks to "excellent" service, you'll feel "like a high roller."

☑ Old Man Rafferty's *American* | 19 | 17 | 18 | $26 |

Hillsborough | 284 Rte. 206 (Triangle Rd.) | 908-904-9731
New Brunswick | 106 Albany St. (George St.) | 732-846-6153
Asbury Park | 541 Cookman Ave. (bet. Bangs & Mattison Aves.) |
732-774-1600
www.oldmanraffertys.com

"Come hungry" to these "dependable", "comfy" American standbys
for "affordable" fare (including "out-of-this-world" desserts) that
suits any occasion, whether for "family" meals or "first dates";
N.B. the New Brunswick locale has a to-go gourmet deli.

☑ Ombra Ⓜ *Italian* | 25 | 27 | 22 | $52 |

Atlantic City | Borgata Hotel, Casino & Spa | 1 Borgata Way
(Atlantic City Expwy., exit 1) | 866-692-6742 | www.theborgata.com
Capturing the ambiance of a wine cellar, albeit one that's as "beautiful" as it is "comfortable", this Borgata Italian features stone, wood
and glass decor, "fantastic" Italian cooking and an "amazing" vino
selection sourced from some of Italy's smaller producers; it all goes
down well with fans, as long as they're ready for the "pricey" bills;
N.B. new executive chef James Hennessey recently replaced Luke
Palladino, which may outdate the above Food score.

One 53 *American* | - | - | - | E |

Rocky Hill | 153 Washington St. (Princeton Ave.) | 609-924-1019 |
www.restaurantone53.com
Start with seasonal New American fare, add a roster of boutique
wines, place them in a warm setting and you get this bistro in Rocky
Hill; not surprisingly, fans hope that all the above supplies a recipe
for success, given the imminent arrival of a new chef; N.B. a private
dining room recently opened in the wine cellar.

Onieal's *American* | 19 | 17 | 18 | $31 |

Hoboken | 343 Park Ave. (4th St.) | 201-653-1492 |
www.oniealshoboken.com
Although its scene is "typical" for a Hoboken pub (i.e. it's "packed
solid"), this "dark" "perennial" turns out New American eats that

range from "above average" to "good"; Casanovas advise "fighting your way past the bar" and into the back room for a "perfect date."

Opah Grille *Seafood* 24 | 22 | 22 | $52

Gladstone | 12 Lackawanna Ave. (Main St.) | 908-781-1888 | www.opahgrille.com

Somehow, the "Shore" seems so close when you're dining in this suburban seafooder in Gladstone noted for "so-fresh" seafood and the "best martinis on earth" augmented by generally "helpful" service; the "beautiful" freshwater tanks "transport" you closer to the beach, as does the recently added outdoor dining area.

Orbis Bistro Ⓜ *American* 22 | 15 | 19 | $41

Upper Montclair | 128 Watchung Ave. (N. Fullerton Ave.) | 973-746-7641 | www.orbisbistro.com

Its "delectable" New American food (and newly added tapas menu) is as "special" as the treatment you'll get if you travel to this Upper Montclair BYO fronted by Nancy Caballes, who also presides over the kitchen; the setting is akin to a "comfortable" "dining room in someone's home"; N.B. lunch is served Tuesdays–Fridays.

Ⓩ Origin Ⓜ *French/Thai* 26 | 20 | 20 | $36

Morristown | 10 South St. (DeHart St.) | 973-971-9933
Somerville | 25 Division St. (Main St.) | 908-685-1344
www.originthai.com

Whether you dine at the origin-al Somerville locale or the Morristown offshoot, these "bustling" BYO French-Thai fusionists are idolized for "spectacularly" conceived and executed preparations accompanied by "friendly", if "quick", service; at both expect to sit "in close proximity" to your neighbors and "deafening" acoustics, but meals at these "winners" are "worth anything"; N.B. a new location in Basking Ridge is scheduled to open in summer 2008.

Osteria Dante *Mediterranean* 19 | 17 | 17 | $39

Red Bank | 91 Broad St. (Linden Pl.) | 732-530-0602 | www.osteriadante.net
The fare "rises above the typical" tout followers of this Red Bank BYO who choose from an "expansive" selection of "down-to-earth" Mediterranean items; acolytes applaud the "pleasant" setting, and "sidewalk seating is still tops."

Osteria Giotto *Italian* 25 | 18 | 21 | $40

Montclair | 21-23 Midland Ave. (Bloomfield Ave.) | 973-746-0111 | www.osteria-giotto.com
Everything's "spot on" at this Italian BYO, whether it's the "sublime" dishes (accompanied by "hearty", housemade breads), "warm", "informal" wood setting and "good" service; no doubt, "you'll need a lot of pull" to secure a reservation, but for a "best-of-Montclair" experience, seek divine intervention if necessary; N.B. closed Tuesdays.

Ota-Ya Ⓜ *Japanese* 23 | 14 | 19 | $31

Lambertville | 21 Ferry St. (S. Union St.) | 609-397-9228 | www.ota-ya.com
"Fresh", "unique" raw fare comes from sushi "masters" while the "delicious" cooked items delight just about everyone else at this

"cozy" albeit "pedestrian"-looking Japanese spot in Lambertville warmed by a "friendly" staff that "knows its customers."

NEW Ox M *American* | - | - | - | E |

Jersey City | 176 Newark Ave. (bet. Erie St. & Jersey Ave.) | 201-860-4000 | www.oxrestaurant.com

It's no surprise that braised oxtail's in the offing at this high-end, high-energy, Jersey City New American newcomer, but the menu's also bullish on unusual options (e.g. scallop, cockle and spicy lobster sausage stew); a snazzy, industrial interior replete with a lively bar (and interesting wines by the glass) adds to the festive vibe; N.B. the prix fixe Sunday brunch is a deal.

Oyako Tso's *Japanese* | 21 | 20 | 19 | $30 |

Freehold | 6 W. Main St. (bet. South & Throckmorton Sts.) | 732-866-1988 | www.oyakotsos.com

Things are tso "good" at this "fun" Freehold Japanese BYO that's a "big hit with families" on account of the "entertaining" hibachi and "fresh" sushi; though service sometimes seems "lost in translation", the staff is always "respectful of any requests."

Pad Thai *Thai* | 22 | 13 | 17 | $20 |

Highland Park | 217 Raritan Ave. (bet. 2nd & 3rd Aves.) | 732-247-9636 | www.pad-thai.com

"Plentiful", "cheap" and "authentic" are the vittles at this Highland Park Thai; the prices are "right", and the "incredible", "knock-your-socks-off" spicy specialties draw a "packed" house, especially the "best pad Thai" in this neck of the woods.

Palm, The *Steak* | 24 | 21 | 24 | $61 |

Atlantic City | The Quarter at the Tropicana | 2801 Pacific Ave. (S. Iowa Ave.) | 609-344-7256 | www.thepalm.com

Now, "that's dining" marvel backers of this Quarter at the Tropicana chainlet and "carnivore's palace" sending out "X-large", "expertly prepared" steaks and lobsters into its signature dining room complete with caricatures of celebs on the walls; the "big bucks" tabs and "loud" acoustics are soothed by "top" service.

Pamir *Afghan* | 21 | 16 | 20 | $27 |

Morristown | 85 Washington St. (bet. Cobb Pl. & Phoenix Ave.) | 973-605-1095 | www.pamirrestaurant.com

"Low-cost", "traditional" Afghan cuisine comes in "large" portions and with a "bouquet of flavors" at this Morristown BYO, a "welcome change" catering to vegetarians and kebab lovers; the location may be "inauspicious", but all the rugs and pillows here add an "exotic" note.

Panico's *Italian* | 24 | 21 | 24 | $52 |

New Brunswick | 103 Church St. (Neilson St.) | 732-545-6100 | www.panicosrestaurant.com

Book a table here to "impress your boss" with the "top-notch" Italian food, the specialty of this "classy", "dress-up" New Brunswick mainstay (now in its 21st year) also noted for "sophisticated" service;

"expense" tabs notwithstanding, its many admired attributes factor into its "delightful-dining" reputation.

☒ Park & Orchard *Eclectic*

	22	13	20	$39

East Rutherford | 240 Hackensack St. (Union Ave. W.) | 201-939-9292 | www.parkandorchard.com

The "unusual", "healthy" assortment (from Italian to stir fries) is as "tasty" as ever for fans of this "extremely popular" East Rutherford Eclectic; though the space looks somewhat "spartan", "oh, that wine list" – 2,400 labels at last count – it's "nirvana for oenophiles."

NEW Park Avenue
Bar & Grill ● *American/Pan-Latin*

	–	–	–	E

Union City | 3417 Park Ave. (34th St.) | 201-617-7274 | www.parkavenuebarandgrill.com

Park yourself in style at this new Pan-Latin–American sparkler in Union City where the pricey menu navigates toward seafood; sample ceviche or pan-roasted mahi mahi while glimpsing the NYC skyline from one of the dining rooms in the dramatic, multilevel Georgian brick building or sip a Malbec margarita in the zebra-striped bar; N.B. there's entertainment and dancing on weekends.

Park Steakhouse, The *Seafood/Steak*

	24	19	21	$55

Park Ridge | 151 Kinderkamack Rd. (bet. Grand & Park Aves.) | 201-930-1300 | www.theparksteakhouse.com

Some of the "best" steaks in Northern Jersey turn up in this "traditional" Park Ridge chophouse also known for its "particularly well-prepared" seafood; what it lacks in the bang-for-the-buck category (think "NYC prices") is partially recovered by the place's "reliability."

Passage to India Ⓜ *Indian*

	23	17	20	$27

Lawrenceville | Lawrence Shopping Ctr. | 2495 Brunswick Pike/Rte. 1 (bet. Colonial Lake Dr. & Texas Ave.) | 609-637-0800

It's hard to pass up this Lawrenceville Indian BYO making believers out of clientele with "flavorful" fare paired with "helpful" service and "attractive", "peaceful" quarters; for the best "bargain" for miles, check out the "standout" lunch buffet.

Passionne Ⓜ *French*

	▽ 23	19	21	$42

Montclair | 77 Walnut St. (Grove St.) | 973-233-1006 | www.restaurantpassionne.com

A "wonderful" assortment of "classic" Gallic items appears in this "traditional" Montclair French BYO, a "reliable" option comforting diners with its fare, setting and "attentive" service; N.B. there's sidewalk seating and weekend tasting menus available.

Pasta Fresca Café and Market *American*

	▽ 22	15	19	$26

Shrewsbury | Grove Shopping Ctr. | 637 Broad St. (Shadow Brook Rd.) | 732-747-5616

"Soccer moms in SUVs" "love coming" to this Shrewsbury New American BYO offering a "casual" atmosphere and "tasty" fare that seem just right "after shopping" in the "upscale" Grove mall; "strollers" and "alfresco" eating are both popular here.

| | FOOD | DECOR | SERVICE | COST |

NEW Pearl of Lisbon *Portuguese* | - | - | - | M |
(fka Pearl of the Sea)

Long Branch | 609 Broadway (bet. Bath & Norwood Aves.) | 732-263-1050
The Long Branch locale and the name of this Portuguese gem may
have changed, but loyalists have followed it to its trendy new
Uptown quarters for moderately priced classic fare (pork with
clams, paella) and sangria that sings; N.B. there's a seasonal patio.

Penang *Malaysian/Thai*   20 | 15 | 16 | $24

East Hanover | 200 Rte. 10 W. (bet. Ridgedale Ave. & River Rd.) |
973-887-6989
Edison | 505 Old Post Rd. (bet. Rte. 1 & Vineyard Rd.) | 732-287-3038
West Windsor | Nassau Park Pavilion | 635 Nassau Park Blvd.
(Brunswick Pike/Rte. 1 S.) | 609-897-9088
www.penangnj.com
This "tasty" BYO trio vends the "real deal" when it comes to
Malaysian (with some Thai) cooking with a slate of "spicy", "comforting" items and a number of noodle dishes brought to table
"quickly"; in all, the three are as "good" as they are "busy", and the
prices are a "bargain."

Z Perryville Inn M *American*   26 | 24 | 22 | $56

Union Township | 167 Perryville Rd. (I-78, exit 12) | 908-730-9500 |
www.theperryvilleinn.com
"Superlative experiences" are the norm at this Hunterdon County
"class act" set in a historic Colonial tavern, where the "wonderful"
Traditional American creations seem ideally suited to the "intimate"
setting complete with fireplaces; it all adds up to a "great destination at the end of a drive in the country."

Pete & Elda's ◐ *Pizza*   - | - | - | I

Neptune City | 96 Woodland Ave. (Laurel Ave.) | 732-774-6010 |
www.peteandeldas.com
Thin-crust lovers line up for this Shore Italian, a must-stop for its
crackerlike pies topped with zesty red gravy and fresh toppings; the
old-school fare (in the chicken parm vein) carries its own attraction
for this staple's supporters.

Z Peter Shields Inn M *American*   26 | 27 | 25 | $55

Cape May | 1301 Beach Dr. (Trenton Ave.) | 609-884-9090 |
www.petershieldsinn.com
It's all "truly wonderful" at this "very special" Cape May BYO where
"memorable" New American dinners are the norm, as are "excellent" service, "great" views of the ocean from the veranda and a
"beautiful" setting, thanks in part to the Georgian Revival B&B the
eatery is housed in; after all that, it's no wonder this "romantic" restaurant is such a "favorite"; N.B. open Mondays on-season.

Z P.F. Chang's China Bistro *Chinese*   21 | 21 | 19 | $31

West New York | 10 Port Imperial Blvd. (Halfmoon Ct.) |
201-866-7790
Freehold | Freehold Raceway Mall | 3710 Rte. 9 (bet. Rtes. 33 & 537) |
732-308-1840

(continued)

P.F. Chang's China Bistro

Atlantic City | The Quarter at the Tropicana | 2801 Pacific Ave. (Iowa Ave.) | 609-348-4600 ◗

Marlton | Promenade at Sagemore | 500 Rte. 73 S. (Rte. 70) | 856-396-0818

www.pfchangs.com

Hordes "go out of their way" for the "yum" vittles and to put up with "long, long waits" that are standard at this somewhat "high-end", extra-"busy" Chinese chain that's about as "loud" as they come; the drinks are "good" too, and if a few notice a "formula", at least "the formula works."

Pheasants Landing Ⓜ *American/Continental* | 17 | 16 | 17 | $31 |

Hillsborough | 311 Amwell Rd. (Willow Rd.) | 908-281-1288 | www.pheasantslanding.com

For cross-cultural Continental (German, Swiss, Italian) and American fare, locals land at this "comfortable", "homey" Hillsborough eatery for game and other seasonal eats, and for its downstairs pub; while the "good" offerings "aren't particularly exciting", the place is "one of the few around" that serves this kind of food; N.B. dine alfresco on the recently installed patio.

Phillips Seafood *Seafood* | - | - | - | E |

Atlantic City | Pier at Caesars | 1 Atlantic Ocean (Arkansas Ave.) | 609-348-2273 | www.phillipsseafood.com

Eastern Shore meets Jersey Shore at this old-school Maryland-based seafooder in the Pier at Caesars; with a rolling oyster cart offering tableside shucking, it's a classy destination to burn through gambling winnings.

Pho Binh *Vietnamese* | - | - | - | I |
(fka Pho Thang Long)

Jersey City | 749 Bergen Ave. (Montgomery St.) | 201-209-9140

Vietnamese standards stock the extensive menu at this spartan Jersey City BYO that's built its reputation not only upon warming regional dishes but also on its rolls and salads; nice prices make this place long on appeal.

Pic-Nic *Portuguese/Spanish* | - | - | - | M |

East Newark | 224 Grant Ave. (Central Ave.) | 973-481-3646 | www.picnicrestaurant.com

No picnic fare here, just bountiful portions of robust Portuguese (and Spanish) cooking is what it's all about at this East Newark hideaway that quietly competes with its more famous Ironbound brethren; pictures of the motherland, handmade tiles and an overall rustic ambiance is the deal when it comes to decor.

Pierre's Ⓜ *French* | 23 | 22 | 23 | $50 |

Morristown | 995 Mt. Kemble Ave. (bet. N. Maple Ave. & Tempe Wick Rd.) | 973-425-1212 | www.pierresbistro.com

For "delightful" French "every time", Michael Peter's "country", "congenial" Morristown bistro "never disappoints"; cronies also consider the "fantastic" lunch buffet (currently $16.50) deemed a "bargain for such high-quality food", a "great value" treat; N.B. the latest addition is a wine bar proffering 30 vinos by the glass.

Pine Tavern *American*

| 22 | 15 | 20 | $33 |

Old Bridge | 151 Rte. 34 (Cottrell Rd.) | 732-727-5060 | www.pinetavern.net
The "unlikely setting" stands in contrast to the New American menu served at this "rusticated", wood-filled Old Bridge tavern applauded for "spot-on" preparations and a "charming", "put-you-at-ease" vibe; it's a true "solid-neighborhood" eatery, where patrons are known to drop by for the "great" live music.

Pino's La Forchetta *Italian*

| 18 | 20 | 19 | $40 |

Marlboro | 448 Rte. 9 N. (Union Hill Rd.) | 732-972-6933 | www.pinoslaforchetta.com
"Old-world Brooklyn" comes to Marlboro with this Italian where pizza reigns on one side, and the main dining room is the site for more formal affairs; if the entrees are only "decent" for some, most appreciate that the "'za's are the best thing here" and that the staff "makes you feel special"; N.B. live entertainment Tuesdays-Sundays.

Piquant Bread Bar & Grill Ⓜ *Indian*

| - | - | - | E |

New Brunswick | 349A George St. (Bayard St.) | 732-246-2468 | www.piquantfoods.com
A hip and trendy destination in Downtown New Brunswick, this up-scale new Indian features a menu built upon organic ingredients while taking its inspiration from all over the globe with items such as spicy Scottish salmon accompanied by a tomato-yogurt sauce; every stylish detail in the decor syncs up with the food.

Pithari Taverna Ⓜ *Greek*

| - | - | - | M |

Highland Park | 28 Woodbridge Ave. (Raritan Ave.) | 732-572-0616 | www.thepithari.com
Classic Greek – dolmades, souvlaki and the like – is the hallmark of this Highland Park BYO that sits next door to a grocery (where, conveniently, wines from the motherland are offered); moderate pricing gives the goods more appeal.

Pizzicato *Italian*

| 20 | 16 | 18 | $31 |

Marlton | Promenade at Sagemore | 500 Rte. 73 (Rte. 70) | 856-396-0880
Its "reasonably" priced "quality" food shows a "surprising consistency" and encourages "repeat visits" to this "laid-back" Marlton Italian BYO good for "quick bites" before (or after) shopping.

P.J. Whelihan's ● *Pub Food*

| 17 | 16 | 17 | $21 |

Cherry Hill | 1854 E. Marlton Pike (Greentree Rd.) | 856-424-8844
Haddonfield | 700 Haddon Ave. (Ardmore Ave.) | 856-427-7888
Maple Shade | 396 S. Lenola Rd. (Kings Hwy.) | 856-234-2345
Medford Lakes | 61 Stokes Rd. (Hampshire Rd.) | 609-714-7900
Sewell | 425 Hurffville-Cross Keys Rd. (Regulus Dr.) | 856-582-7774
www.pjspub.com
The "best" pub grub and brew (and "hot waitresses") bring "crowds" to this quintet of South Jersey taverns purveying "good ol'" American

"game food"; they're "always fun", plus there are "enough flat-screens to make sports fans happy."

Plantation *American* | 19 | 20 | 17 | $42 |

Harvey Cedars | 7908 Long Beach Blvd. (79th St.) | 609-494-8191 | www.plantationrestaurant.com

Those "mojitos at happy hour are worth leaving the beach for" at this Harvey Cedars New American whose islandy ambiance pairs nicely with the "different", "reliable" menu; even in off-season, this "favorite hang" seems to be "always happening."

☑ Pluckemin Inn *American* | 25 | 26 | 24 | $68 |

Bedminster | 359 Rte. 202/206 S. (Pluckemin Way) | 908-658-9292 | www.pluckemininn.com

In Bedminster, this New American "covers all the bases" with a "gorgeous" modern-Colonial setting (evocative of a 19th-century farmhouse) that's centered by an "amazing" three-story wine tower and list (overseen by a "pro" sommelier), not to mention chef David C. Felton's "exceptional" dishes and "doting" service; you "won't regret emptying your wallet", since the "prices reflect the quality"; N.B. the adjacent Plucky Tavern offers quicker, more casual dining.

Ponzio's ❶ *Diner* | 16 | 11 | 16 | $22 |

Cherry Hill | 7 Rte. 70 W. (Kings Hwy.) | 856-428-4808 | www.ponzios.com

Cherry Hill's unofficial "town hall" and South Jersey's "ultimate" diner (with a staff that "keeps things moving") continues to serve "consistent" coffee-shop chow and "freshly" made sweets from the on-site bakery; if it is "not the Ponzio's of yore", many still make it their "landmark"; N.B. the remodeled bar is outfitted with plasma TVs.

🆕 Pop's Garage 🅱️🅼 *Mexican* | - | - | - | I |

Normandy Beach | 560 Rte. 35 N. (6th Ave.) | 732-830-5700 | www.kitschens.com

This funky Normandy Beach BYO newcomer offers an eclectic low-cost Mexican menu (think lobster enchiladas) and diversions such as an adjacent camper-cum-art galley speckled in sea glass and a seasonal garden where you can eat dinner and watch a movie.

Pop Shop *American* | 18 | 19 | 18 | $16 |

Collingswood | 729 Haddon Ave. (Collings Ave.) | 856-869-0111 | www.thepopshopusa.com

"Kids" have so much "fun" wearing "PJs" and noshing on "tasty" treats from the "enormous" American menu at this "old-timey" Collingswood soda shop from "yesteryear", where shakes, burgers and grilled cheese sandwiches rule; the "retro" spot is ultra-"friendly", and the only thing missing is "The Fonz."

Portobello *Italian* | 20 | 16 | 17 | $34 |

Oakland | 155 Ramapo Valley Rd. (Long Hill Rd.) | 201-337-8990 | www.portobello-restaurant.com

"Solid" is the cooking dished up in "large" portions at this Oakland Northern Italian "value" and neighborhood "favorite" that some supporters say is just the ticket for those who need to throw a "big party"; others, however, cite an "erratic" operation, noting the "inattentive service"; N.B. all-new furniture has been installed post-Survey, which may outdate the above Decor score.

Portofino ⓜ *Italian* | 25 | 18 | 23 | $46 |

Tinton Falls | 720 Tinton Ave. (Sycamore Ave.) | 732-542-6068 | www.portofino-ristorante.com

"Excellent" Italian cookery reigns at this Tinton Falls eatery opposite an old grist mill; with its "exceptional" 400-label wine list focused on Italy and "pleasant", "knowledgeable" service, locals looking for a cut-above dining experience consider it one of Monmouth County's "finer" restaurants.

Porto Leggero ⓢ *Italian* | 23 | 24 | 22 | $50 |

Jersey City | Harborside Financial Plaza 5 (Pearl St.) | 201-434-3200 | www.portoleggero.net

"Fine dining" comes to Jersey City via this "hidden" restaurant (the brainchild of the Scalini Fedeli outfit) whose Downtown location draws a diverse crowd (including financial types) that discovers a treasure trove of "terrific" Italian cookery served in "spacious", "beautiful" quarters, which mixes modern and old world; yes, it's a "touch of class" that comes with a "high" price tag, but most are "happy to find this culinary surprise."

Portuguese Manor *Portuguese/Spanish* | 21 | 15 | 20 | $33 |

Perth Amboy | 310 Elm St. (bet. Fayette & Smith Sts.) | 732-826-2233 | www.portuguesemanorrestaurant.com

They "accommodate" you well at this Perth Amboy Iberian that fills the bill with "dependable", "hearty" Portuguese cooking that stops some from trekking all the way to Newark; supporters add the "rough-around-the-edges" bar and dining room may even look better post-sangrias.

Posillipo ⓜ *Italian* | 22 | 16 | 21 | $39 |

Asbury Park | 715 Second Ave. (Bond St.) | 732-774-5819 | www.posilliporestaurant.com

Exemplifying "what class without fuss" is all about, this "warm" Asbury Park Italian (now in its 79th year) prepares "very good" "Mulberry Street"-style food like "nonna"; opera and 'Broadway' night on Wednesday is the star, and supporters sing about the "bargain" early-bird, offered every day.

NEW Prana Restaurant & Lounge ⓢⓜ *Indian/Mideastern* | - | - | - | E |

Bloomfield | 21 Belleville Ave. (Stephens St.) | 973-748-6669 | www.prananj.com

Locals looking for a lively time turn to this stylish, bi-level Bloomfield restaurant-cum-club combining high-end, innovative Middle Eastern–Indian cuisine (e.g. coconut-poached lobster) with a seductive setting (curtain-draped booths) and post-11 PM dancing; overall, the scene's in sync with the name, which refers to 'energy' in Sanskrit.

	FOOD	DECOR	SERVICE	COST

Primavera *Italian*
| 20 | 17 | 19 | $47 |

West Orange | Wilshire Grand | 350 Pleasant Valley Way
(bet. Marmon Terr. & Sullivan Dr.) | 973-731-4779 |
www.primaverawestorange.com

"Enormous" portions of "steady" Italian cooking are the prima reason
why diners go to this West Orange hotel standby in "not the best" of
settings; however, things seem more settled now that management
has heeded guests pleas to "print the [lengthy list] of specials."

Pub, The *Steak*
| 18 | 14 | 16 | $29 |

Pennsauken | Airport Circle | 7600 Kaighns Ave. (S. Crescent Blvd.) |
856-665-6440 | www.thepubnj.com

"If you're looking for something cozy, this is not the place" opine ob-
servers of this "huge" "hall" in Pennsauken putting out the "best"
salad bar and "same-as-it-ever-was" steaks many find "good", but a
few "not mouthwatering", in a medieval, knights-and-armor setting
that "has a certain charm"; "they don't try to be something they're
not" profess advocates who add "they don't mess with what's
worked" for over a half century.

🆕 Queen Victoria Tea Room Ⓜ *Tearoom*
| - | - | - | I |

Toms River | Victoria on Main | 600 Main St. (Broad St.) | 732-818-7580 |
www.victoriaonmain.com

This 1895 Victorian landmark and B&B now offers a taste of something different in Toms River – high tea; scones, finger sandwiches
and pastries, all homemade by the lady of this historic house, are
served on antique china amid atmospheric parlors, sitting rooms
and a veranda; N.B. it's prix fixe ($17), with seatings at 1:30 PM and
3:30 PM Wednesdays–Sundays, March–December.

Quiet Man, The *Pub Food*
| 22 | 16 | 18 | $32 |

Dover | 64 E. McFarlan St. (Hudson St.) | 973-366-6333 |
www.quietmanpub.com

Decked out in memorabilia from the movie of the same name, this
quintessential Irish pub provides "Guinness" and "fast bites" of
"tasty" treats of the Old Sod along with American offerings; what's
more, all the above comes with an authentically "friendly" vibe.

Raagini *Indian*
| 22 | 20 | 21 | $36 |

Mountainside | 1085 Rte. 22 E. (Mill Ln.) | 908-789-9777 |
www.raagini.com

The "excellent" lunch buffet and "super" Sunday brunch are big
draws when it comes to this "upscale" Mountainside Indian sporting
a "nice-looking" room; if dinners are slightly "expensive", the "consistently delicious", "far-above"-the-norm cooking compensates.

Radicchio *Italian*
| 23 | 19 | 20 | $46 |

Ridgewood | 32 Franklin Ave. (Chestnut St.) | 201-670-7311 |
www.radicchiorestnj.com

"Inspired" Northern Italian cuisine of "consistently high-quality"
sets apart this "relaxed" Ridgewood BYO, where a bevy of the

"best", "unusual" daily specials complements the "small" regular menu; "high prices" don't seem to offend its loyal clientele, who bestow on it "favorite" status.

Raimondo's *Italian*

23 | 15 | 20 | $44

Ship Bottom | 1101 Long Beach Blvd. (11th St.) | 609-494-5391
For "good-for-the-soul" Italian, try this ever-"popular" Ship Bottom BYO, "one of LBI's most consistent", with a staff that "takes pride" in its work; prepare for "loud" acoustics, and some say "off-season" is your best bet.

☑ Ram's Head Inn Ⓜ *American*

26 | 27 | 25 | $55

Galloway | 9 W. White Horse Pike (bet. Ash & Taylor Aves.) | 609-652-1700 | www.ramsheadinn.com
It's "nice to see all the men in jackets" and to "actually hear your conversation" at this Galloway "old favorite" turning out Caesars prepared tableside ("where else do they do that these days?") along with other Traditional American fare that would "please those with the highest standards"; overall, it's a "true charmer" for patrons who put it in the "solidly classic" category; N.B. there are plans for patio dining.

☑ Rat's Ⓜ *French*

24 | 28 | 24 | $63

Hamilton | Grounds for Sculpture | 16 Fairgrounds Rd. (Sculptors Way) | 609-584-7800 | www.ratsrestaurant.org
"Step into a Wonderland" of a setting when you visit this destination New French ranked NJ's No. 1 for Decor, where the "beautiful" Grounds for Sculpture (inspired by Monet's legendary Giverny) afford pre- or post-repast strolls; within the restaurant, "exciting" cuisine and "phenomenal" wines reign, both delivered by "excellent" servers; N.B. there's also a less formal cafe that accepts walk-ins.

Rattlesnake Ranch Café *Southwestern*

16 | 14 | 16 | $25

Denville | Foodtown Shopping Ctr. | 559 E. Main St. (bet. Fox Hill Rd. & Front St.) | 973-586-3800 | www.rattlesnakeranchcafe.com
"The only place around to fulfill a craving for alligator" is this Denville strip-mall Southwesterner whose "interesting" lineup also includes elk and ostrich; happily, "great" margaritas and "moderate" pricing take some of the sting out of "so-so decor" and "unremarkable" eats.

Raven and the Peach *American*

24 | 25 | 24 | $56

Fair Haven | 740 River Rd. (Fair Haven Rd.) | 732-747-4666 | www.ravenandthepeach.net
"Romance", "celebrations" and "entertaining clients" all come easy over "delightful" New American food at this Fair Haven "special-occasion" spot sporting a *Casablanca*-esque" ambiance; thanks to "professional", "attentive" service, you may even be less inclined to notice it's "one of the most expensive meals" you may ever have.

Raymond's *American*

21 | 18 | 19 | $27

Montclair | 28 Church St. (bet. Fullerton Ave. & Park St.) | 973-744-9263 | www.raymondsnj.com
"Everyone should love" Raymond Badach's "insanely popular" Montclair "institution" that's "always a pleasure" for its "perfectly

satisfying" New American "comfort food" all day long; the BYO's "cozy", "retro" look and "friendly" floor crew are "just what you want out of a local restaurant."

Ray's Little Silver Seafood ⓂⒷ *Seafood* | 23 | 10 | 18 | $33 |

Little Silver | Markham Place Plaza | 125 Markham Pl. (Prospect Ave.) | 732-758-8166

Everything arrives "piping hot" and tastes "delicious" at this store-front BYO in Little Silver vending the "freshest" fish at "reasonable" prices; "helpful", "efficient" service supplies a ray of sunshine in these "plain"-Jane digs.

Rebecca's Ⓜ *Cuban* | 24 | 19 | 22 | $44 |

Edgewater | 236 Old River Rd. (River Rd.) | 201-943-8808 | www.rebeccasedgewater.com

Layout and size help supply the "romance" that fuels this Edgewater Cuban-Caribbean BYO where the "intimate" ambiance is matched by "wonderful", "vibrant" food; for an even "quieter tête-à-tête", fans endorse the "charming" back patio.

Red *American* | 20 | 22 | 19 | $45 |

Red Bank | 3 Broad St. (Front St.) | 732-741-3232 | www.rednj.com

More about the "chic" ambiance and "social scene" than its "solid" New American cuisine (with an extensive sushi menu), this "dark", "late-night" Red Bank site hosts "beautiful" people "cocktailing" along with sometimes "friendly", sometimes "pretentious" service; all agree, though, that as lounges go, the upstairs one is "great."

Red's Lobster Pot *Seafood* | 24 | 13 | 19 | $35 |

Point Pleasant Beach | 57 Inlet Dr. (Ocean Ave.) | 732-295-6622 | www.redslobsterpot.com

This Point Pleasant Beach waterside BYO, "shack" and "mainstay" features an "excellent" outside area (inside's the "size of a phone booth") to "watch the boats go by" while chowing down on "amazingly fresh" lobsters and other sea fare; P.S. the dockside raw bar is "excellent" too.

Red Square *Eclectic/Russian* | - | - | - | VE |

Atlantic City | The Quarter at the Tropicana | 2801 Pacific Ave. (S. Iowa Ave.) | 609-344-9100 | www.chinagrillmgt.com

The spirits of Lenin and co. are alive and well at Jeffrey Chodorow's Soviet-kitschy lounge/restaurant in the Quarter at the Tropicana, where caviar, Eclectic fare and martinis (try the 'Chernobyl') are served in a setting filled with agitprop, red velvet, banquettes and a 60-ft. bar made partly of ice; comrades richer than Croesus can lease one of several vodka lockers, all icily chilled in the 0-degree Fahrenheit vault.

Redstone American Grill *American* | - | - | - | E |

Marlton | Promenade at Sagemore | 500 Rte. 73 S. (Brick Rd.) | 856-396-0332 | www.redstonegrill.com

A stone exterior helps define the modern, rustic design philosophy of this Marlton seafood/steak-focused New American, an East

| | FOOD | DECOR | SERVICE | COST |

Coast outpost of a Twin Cities mini-chain; not surprisingly, the bar is a major attraction, drawing South Jersey singles from far and wide.

Renault Winery ⓂⒶ *American* — 22 | 24 | 22 | $47
Egg Harbor | 72 N. Bremen Ave. (Moss Mill Rd.) | 609-965-2111 | www.renaultwinery.com

One of the oldest wineries in America provides an "enchanting" backdrop for this Egg Harbor New American serving up "a treat" of a menu and "romance at dinner"; the "unique" setting also includes a hotel and golf course; N.B. dinner on Fridays (5 PM–7:30 PM) and Saturdays (5–8 PM); brunch Sundays (10 AM–3:30 PM).

Reservoir Tavern ⒵Ⓜ *Italian* — 22 | 8 | 16 | $24
Boonton | 92 Parsippany Blvd. (Intervale Rd.) | 973-334-5708

"Exquisite" thin-crust pizza is the story of this Boonton red-saucer, a family-run feedery (since 1936) dispensing 'zas and "no-nonsense" Italiana in "divey", "no-decor" digs; the "consistently delicious" goods keep inspiring all the "committed clientele" to line up.

Restaurant, The Ⓜ *Italian* — 21 | 23 | 22 | $54
Hackensack | 160 Prospect Ave. (bet. American Legion Dr. & Beech St.) | 201-678-1100 | www.therestaurant.net

"High style" comes with "high prices" at this "classy", "dark" and "intimate" Italian bar/restaurant improbably located in a Hackensack condo complex; all told though, the "pretty-good" food "takes a backseat" to the "pickup" central scene, a "wolf's den of middle-aged men" and divorcées.

Restaurant L *Continental* — - | - | - | E
Allendale | 9 Franklin Tpke. (bet. Mackay Ave. & Waibel Dr.) | 201-785-1112 | www.go2l.com

Comfortable leather seats and a convivial bar set an inviting tone and frame the warming Continental food (from short ribs to veal piccata) at this moderately expensive Allendale eatery; N.B. they can seat up to 40 guests for private parties, and now there's patio service.

Restaurant Latour Ⓜ *American* — - | - | - | VE
Hamburg | Crystal Springs Resort | 1 Wild Turkey Way (Crystal Springs Rd.) | 973-827-0548 | www.crystalgolfresort.com

Part of northwest New Jersey's 4,000-acre golf and spa destination, the Crystal Springs Resort, this 40-seat New American boasts cuisine from new chef Michael Weisshaupt (ex The Manor), who replaces John Benjamin (an alum of the French Laundry and Aureole), formal service and a glass window in the main dining room that affords views of the surrounding mountains; for oenophiles, the uncommonly deep vino list is one of the world's best, featuring 3,700 labels and 54,000 bottles; N.B. there are two eating areas in the wine cellar.

restaurant.mc *American/Eclectic* — - | - | - | E
Millburn | 57 Main St. (Millburn Ave.) | 973-921-0888 | www.restaurantmc.com

This pricey Millburn Eclectic-American attracts attention for its globe-spanning ingredients and chic bar scene; the hot spot is helmed by chef Steve Permaul, who regularly reinvents the menu to keep up with the town's sophisticated clientele.

Richard's ⊭ *Deli*   20 | 12 | 19 | $18

Long Branch | 155 Brighton Ave. (Sairs Ave.) | 732-870-9133

"Anything and everything you can imagine or want" from a deli is in this Long Brancher whose artery-"clogging" comestibles (e.g. corned beef and pastrami sandwiches) "satisfy"; the only complaint: "they close too early to be able to eat dinner": 3 PM Mondays–Tuesdays, 8 PM Wednesdays–Sundays.

Richie Cecere's   21 | 23 | 21 | $68
Restaurant & SupperClub ⓈItalian

Montclair | 2 Erie St. (Label St.) | 973-746-7811 | www.richiececere.com

"For a big night out", this "cosmopolitan" tri-level supper club-cum-Italian restaurant in Montclair shines with its "good" food, "high-end" space and happening weekend cabaret that includes an 18-piece orchestra, crooner and showgirls ("you expect Ricky Ricardo to waltz in"); this adult "playground" may be "flamboyant" and "pricey", but it's a "favorite" nonetheless.

Rick's Ⓜ *Italian*   - | - | - | M

Lambertville | 19 S. Main St. (Ferry St.) | 609-397-0051 | www.ricksitalian.com

This popular Lambertville BYO offers modestly priced preparations and a warm ambiance, the latter partly due to co-owner Dana Cormier, who presides over the dining room; though the menu is focused on Italian home cooking, chef Alex Cormier's blackboard specials (foie gras, sweetbreads) provide a contrast to the restaurant's looks, with its knotty pine paneling and red-and-white checkered tablecloths.

Ristorante da Benito *Italian*   25 | 21 | 24 | $53

Union | 222 Galloping Hill Rd. (Walton Ave.) | 908-964-5850 | www.dabenito.com

"Great" Italian food and an "excellent" wine list attract local politicians and pedestrians alike head to this "swanky" Union spot whose "top-notch" staff "rolls out the red carpet" for the "see-and-be-seen" clientele; "costly" tabs notwithstanding, fans find it "as good as it gets."

Ritz Seafood Ⓜ *Pan-Asian/Seafood*   24 | 15 | 20 | $38

Voorhees | Ritz Shopping Ctr. | 910 Haddonfield-Berlin Rd. (Voorhees Dr.) | 856-566-6650 | www.ritzseafood.com

"Creative" fare, all so "fabulous" and "tasty", is the real appeal of this slightly "cramped" Voorhees BYO Pan-Asian–seafooder near the Ritz movie complex; a "gracious", "efficient" front of the house is a bonus, as is the "exotic" tea selection (at nearly 40 varieties).

Ⓩ River Palm Terrace *Steak*   25 | 19 | 20 | $58

Edgewater | 1416 River Rd. (Palisade Terr.) | 201-224-2013
Fair Lawn | 41-11 Rte. 4 W. (Plaza Rd.) | 201-703-3500

(continued)

(continued)

River Palm Terrace

Mahwah | 209 Ramapo Valley Rd. (bet. W. Ramapo Ave. & Rte. 17) |
201-529-1111
www.riverpalmterrace.com

"If you love steak you can't miss" this triad of "classy", "very
popular" North Jersey meat emporiums that also deliver
"consistently good" Continental cuisine and seafood; expect to blow
"lots of money", and note that many beef "reservations are mean-
ingless", since you'll likely wind up waiting "too long a time" even if
you have one.

Roberto's Dolce Vita *Italian*   22 | 18 | 21 | $38

Beach Haven | 12907 Long Beach Blvd. (Indiana Ave.) |
609-492-1001

The staff's "extra-warm touch" lights up this "crowded" Beach
Haven BYO "favorite" of LBlers, serving Northern Italian dishes that
"never disappoint" in "comfy" quarters; pros profess "sitting fireside" in the winter couldn't be sweeter.

Roberto's II Ⓜ *Italian*   19 | 13 | 20 | $45

Edgewater | 936 River Rd. (bet. Dempsey & Hilliard Aves.) | 201-224-2524 |
www.robertos2.com

Think "Sinatra and the '50s" and you have this family-run Edgewater
Italian "landmark" that's been dishing out ample portions of "solid"
red-sauce numbers since 1972; things seemingly "haven't changed"
here, as evidenced by decor that could "use an update."

Robin's Nest *American*   22 | 20 | 22 | $32

Mount Holly | 2 Washington St. (White St.) | 609-261-6149 |
www.robinsnestmountholly.com

A "quaint", "unpretentious" setting frames the "delicious" goings on
within this Mount Holly American, a showcase for "superb" sweets,
"impressive" dishes and beverages ("even the iced tea is special
here"), backed by "attentive" servers; N.B. check out the
new alfresco bar.

Robongi *Japanese*   25 | 16 | 21 | $31

Hoboken | 520 Washington St. (bet. 5th & 6th Sts.) |
201-222-8388

"Super-friendly" staffers serve the "freshest" fish at this Hoboken
Japanese BYO, the town's "popular" mainstay for "excellent" sushi;
yes, the "kitschy" decor is very *"Gilligan's Island"*, but given the
food – and "reasonable" prices – no one seems to mind.

Rocca Ⓜ *Italian*   22 | 18 | 20 | $38

Glen Rock | 203 Rock Rd. (bet. Glen Ave. & Main St.) | 201-670-4945 |
www.roccaitalianrestaurant.com

Chef-owner Craig Levy's (ex NYC's Gotham Bar & Grill) "consistently enjoyable" fare (including the "best" pastas) rules at this "inviting" Glen Rock Italian that overall "does everything well";
N.B. takeout fans can pick up savories and pastries at the market
around the corner.

	FOOD	DECOR	SERVICE	COST

Rod's Olde Irish Tavern *Pub Food*

| 19 | 16 | 19 | $29 |

Sea Girt | 507 Washington Blvd. (5th Ave.) | 732-449-2020 | www.rodstavern.com

"The *Cheers* of Sea Girt" is filled with folks who settle in for the "hospitality" and reliably "good" pub provisions and entrees, not to mention to check out games on the myriad TVs; this American "stalwart of suds" has the "right" prices, so it's no surprise that "my husband would eat all his meals there if he could."

Rod's Steak & Seafood Grille · *Seafood/Steak*

| 21 | 23 | 21 | $49 |

Convent Station | Madison Hotel | 1 Convent Rd. (Madison Ave.) | 973-539-6666 | www.rodssteak.com

"All aboard" for the "delicious" steaks and seafood that drive the success of this "classy" Convent Station American where patrons dine in one of the restored antique Pullman Parlour cars, while others opt for the "charming" main dining room decked out in Victoriana; regardless of venue, meals here are "consistently good."

Roman Cafe, The *Italian*

| 19 | 16 | 19 | $43 |

Harrington Park | 12 Tappan Rd. (Schraalenburgh Rd.) | 201-767-4245 | www.romancafe.com

"Meet up with friends for a leisurely dinner" at this "go-to neighborhood place" in Harrington Park that's "always a solid performer", proffering a "typical but well-done" classic Italian menu; though some say the "decor needs improvement", this establishment compensates with a "quiet" ambiance and "friendly" staff; N.B. closed Tuesdays.

Rooney's Oceanfront *Seafood*

| 18 | 21 | 17 | $43 |

Long Branch | 100 Ocean Ave. N. (Cooper Ave.) | 732-870-1200 | www.rooneysocean.com

A "breathtaking" scenery (namely, the Atlantic) explains why you have to "fight the crowds" to get a seat at this waterside Long Branch seafooder (with a recently installed raw bar) whose accommodating staff only "rushes you out if there's a hurricane coming"; for some, however, the "passable fare" is certainly "not as good as the view."

Roots Steakhouse *Steak*

| - | - | - | VE |

Summit | 401 Springfield Ave. (Maple St.) | 908-273-0027 | www.rootssteakhouse.com

Contemporary classics in steak (think Kobe beef sliders) can be found at this marble-and-wood Summit chophouse proffering a diverse menu backed by a mostly American wine list; naturally, the expense-account tabs come with the turf.

Rosemary and Sage ⧄Ⓜ *American*

| 26 | 18 | 23 | $51 |

Riverdale | 26 Hamburg Tpke. (bet. Haycock & Morris Aves.) | 973-616-0606 | www.rosemaryandsage.com

For an "outstanding", "lovingly prepared" meal and "friendly" service in "out-of-the-way" Riverdale, look no further than chef and co-owner Brooks Nicklas' perennially popular, "simply" spruced-up New American recognized for its popular tasting menu; one gripe: "too bad it's only open" Wednesdays–Saturdays for dinner.

	FOOD	DECOR	SERVICE	COST

Ruga 🗷Ⓜ️ *American* — 20 | 18 | 18 | $48

Oakland | 4 Barbara Ln. (W. Oakland Ave.) | 201-337-0813 |
www.rugarestaurant.com

The results on this Oakland New American are mixed: while
backers applaud the "beautiful" decor and quality of the preparations (they're "good" and "varied"), some say it's "not what it
used to be", countering the "service slow" and the fare "unimag-
inative"; N.B. the addition of a new chef might alter that view –
and the above Food score.

Rupee Room *Indian* — – | – | – | M

North Brunswick | Shop at Commerce Ctr. | 2155 Commerce Ctr.
(Rte. 1 S.) | 732-398-9022 | www.therupeeroom.us

Unique is the word for this innovative Indian BYO that transports
you from its North Brunswick strip-mall setting to a fantasyland of
fountains, flashing lights and – trust us – swings for chairs; the
food is in sync with the mood, ranging from flaming skewers from
the tandoor (all the meat is Halal) to fried ice cream to colorful buffets, all comfortably priced.

🗹 Ruth's Chris Steak House *Steak* — 24 | 20 | 23 | $60

Weehawken | Lincoln Harbor | 1000 Harbor Blvd. (19th St.) |
201-863-5100
Parsippany | Hilton Hotel | 1 Hilton Ct. (Campus Dr.) | 973-889-1400
Atlantic City | The Walk | 2020 Atlantic Ave. (bet. Arkansas &
Michigan Aves.) | 609-344-5833
www.ruthschris.com

Meat eaters have "no beef" with these "classic" chain chophouses
known for their "juicy", "sizzling" "butter-covered" chops that are as
"rich" as the tabs; carnivores confirm "these are places to go if on a
cholesterol holiday"; P.S. equally mouthwatering is the "nice" view
of NYC from the Weehawken location.

Sabor *Nuevo Latino* — 22 | 20 | 19 | $43

Hawthorne | 1060 Goffle Rd. (Rte. 208) | 973-238-0800
North Bergen | 8809 River Rd. (Churchill Rd.) | 201-943-6366
www.saborlatinbistro.com

These "snazzy" Nuevo Latinos spotlight "upscale", "vivid" cooking
backed by "trendy" decor, thus attracting a "hip" crowd intent on
"people-watching"; as the night wears on, expect more of a night-
club ambiance, with live entertainment and "skillful" bartenders
concocting "fab" cocktails, mojitos naturally among them.

🗹 Saddle River Inn 🗷Ⓜ️ *American/French* — 27 | 25 | 26 | $62

Saddle River | 2 Barnstable Ct. (W. Saddle River Rd.) | 201-825-4016 |
www.saddleriverinn.com

"Top flight" is another name for this "rustic" yet "civilized" French-
New American near the Saddle River that's been dealing in delightful dining for more than 25 years, serving "haute", "sublime" fare
that lends the "quaint" converted farmhouse setting an "elegant"
touch; blessedly, BYO helps suppress the cost of this "superlative"
restaurant that easily rivals the best.

	FOOD	DECOR	SERVICE	COST

Saffron Indian Cuisine *Indian* | 23 | 19 | 19 | $29 |

East Hanover | 249 Rte. 10 E. (New Murray Rd.) | 973-599-0700 | www.saffronnj.com

"High-class" Indian is the name of the game at this East Hanover BYO where "fantastic" food (and a "not-to-be-missed" lunch buffet) arrives via "helpful" staffers within quarters "more elegant" than the genre usually offers – along with tabs perhaps a tad "pricier"; but overall, when the check comes, it's "worth it."

ⓩ Sagami Ⓜ *Japanese* | 26 | 14 | 21 | $36 |

Collingswood | 37 Crescent Blvd. (bet. Haddon & Park Aves.) | 856-854-9773

The fish is "all it's cut up to be" at this Collingswood BYO, at 34-years-old the birthplace of South Jersey's Japanese scene where the "best sushi around" is still served in a "dark", "low-ceilinged" space; but since you can expect "heaven in the raw", "who cares how the place looks?"

NEW Sage Ⓜ⇗ *Mediterranean* | - | - | - | M |

Ventnor | 5206 Atlantic Ave. (Weymouth Ave.) | 609-823-2110

Savvy locals find this arty, earth-toned Ventnor BYO storefront a welcome addition for reasonably priced Mediterranean meals with an eclectic twist (e.g. black bass with shiitake mushrooms); N.B. the chef's specialties can be purchased at the adjacent Italian market, which she also owns.

Sakura-Bana Ⓜ *Japanese* | 25 | 13 | 21 | $34 |

Ridgewood | 43 Franklin Ave. (bet. Chestnut & Oak Sts.) | 201-447-6525 | www.sakurabana.com

Ardent believers in this longtime Japanese Ridgewood BYO (two decades and counting) still hold it up as the best example "this side of the Hudson" for its "deliciously super-fresh" sushi, dubbing it the "gold standard" in raw fare; N.B. recently expanded quarters may outdate the above Decor score.

Sakura Spring *Chinese/Japanese* | ▽ 23 | 19 | 22 | $27 |

Cherry Hill | 1871 Marlton Pike E. (Greentree Rd.) | 856-489-8018 | www.sakuraspring.com

A "wide", unusual mix of "tasty" Chinese and Japanese specialties greets diners at this Cherry Hill BYO that's good "when you want more than just a take-out" experience; if dinner's out of the picture, lunch is a perfect time to drop by, thanks to modest pricing.

Sallee Tee's Grille *American/Eclectic* | 21 | 18 | 18 | $34 |

Monmouth Beach | 33 West St. (Channel Dr.) | 732-870-8999 | www.salleeteesgrille.com

"Where else can you eat a great corned beef sandwich while your partner enjoys sushi?" before "great" water views than at this Monmouth Beach Eclectic catering to "every taste" imaginable with an "interesting", expansive menu; "mobbed in the summer" and "busy the rest of the year" sums up the scene at this "slam for the buck."

	FOOD	DECOR	SERVICE	COST

Sally Ling *Chinese* | 19 | 15 | 17 | $28 |

Fort Lee | 1636 Palisade Ave. (Main St.) | 201-346-1282

For its many admirers, the food at this popular Fort Lee Chinese is consistently "yummy", with "quick", "efficient" service and a "friendly" vibe as part of the appeal; a few foes, however, find fare that's "nothing special" and a floor staff that's "indifferent."

Salt Creek Grille *American* | 20 | 24 | 20 | $43 |

Rumson | 4 Bingham Ave. (River Rd.) | 732-933-9272
Princeton | Princeton Forrestal Vill. | 1 Rockingham Row (Rte. 1) | 609-419-4200
www.saltcreekgrille.com

The "amazing" architecture of these Traditional Americans are Craftsman-inspired, and while the Rumson location is "perfectly situated" to take in the "wonderful sunsets" across the Navesink, the newer, larger Princeton locale sports an airy, contemporary look; the food is "nicely cooked" if "unremarkable", but the wines are "excellent" and the bar scenes are "hip and happening."

NEW Salt Water Beach Café *American* | – | – | – | M |

Asbury Park | 1200 Ocean Ave. (Fourth Ave.) | 732-774-1400

You can't get much closer to the ocean than sitting on the boardwalk patio at local restaurateur Tim McLoone's latest entry, an Asbury Park New American (in the old Howard Johnson's) with creative combos culled from local fleets and farms (like truffled lobster with mac 'n' cheese); N.B. Tim McLoone's Supper Club – a 1940s-style dinner and dancing nightspot – is scheduled to open upstairs in summer 2008.

Samdan *Turkish* | 22 | 14 | 19 | $31 |

Cresskill | 178 Piermont Rd. (Union Ave.) | 201-816-7343 | www.samdanrestaurant.com

Those with a taste for Turkish head straight for this "cheerful", "always busy" Cresskill Middle Eastern "delight" dispensing "delicious" mezes and meat kebabs; they've got the "right" prices, plus the "nicest" folks work there; N.B. a recent redecoration may alter the above Decor score.

Sammy's Ye Old Cider Mill *Steak* | 21 | 9 | 16 | $59 |

Mendham | 353 Mendham Rd. W. (Oak Knoll Rd.) | 973-543-7675 | www.sammyscidermill.com

"There's no sign", "other than the convoy of Lexuses" outside, "but that doesn't keep away the throngs" who "love" this Mendham "icon", a "speakeasy-turned-restaurant" serving "amazing" if "pricey" steaks and lobsters in "nothing-special" quarters.

San Remo *Italian* | 22 | 15 | 19 | $39 |

Shrewsbury | 37 E. Newman Springs Rd. (Rte. 35) | 732-345-8200 | www.sanremoitaliana.com

"Appearances can be deceiving" say followers of this "unassuming" Shrewsbury Italian BYO cooking up "good", "solid" specialties served by "so-friendly" staffers; a "busy" room and "loud" acoustics go to show that everyone seems to be having an "excellent night" here.

	FOOD	DECOR	SERVICE	COST

Sapori *Italian*
24 | 22 | 22 | $34

Collingswood | 601 Haddon Ave. (Harvard Ave.) | 856-858-2288 |
www.sapori.info

"You can taste" the work that goes into the "great" Italian preparations at this rustic Collingswood BYO fronted by a "delightful" owner
who often stops by tables to greet guests; it all seems so "authentic"
here, some say they "thought they were dining in a trattoria in Italy";
N.B. closed Tuesdays.

Sapo Verde Ⓜ *Mexican*
- | - | - | M

Atlantic Highlands | 99 First Ave. (W. Mt. Ave.) | 732-291-8003

A former ice cream parlor on Atlantic Highlands' main drag has
morphed into this affordable Mexican BYO eatery with all the expected favorites plus more upscale specialties; the red, orange and
yellow hues of the setting are as enticing as the town's hipness.

Savanna *Spanish*
20 | 20 | 19 | $37

Red Bank | The Galleria | 10 Bridge Ave. (W. Front St.) | 732-741-6333 |
www.savannaredbank.com

"Worthy" tapas are dished up in "modern", "warmly comforting"
quarters (featuring low-hanging lanterns and rich woods) at this
Spanish BYO set in an "old-factory" space in Red Bank's historic
Galleria complex; one thing: all those small plates can "run
up the bill."

Savannah's Ⓜ *Eclectic*
- | - | - | M

Stockholm | 2700 Rte. 23 N. (Rte. 515) | 973-697-6000 |
www.savannahsfinedining.com

Sitting on the outskirts of Sussex County ski country is this scenic,
snazzy and spacious Eclectic in Stockholm that's part jazz club and
part lounge; while only open Thursdays through Sundays, it's become home for a crowd of night owls.

SAWA Steakhouse &
Sushi Bar *Japanese*
22 | 20 | 21 | $32

Eatontown | 42 Rte. 36 (Rte. 35) | 732-544-8885
Long Branch | Pier Vill. | 68 Ocean Ave. (Chelsea Ave.) | 732-229-0600
www.sawasteakhouse.com

Fans "go back" to these "islands in the ocean" of Japanese after
sampling the cooked goods at the "entertaining" hibachi tables and
sushi that may be "West Coast" quality; the "marvelous", massive
fish tanks are a hit with the crowds.

❑ Scalini Fedeli Ⓩ *Italian*
27 | 25 | 26 | $69

Chatham | 63 Main St. (bet. Parrott Mill Rd. & Tallmadge Ave.) |
973-701-9200 | www.scalinifedeli.com

"Prepare to be wowed" at top toque Michael Cetrulo's "magical"
Northern Italian "in the woods" of Chatham, where the "truly amazing" dining experience "from start to finish" consists of a "sublime"
prix fixe meal enhanced by "wonderful" wines, "superb" service and
a "lovely, intimate" setting; true, it's "expensive", but all agree it's
"worth every penny" you'll have to give up.

	FOOD	DECOR	SERVICE	COST

Scarborough Fair ⓜ American
20 | 23 | 19 | $44

Wall | 1414 Meetinghouse Rd. (Rte. 35) | 732-223-6658 |
www.scarboroughfairrestaurant.com

At this "warm", "low-key" Wall New American, the food is "pretty good" and various alcoves along the winding stairway and small rooms guarantee "intimacy"; it's "a little expensive" for some, but "oh, what a lovely place"; N.B. the presence of a new chef may outdate the above Food score.

ⓃⒺⓌ Scorpio's Steakhouse Steak
– | – | – | E

Jackson | Jackson Crossings Shopping Ctr. | 21 S. Hope Chapel Rd.
(Veterans Hwy.) | 732-901-3100 | www.scorpiossteakhouse.net

This swanky NY-style steakhouse is a welcome addition to Jackson, a burg abundant in chains and mom 'n' pop spots; the handsome red-and-black, booth-lined dining room suits the upscale meat-lover's menu, which ranges from certified Angus beef to veal chops; N.B. dress is casual – and there's a children's menu too.

☑ SeaBlue ⓜ Seafood
27 | 25 | 25 | $73

Atlantic City | Borgata Hotel, Casino & Spa | 1 Borgata Way
(Atlantic City Expwy., exit 1) | 609-317-8220 | www.theborgata.com

Michael Mina, the celebrated chef of the eponymous San Fran restaurant, has landed in AC's Borgata with this highly rated outpost, a "clear winner" thanks to its "extremely fresh" and "incredibly" prepared, wood-grilled seafood (with fish sourced from around the world), "well-developed" wine list and Adam Tihany's "beautiful" room filled with reds and oranges; in all, this expense-account delight is an undeniable "home run."

Sea Shack ☒ Seafood
20 | 16 | 20 | $44

Hackensack | 293 Polifly Rd. (Rte. 17) | 201-489-7232 | www.seashack.com

Aficionados get shack attacks for this "oldie-but-goodie" Hackensack seafooder where "top-of-the-line" fish is "prepared any way you like it" (and the martinis are "superb"); some argue that the place needs a "face-lift", and you should look out for "high prices", but at least the service ("you feel like family") helps to soothe wounded wallets.

Segovia Portuguese/Spanish
22 | 13 | 20 | $37

Moonachie | 150 Moonachie Rd. (Garden St.) | 201-641-4266 |
www.segoviarestaurant.com

"Paella paradise", this "noisy" Moonachie Iberian in the shadows of the Meadowlands serves "excellent" Portuguese and Spanish (with Continental touches) in "abundance"; a "friendly" staff has "been there for years – and so, unfortunately, has the decor", but just about everyone ignores the "dark" digs and focuses on their "leftovers."

Senorita's Mexican Grill Mexican
20 | 19 | 19 | $24

Bloomfield | 285 Glenwood Ave. (Conger St.) | 973-743-0099 |
www.senoritasmexicangrill.com

A "lively" Mexican in gentrifying Bloomfield, this colorful spot offers a "reasonably priced" menu that's a "fiesta for the palate" with its

| | FOOD | DECOR | SERVICE | COST |

combination of "tasty", "straight-up classics" and "inventive new tastes"; there's also a long list of tequilas and some "very strong margaritas", all brought to table by an "accommodating" staff.

Sens Asian *Asian*
▽ 22 | 20 | 20 | $23

South Brunswick | South Brunswick Square Mall | 4095 Rte. 1 S. (bet. New & Wynwood Rds.) | 732-355-1919 | www.sensasiancuisine.com
"Nondescript" strip-mall environs can't hide the "surprisingly good" Asian dishes or the "hip" decor (with a fish pond in back) at this South Brunswick BYO; the consensus is that it "makes a nice impression", as does its "friendly" staff.

☒ Serenade *French*
27 | 26 | 26 | $70

Chatham | 6 Roosevelt Ave. (Main St.) | 973-701-0303 | www.restaurantserenade.com
"Perfect in every way" is the refrain sung by fans of this "charming" New French in Chatham, which hums with "delighted" diners who "never tire" of the "impeccable" "fine dining", courtesy of husband-wife team James Laird and Nancy Sheridan Laird (chef and manager, respectively); the "superb" cuisine and wines, an "elegant" dining room and an "excellent" staff all add up to make it like a "top NYC restaurant transplanted to the suburbs."

Sergeantsville Inn, The Ⓜ *American*
23 | 24 | 21 | $48

Sergeantsville | 601 Rosemont-Ringoes Rd. (Rtes. 523 & 604) | 609-397-3700 | www.sergeantsvilleinn.com
Emitting a "romantic" ambiance in Sergeantsville, this roadside New American set in a 1734 Colonial building provides "well-prepared" selections (in the main room and more casual tavern) and "great" martinis, both adding to "joyful" repasts; even better, some say, is supping "in winter when the fireplaces are crackling"; N.B. closed for lunch Tuesdays.

Settebello Cafe ☒ *Italian*
22 | 19 | 21 | $37

Morristown | 2 Cattano Ave. (Speedwell Ave.) | 973-267-3355 | www.settebellocafe.com
The "welcoming" atmosphere and "all sorts of delicious" food add up to the "perfect combination" for advocates of this Morristown Northern Italian BYO; high marks go to the outdoor courtyard, a "lovely" choice that somehow feels "like being in Tuscany."

Seven Hills of Istanbul *Turkish*
21 | 19 | 19 | $29

Highland Park | 441 Raritan Ave. (5th Ave.) | 732-777-9711
"Superb" grilled meats and "good" salads are on offer at this BYO "breath of fresh air" for Highland Park serving Turkish specialties at "hard-to-beat" prices; reinforcing the "authentic" aura is the "attractive" decor, with its various rugs and "enormous" samovar.

Shaker Cafe ☒⇩ *American/Eclectic*
- | - | - | M

Flemington | 31 Main St. (bet. Bloomfield Ave. & Capner St.) | 908-782-6610 | www.shakercafe.com
Not named for a religious order but rather referring to the salt and pepper shakers, this quirky American-Eclectic BYO in outlet-clogged

| | FOOD | DECOR | SERVICE | COST |

Flemington is where shoppers stop for omelets, salads and sandwiches; another plus: your pocketbook leaves in generally good shape.

Shanghai Jazz Ⓜ Chinese
`21` `19` `21` `$39`

Madison | 24 Main St. (Green Village Rd.) | 973-822-2899 | www.shanghaijazz.com

Chinese and jazz hit the right note at this Madison restaurant-cum-nightclub featuring a "widely diverse" menu of "high-quality" cooking accompanied by a "backdrop of hot and cool jazz", "some of the best" you can find; factor in the "lively" mood and "efficient" service, and it's no stretch to say things are "in harmony" here.

Ship Inn, The Pub Food
∇ `19` `19` `17` `$28`

Milford | 61 Bridge St. (Rte. 519) | 908-995-0188 | www.shipinn.com

If you're "in the mood for a pint and shepherd's pie", head to this "very comfortable" Milford mainstay that's nautically themed and, appropriately, located just a stone's throw from the Delaware; it's a "real pub" for "sampling microbrews" plus "classic" British bar food that's "good without pretension" and served by a "friendly staff."

Shipwreck Grill American
`25` `17` `20` `$46`

Brielle | 720 Ashley Ave. (Evergreen Ave.) | 732-292-9380 | www.shipwreckgrill.com

"Why would anyone think of going to NYC when we have this in our backyard?" is the question many would ask after time spent at this Brielle New American seafooder whose "wonderful" dinners, "great" bar and servers who make sure to "satisfy their customers" all bring accolades; despite "high-level" acoustics, things in this "tip-top" restaurant seem shipshape.

Shogun Japanese/Steak
`18` `15` `18` `$30`

East Brunswick | Center 18 Mall | 1020 Rte. 18 N. (bet. Gunia St. & Hillsdale Rd.) | 732-390-1922 | www.shogun18.net
Green Brook | 166 Rte. 22 (Washington Ave.) | 732-968-3330 | www.shogun22.net
Kendall Park | 3376 Rte. 27 (Sand Hills Rd.) | 732-422-1117 | www.shogun27.com
Toms River Township | Bey Lea Golf Course | 1536 N. Bay Ave. (Oak Ave.) | 732-286-9888 | www.shogunbeylea.com

Shogun Legends Japanese/Steak
NEW **Wall** | 1969 Rte. 34 S. (Allenwood Rd.) | 732-449-6696

The hibachi chefs "put on a spectacular show" at these Japanese cousins that are "fun for kids" and "a favorite for celebrations", proffering "plentiful" portions of "above-average" sushi and grill items; nevertheless, some feel the food is "nothing special" and note the "chainlike decor" "needs a makeover" (the Kendall Park branch took heed and has reopened, post-redo).

Shumi Ⓜ Japanese
`25` `12` `22` `$35`

Somerville | 30 S. Doughty Ave. (bet. Veterans Memorial Dr. W. & W. Main St.) | 908-526-8596 | www.shumirestaurant.com

"Hidden" in the recesses of a strip mall, this Somerville BYO is "absolutely worth" seeking out for "incredible" raw fin fare that "sets the standard"; the decor may "leave a lot to be desired" but you can't go wrong "sitting at the sushi bar", where the "wonderfully talented chef-owner" "will guide you to interesting" specials that are "expensive but worth it"; N.B. a recent redecoration might brighten things up – and alter the above Decor score.

Siam M⊄ *Thai*

21	7	14	$25

Lambertville | 61 N. Main St. (bet. Coryell & York Sts.) | 609-397-8128

"If you're looking for authentic, delicious, reasonably priced Thai food", this "casual" storefront BYO in Lambertville will "leave you tongue-Thai-ed"; despite "extremely slow" service and "bland", "unappealing" decor, it's "very popular and deservedly so", making reservations "a must"; P.S. "it's cash-only."

Siam Garden *Thai*

23	20	20	$31

Red Bank | The Galleria | 2 Bridge Ave. (W. Front St.) | 732-224-1233 | www.siamgardenrestaurant.com

The menu at this "tasty" Red Bank Thai BYO is "large" enough to "cater to everyone, including children and vegetarians" who'll find some "delicious" dishes; the staff seems "eager to please", and acolytes add up the ways why this place is a "delightful change of pace."

NEW Siena Grille *Italian*

-	-	-	M

Red Bank | 141 Shrewsbury Ave. (bet. Chestnut & Herbert Sts.) | 732-747-1470 | www.sienagrille.com

This Red Bank Italian yearling is two restaurants in one; while the casual tavern/bar area features moderately priced, familiar fare (ranging from burgers to pizza), those seeking a finer (and pricier) experience will find it in the formal dining room, proffering updated dishes like prosciutto-wrapped scallops over a blood-orange risotto; N.B. on-site parking is a plus.

Silver Oak Bistro M *American/Southern*

23	12	19	$41

Ridgewood | 26 Wilsey Sq. (W. Ridgewood Ave.) | 201-444-4744 | www.silveroakbistro.com

At this "charming" BYO in Ridgewood, chef/co-owner Gary Needham makes a "serious effort at being different", doling out "generous portions" of "innovative", Southern-style New American cuisine that's "great on the taste buds" if "less so on the waistline"; while the "incredible food" "trumps the noisy, shoebox surroundings", the "tiny" interior nevertheless has surveyors suggesting you "arrive early" or reserve in advance.

Silver Spring Farm M *French*

▽ 23	20	20	$53

Flanders | 60 Flanders Drakestown Rd. (Theresa Dr.) | 973-584-0202 | www.silverspringfarm.com

"Run by a French family that's been at it for [nearly] 50 years", this "fantastic" Flanders favorite "only gets better with age", offering "country-style" Gallic cuisine in a "quaint", refurbished 1870s inn accessed via "a winding, tree-lined road"; all in all, the "wonderful" experience provides "old-world comfort and elegance" "at a decent price"; N.B. dinner only.

	FOOD	DECOR	SERVICE	COST

Simply Radishing ⚅ *American* — 18 | 9 | 15 | $20

Lawrenceville | Lawrence Shopping Ctr. | 2495 Brunswick Pike/Rte. 1 (bet. Colonial Lake Dr. & Texas Ave.) | 609-882-3760 | www.simplyradishing.com

If you want "a quick lunch or snack between errands", this strip-mall New American in Lawrenceville offers salads "so big a family could share just one" plus a "carb-loading extravaganza" of a bread bar boasting "a tasty assortment of butters"; while it also serves dinner, patrons protest its "dreary-looking" decor, declaring "it desperately needs a makeover"; N.B. it's BYO.

Z Sirena *Italian* — 23 | 26 | 19 | $53

Long Branch | 27 Ocean Ave. (Laird St.) | 732-222-1119 | www.sirenaristorante.com

A "fantastic" setting overlooking the ocean partnered with "high-quality" cuisine is the deal at this "classy" Long Branch Italian situated waterside; although some assert that the "uneven service" could come with less "attitude", the "excellent" eats help compensate.

Sirin *Thai* — 22 | 19 | 20 | $33

Morristown | 3 Pine St. (South St.) | 973-993-9122 | www.sirinthairestaurant.com

For "quick and easy dining" before or after a show at the Community Theater, head to this "above-average" BYO Thai in Morristown that's "a great find" for an "interesting variety" of "well-prepared food"; it's situated in a "cozy, houselike setting" that seems "understated" and "pleasant" to some and "dark" to others; N.B. closed Tuesdays.

Siri's Thai French Cuisine *French/Thai* — 25 | 20 | 23 | $37

Cherry Hill | 2117 Rte. 70 W. (Haddonfield Rd.) | 856-663-6781 | www.siris-nj.com

The strip-mall locale "deceives" but the cooking doesn't at this Cherry Hill BYO that knits Thai and French in its "amazingly good" fare; though outside is all shopping center, the inside, with its white tablecloths, pleases, as does the "friendly" service.

Sister Sue's *Caribbean* — ∇ 21 | 14 | 20 | $27

Asbury Park | 311 Bond St. (Mattison Ave.) | 732-502-8383 | www.sistersueroti.com

"Trek no further than Asbury Park" to experience "true Trini tastes" turning up in this Caribbean BYO whose "pleasant" staff serves "authentic" Trinidadian cookery such as curried goat and oxtail stew; aside from its "good" value it's a "great change" from the usual.

Skylark Fine Diner & Lounge ☽ *American* — 19 | 22 | 19 | $23

Edison | 17 Wooding Ave. (bet. Old Post Rd. & Rte. 1 N.) | 732-777-7878 | www.skylarkdiner.com

"More silver spoon than greasy spoon", this "lively" "upscale diner" in Edison is flying high in the eyes of fans who praise its almost "offensively large portions" of "spiffed-up" comfort food, its "ultra-modern", "meet-George-Jetson" decor and its "friendly" service; it also boasts an attached bar/lounge with an "impressive drink menu", regular DJs and trivia nights.

	FOOD	DECOR	SERVICE	COST

Smithville Inn *American*

18 | 21 | 19 | $36

Smithville | 1 N. New York Rd. (Moss Mill Rd.) | 609-652-7777 | www.smithvilleinn.com

Exposed wooden beams and various fireplaces lend "charm" to this Smithville site whipping up Traditional American "throwback" goods to complement the "early American" ambiance; the fare may be "uneven", but there's nothing like "sitting by the fire" to soak up some "coziness."

Smoke Chophouse & Cigar Emporium *Seafood/Steak*

22 | 19 | 20 | $56

Englewood | 36 Engle St. (Palisade Ave.) | 201-541-8530 | www.smokechophouse.com

"The place to go for a great meal and a cigar afterwards", this Englewood steak-and-stogie site offers "fantastic" beef and seafood in an "old-world, gentlemen's club" ambiance; if you can't take the "smoky haze", there's a nonsmoking room downstairs, where you'll find the same "top-shelf wine list" and "attentive service"; N.B. you can BYO for a $20 corkage fee.

Sogno *Italian*

23 | 18 | 20 | $44

Red Bank | 69 Broad St. (bet. Monmouth & Wallace Sts.) | 732-747-6969 | www.sognoredbank.com

"Excellent" Italian food fills the room, as does lots of "noise" ("what's that?") and "crowds" at this "narrow", "tightly" packed Red Bank BYO, for some the town's "restaurant of choice" that "bustles" just about every night; no shock – it's best to "call for a reservation."

SoHo on George *American*

23 | 22 | 21 | $48

New Brunswick | 335 George St. (bet. Bayard & Liberty Sts.) | 732-296-0533 | www.sohoongeorge.com

This New American New Brunswick "winner" succeeds with "tasty" savories (and "sinful" desserts), an "elegant" yet "trendy" vibe (complemented by an "airy" space) and "efficient" service; thanks to its "always-hot" bar, expect "loud" acoustics, but for the area, "this is one of the best for a night out."

Soho 33 *Eclectic*

19 | 15 | 17 | $33

Madison | 33 Main St. (bet. Green Village Rd. & Waverly Pl.) | 973-822-2600 | www.soho33.com

"Salads, sandwiches and wraps" sum up the "light" lunches that "ladies" show up for at this "casual" Madison BYO Eclectic that seems "to the point"; "when dining locally", it's a "reliably" sound choice.

Solaia Restaurant *Italian*

20 | 21 | 18 | $52

Englewood | 22 N. Van Brunt St. (Palisade Ave.) | 201-871-7155 | www.solaiarestaurant.com

Situated "next to the bustling Bergen Performing Arts Center", this "chic", "upscale" Italian in Englewood is just the ticket "for dinner or drinks before a show" with its "imaginative" seafood-centric menu and equally "lively" bar scene (there are two of them); whether you opt to sit in the "pretty interior" or "outside on warm days", expect to have a "pleasant" if "pricey" experience.

Solari's ☒ *Italian*   21 | 16 | 19 | $41
Hackensack | 61 River St. (Bridge St.) | 201-487-1969 |
www.solarisrestaurant.com

Just shy of its 75th anniversary, this "traditional" Italian has been a "Hackensack haven" for lunching "lawyers, judges and politicos" "from the nearby Bergen County courthouse" "for three generations"; it's also a "warm and inviting" destination for dinner courtesy of "gracious" chef, owner and host Marco Solari; P.S. live music keeps it "swinging" on weekends.

Solo Bella *Italian*   ∇ 21 | 19 | 19 | $31
Jackson | 426 Chandler Rd. (Genova Ave.) | 732-961-0951 |
www.solobella.com

"Dependable" Italian dinners are nice to have around say gratified eaters at this Italian BYO seemingly operating solo in virtually "restaurant-less" Jackson; for "family-style" dining, it scores points, and for the folks in town, it's "worth the wait."

So Moon Nan Jip ◐ *Korean*   ∇ 23 | 11 | 17 | $26
Palisades Park | 238 Broad Ave. (Brinkerhoff Ave.) | 201-944-3998

There's nothing so-so about the "delicious" Korean barbecue and other "homestyle" "standards" served up at this "comfortable" "value" in Palisades Park; there are "many side dishes" to tempt the taste buds plus "great sushi and sashimi", but you'll likely leave "smelling like the food you just grilled", so "don't go in a suit."

Somsak *Thai*   23 | 14 | 20 | $24
Voorhees | Echo Shops | 200 White Horse Rd. (bet. 4th & 5th Sts.) |
856-782-1771

The chef-owners take "great care" in what they prepare at this "popular" Voorhees Thai BYO known for "consistently excellent" cuisine that uses "fresh" ingredients (the "homemade ice creams are a must"); "attentive" service and "bargain" prices also please.

Sono Sushi *Japanese*   26 | 16 | 22 | $32
Middletown | Village Mall | 1098 Rte. 35 S. (New Monmouth Rd.) |
732-706-3588 | www.sonosushi.com

Watch the "happiest patrons" walk out of this "friendly" Middletown Japanese BYO, the "best sushi house in the area", with "super-fresh", "high-quality" raw fish employed in the "beautiful" morsels; tips: check out the "nicely prepared" hot dishes, and "take advantage of the amazing lunch specials."

Sonsie *American*   - | - | - | E
Atlantic City | Pier at Caesars | 1 Atlantic Ocean (Arkansas Ave.) |
609-345-6300 | www.sonsieac.com

Boston's upscale, casual eclectic American brings its European brasserie-style setting to NJ with this outpost in the Pier at Caesars; in addition to the hearty selection at lunch and dinner, there's a breakfast menu of eggs and croissants to fuel a busy day at the slot machines.

Sophie's Bistro ⓜ *French*

`22` `20` `21` `$36`

Somerset | 700 Hamilton St. (bet. Baier & Dewald Aves.) | 732-545-7778 | www.sophiesbistro.net

In the "unlikeliest of places" dwells this Somerset French "charmer" lauded for its "affordable" bistro fare accompanied by Gallic wines, "quaint" banqueted quarters (with a copper bar), "congenial" hosts and staff; overall, it easily transports to "gay Paree."

Soufflé ⓜ *French*

`23` `18` `21` `$48`

Summit | 7 Union Pl. (Summit Ave.) | 908-598-0717 | www.soufflerestaurant.com

"Quiet, understated and worth a visit", this Summit storefront draws praise for its "fine" French cuisine, especially the "spectacular soufflés" "that are certain to please"; factor in "charming decor" and a "wonderful staff", and this Gallic "sleeper" seems "a rare pleasure" "in an area dominated by Italian restaurants"; P.S. the "BYO takes the sting out of the prices."

ⓩ South City Grill *American*

`23` `23` `20` `$47`

Jersey City | 70 Town Square Pl. (Rochelle Ave.) | 201-610-9225
Rochelle Park | 55 Rte. 17 S. (Passaic St.) | 201-845-3737
Mountain Lakes | 60 Rte. 46 E. (Crane Rd.) | 973-335-8585
www.southcitygrill.com

Whether you're looking for a "fabulous" meal in a "modern setting" or a "happening bar" with a "hip, young singles scene", you'll have "an amazing experience" at this trio of "trendy", seafood-centric Americans offering a "diverse" menu of "delectable" delights; while the "speed and friendliness of service varies", however, the decibel levels do not: "the food's fine if you can stand the noise, but oh that noise!"

NEW South Street Steakhouse ⓜ *Steak*

`-` `-` `-` `E`

Freehold | 24 South St. (bet. Main & Throckmorton Sts.) | 732-780-2929 | www.southstreetsteakhouse.com

Serious beef eaters can have their hand-cut certified black Angus porterhouse and NY sirloin too at this classy new Freehold chophouse that also proffers seafood – and some surprises (like chicken tagine), in elegant, draped-ceiling surroundings; it's pricey but BYO – and oenophiles can have their vinos at the ready by renting personal, on-site, temperature-controlled wine lockers.

Spain *Portuguese/Spanish*

`21` `15` `20` `$35`

Newark | 419 Market St. (Raymond Blvd.) | 973-344-0994 | www.spainrestaurant.com

"Mammoth amounts" of "tasty" Spanish-Portuguese fare – including "giant lobsters", "brontosaurus-sized steaks" and "hefty desserts" – ensures "everyone carries out a doggy bag" at this Ironbound institution that "caters to families and NJPAC visitors"; while the decor "appears a bit worn"(a recent redecoration might brighten things up), the service here remains "as good as ever."

	FOOD	DECOR	SERVICE	COST

Spanish Tavern *Spanish* — 22 | 17 | 21 | $39

Mountainside | 1239 Rte. 22 E. (Locust Ave.) | 908-232-2171
Newark | 103 McWhorter St. (Green St.) | 973-589-4959
www.spanishtavern.com

"Does paella get any better?" ask aficionados of this "reliable" Iberian duo that delivers "huge" helpings of "Spanish food at its best" – "just come with a loose outfit and enjoy"; "friendly", "attentive service" is also a plus, but while the "more elegant Mountainside branch" boasts a "warm" ambiance, the Ironbound original may be "a little dated" (though a recent spruce-up might enliven the environment).

Spargo's Grille Ⓜ *American* — 25 | 18 | 20 | $40

Manalapan | Andee Plaza | 130 Rte. 33 W. (Millhurst Rd.) | 732-294-9921 |
www.spargosgrille.com

"Don't judge" this place by its strip-mall locale argue fans of this Manalapan BYO presenting "attractive", "well-prepared" New American food that's a "bargain" considering the quality of the preparations; while service gets "spotty when the house is full", it still comes across as "friendly."

Specchio Ⓢ Ⓜ *Italian* — 25 | 25 | 24 | $63

Atlantic City | Borgata Hotel, Casino & Spa | 1 Borgata Way (Atlantic City Expwy., exit 1) | 609-317-1000 | www.theborgata.com

An "ethereal" experience awaits at this "high-end" Italian in the Borgata, where the modern cuisine is "nothing short of outstanding" (and features "fresh" vegetarian options, thanks in part to local sourcing) and where tables are spaced "far enough apart" to lend a "romantic" ambiance to the "beautiful" room; the consensus: "double down your bet – this one's worth the chips" (except Sundays–Tuesdays, when they're closed); N.B. new chef James Hennessey has replaced Luke Palladino, which may outdate the above Food score.

Spice Cuisine *Eclectic* — - | - | - | M

Bloomfield | 26 Belleville Ave. (Willet St.) | 973-748-0056
Thailand and Italy meet up at this Eclectic low-frills Bloomfield BYO, where the dishes go either way, sporting Asian or Italian accoutrements; modest pricing easily appeals to fans of East and West.

Spike's *Seafood* — 22 | 7 | 17 | $26

Point Pleasant Beach | 415 Broadway (bet. Channel Dr. & Rte. 35) |
732-295-9400

"Fabulously" fresh catch in digs that look "like a shack should" is the appeal of this Point Pleasant Beach BYO seafooder/market that "knows how to cook" and where they serve the stuff "without any hoopla"; if the "waits" are the equivalent to "getting hazed when rushing a fraternity", few mind when they keep in mind the "ultimate goal" – chowing down on the eats.

NEW Splash Ⓜ *Seafood* — - | - | - | M

Long Valley | 1 W. Mill Rd. (Fairmount Rd.) | 908-876-9307
This Long Valley seafooder proffers swimmingly fresh dishes from the deep (from classy to casual, plus a children's menu) and land-

lubber options at reasonable prices; get in a mermaid-mood via flat-screen TVs featuring underwater scenes that line the dining room.

Squan Tavern 🅼 *Italian*

19 | 13 | 19 | $27

Manasquan | 15 Broad St. (Main St.) | 732-223-3324 | www.squantavern.com

The "absolute friendliest" folks serve the "best" pizzas that steal the show at this family-run feedery that's been dispensing solidly "good", "heavy" Southern Italian "home cooking" (since 1964) in Manasquan; P.S. the kitchen's been known to "prepare special requests when they're not on the menu."

Sri Thai *Thai*

24 | 9 | 17 | $19

Hoboken | 234 Bloomfield St. (3rd St.) | 201-798-4822

Although "low on decor", this tiny Thai BYO in Hoboken beckons fans with its "sensational" Siamese chow; prices are "cheap", the food "filling" and the staff "friendly", so no wonder lots of folks think it "worth a try"; N.B. closed Tuesdays.

Stage House Restaurant & Wine Bar *American*

23 | 22 | 21 | $56

Scotch Plains | 366 Park Ave. (Front St.) | 908-322-4224 | www.stagehouserestaurant.com

"Prepare to be spoiled" at this "expensive-but-worth-it" New American in Scotch Plains that's tucked away in a "charming", "rustic" 1737 inn highlighted by a "fireplace [for] cold evenings" and "patio dining in the summer"; they've recently added a "more casual tavern" side, which some say "has taken away from the restaurant" but most consider a "wonderful", "lower-cost alternative" for "lighter fare"; N.B. two prix fixe dinner menus ($24 or $33) are now offered.

🆉 Stage Left *American*

26 | 23 | 25 | $64

New Brunswick | 5 Livingston Ave. (George St.) | 732-828-4444 | www.stageleft.com

"A perfect place for a before- or after-theater meal" or "a celebration night", this "consistent winner" in New Brunswick "keeps getting better with age", proffering "excellent" New American cuisine that's complemented by an "incredible cheese table" and "to-die-for wine list"; factor in "superb service" and an "elegant atmosphere" and this is "the definition of fine dining", which to some means you'd better "bring two credit cards."

Steve & Cookie's By the Bay *American*

25 | 20 | 22 | $47

Margate | 9700 Amherst Ave. (N. Monroe Ave.) | 609-823-1163 | www.steveandcookies.com

"Consistently good" deliciousness keeps the house "packed" at this "favorite" of a New American with a "gorgeous" Margate location and "wonderful" service (including the "best bartenders" at the "great" bar); off-peak is an ideal time to visit – things are a "little quieter" and you can enjoy the fare before one of the "blazing" fireplaces.

| | FOOD | DECOR | SERVICE | COST |

NEW Stonehouse at
Stirling Ridge Ⓜ *American*   - | - | - | E

Warren | Stirling Ridge | 50 Stirling Rd. (Stiles Rd.) | 908-754-1222 |
www.stirlingridgeevents.com

Though catering is the mainstay at this new upscale Warren
Township establishment (set in the sprawling venue of the old
Chanticler Chateau), its stylish on-site New American restaurant
caters to those with an appetite for the likes of braised short ribs (or
brownie s'mores); all eyes are on the floor-to-ceiling 'wine tower'
showcasing 150 labels; N.B. a five- ($65) or seven-course ($75)
chef's tasting menu is available.

Stony Hill Inn *Continental/Italian*   23 | 25 | 22 | $54

Hackensack | 231 Polifly Rd. (Rte. 80) | 201-342-4085 |
www.stonyhillinn.com

"Romance abounds" at this "charming" Italian-Continental in
Hackensack that's set in the "elegant, old-world" ambiance of a converted 1818 farmhouse; you "won't be rushed", "whether you're
having an intimate dinner", a "gathering with friends" or a "special
event" at this "place to go for posh."

Strip House *Steak*   23 | 23 | 21 | $63

Livingston | Westminster Hotel | 550 W. Mt. Pleasant Ave.
(bet. Daven Ave. & Microlab Rd.) | 973-548-0050 |
www.striphouse.net

You "don't have to go through any tunnels" to reach this "swanky"
Livingston spin-off of the Gotham original vending "lusciously" good
steaks proffered in, as the name implies, "sexy", "reddish" boudoirlike
quarters; some say if only they could strip away some of the "NYC
pricing", but for surf 'n' turf supping, it's "major league all the way."

Suez Canal ⌀ *Seafood*   - | - | - | I

Jersey City | 117 Tonnele Ave. (bet. Broadway & Newark Ave.) |
201-333-5305

Serving all things aquatic in nautical, neon-accented quarters, this
Egyptian seafooder in Jersey City is noted for its fresh catch, from
fried items to charcoal-grilled options; affordable tabs transform it
into a must-try for fish fans.

Sumo *Japanese*   - | - | - | M

Wall | 1933 Rte. 35 (Allaire Rd.) | 732-282-1388 |
www.sumowalltwp.com

This roomy Wall Japanese BYO has emerged as a favorite among
Shore dwellers, with a sizable sushi selection in addition to cooked
foods created hibachi style – with sizzle and a show.

Sunny Garden *Chinese*   22 | 20 | 20 | $28

West Windsor | 15 Farber Rd. (Rte. 1) | 609-520-1881 |
www.sunnygarden.net

"Tucked away just off Route 1" in West Windsor, this hard-to-find
"upscale Chinese" has "a loyal crowd of regulars" that rave about its
"flavorful soups", "elegant entrees" and sushi selection, all "pre-

pared with care and attractively presented"; factor in "attentive ser-vice" and "the atmosphere of a four-star hotel", and this BYO is "truly a fine-dining experience."

Surf Taco *Mexican*

| 20 | 14 | 16 | $13 |

Belmar | 1003 Main St. (10th Ave.) | 732-681-3001
Jackson | 21 Hope Chapel Rd. (E. Veteran's Hwy.) | 732-364-8226 ◐
Manasquan | 121 Parker Ave. (Stockton Lake Blvd.) | 732-223-7757
Point Pleasant Beach | 1300 Richmond Ave. (Marcia Ave.) | 732-701-9000
Seaside Park | 212 SE Central Ave. (bet. Franklin & Lincoln Aves.) | 732-830-2111
Toms River | 1887 Hooper Ave. (bet. Church & Moore Rds.) | 732-255-3333
www.surftaco.com

Bringing "West Coast" Cal-Mex to NJ, these BYO counter-service spots offer up "quick and easy" items – tacos, burritos, wraps and smoothies – that are "fresh" and "cheap"; overall, these "fun" and "casual" spots have quickly become a "necessity on the Shore."

Sushi by Kazu *Japanese*

| ▽ 28 | 14 | 20 | $35 |

Howell | 2724 Rte. 9 S. (bet. 2nd & 3rd Sts.) | 732-370-2528

Devotees give "thanks" for this Japanese BYO in Howell, chef Kazu Mukai's showcase for "extremely fresh" fish used for his undeniably "great" sushi and other near "perfect" fare; to experience "top qual-ity", get there early – the "very small" space "fills up fast"; N.B. closed Tuesdays.

Sushi Lounge *Japanese*

| 24 | 22 | 20 | $37 |

Hoboken | 200 Hudson St. (2nd St.) | 201-386-1117
Totowa | 235 Rte. 46 W. (bet. Minnisink Rd. & Union Blvd.) | 973-890-0007
Morristown | 12 Schuyler Pl. (Washington St.) | 973-539-1135
www.sushilounge.com

For "high-quality" sushi and a "hip", "clublike" scene, check out these "extra-loud" Hoboken, Morristown and (newest) Totowa Japanese dens and make like sardines ("you have to weigh about 80 pounds to squeeze in when it's full"); with the "best" DJs around, they please lounge lizards who say "the beats are even better than the eats."

Table 🖫 Ⓜ *American*

| - | - | - | VE |

Little Silver | Markham Place Plaza | 151 Markham Pl. (Prospect Ave.) | 732-747-2008 | www.tablenj.com

Set in a Little Silver shopping mall that already sports several restau-rants, chef Martin Bradley's BYO distinguishes itself with its fine haute New American fare; the tabs are high, but the folks waiting in line don't seem to mind.

Table 8 Ⓜ *American*

| 23 | 21 | 21 | $45 |

Montclair | 615 Bloomfield Ave. (bet. Midland Ave. & Valley Rd.) | 973-746-2233 | www.table8nj.com

"In a town full of surprises", this Montclair BYO is an undeniable "delight" that's easy on the eyes (thanks to a "chic" red-and-brown design scheme) and on the palate, with a "delicious" roster of New

American preparations delivered by "terrific" servers; it's all overseen by a "charming" owner, so it's no surprise this "lively" addition is "worth the price."

NEW Tabor Road Tavern American — | — | — | E

Morris Plains | 510 Tabor Rd. (Rte. 10) | 973-267-7004 | www.harvestrestaurants.com

Fireplaces and a soaring atrium evoke the rustic elegance of an Aspen ski lodge and warm first-time guests at this instantly popular, pricey Morris Plains New American newcomer; cozy up to a varied menu (from chic tuna tartare crisps to comfy red velvet cake), but keep in mind you're on a slippery slope sans weekend reservations.

Tacconelli's Pizzeria Ⓜ ⇗ Pizza   24 | 9 | 15 | $18

Maple Shade | 450 S. Lenola Rd. (Rte. 38) | 856-638-0338 | www.tacconellispizzerianj.com

"Order your dough in advance" or risk going home with nothing advise aficionados of this "legendary" "no-frills" pizzeria in Maple Shade; it's "well worth the effort" once you taste the "best thin-crust pizza anywhere" (especially the "white with spinach"), though just be prepared to smell "garlicky"; N.B. also closed Tuesdays.

Z Taka Ⓜ Japanese   26 | 26 | 24 | $37

Asbury Park | 632 Mattison Ave. (Main St.) | 732-775-1020 | www.takaapnj.com

"Beautiful", "sophisticated" and "sleek" in setting, this Asbury Park BYO is the "current fave", serving "super-fresh", "cleverly" assembled sushi and other "excellent" Japanese "delights" supported by a "pro" staff; in all, admirers are entranced with this "winning" spot that seems "straight out of Manhattan."

Takara Japanese   ▽ 25 | 26 | 19 | $28

Ocean Township | Orchard Plaza | 1610 Rte. 35 S. (Willow Dr.) | Oakhurst | 732-663-1899 | www.takarajapaneserestaurant.com

Hibachi tables, tatami rooms and a koi pond lend allure to this "lovely" Ocean Township Japanese that "deserves much praise" since the cooked fare is "really good", the decor "really nice" and "the kids love it"; overall, expect an "enjoyable" dining experience.

Tapas de Espana Spanish   20 | 17 | 18 | $36

Englewood | 47 N. Dean St. (bet. Palisade Ave. & Park Pl.) | 201-569-9999

North Bergen | 7909 Bergenline Ave. (79th St.) | 201-453-1690

"*Viva España!*" is what unprompted acolytes exclaim after hitting these "lively" tapas experts serving a "long" menu of Spanish "tasty" bites in old-world Spain environs; though larger portions are available, "bring a group", "explore the menu" then "stick with the small plates."

NEW Tap Room Bar & Grille American   — | — | — | E

Northfield | Atlantic City Country Club | 1 Leo Fraser Dr. (Shore Rd.) | 609-641-7575 | www.accountryclub.com

Dinners hit the mark at this Traditional American at Northfield's historic 1897 Atlantic City Country Club (the birthplace of the 'birdie'), which recently opened to the public; dishes like prime rib and crab cakes are proffered in a candlelit setting with a pianist or out on the patio overlooking the legendary greens; N.B. breakfast, lunch and Sunday brunch are also served.

Taqueria Ⓜ Mexican
▽ 20 | 12 | 17 | $15

Jersey City | 236 Grove St. (Grand St.) | 201-333-3220
"Roll up your sleeves and enjoy some of the best" – and "cheapest" – Mexican eats around rave admirers of this "friendly" family-run Jersey City BYO whose "honest", "authentic" cooking counterbalances the modest looks; N.B. a patio is available for warm weather dining.

Taro Pan-Asian
21 | 22 | 19 | $36

Montclair | 32 Church St. (bet. S. Fullerton Ave. & S. Park St.) | 973-509-2266 | www.tarorestaurant.com
With food as "tasty as it looks", fans are "hooked" on this Pan-Asian Montclair BYO with "austere", "minimalist" decor that "soothes" and seems suited to the menu; N.B. though they've been serving it for some time, dim sum rolls around on weekends.

Tashmoo Pub Food
- | - | - | M

Morristown | 8 Dehart St. (South St.) | 973-998-6133
Settling in swimmingly off the green in Morristown, this Traditional American pays homage to an inlet of the same name on Martha's Vineyard and seeks to emulate the summery vibe there; for the food, the burgers and other comfort eats are complemented by boutique brews in an upscale-pub setting.

Taste of Asia, A Ⓜ Malaysian
21 | 13 | 19 | $30

Chatham | 245 Main St. (N. Passaic Ave.) | 973-701-8821 | www.atasteofasianj.com
"Chase away the malaise" at this storefront Malaysian in Chatham that "excites the taste buds" with its "diverse menu" of "well-prepared food"; though some find the space "cavernous" and "bare", this BYO proves a "real bargain" and "a nice alternative to Chinese."

Tattoni's Restaurant Ⓢ Italian
- | - | - | I

Hamilton Township | 1280 Hwy. 33 (Hamilton Sq.) | 609-587-9700
Red sauce – make that gravy – reigns supreme at this family-run, strip-mall BYO Italian that recently relocated to Hamilton Township after a 37-year stint in Trenton's Chambersburg; loyalists followed suit for the wallet-friendly fare, including a signature chicken cacciatore and tiramisu; overall, it always feels like Sunday dinner here.

Teak Pan-Asian
23 | 22 | 19 | $42

Red Bank | 64 Monmouth St. (Drummond Pl.) | 732-747-5775 | www.teakrestaurant.com
"The food's very good, the drinks are better and the people-watching is the best" ("am I pretty enough?") at "one of Red Bank's hippest" parlors, a Pan-Asian where "low lighting" and "cool" decor suit the young "singles" scene; P.S. for some "quiet" with dinner, sit in one of the "more intimate back rooms"; if you like it loud, there's live music on some Friday nights.

	FOOD	DECOR	SERVICE	COST

Ted's on Main 🅱️Ⓜ️ *American* — | - | - | - | M

Medford | 20 S. Main St. (Bank St.) | 609-654-7011 | www.tedsonmain.net
It's casual at this New American BYO on Medford's main drag that
oozes white-tablecloth elegance and big-city aspirations – not surprising, since Ted is chef Ted Iwachiw, whose background includes Philly's
Striped Bass; count on large flavorful portions at medium prices.

Teresa Caffe *Italian* — 21 | 16 | 18 | $29

Princeton | Palmer Sq. | 23 Palmer Sq. E. (Nassau St.) | 609-921-1974 |
www.terramomo.com
For most, there are no reservations about this no-reservations strip-
mall Italian, "one of the best things about" Princeton since the
"solid", "high-quality" *ciao* is "affordable and delicious", the atmosphere "bubbly" and the service "friendly" (if "uneven") – oh, and
"getting a table on weekends can take as long as getting a PhD."

Terrace Restaurant *Mediterranean* — 22 | 22 | 23 | $48

Short Hills | Hilton at Short Hills | 41 JFK Pkwy. (Rte. 24, exit 7C) |
973-912-4757 | www.hiltonshorthills.com
This "elegant" Hilton at Short Hills' eatery delivers "fine"
Mediterranean food and "unrushed service" in a "sumptuous" setting;
while the "spectacular" "Sunday brunch is their forte" (there's "truly
something for everyone"), they also offer light fare at the bar.

Tewksbury Inn *American* — 22 | 20 | 19 | $45

Oldwick | 55 Main St./Rte. 517 (King St.) | 908-439-2641 |
www.thetewksburyinn.com
"Mingle with the horsey set" and "rub elbows with the upper crust"
at this "rural gem" in "gentrified" Oldwick that proffers "unusual"
New American offerings and fine wines in a "charming" former inn;
whether you opt for the "warm, comfortable" dining room, the
"clubby", "social" tavern, the weekends-only upstairs quarters or
the "lovely outside seating in summer", expect a "relaxing" meal.

Thai Chef *Thai* — 21 | 17 | 19 | $32

Hackensack | Riverside Square Mall | 169 Hackensack Ave. (off Rte. 4) |
201-342-7257
Montclair | 664 Bloomfield Ave. (bet. Orange & Valley Rds.) | 973-783-4994
www.thaichefusa.com
Although distinct in their own ways (Hackensack incorporates
French fare and serves alcohol), the Thais that bind these "treasures"
are their "large" menus, "tasty" cooking and "Zen-like" settings even
when "busy"; overall, they're "impressively consistent" performers.

Thai Kitchen *Thai* — 23 | 14 | 20 | $22

Bridgewater | 1351 Prince Rodgers Ave. (I-287, exit 14B) | 908-231-8822
Bridgewater | Somerset Shopping Ctr. | 327 Hwy. 202/206 (off Rte. 22) |
908-722-8983
Hillsborough | Hillsborough Shopping Ctr. | 649 Hwy. 206 (Amwell Rd.) |
908-904-8038
www.thaikitchennj.com
So what if "the decor is lacking"? ask fans, for these "friendly"
Somerset County BYOs offer an "incredible bargain" (lunch is "a

steal") on some of the "best" Thai in the Garden State; "fast" "pros"
for servers keep the "busy" rooms in order.

Thai Thai *Thai*

25	16	21	$27

Stirling | 1168 Valley Rd. (bet. Poplar Dr. & Warren Ave.) | 908-903-0790 |
www.thaithaifinecuisine.com

"Always crowded" with "a loyal following", this strip-mall "favorite" in
Stirling serves up "Thai-riffic food" with such "presentation, taste and
quality" that "you'll swear you're in a popular NYC restaurant"; the
"fresh, creative" curries come at an "excellent value" that's made
even better by the BYO policy and the presence of a "friendly staff."

▮▮▮ Thai Tida *Thai*

–	–	–	M

Lambertville | 236 N. Union St. (bet. Cherry & Elms Sts.) |
609-397-6701 | www.thaitida.com

Lambertville locals with a taste for something different turn up at
this budget-friendly, family-run BYO Thai newcomer with Laotian
twists (and a hint of Malaysia); the cozy spot is a trek from trendy
Downtown, so don your walking shoes – or drive – to sample *larb
moo* (pork) with mint and ground roasted rice.

Theater Square Grill *American/Continental*

20	23	18	$50

Newark | New Jersey Performing Arts Ctr. | 1 Center St. (McCarter Hwy.) |
973-642-1226 | www.theatersquaregrill.com

"Your best bet" for "good" pre-performance repasts, this Newark
Continental-American in NJPAC proffers a "high-end" menu amid a
"beautiful" retro "modern" space; though "hardly cheap", you gain
ground by making "curtain call" on time; N.B. reservations required
on theater nights.

Theresa's *Italian*

23	17	21	$37

Westfield | 47 Elm St. (bet. E. Broad St. & North Ave.) | 908-233-9133 |
www.theresasrestaurant.com

"Good", "solid" "old-time" Italian food and "hard-to-beat" prices
add up to a "packed" room at this Westfield BYO "festive" "favorite"
that "always satisfies" – except for the "loud", "overwhelming"
acoustics and, thanks to no reservations, "waits worse than what
you get at Great Adventure."

3 Forty Grill *American*

21	23	20	$40

Hoboken | 340 Sinatra Dr. (Washington St.) | 201-217-3406 |
www.3fortygrill.com

Devotees of this "upscale" Hoboken New American stream in for
"fresh" seafood and "interesting" martinis at the "active" bar;
"great" views of the NYC skyline and a "trendy" setting augment the
"love" factor for many; N.B. validated parking is offered to those
who spend over $50.

▮ 3 West *American*

23	24	21	$49

Basking Ridge | 665 Martinsville Rd. (Independence Blvd.) | 908-647-3000 |
www.3westrest.com

"Imaginative" "haute comfort food" keeps admirers attracted to this
"frenetic" Basking Ridge American, a "winner" equally prized for its

fare and "hot" bar, where "hanging out becomes a career" for some; the "chic", "rustic" space is suited to both "intimate" dinners or "business" meetings, the latter appropriate given the tabs ("the bill can really sneak up on you").

NEW Thyme Restaurant & Bar Ⓜ *American*

| | | | E |

Phillipsburg | Architects Golf Club | 700 Strykers Rd. (bet. Meadowview & Powderhorn Drs.) | 908-213-3080 | www.thearchitectsclub.com

Taking a time-out at the (open-to-the-public) Architects Golf Club in Phillipsburg could mean dining in this formal, upscale New American tucked in the new Clubhouse; you might also consider a fireside drink in the bar that sports flat-screen TVs; N.B. a Thursday night, three-course prix fixe prime rib dinner for two costs $49.95.

Thyme Square Ⓜ *Mediterranean*

| 21 | 18 | 19 | $41 |

Red Bank | 45 Broad St. (White St.) | 732-450-1001 | www.thymesquarerestaurant.com

"Winning" is the word at this Red Bank BYO that's "highly recommended" for its "warm", sophisticated ambiance, not to mention the "interesting" "innovative" New American–Med menu; advocates acknowledge the staff "tries hard" here, usually with gratifying results.

Tick Tock Diner ◑ *Diner*

| 17 | 12 | 17 | $18 |

Clifton | 281 Allwood Rd./Rte. 3 W. (bet. Bloomfield & Passaic Aves.) | 973-777-0511

Time marches on at this 24/7 "roadside" Clifton "classic" diner (since 1948), "ticking along" with its "something-for-everybody" menu and "huge" quantities of "cheaply" priced chow; it "won't let you down", and admirers add it more than transcends the "truck-stop" category.

Tim Schafer's Cuisine *American*

| 25 | 17 | 22 | $46 |

Morristown | 82 Speedwell Ave. (bet. Cattano Ave. & Clinton Pl.) | 973-538-3330 | www.timschafersrestaurant.com

This "newly decorated" New American Morristown BYO storefront stays "at the top of the pack" courtesy of its "exotic", "well-prepared" lineup (elk, buffalo and ostrich, many enlivened by beer) coupled with an "effective" front of the house; P.S. it "hasn't skipped a beat" even though Tim Schafer is no longer affiliated with the restaurant.

Tina Louise Ⓜ *Asian*

| 24 | 15 | 20 | $28 |

Carlstadt | 403 Hackensack St. (bet. Broad St. & Division Ave.) | 201-933-7133 | www.villagerestaurantgroup.com

A "charming" sister-team of Tina (chef) and Louise (manager) Wong run this "friendly", "little" Carlstadt BYO that spotlights "clean", "light" flavors in its "excellent" fare; best of all, this "fresh approach" to Asian cooking comes at a "bargain."

Tisha's Fine Dining *American*

| 25 | 21 | 21 | $44 |

Cape May | 714 Beach Ave. (Stockton Ave.) | 609-884-9119 | www.tishasfinedining.com

"Fabulous" views sync up with the "fantastic" food at this Cape May New American BYO that's "about as close to the water" as possible;

	FOOD	DECOR	SERVICE	COST

acolytes advise alfresco dining is key at this Victorian destination that offers the "best oceanside dining in the area."

NEW Tokyo Bleu *Japanese*
| - | - | - | M |

Cinnaminson | 602 Rte. 130 N. (Westfield Lees Dr.) | 856-829-8889 | www.tokyobleusushi.com

The sushi bar at this sexy Cinnamonson BYO puts out rolls in dozens of raw fish varieties, both exotic and familiar; its kitchen executes straight-ahead Japanese dishes, including udon, tempura and teriyaki – and the price won't leave you blue.

Tomatoes *Californian/Eclectic*
| 24 | 23 | 20 | $47 |

Margate | 9300 Amherst Ave. (Washington Ave.) | 609-822-7535 | www.tomatoesmargate.com

Its "trendy", "upscale" decor attracts a "glitzy", "jet-set" clientele at this "sleek" Margate Cal-Eclectic where "every dish is delicious" and the service "good"; in the "ultimate-scene" restaurant at the Shore, dessert is really "all the eye candy at the bar."

Tomo's Cuisine M *Japanese*
| - | - | - | E |

Little Falls | 113 Rte. 23 (bet. 1st & 2nd Sts.) | 973-837-1117

Purists may be pleased with this relatively expensive Japanese BYO in Little Falls offering sushi and a slate of authentic, artistically presented cooked dishes; it's small and frills-free, but raw-fish experts may see a sea dream come true.

Tony Da Caneca *Portuguese/Spanish*
| 24 | 15 | 22 | $38 |

Newark | 72 Elm Rd. (Houston St.) | 973-589-6882 | www.tonydacanecarestaurant.com

"So much incredible" Portuguese and seafood – "huge" servings of it – are why backers "come back" to this "slightly off-the-beaten-path" Iberian that's branded "one of the best" in Newark; via scene and cuisine, this "unpretentious" place successfully "transports you" to Portugal.

Tony Luke's ● *Sandwiches*
| - | - | - | I |

Atlantic City | Borgata Hotel, Casino & Spa | 1 Borgata Way (Atlantic City Expwy., exit 1) | 609-317-1000 | www.theborgata.com

A Philly favorite has settled into Casino City in the form of this Borgata sandwich specialist drawing slot players with the signature broccoli rabe-topped pork- and steak-stuffed rolls; the spin-off of the original is going down well with the crowds; N.B. open until midnight Sundays–Thursdays.

Tony's Baltimore Grill ● *Pizza*
| - | - | - | I |

Atlantic City | 2800 Atlantic Ave. (Iowa Ave.) | 609-345-5766 | www.baltimoregrill.com

For a taste of 'old' Atlantic City at budget prices, this 40-year-old, family-owned pizza place–cum–sandwich shop (where a meal costs around $10) fits the bill; jukeboxes still play 45s – and the only thing new since the '60s (including the customers) is the upholstery on the booths.

	FOOD	DECOR	SERVICE	COST

Tortilla Press *Mexican* — 23 | 19 | 21 | $26

Collingswood | 703 Haddon Ave. (Collings Ave.) | 856-869-3345 |
www.thetortillapress.com

Supporters "can't say enough" about the "excellent" fare that's
"strong on creativity" at this Collingswood Mexican BYO that's also
recognized for its "colorfully decorated" digs; sage respondents say
if you like "very flavorful" "real" deal *comidas*, "go to this place."

NEW Tortilla Press Cantina *Mexican* — - | - | - | M

Pennsauken | 7716 Maple Ave. (Haddonfield Rd.) | 856-488-0005 |
www.tortillapresscantina.com

Collingswood's almost too popular Tortilla Press expanded into a
much larger but still festive space in nearby Pennsauken offering a
little something extra: a liquor license and large juicer for fresh margaritas to wash down the savory midpriced Mex dishes.

Tortuga's Mexican Village ≠ *Mexican* — 21 | 10 | 17 | $22

Princeton | 44 Leigh Ave. (bet. John & Witherspoon Sts.) | 609-924-5143 |
www.tortugasmv.com

It's "the bomb" when it comes to food swear fans of this "not-your-
ordinary" south-of-the-border Princeton BYO dispensing "down 'n'
dirty" Mexican; the "best" prices spur "rowdy" crowds to keep coming; N.B. a post-Survey redo may alter the above Decor score.

Tosca Ristorante *Italian* — 20 | 23 | 21 | $49

Kenilworth | 572 Boulevard (bet. N. 23rd & 24th Sts.) | 908-709-1200 |
www.toscaristorante.net

There's "fine dining" afoot in Kenilworth with this Northern Italian, a
"palatial" venue with elegant rooms and a "cool" lounge; despite
disagreements about the food (it ranges from "quite good" to "ok"),
the place is always packed; N.B. the wine cellar holds 20 for parties.

Trap Rock *American* — 21 | 21 | 19 | $44

Berkeley Heights | 279 Springfield Ave. (bet. Snyder & Union Aves.) |
908-665-1755 | www.traprockrestaurant.net

"This place rocks" may be the first thing folks say of this "upmarket"
Berkeley Heights pub and microbrewery serving "excellent" beers and
distinguished by "first-rate" New American fare; the "attractive ski-
lodge" decor adds appeal to this "lively gathering place."

Tre Figlio ⊠ *Italian* — 24 | 21 | 23 | $42

Egg Harbor | 500 W. White Horse Pike (Mannheim Ave.) |
609-965-3303 | www.trefiglio.com

"Not to be missed", this Egg Harbor City Italian is a purveyor of
"truly fine" cooking with a "courteous" staff to back it up; plus, the
wines are "wonderful", the surroundings "lovely" and bargain-
hunters adore the "great" early-bird.

Tre Piani *Italian/Mediterranean* — 21 | 20 | 20 | $42

Princeton | Forrestal Village Shopping Ctr. | 120 Rockingham Row
(College Rd. W.) | 609-452-1515 | www.trepiani.com

"Local ingredients" are given their due at this spacious, "open"
Plainsboro Italian-Mediterranean whose fare takes its inspiration from

Slow Food U.S.A. (an organization dedicated to upholding the culinary traditions of the country, and to sustainable agriculture); the dishes, however, are sometimes "good", and sometimes "decent"; N.B. The Bar, an adjacent drinks and tapas spot, opened post-Survey.

Triumph Brewing Company *Eclectic*   18 | 20 | 16 | $28

Princeton | 138 Nassau St. (Washington Rd.) | 609-924-7855 | www.triumphbrewing.com

"Gotta love the beers" – all of them "excellent" – marketed to the "bustling" crowds that populate this "energetic" Princeton microbrewery that also feeds fans with "unexpectedly" good Eclectic pub vittles; the "spacious", "neo-modern" industrial space (with high vaulted ceilings and an exposed, glass-enclosed brewery) seats 260, "so don't expect a quiet meal."

Tsuki 🖾 *Japanese*   22 | 14 | 17 | $30

Bernardsville | 23 Mine Brook Rd. (Mt. Airy Rd.) | 908-953-0450

The "strong suit" is the "consistently fresh" sushi sold at this Japanese Bernardsville BYO also purveying "tasty" cooked morsels; while the "lacking atmosphere" and "not-so-hot service" are less appealing, thanks to the fare, few seem to care.

Tuckers Eating &   18 | 18 | 17 | $31
Drinking Establishment *American*

Beach Haven | 101 West Ave. (Engleside Ave.) | 609-492-2300

"Full of cheer", this "nautical" Beach Haven "staple" remains "popular" and the "only game in town" on account of "reliable" Eclectic pub food, TVs and, as the name suggests, a "great" bar dispensing assorted drinks; when sports aren't on, at least the bay views are.

Tucker's Steak &   ▽ 19 | 19 | 18 | $44
Seafood House *Seafood/Steak*

Somers Point | 800 Bay Ave. (E. New Jersey Ave.) | 609-927-3100

The water view's "spectacular" at this Somers Point house of "above-average" reef 'n' beef set in a Victorian inn by the bay; porch dining has been replaced by an outdoor bar, and the addition of moderately priced meals might offset what some cite as "overpriced" vittles.

Tun Tavern ❶ *American*   18 | 17 | 17 | $24

Atlantic City | Sheraton Hotel | 2 Miss America Way (Baltic Ave.) | 609-347-7800 | www.tuntavern.com

"They should call it fun tavern" aver acolytes of this Atlantic City American featuring Marine Corps. memorabilia, burgers and "great" microbrews; thanks to "reasonable" prices, most maintain it's "good for a hearty meal after shopping the outlets."

Tuptim *Thai*   22 | 16 | 21 | $29

Montclair | 600 Bloomfield Ave. (bet. Park St. & Valley Rd.) | 973-783-3800 | www.tuptimthaicuisine.com

"Always worth a visit", this Montclair Thai BYO servicing vegetarians and meat eaters offers "delicious" dishes in a "calming", "down-to-earth" setting; "attention to detail" from a "caring" staff helps it "hold its own" against newer competitors.

Tuzzio's *Italian*
21 | 11 | 21 | $28

Long Branch | 224 Westwood Ave. (Morris Ave.) | 732-222-9614 |
www.tuzzioscatering.com

The "veal parms" are the best at this "no-frills" Long Branch long-
timer (over 40 years) still delivering the "best in classic red-sauce"
Italian cooking accompanied by an "old-fashioned", "friendly" atmosphere; when factoring everything in, it's not surprising this
place remains "rock solid."

2Senza Ristorante Ⓜ *Mediterranean*
20 | 18 | 20 | $42

Red Bank | The Galleria | 2 Bridge Ave. (W. Front St.) | 732-758-0999 |
www.2senza.com

It's "bustling" at this Red Bank Mediterranean that stays "a cut
above" its competitors with "good" food and an ambiance "full of vi-
tality", the latter thanks to its brick-walled setting and open kitchen;
if some get a senza "pricey" tabs, most find it a "dependable"
choice; N.B. plans to expand are underway.

Ugly Mug *American*
16 | 14 | 18 | $21

Cape May | 426 Washington St. (Decatur St.) | 609-884-3459 |
www.uglymugenterprises.com

Downing burgers and brews, it's hard not to "feel like a local" at this
"classic" Cape May watering hole selling "standard" American pub
chow and eponymous cups, T-shirts and other items; those who
"keep returning" do it out of "tradition" as much as for the "convivial" vibe, enhanced by the addition of bands five nights a week.

Underground Café Ⓜ *E Euro.*
13 | 17 | 18 | $28

Princeton | 4 Hulfish St. (Witherspoon St.) | 609-924-0666 |
www.cafe-underground.com

"Filling in for Eastern European", this "different" Princeton
BYO vends "large" servings of Bulgarian items (along with
French and Italian dishes) in a suitably "funky", "Euro" ambiance; despite "shaky" vittles, adherents insist this addition is
bound for "landmark" status.

NEW Undici *Italian*
- | - | - | E

Rumson | 11 W. River Rd. (Bingham Ave.) | 732-842-3880 |
www.undicirestaurant.com

This new Rumson Italian has the makings of a showstopper – a soaring, bi-level space with a rustic Tuscan design (exposed brick, stone
columns, wood-fired oven), market-fresh menu and 350-label vino
list (many featured at frequent wine dinners); it's aiming to be a 10 -
make that 11 (the English translation of its name).

Ⓩ Union Park Dining Room *American*
26 | 25 | 25 | $52

Cape May | 727 Beach Ave. (Howard St.) | 609-884-8811 |
www.unionparkdiningroom.com

"Carefully prepared" New American food served on "good china"
makes for "lovely" dining at this "surprise" of a Victorian BYO (with NJ
wines) whose "romantic", "special-occasion" appeal is supported by
white tablecloths and "informative" service; although the wrap-

around porch features views of the Atlantic, many marvel "you can't believe" you're in Cape May given the wonderfully "formal" airs here.

Union Station Grill Ⓜ American
(fka Wardell Steakhouse & Raw Bar)

`- | - | - | M`

Phillipsburg | 9 Union Sq. (S. Main St.) | 908-387-1380 | www.theunionstationgrill.com

This affordable, family-friendly Phillipsburg New American (formerly the Wardell Steakhouse & Raw Bar) offers three distinct eating areas, among them a spacious dining room, a bar – and for train buffs, a renovated railroad car (an occasional locomotive rumbling on a track out back adds to the all-aboard aura).

Vanthia's Seafood

`- | - | - | I`

West Cape May | 106 Sunset Blvd. (Broad St.) | 609-884-4020 | www.vanthias.com

Zorba-size portions of affordable, Mediterranean-style seafood inform this West Cape May family-run, family-friendly BYO also favored for its bountiful weekend breakfasts, coffee bar and homemade desserts; what's more, the perky yellow-and-plum decor pleases; N.B. hours vary by season.

Varka Fish House Greek/Seafood

`25 | 24 | 23 | $54`

Ramsey | 30 N. Spruce St. (E. Main St.) | 201-995-9333 | www.varkarestaurant.com

"Terrific" treats from the sea are the lure at this "chic" Greek, a fish lover's "delight" in Ramsey that impresses with other "amazingly" good Mediterranean fare, all arriving via "efficient" servers; in keeping with the genre, per-the-pound pricing "creeps up on you."

Ventura's Greenhouse Italian

`17 | 15 | 17 | $31`

Margate | 106 S. Benson Ave. (Atlantic Ave.) | 609-822-0140

"For a taste of the Shore", voters visit this "casual" Margate Italian that's "insanely crowded" when summer rolls around, when most hit the outdoor deck; "so-so" food simply doesn't measure up to checking out the "so-good-looking" people and indulging in "bikini watching."

Verdigre ⓈⓂ American

`∇ 22 | 25 | 21 | $49`

New Brunswick | 25 Liberty St. (bet. George & Neilson Sts.) | 732-247-2250 | www.verdigrenb.com

Head for this New American–Med in New Brunswick for a deliciously "hip mix" of club scene and "interesting" (and "expensive") fare within a "dark", "eye-catching" interior; the lounge is a pleasant space for sipping and chatting.

Verjus Ⓜ French

`25 | 19 | 22 | $48`

Maplewood | 1790 Springfield Ave. (Rutgers St.) | 973-378-8990 | www.verjusrestaurant.com

"Fine dining" in a "comfortable" setting is key to the success of this "superb" Maplewood French (helmed by a wife and husband) where "fantastic" dishes meet up with "pampering" service in decor filled with the works of local artists; whether or not you go for the "bargain" Sunday brunch, this "lovely" restaurant is "well-worth" visiting.

	FOOD	DECOR	SERVICE	COST

Verve ⊠ *American/French*   23 | 19 | 22 | $45

Somerville | 18 E. Main St. (bet. Grove & N. Bridge Sts.) | 908-707-8655 | www.vervestyle.com

Voters vouch for the vibe at this "classy" triple-decker, a "treasure" for Somerville offering "well-done" New American–French bistro meals (and "great" steaks), "quality" service, "good" live jazz and an "appreciated" "way-cool" lounge; N.B. seasonal alfresco dining is a welcome addition.

Vic's Ⓜ *Pizza*   20 | 10 | 19 | $22

Bradley Beach | 60 Main St. (Evergreen Ave.) | 732-774-8225 | www.vicspizza.com

"Fill up on the cheap" with "excellent" "thin-crust" pizzas at this "venerable" Bradley Beacher that's been owned by one family for four generations; sure, the main attraction may not be the "old-school" digs, but for the "perfect balance of crust, sauce and cheese", it's hard to go wrong here.

NEW Victor's Pub, The ◕ *Pub Food*   – | – | – | M

Camden | Victor Luxury Lofts | 1 Market St. (Delaware Ave.) | 856-635-0600 | www.victorspub.com

Camden's waterfront, already home to an aquarium, ballpark and concert hall, also boasts this American pub located in the Victor Luxury Lofts offering a midpriced bar menu that draws residents and local workers; N.B. despite the requisite 20 plasma-screen TVs, the best view is of the Philly skyline across the Delaware.

Village Gourmet *Eclectic*   21 | 17 | 17 | $29

Rutherford | 73-75 Park Ave. (Ridge Rd.) | 201-438-9404 | www.villagerestaurantgroup.com

This BYO in Rutherford is favored for its "reasonably" priced food, an Eclectic array of New American, Asian and Southwestern, served in "quaint, casual" quarters; "solidly satisfying" sums up the dining, and there's no question – the "liquor store right inside" the dining room is a nice touch.

Village Green *American*   25 | 18 | 23 | $53

Ridgewood | 36 Prospect St. (Hudson St.) | 201-445-2914 | www.villagegreenrestaurant.com

The "small" plates pack "fabulous" flavors at this "sophisticated" New American BYO featuring "courteous", "knowledgeable" service and multicourse prix fixes with "selections to satisfy any palate"; the "high-quality" cooking comes with equally high prices, but tabs are little concern to fans who like "the best Ridgewood has to offer."

Villa Vittoria *Italian*   22 | 17 | 20 | $36

Brick | 2700 Hooper Ave. (Cedar Bridge Ave.) | 732-920-1550 | www.villavittoria.com

Italian food "fixes" are fulfilled at this Brick standby serving "very good" specialties amid the sound of live entertainment; "attentive" service helps keep the operation "consistent", and fans tip their hats to the "fair" tabs that come with the drinks.

	FOOD	DECOR	SERVICE	COST

Vine ⊠ *American/Mediterranean* — 22 | 21 | 21 | $54

Basking Ridge | 95 Morristown Rd. (bet. Maple & N. Finley Aves.) | 908-221-0017 | www.vinerestaurant.net

The "vastly improved" decor's now "more modern" and the reworked fare often "delicious" at this retooled Basking Ridge Med-New American that boasts some "energy"; factor in "attentive" service, and the consensus is a version for "success."

NEW Vivas Classic Latin Cuisine *Nuevo Latino* — - | - | - | M

Belmar | Belmar Plaza | 801 Belmar Plaza (bet. 8th & 10th Aves.) | 732-681-1213 | www.vivasrestaurant.com

Viva! to chef/co-owner Will Vivas' (ex Bistro Olé) nuevo Nuevo Latino BYO in Belmar, where aficionados savor midpriced, signature *comidas* (e.g. halibut in a bacon sofrito sauce) in casual, tapestry-lined quarters (or on a seasonal patio); N.B. closed Mondays in winter.

Walpack Inn M *American* — 19 | 22 | 18 | $35

Wallpack Center | Rte. 615 (Rte. 206 N.) | 973-948-3890 | www.walpackinn.com

Wall-mounted deer and elk heads "fit in with the surrounding woods" and line up nicely with a menu of "good", "old-style" Americana at this Walpack staple whose "rustic" ambiance charms; sure, the all-you-can-eat salads and breads are "great", but everyone agrees the "view out back" is worth the trip alone; N.B. open Fridays-Sundays and for lunch Saturdays-Sundays.

Wasabi Asian Plates *Japanese* — 24 | 19 | 21 | $31

Somerville | 12 W. Main St. (N. Bridge St.) | 908-203-8881

Wasabi House *Japanese*

East Brunswick | Colchester Plaza | 77 Tices Ln. (Rte. 18) | 732-254-9988

"Inspired" if not "dazzling" food is common to these Asians in East Brunswick and Somerville, with both prized for their "efficient" and "friendly" servers; the "chic" Somerville satellite serves "great" drinks and is roomier than BYO East Brunswick, which offers more traditional Japanese cuisine, notably "terrific" sushi.

Z Washington Inn *American* — 26 | 26 | 26 | $58

Cape May | 801 Washington St. (Jefferson St.) | 609-884-5697 | www.washingtoninn.com

"High elegance" is achieved at this "pinnacle of Cape May dining", an "exceptional" Traditional American proffering "gracious" service and an "excellent" wine list, all within a "lovely" "old" space that was once a plantation home; steep prices do nothing to dissuade patrons from describing the "across-the-board" quality here.

Waterfront Buffet *Eclectic* — 17 | 18 | 16 | $27

(fka Fantasea Reef Buffet)

Atlantic City | Harrah's | 777 Harrah's Blvd. (Brigantine Blvd.) | 609-441-5052 | www.harrahs.com

"Help forget gambling losses" by indulging in the array of Eclectic offerings (especially a "good" variety of seafood) at this "undersea-

| | FOOD | DECOR | SERVICE | COST |

themed" "traditional" buffet docked in Harrah's; the fare's "above average" for some, but critics disagree.

Water Lily ⓜ *Asian/French* | 24 | 21 | 23 | $35 |

Collingswood | 653 Haddon Ave. (Collings Ave.) | 856-833-0998 | www.waterlilybistro.com

"Fabulous" fusion fare backed by "stunning" green-and-burgundy decor justify the accolades given to this Collingswood BYO, where the "interesting" menu combines Asian and French; supporters "can't rave enough" – and that's before they talk about the "outstanding" servers; N.B. a four-course prix fixe dinner is $30 per person.

West Lake Seafood Restaurant *Chinese* | ▽ 25 | 15 | 18 | $25 |

Matawan | Pine Crest Plaza | 1016 Rte. 34 (Broad St.) | 732-290-2988 | www.westlakeseafood.com

That "many customers order from the Chinese language menu" is a sign that this Matawan BYO is serving "exquisitely pure" Cantonese selections, especially "fresh" seafood you "select from one of the fish tanks"; some say it offers one of the more "authentic" experiences in the area.

What's Your Beef? *Steak* | 20 | 13 | 18 | $39 |

Rumson | 21 W. River Rd. (Lafayette St.) | 732-842-6205 | www.whatsyourbeefrumson.com

It's "been around since 1969, and looks it", but this Rumson red-meat staple (also serving seafood) has been "solidly" standing by the neighborhood with "slabs" o' beef that you "walk up to a window" and choose pre-gnawing; if the steaks don't sate, the "extensive" salad bar will.

☒ Whispers *American* | 27 | 23 | 25 | $56 |

Spring Lake | Hewitt Wellington Hotel | 200 Monmouth Ave. (2nd Ave.) | 732-974-9755 | www.whispersrestaurant.com

In a "fabulous" Victorian hotel near "beautiful" Spring Lake "lies a mecca of gourmet treats" in the form of this "serene" New American BYO, which specializes in "memorable" meals enhanced by "polished" servers and "consistently excellent" preparations; devoted fans concur the positives easily outweigh any concerns about the "expense" associated with this "oasis of elegance."

☒ White House ⊅ *Sandwiches* | 27 | 7 | 15 | $13 |

Atlantic City | 2301 Arctic Ave. (Mississippi Ave.) | 609-345-1564

"Sub lovers" surrender to the "world's best" hoagies doled out at this South Jersey "legend" (since 1946) where the service is "gruff, the meat ain't tough" and "unreal" bread makes the sandwiches "great"; once you've tasted the goods, you'll understand the "crazed" scene and "lines down the street."

☒ Wild Ginger ☒ⓜ *Japanese* | 25 | 15 | 19 | $46 |

Englewood | 6 E. Palisade Ave. (bet. Dean & S. Van Brunt Sts.) | 201-567-2660 | www.wild-ginger.biz

At this Englewood Japanese BYO, let the "chef choose" and then receive "memorable" sushi served by "lovely" staffers within "cramped" quarters; those "shocked" by "sky-high" tabs reason they'll have to "pay dearly" for "Bergen County's answer to Nobu" but add "ask the price of the specials before ordering."

Windansea *Seafood*　　　　　| 20 | 21 | 18 | $38 |
Highlands | 56 Shrewsbury Ave. (Bay Ave.) | 732-872-2266 | www.windanseanj.com

"Gorgeous" water views mean many go to this Highlands seafooder where the food's "fresh"; "families" applaud the scene for lunch or during early-dinner hours on Saturdays, all before "lively" crowds "invade the place" on the lookout for drinks and a "meat market."

WindMill, The *Hot Dogs*　　　| - | - | - | I |
Westfield | 256 E. Broad St. (Central Ave.) | 908-233-2001
Belmar | 1201 River Rd. (Rte. 71) | 732-681-9628 ◐
Brick | 856 Rte. 70 (Jct. Rtes. 88 & 70) | 732-458-7774
Freehold | 3338 S. Hwy. 9 (Jackson Mills Rd.) | 732-303-9855
Long Branch | 200 Ocean Ave. (Morris Ave.) | 732-870-6098
Long Branch | 586 Ocean Ave. (Brighton Ave.) | 732-229-9863 ◐
Ocean Grove | 18 S. Main St. (Main Ave.) | 732-988-5277 ◐
Red Bank | 22 N. Bridge Ave. (W. Front St.) | 732-530-7228
www.windmillhotdogs.com

Wiener worshipers affirm that there's none better than a crackling frank hot off the grill at these Shore (and solo Central NJ) hot dog havens – particularly at the original 1964 windmill-shaped outpost at 586 Ocean Avenue in Long Branch; N.B. all are BYO except 200 Ocean Avenue which sells beer and wine year-long and rum drinks summer months only.

Witherspoon Grill *Seafood/Steak*　　| - | - | - | E |
Princeton | 57 Witherspoon St. (bet. Hulfish & Wiggins Sts.) | 609-924-6011 | www.jmgroupprinceton.com

This fashionable, pricey Princeton beef 'n' reefer decked out with dark wood and candles is popular for its steaks, crab cakes – and happening bar; keep in mind there's a no-reservations policy.

Wolfgang Puck
American Grille *American*　　| 23 | 23 | 21 | $50 |
Atlantic City | Borgata Hotel, Casino & Spa | 1 Borgata Way (Atlantic City Expwy., exit 1) | 609-317-1000 | www.theborgata.com

"Don't ever leave!" is what enthusiasts demand of Wolfgang Puck, whose AC Borgata spot brings plaudits for his "oh-so-good" New American dinner fare; designer Tony Chi has divided the "cool" space into two distinct dining areas: one a "wonderful" tavern and the other for more formal meals; "regardless of where you sit", how-ever, it's a "real winner"; N.B. closed on Tuesdays.

Wondee's Thai Café *Thai*　　| - | - | - | I |
Hackensack | 296 Main St. (Camden St.) | 201-883-1700 | www.wondeenj.com

The Thai comestibles satisfy at this BYO in Hackensack that oper-ates in obscurity; there's not much in the way of scenery, but bargain tabs mean you leave with cash in your pocket.

Wonder Seafood *Chinese*

▽ 24 | 12 | 16 | $25

Edison | 1984 Rte. 27 (Langstaff Ave.) | 732-287-6328

"You'll have a memorable meal" at this BYO establishment in Edison that gets "crowded on weekends" for its "variety" of "authentic Chinese" ("not Chinese-American") cuisine, including "must-try dim sum" and lots of seafood; some naysayers note a "lack of service and decor" – it's set in a "noisy, auditoriumlike hall" – but the "Chinatown-quality" eats are "worth it."

Word of Mouth Ⓜ *American*

24 | 24 | 21 | $40

Collingswood | 729 Haddon Ave. (bet. Collings & Washington Aves.) | 856-858-2228

For "tasteful" dining, try this BYO, an "excellent" choice in Collingswood for its "comforting" New American food, stained-window ambiance that's "great for special dinners, including dates", and "personable" service.

Yankee Doodle Tap Room *American*

14 | 20 | 15 | $32

Princeton | Nassau Inn | 10 Palmer Sq. (Nassau St.) | 609-921-7500 | www.nassauinn.com

"Tradition is everything in Princeton" and this "classic Ivy League taproom" beneath the "historic" Nassau Inn (circa 1756) "has it all": "simple" American fare, a "warm fireplace", "pictures of famous alumni on the walls" and "a one-of-a-kind Norman Rockwell mural"; some dis the eats as "uninspired", but "for a burger and a beer, it can't be beat."

Ya Ya Noodles *Chinese*

- | - | - | M

Skillman | Montgomery Shopping Ctr. | 1325 Rte. 206 N. (Rte. 518) | 609-921-8551 | www.yayanoodles.com

This relatively unknown Chinese BYO located in a Skillman shopping center hits the spot with its authentic dishes from a long menu; N.B. the bubble tea bar that's adjacent to the dining room is worth a look-see.

Yellow Fin *American*

25 | 18 | 21 | $50

Surf City | 104 24th St. (Long Beach Blvd.) | 609-494-7001

It "would be great anywhere" aver regulars of this "packed" Surf City New American BYO that keeps a following in light of "eclectic", "delicious" (albeit "expensive") dinners and a "chic" vibe; though "good" service can run "snobby", cronies call the place "worth it" just for the "quality of the food"; N.B. the owners recently opened Cafe Altetta in Surf City.

Yumi *Pan-Asian*

26 | 17 | 22 | $39

Sea Bright | 1120 Ocean Ave. (Church St.) | 732-212-0881 | www.yumirestaurant.com

Patrons walk away feeling "wonderful" after making their way through the "diverse" offerings at this Sea Bright BYO, proffering flavors of the Pacific Rim while especially noted for "delicious" Japanese items; "super-sweet" service brings a bit of light to the "dark" digs.

	FOOD	DECOR	SERVICE	COST

Zafra *Pan-Latin*

24 | 16 | 19 | $31

Hoboken | 301 Willow Ave. (3rd St.) | 201-610-9801

"If you can get a table" at this colorful, compact Hoboken BYO "hideaway" (the casual precursor to nearby Cucharamama), the payoff is "great", since celeb chef and co-owner Maricel Presilla's Pan-Latin fare is "outstanding", the menu "wide-ranging" and the drinks "amazing"; P.S. the "fantastic" brunch is somewhat of a "secret" in this "land of bars and grills."

🆕 Zen Palate 🅂Ⓜ *Vegetarian*

- | - | - | M

Princeton | Princeton Shopping Ctr. | 301 N. Harrison St. (Valley Rd.) | 609-279-9888 | www.zenpalate.com

The cafeteria-style setting of this new Princeton BYO – the lone NJ branch of the NYC chainlet – is trumped by the vast variety of economical vittles for vegetarians (and curious carnivores); despite the bare-bones decor and brisk service, where else can you find shiitake mushroom caps with soy pâté or wheat gluten filet à l'orange?

Ⓩ Zoe's by the Lake Ⓜ *French*

26 | 24 | 24 | $54

Sparta | 112 Tomahawk Trail (2 mi. east of Rte. 15) | 973-726-7226 | www.zoesbythelake.com

"NYC and Paris" meet in Sussex County at this "out-of-the-way" Sparta French, where the "exceptional" (and "expensive") country-style fare is matched by a "lovely, spacious" bi-level dining room and a "fantastic" lake setting (not surprisingly, "sitting outside is best"); with a staff that "goes above and beyond" to cater to the clientele, few hold no qualms about calling this "jewel" "superb on all fronts."

INDEXES

Cuisines

Includes restaurant names, locations and Food ratings. ☑ indicates places with the highest ratings, popularity and importance.

AFGHAN

Pamir | **Morristown**	21

AMERICAN (NEW)

Acacia | **Lawrenceville**	25
☑ Amanda's | **Hoboken**	26
☑ André's | **Newton**	27
Anton's/Swan | **Lambertville**	22
Arthur's Landing | **Weehawken**	20
Atlantic B&G | **S Seaside Pk**	24
Bacari Grill | **Washington Twp**	21
Bazzini | **Ridgewood**	21
Bell's Mansion | **Stanhope**	18
☑ Bernards Inn | **Bernardsville**	26
NEW Blackbird | **Collingswood**	–
Black Trumpet | **Spring Lake**	23
Blu | **Montclair**	25
Blue | **Surf City**	23
☑ Blue Bottle | **Hopewell**	27
Boulevard Grille | **Mahwah**	18
Brandl. | **Belmar**	24
Brass Rail | **Hoboken**	19
Buttonwood Manor | **Matawan**	18
Cafe at Rosemont | **Rosemont**	22
Cafe Loren | **Avalon**	25
☑ Chakra | **Paramus**	21
City Bistro | **Hoboken**	19
Clydz | **New Bruns.**	23
☑ CoccoLa | **Hillsborough**	22
Continental | **A.C.**	–
Copeland | **Morristown**	25
Copper Fish | **Cape May**	20
Cork | **Westmont**	21
☑ CulinAriane | **Montclair**	27
daddy O | **Long Beach**	18
NEW Daryl | **New Bruns.**	–
☑ David Burke | **Rumson**	26
☑ David Drake | **Rahway**	27
Dish | **Red Bank**	22
Doris & Ed's | **Highlands**	25
Drew's Bayshore | **Keyport**	28
☑ Ebbitt Room | **Cape May**	27

Elements | **Haddon Hts**	21
NEW Embers Grill | **Cherry Hill**	–
NEW Equus | **Bernardsville**	–
Esty Street | **Park Ridge**	23
☑ Ferry Hse. | **Princeton**	25
NEW 55 Main | **Flemington**	–
Food/Thought | **Marlton**	24
☑ Frog/Peach | **New Bruns.**	26
Gazelle Café | **Ridgewood**	–
Grenville | **Bay Hd.**	21
Grill 73 | **Bernardsville**	22
Harrison | **Asbury Pk**	24
Harvest Moon | **Ringoes**	24
☑ Highlawn | **W Orange**	24
High St. Grill | **Mt Holly**	23
☑ Huntley Taverne | **Summit**	22
NEW Inlet, The | **Somers Point**	–
Isabella's | **Westfield**	22
Island Palm Grill | **Spring Lake**	18
NEW Javier's | **Haddonfield**	–
Karen & Rei's | **Clermont**	27
Kitchen 233 | **Westmont**	22
Krave Café | **Newton**	–
Light Horse | **Jersey City**	22
NEW Luke's | **Maplewood**	–
Madison B&G | **Hoboken**	21
Mahogany Grille | **Manasquan**	23
Main St. Bistro | **Freehold**	21
Main St. Euro-Amer. | **Princeton**	18
NEW Manna | **Margate**	–
Marco & Pepe | **Jersey City**	22
Marie Nicole's | **Wildwood**	23
Matisse | **Belmar**	22
Mattar's | **Allamuchy**	24
Matt's Rooster | **Flemington**	25
Metuchen Inn | **Metuchen**	22
Mill/Spring Lake | **Spring Lake Hts**	20
☑ Moonstruck | **Asbury Pk**	24
Napa Valley | **Paramus**	22
☑ Nauvoo Grill | **Fair Haven**	16
Neil's Oyster | **Highlands**	–

☑ Nicholas | **Middletown**	29
NEW 947 B&G | **Clementon**	–
No. 9 | **Lambertville**	24
One 53 | **Rocky Hill**	–
Onieal's | **Hoboken**	19
Orbis Bistro | **Upper Montclair**	22
NEW Ox | **Jersey City**	–
NEW Park Ave. | **Union City**	–
Pasta Fresca | **Shrewsbury**	22
☑ Peter Shields | **Cape May**	26
Pine Tavern | **Old Bridge**	22
Plantation | **Harvey Cedars**	19
☑ Pluckemin Inn | **Bedminster**	25
Raven & Peach | **Fair Haven**	24
Raymond's | **Montclair**	21
Red | **Red Bank**	20
Renault Winery | **Egg Harbor**	22
Restaurant Latour | **Hamburg**	–
restaurant.mc | **Millburn**	–
Rosemary & Sage | **Riverdale**	26
Ruga | **Oakland**	20
☑ Saddle River Inn | **Saddle R.**	27
NEW Salt Water | **Asbury Pk**	–
Scarborough Fair | **Wall**	20
Sergeantsville Inn | **Sergeantsville**	23
Shipwreck Grill | **Brielle**	25
Silver Oak Bistro | **Ridgewood**	23
Simply Radishing | **Lawrenceville**	18
Skylark Diner | **Edison**	19
SoHo on George | **New Bruns.**	23
Sonsie | **A.C.**	–
Spargo's Grille | **Manalapan**	25
Stage Hse. | **Scotch Plains**	23
☑ Stage Left | **New Bruns.**	26
Steve & Cookie's | **Margate**	25
NEW Stonehouse | **Warren**	–
Table | **Little Silver**	–
Table 8 | **Montclair**	23
NEW Tabor Rd. | **Morris Plains**	–
Ted's on Main | **Medford**	–
Tewksbury Inn | **Oldwick**	22
3 Forty Grill | **Hoboken**	21
NEW Thyme Rest. | **Phillipsburg**	–

Tim Schafer's | **Morristown**	25
Tisha's | **Cape May**	25
Trap Rock | **Berkeley Hts**	21
☑ Union Park | **Cape May**	26
Union Station | **Phillipsburg**	–
Verdigre | **New Bruns.**	22
Verve | **Somerville**	23
Village Green | **Ridgewood**	25
Vine | **Basking Ridge**	22
☑ Whispers | **Spring Lake**	27
Wolfgang Puck | **A.C.**	23
Word of Mouth | **Collingswood**	24
Yellow Fin | **Surf City**	25

AMERICAN (TRADITIONAL)

Alchemist/Barrister | **Princeton**	16
Allendale B&G | **Allendale**	16
NEW A Toute Heure | **Cranford**	–
Avon Pavilion | **Avon-by-Sea**	18
Barnacle Bill's | **Rumson**	21
Basil T's | **Red Bank**	20
☑ Baumgart's Café | **multi.**	19
☑ Bay Ave. | **Highlands**	28
Bay Head Bistro | **Bay Hd.**	21
Bell's | **Lambertville**	19
Bell's Mansion | **Stanhope**	18
Bistro 44 | **Toms River**	25
Black Horse | **Mendham**	19
Blue Pig Tavern | **Cape May**	20
Braddock's | **Medford**	22
Brickwall Tavern | **Asbury Pk**	19
Cabin | **Howell**	18
Charley's | **Long Branch**	19
☑ Cheesecake Factory | **multi.**	19
Christopher's | **Colts Neck**	21
Clark's Landing | **Pt. Pleas.**	17
Country Pancake | **Ridgewood**	19
Cranbury Inn | **Cranbury**	17
Cup Joint | **Hoboken**	20
Doris & Ed's | **Highlands**	25
Gaslight | **Hoboken**	20
Gladstone Tavern | **Gladstone**	–
Gusto Grill | **E Brunswick**	–
Hard Grove | **Jersey City**	14
Harry's Lobster | **Sea Bright**	22
Holsten's | **Bloomfield**	–

Inn at Millrace | **Hope**	21
Inn at Sugar Hill | **Mays Landing**	-
Inn/Hawke | **Lambertville**	18
Java Moon | **multi.**	19
Laguna Grill | **Brigantine**	22
Lambertville Station | **Lambertville**	17
Liberty House | **Jersey City**	20
Limestone Cafe | **Peapack**	22
Lucky Bones | **Cape May**	18
Mad Batter | **Cape May**	21
Maize | **Newark**	21
Z Manor | **W Orange**	23
Mastoris | **Bordentown**	19
McLoone's | **multi.**	17
Meil's | **Stockton**	23
NEW Merchant Hse. | **Fairfield**	-
Merion Inn | **Cape May**	20
Meyersville Inn | **Gillette**	-
Molly Pitcher | **Red Bank**	22
Nag's Head | **Ocean City**	26
NEW Next Door | **Montclair**	-
Z Old Man Rafferty's | **multi.**	19
Z Perryville Inn | **Union Twp**	26
P.J. Whelihan's | **multi.**	17
Ponzio's | **Cherry Hill**	16
Pop Shop | **Collingswood**	18
Quiet Man | **Dover**	22
Z Ram's Head Inn | **Galloway**	26
Redstone | **Marlton**	-
Robin's Nest | **Mt Holly**	22
Rod's Olde Irish | **Sea Girt**	19
Sallee Tee's | **Monmouth Bch**	21
Salt Creek | **multi.**	20
Shaker Cafe | **Flemington**	-
Smithville Inn | **Smithville**	18
Z South City Grill | **multi.**	23
NEW Tap Rm. | **Northfield**	-
Theater Sq. Grill | **Newark**	20
Z 3 West | **Basking Ridge**	23
Tuckers | **Beach Haven**	18
Tun Tavern | **A.C.**	18
Ugly Mug | **Cape May**	16
Walpack Inn | **Wallpack**	19
Z Washington Inn | **Cape May**	26
Yankee Doodle | **Princeton**	14

ASIAN

Chez Elena Wu | **Voorhees**	24
Coconut Bay | **Voorhees**	21
Ginger & Spice | **Ramsey**	-
Metropolitan Cafe | **Freehold**	22
Sens Asian | **S Brunswick**	22
Taro | **Montclair**	21
Tina Louise | **Carlstadt**	24
Water Lily | **Collingswood**	24

ASIAN FUSION

NEW Fusion | **Flemington**	-

BAKERIES

Mastoris | **Bordentown**	19
Ponzio's | **Cherry Hill**	16

BARBECUE

Big Ed's BBQ | **Old Bridge**	17
Corky's | **A.C.**	16
Cubby's BBQ | **Hackensack**	17
NEW D & L BBQ | **Asbury Pk**	-
GRUB Hut | **Manville**	-
Indigo Smoke | **Montclair**	22
Memphis Pig Out | **Atlantic H.**	19

BELGIAN

NEW KC's | **Mendham**	-

BRAZILIAN

Brasilia | **Newark**	23

BRITISH

Elephant/Castle | **Cherry Hill**	10
Ship Inn | **Milford**	19

BURGERS

Barnacle Bill's | **Rumson**	21
Five Guys | **multi.**	-
Pop Shop | **Collingswood**	18
WindMill, The | **Belmar**	-

CAJUN

Bayou Cafe | **Manasquan**	23
Creole Cafe | **Sewell**	27
Luchento's | **Millstone**	20
Oddfellows | **Hoboken**	19
Old Bay | **New Bruns.**	17

CALIFORNIAN

Napa Valley | **Paramus**	22
Surf Taco | **multi.**	20
Tomatoes | **Margate**	24

CARIBBEAN

Bahama Breeze | **Cherry Hill**	16
Caneel Bay | **Harvey Cedars**	17
Sister Sue's | **Asbury Pk**	21

CHINESE

(* dim sum specialist)

Cathay 22 | **Springfield**	23
Chengdu 46 | **Clifton**	24
Crown Palace* | **multi.**	22
Dim Sum Dynasty* | **Ridgewood**	21
Edo Sushi | **Pennington**	20
☑ Far East Taste | **Eatontown**	26
Hunan Chinese | **Morris Plains**	23
Hunan Spring | **Springfield**	19
Hunan Taste | **Denville**	23
Joe's Peking | **Marlton**	23
Look See | **Ramsey**	19
Lotus Cafe | **Hackensack**	24
Meemah | **Edison**	24
Ming | **Edison**	23
Mr. Chu | **E Hanover**	22
☑ P.F. Chang's | **multi.**	21
Sakura Spring | **Cherry Hill**	23
Sally Ling | **Fort Lee**	19
Shanghai Jazz | **Madison**	21
Sunny Gdn. | **W Windsor**	22
West Lake | **Matawan**	25
Wonder Seafood* | **Edison**	24
Ya Ya Noodles | **Skillman**	-

COFFEE SHOPS/DINERS

☑ Baumgart's Café | **multi.**	19
Fedora Cafe | **Lawrenceville**	19
Hard Grove | **Jersey City**	14
Mastoris | **Bordentown**	19
Ponzio's | **Cherry Hill**	16
Skylark Diner | **Edison**	19
Tick Tock | **Clifton**	17

COLOMBIAN

El Familiar | **Toms River Twp**	-

CONTINENTAL

Alessio 426 | **Metuchen**	20
☑ Black Forest Inn | **Stanhope**	23
Café Gallery | **Burlington**	21
Court Street | **Hoboken**	21
Farnsworth Hse. | **Bordentown**	21
Ho-Ho-Kus Inn | **Ho-Ho-Kus**	21
Inn at Millrace | **Hope**	21
Lahiere's | **Princeton**	21
Lincroft Inn | **Lincroft**	18
Madeleine's | **Northvale**	24
Main St. Euro-Amer. | **Princeton**	18
NEW Mi Sueño | **Middlesex**	-
Pheasants Land. | **Hillsborough**	17
Restaurant L | **Allendale**	-
Stony Hill Inn | **Hackensack**	23
Theater Sq. Grill | **Newark**	20

CREOLE

Bayou Cafe | **Manasquan**	23
Creole Cafe | **Sewell**	27
☑ 410 Bank St. | **Cape May**	27
Luchento's | **Millstone**	20
☑ Mélange | **Cherry Hill**	26
Oddfellows | **Hoboken**	19
Old Bay | **New Bruns.**	17

CUBAN

Azúcar | **Jersey City**	19
Casona | **Collingswood**	24
Cuba Libre | **A.C.**	21
Cuban Pete's | **Montclair**	17
Habana Latin | **Ridgefield Pk**	-
Hard Grove | **Jersey City**	14
NEW Havana | **Highlands**	-
☑ La Isla | **Hoboken**	26
Martino's | **Somerville**	21
Rebecca's | **Edgewater**	24

DELIS/SANDWICH SHOPS

Eppes Essen | **Livingston**	18
Jack Cooper's | **Edison**	19
Jerry & Harvey's | **Marlboro**	18
Kibitz Room | **Cherry Hill**	24
NEW Mr. Bill's | **Hammonton**	-
Richard's | **Long Branch**	20

DESSERT

Z Cheesecake Factory | **multi.** 19

Holsten's | **Bloomfield** –

Z Old Man Rafferty's | **multi.** 19

EASTERN EUROPEAN

Blue Danube | **Trenton** 22

Underground Café | **Princeton** 13

ECLECTIC

NEW Alstarz | **Bordentown** –

Anthony David's | **Hoboken** 25

Bistro at Red Bank | **Red Bank** 21

Z Black Duck | **W Cape May** 26

Blue | **Surf City** 23

Brix 67 | **Summit** 18

Z Cafe Matisse | **Rutherford** 27

Cafe Metro | **Denville** 21

Z Cafe Panache | **Ramsey** 28

California Grill | **Flemington** 20

Echo | **Red Bank** 19

Eurasian Eatery | **Red Bank** 20

Fedora Cafe | **Lawrenceville** 19

503 Park | **Scotch Plains** 20

Frenchtown Inn | **Frenchtown** 23

Full Moon | **Lambertville** 17

Z Gables, The | **Beach Haven** 26

Garlic Rose | **multi.** 21

Grand Colonial | **Union Twp** 25

Joel's Malibu | **Ridgewood** –

Labrador | **Normandy Bch** 23

Laguna Grill | **Brigantine** 22

Lilly's/Canal | **Lambertville** 21

Little Café | **Voorhees** 25

Mkt. in the Middle | **Asbury Pk** 23

Market Roost | **Flemington** 22

Mattar's | **Allamuchy** 24

Metropolitan Cafe | **Freehold** 22

Z Park/Orchard | **E Rutherford** 22

Red Square | **A.C.** –

Sallee Tee's | **Monmouth Bch** 21

Savannah's | **Stockholm** –

Shaker Cafe | **Flemington** –

Soho 33 | **Madison** 19

Spice Cuisine | **Bloomfield** –

Tomatoes | **Margate** 24

Triumph Brewing | **Princeton** 18

Village Gourmet | **Rutherford** 21

Waterfront Buffet | **A.C.** 17

ETHIOPIAN

Makeda | **New Bruns.** 23

FONDUE

Magic Pot | **Edgewater** 19

Melting Pot | **multi.** 19

FRENCH

Alexander's | **Cape May** 24

Alisa Cafe | **Cherry Hill** 22

Andaman | **Morristown** 23

Z Aozora | **Montclair** 25

Benihana | **Short Hills** –

Bistro En | **Teaneck** 22

Brothers Moon | **Hopewell** 22

Z Chez Catherine | **Westfield** 27

Chez Elena Wu | **Voorhees** 24

Claude's | **N Wildwood** 25

NEW Dream Café | **Cherry Hill** –

Z Ferry Hse. | **Princeton** 25

Frenchtown Inn | **Frenchtown** 23

Z Grand Cafe | **Morristown** 25

NEW KC's | **Mendham** –

La Campagne | **Cherry Hill** 24

Lahiere's | **Princeton** 21

Z Latour | **Ridgewood** 27

Le Petit Chateau | **Bernardsville** 25

Z Lorena's | **Maplewood** 27

Madeleine's | **Northvale** 24

Manon | **Lambertville** 25

Z Origin | **multi.** 26

Passionne | **Montclair** 23

Z Rat's | **Hamilton** 24

Z Saddle River Inn | **Saddle R.** 27

Z Serenade | **Chatham** 27

Silver Spring | **Flanders** 23

Siri's | **Cherry Hill** 25

Soufflé | **Summit** 23

Verjus | **Maplewood** 25

Verve | **Somerville** 23

Water Lily | **Collingswood** 24

Z Zoe's | **Sparta** 26

FRENCH (BISTRO)

Bienvenue | **Red Bank**	24
Bistro 44 | **Toms River**	25
☑ Chef's Table | **Franklin Lakes**	28
Circa | **High Bridge**	20
Elysian Cafe | **Hoboken**	21
Epernay | **Montclair**	21
Harvest Bistro | **Closter**	22
Le Fandy | **Fair Haven**	26
☑ Le Rendez-Vous | **Kenilworth**	26
Madame Claude | **Jersey City**	23
Pierre's | **Morristown**	23
Sophie's Bistro | **Somerset**	22

FRENCH (BRASSERIE)

☑ Avenue | **Long Branch**	22

GERMAN

Black Forest | **Allentown**	19
☑ Black Forest Inn | **Stanhope**	23

GREEK

Athenian Gdn. | **Galloway Twp**	23
Axia Taverna | **Tenafly**	21
☑ It's Greek To Me | **multi.**	18
Kuzina by Sofia | **Cherry Hill**	-
My Little Greek | **Freehold Twp**	-
Pithari Taverna | **Highland Pk**	-
Varka Fish Hse. | **Ramsey**	25

HOT DOGS

Amazing Hot Dog | **multi.**	22
WindMill, The | **multi.**	-

ICE CREAM PARLORS

Holsten's | **Bloomfield**	-

INDIAN

Aamantran | **Toms River Twp**	23
Aangan | **Freehold Twp**	23
Akbar | **Edison**	18
Amiya | **Jersey City**	21
Bombay Curry | **Basking Ridge**	-
Bombay Gardens | **E Brunswick**	22
Chand Palace | **Parsippany**	22
Chowpatty | **Iselin**	-
DabbaWalla | **Summit**	19
Gagan Bistro | **Marlton**	-

India on Hudson | **Hoboken**	19
NEW Indigo | **N Brunswick**	-
☑ Karma Kafe | **Hoboken**	25
Malabar House | **Piscataway**	-
Mehndi | **Morristown**	-
Ming | **Edison**	23
Moghul | **Edison**	24
Moksha | **Edison**	22
Neelam | **multi.**	18
Passage to India | **Lawrenceville**	23
Piquant Bread | **New Bruns.**	-
NEW Prana | **Bloomfield**	-
Raagini | **Mountainside**	22
Rupee Room | **N Brunswick**	-
Saffron | **E Hanover**	23

IRISH

Egan & Sons | **Montclair**	17
Irish Pub | **A.C.**	18
Quiet Man | **Dover**	22

ITALIAN

(N=Northern; S=Southern)

Acqua | **Raritan**	21
Acquaviva | N | **Westfield**	23
NEW Aglio | **Metuchen**	-
Alan@594 | **Upper Montclair**	20
Al Dente | N | **Piscataway**	23
Aldo & Gianni | **multi.**	21
Alessio 426 | N | **Metuchen**	20
Amarone | N | **Teaneck**	21
Amici Milano | N | **Trenton**	22
Angelo's | **A.C.**	20
Anjelica's | S | **Sea Bright**	25
Anna's Italian | **Middletown**	22
Anthony David's | N | **Hoboken**	25
Anthony's | **Haddon Hts**	23
Aquila Cucina | **New Providence**	21
Arturo's | S | **Midland Pk**	22
A Tavola | **Old Bridge**	23
☑ Augustino's | S | **Hoboken**	26
Bareli's | **Secaucus**	23
Barone's | N | **multi.**	20
Barrel's | **multi.**	19
☑ Basilico | N | **Millburn**	23
Basil T's | **Red Bank**	20
☑ Bay Ave. | **Highlands**	28

Bazzarelli | **Moonachie**	22	Fiorino | N | **Summit**	23
Bella Sogno | **Bradley Bch**	21	Frankie Fed's | **Freehold Twp**	20
Bell's | **Lambertville**	19	Frescos | **Cape May**	24
Belmont Tavern | **Belleville**	24	Gaetano's | **Red Bank**	19
Belvedere | **Clifton**	19	Gaslight | **Hoboken**	20
Benito's | N | **Chester**	24	Gianna's | **Atlantic H.**	25
Berta's Chateau | N | **Wanaque**	22	Girasole | S | **A.C.**	25
Brioso | **Marlboro**	23	Girasole | **Bound Brook**	25
NEW Brio | **Cherry Hill**	-	Giumarello's | N | **Westmont**	25
Cafe Arugula | **S Orange**	20	GoodFellas | N | **Garfield**	-
Café Azzurro | N | **Peapack**	-	Grissini | **Englewood Cliffs**	22
Cafe Coloré | **Freehold Twp**	21	Ho-Ho-Kus Inn | **Ho-Ho-Kus**	21
Cafe Cucina | **Branchburg**	23	Homestead Inn | **Trenton**	23
Cafe Emilia | **Bridgewater**	22	I Cavallini | **Colts Neck**	25
Cafe Graziella | **Hillsborough**	22	Il Capriccio | **Whippany**	26
Cafe Italiano | **Englewood Cliffs**	18	Il Michelangelo | **Boonton**	21
Caffe Aldo | **Cherry Hill**	23	**Z** Il Mondo | N | **Madison**	25
Capriccio | **A.C.**	25	Il Villaggio | **Carlstadt**	23
Carmine's | **A.C.**	20	Jamie's | **Clifton**	-
Carmine's Asbury Pk | S | **Asbury Pk**	-	Jimmy's | S | **Asbury Pk**	24
		Kinchley's Tavern | **Ramsey**	21
Casa Dante | **Jersey City**	22	La Campagna | N | **multi.**	24
Casa Giuseppe | N | **Iselin**	24	Laceno Italian | **Voorhees**	25
Catelli | **Voorhees**	24	La Cipollina | **Freehold**	23
Z Catherine Lombardi | **New Bruns.**	21	La Focaccia | N | **Summit**	24
		La Nonna | **Bradley Bch**	18
Cenzino | **Oakland**	24	La Pastaria | **multi.**	19
Chef Vola's | **A.C.**	26	La Scala | N | **Somerville**	22
Christie's | **Howell**	24	La Spiaggia | **Ship Bottom**	26
Cinque Figlie | **Whippany**	21	La Strada | **Randolph**	22
Z CoccoLa | **Hillsborough**	22	LouCás | **Edison**	24
Columbia Inn | **Montville**	20	Luchento's | **Millstone**	20
Corso 98 | **Montclair**	21	Luigi's | **E Hanover**	19
Cucina Rosa | **Cape May**	23	Luka's | **Ridgefield Pk**	22
da Filippo | **Somerville**	24	Lu Nello | **Cedar Grove**	25
Dante's | **Mendham**	21	Margherita's | **Hoboken**	22
De Anna's | **Lambertville**	-	Marra's | **Ridgewood**	20
NEW Divino | **Berkeley Hts**	-	Mia | **A.C.**	26
NEW Due Terre | **Bernardsville**	-	Michael's Cucina | **Manalapan**	19
E & V | **Paterson**	24	**NEW** Mirabella | **Cherry Hill**	-
Eccola | **Parsippany**	23	Nunzio | **Collingswood**	23
Espo's | S | **Raritan**	21	**Z** Ombra | **A.C.**	25
Z Fascino | **Montclair**	26	Osteria Giotto | **Montclair**	25
Federici's | **Freehold**	21	Panico's | **New Bruns.**	24
Ferrari's | **Freehold Twp**	22	Pete & Elda's | **Neptune City**	-
Filomena | S | **multi.**	20	Pino's | **Marlboro**	18

Pizzicato	**Marlton**	20
Portobello	N	**Oakland**	20
Portofino	**Tinton Falls**	25
Porto Leggero	**Jersey City**	23
Posillipo	**Asbury Pk**	22
Primavera	**W Orange**	20
Radicchio	N	**Ridgewood**	23
Raimondo's	**Ship Bottom**	23
Reservoir Tavern	**Boonton**	22
Restaurant	**Hackensack**	21
Richie Cecere's	**Montclair**	21
Rick's	**Lambertville**	-
Ristorante Benito	**Union**	25
Roberto's	N	**Beach Haven**	22
Roberto's II	**Edgewater**	19
Rocca	**Glen Rock**	22
Roman Cafe	**Harrington Pk**	19
San Remo	**Shrewsbury**	22
Sapori	**Collingswood**	24
Z Scalini Fedeli	N	**Chatham**	27
Settebello	N	**Morristown**	22
NEW Siena Grille	**Red Bank**	-
Z Sirena	**Long Branch**	23
Sogno	**Red Bank**	23
Solaia	**Englewood**	20
Solari's	**Hackensack**	21
Solo Bella	**Jackson**	21
Specchio	**A.C.**	25
Squan Tavern	S	**Manasquan**	19
Stony Hill Inn	**Hackensack**	23
Tattoni's	**Hamilton Twp**	-
Teresa Caffe	**Princeton**	21
Theresa's	**Westfield**	23
Tosca	N	**Kenilworth**	20
Tre Figlio	**Egg Harbor**	24
Tre Piani	**Princeton**	21
Tuzzio's	**Long Branch**	21
NEW Undici	**Rumson**	-
Ventura's	**Margate**	17
Vic's	**Bradley Bch**	20
Villa Vittoria	**Brick**	22

JAPANESE

(* sushi specialist)

Z Ajihei*	**Princeton**	26
Akai Lounge*	**Englewood**	23
Aligado Asian*	**Hazlet**	23
Z Aozora	**Montclair**	25
Benihana	**multi.**	-
Bistro En*	**Teaneck**	22
Brix 67*	**Summit**	18
Dai-Kichi*	**Upper Montclair**	22
East*	**Teaneck**	18
Edo Sushi*	**Pennington**	20
Elements Asia*	**Lawrenceville**	23
NEW Fuji	**Haddonfield**	-
Ichiban*	**Princeton**	17
Ikko*	**Brick**	22
NEW Kanji Steak	**Tinton Falls**	-
Klein's Fish Mkt.*	**Belmar**	20
K.O.B.E.*	**Holmdel**	25
Komegashi*	**Jersey City**	24
Konbu*	**Manalapan**	25
Mahzu*	**multi.**	22
Megu Sushi*	**Cherry Hill**	22
Midori*	**Denville**	24
Mikado*	**multi.**	22
Monster Sushi*	**Summit**	19
Nikko*	**Whippany**	24
Nobi*	**Toms River Twp**	25
Nori*	**multi.**	22
Nouveau Sushi*	**Montclair**	25
Ota-Ya*	**Lambertville**	23
Oyako Tso's*	**Freehold**	21
Robongi	**Hoboken**	25
Z Sagami*	**Collingswood**	26
Sakura-Bana*	**Ridgewood**	25
Sakura Spring	**Cherry Hill**	23
SAWA Steak*	**multi.**	22
Shogun*	**multi.**	18
Shumi*	**Somerville**	25
Sono Sushi*	**Middletown**	26
Sumo	**Wall**	-
Sushi by Kazu*	**Howell**	28
Sushi Lounge*	**multi.**	24
Z Taka*	**Asbury Pk**	26
Takara	**Ocean Twp**	25
NEW Tokyo Bleu	**Cinnaminson**	-
Tomo's Cuisine	**Little Falls**	-
Tsuki*	**Bernardsville**	22
Wasabi*	**multi.**	24
Wild Ginger*	**Englewood**	25
Yumi*	**Sea Bright**	26

JEWISH

Eppes Essen | **Livingston**	18
Kibitz Room | **Cherry Hill**	24

KOREAN

(* barbecue specialist)

Doo Rae Myun Ok | **Fort Lee**	21
So Moon Nan Jip* | **Palisades Pk**	23

MALAYSIAN

Meemah | **Edison**	24
Penang | **multi.**	20
Taste of Asia | **Chatham**	21

MEDITERRANEAN

Europa/Monroe | **Monroe Twp**	–
Frescos | **Cape May**	24
Hamilton's | **Lambertville**	24
Lodos | **New Milford**	21
Marmara | **Manalapan**	–
Mediterra | **Princeton**	20
Z Moonstruck | **Asbury Pk**	24
Oasis Grill | **Cherry Hill**	25
Osteria Dante | **Red Bank**	19
NEW Sage | **Ventnor**	–
Seven Hills | **Highland Pk**	21
Terrace Rest. | **Short Hills**	22
Thyme Square | **Red Bank**	21
Tre Piani | **Princeton**	21
2Senza | **Red Bank**	20
Varka Fish Hse. | **Ramsey**	25
Verdigre | **New Bruns.**	22
Vine | **Basking Ridge**	22

MEXICAN

Aby's | **Matawan**	22
Baja | **multi.**	20
Casa Maya | **multi.**	20
Charrito's | **multi.**	24
Chilangos | **Highlands**	21
El Azteca | **Mt Laurel**	17
El Familiar | **Toms River Twp**	–
Z El Meson | **Freehold**	24
Habana Latin | **Ridgefield Pk**	–
Jose's | **Spring Lake Hts**	22
Jose's Cantina | **multi.**	19
Juanito's | **multi.**	23
La Esperanza | **Lindenwold**	24
La Tapatia | **Asbury Pk**	–
Los Amigos | **multi.**	23
Mexican Food | **Marlton**	18
Mexico Lindo | **Brick**	28
NEW Pop's Garage | **Normandy Bch**	–
Sapo Verde | **Atlantic H.**	–
Senorita's | **Bloomfield**	20
Surf Taco | **multi.**	20
Taqueria | **Jersey City**	20
Tortilla Press | **Collingswood**	23
NEW Tortilla Press Cantina | **Pennsauken**	–
Tortuga's | **Princeton**	21

MIDDLE EASTERN

Ali Baba | **Hoboken**	20
Norma's | **Cherry Hill**	21
NEW Prana | **Bloomfield**	–

MOROCCAN

Oasis Grill | **Cherry Hill**	25

NOODLE SHOPS

Noodle Hse. | **N Brunswick**	19
Penang | **multi.**	20

NORTH AFRICAN

Norma's | **Cherry Hill**	21

NUEVO LATINO

Casona | **Collingswood**	24
Sabor | **multi.**	22
NEW Vivas | **Belmar**	–

PAN-ASIAN

Asia Star Cafe | **Tinton Falls**	–
NEW Bank 34 | **Somerville**	–
Z Baumgart's Café | **multi.**	19
Buddakan | **A.C.**	–
Elements Asia | **Lawrenceville**	23
Grand Shanghai | **Edison**	21
NEW Hotoke | **New Bruns.**	–
Ming II | **Morristown**	–
Nori | **Caldwell**	22
Nouveau Sushi | **Montclair**	25
Ritz Seafood | **Voorhees**	24
Teak | **Red Bank**	23
Yumi | **Sea Bright**	26

CUISINES

Hamilton's | **Lambertville**	24
Harry's Lobster | **Sea Bright**	22
Harvey Cedars | **multi.**	22
Hunt Club | **Summit**	20
Inlet Café | **Highlands**	19
John Henry's | **Trenton**	21
Klein's Fish Mkt. | **Belmar**	20
Kunkel's | **Haddon Hts**	20
Laceno Italian | **Voorhees**	25
Latitude 40N | **Pt. Pleas. Bch**	23
☑ Legal Sea Foods | **multi.**	20
Little Tuna | **Haddonfield**	20
Lobster Hse. | **Cape May**	20
☑ McCormick/Schmick | **multi.**	20
Milford Oyster Hse. | **Milford**	–
Mill/Spring Lake | **Spring Lake Hts**	20
Morgan Fishery | **S Amboy**	–
Mud City | **Manahawkin**	21
Navesink Fishery | **Navesink**	24
Neil's Oyster | **Highlands**	–
Oceanos | **Fair Lawn**	–
Octopus's Gard. | **Stafford**	22
Opah Grille | **Gladstone**	24
Park Steak | **Park Ridge**	24
Phillips Seafood | **A.C.**	–
Ray's | **Little Silver**	23
Red's Lobster | **Pt. Pleas. Bch**	24
Ritz Seafood | **Voorhees**	24
Rooney's | **Long Branch**	18
☑ SeaBlue | **A.C.**	27
Sea Shack | **Hackensack**	20
Shipwreck Grill | **Brielle**	25
Smoke Chophse. | **Englewood**	22
Solaia | **Englewood**	20
☑ South City Grill | **multi.**	23
NEW South St. Steak | **Freehold**	–
Spike's | **Pt. Pleas. Bch**	22
NEW Splash | **Long Valley**	–
Suez Canal | **Jersey City**	–
3 Forty Grill | **Hoboken**	21
Tucker's Steak | **Somers Point**	19
Vanthia's | **W Cape May**	–
Varka Fish Hse. | **Ramsey**	25
Waterfront Buffet | **A.C.**	17
West Lake | **Matawan**	25
Windansea | **Highlands**	20

Witherspoon Grill | **Princeton**	–
Wonder Seafood | **Edison**	24

SMALL PLATES

(See also Spanish tapas specialist)

NEW A Toute Heure | Amer. | **Cranford**	–
NEW Daryl | Amer. | **New Bruns.**	–
Echo | Eclectic | **Red Bank**	19
Elements | Amer. | **Haddon Hts**	21
Grand Colonial | Eclectic | **Union Twp**	25
Lua | Pan-Latin | **Hoboken**	22
Marco & Pepe | Amer. | **Jersey City**	22

SOUL FOOD

Delta's | **New Bruns.**	22
Je's | **Newark**	26

SOUP

NEW Hale/Hearty | **Livingston**	–

SOUTH AMERICAN

☑ Cucharamama | **Hoboken**	26

SOUTHERN

Delta's | **New Bruns.**	22
House of Blues | **A.C.**	16
Indigo Smoke | **Montclair**	22
Je's | **Newark**	26
Niecy's | **S Orange**	20
Silver Oak Bistro | **Ridgewood**	23

SOUTHWESTERN

Copper Canyon | **Atlantic H.**	25
GRUB Hut | **Manville**	–
Los Amigos | **multi.**	23
☑ Mojave Grille | **Westfield**	24
Rattlesnake Ranch | **Denville**	16

SPANISH

(* tapas specialist)

Adega Grill | **Newark**	24
☑ Bistro Olé | **Asbury Pk**	25
Casa Vasca* | **Newark**	24
Don Pepe | **multi.**	21
El Cid | **Paramus**	21
Europa South | **Pt. Pleas. Bch**	20
☑ Fornos of Spain | **Newark**	23
NEW Havana* | **Highlands**	–
Iberia | **Newark**	21

Lola's* | **Hoboken** 22

Mompou* | **Newark** 20

Pic-Nic | **E Newark** -

Portuguese Manor | 21
   Perth Amboy

Savanna* | **Red Bank** 20

Segovia | **Moonachie** 22

Spain | **Newark** 21

Spanish Tavern | **multi.** 22

Tapas de Espana* | **multi.** 20

Tony Da Caneca | **Newark** 24

STEAKHOUSES

Z Arthur's | **multi.** 18

Assembly | **Englewood Cliffs** 16

BayPoint Prime | 24
   Pt. Pleas. Bch

Beau Steak | **Medford** 22

Blue Eyes | **Sewell** 20

Bobby Flay Steak | **A.C.** 24

Brennen's | **Neptune City** 22

Capt'n Ed's | **Pt. Pleas.** 19

Chophouse | **Gibbsboro** 23

Danny's Steak | **Red Bank** -

Don Pepe's Steak | **Pine Brook** 22

Z Fernandes Steak | **Newark** 26

Fleming's | **Edgewater** 22

Frankie & Johnnie | **Hoboken** 23

Fresco Steak | **Milltown** 23

Gallagher's Steak | **A.C.** 22

NEW Havana | **Highlands** -

Hunt Club | **Summit** 20

NEW Kanji Steak | **Tinton Falls** -

Kunkel's | **Haddon Hts** 20

Manhattan Steak | **Oakhurst** 22

Mignon Steak | **Rutherford** 23

Mill/Spring Lake | 20
   Spring Lake Hts

Morton's Steak | **Hackensack** 24

Nero's Grille | **Livingston** 17

Old Homestead | **A.C.** 25

Palm | **A.C.** 24

Park Steak | **Park Ridge** 24

Pub | **Pennsauken** 18

Z River Palm | **multi.** 25

Rod's Steak | **Convent Station** 21

Roots Steak | **Summit** -

Z Ruth's Chris | **multi.** 24

Sammy's Cider | **Mendham** 21

NEW Scorpio's Steak | **Jackson** -

Shogun | **multi.** 18

Smoke Chophse. | **Englewood** 22

NEW South St. Steak | **Freehold** -

Strip House | **Livingston** 23

Tucker's Steak | **Somers Point** 19

What's Your Beef? | **Rumson** 20

Witherspoon Grill | **Princeton** -

TAIWANESE

China Palace | **Middletown** -

THAI

Aligado Asian | **Hazlet** 23

NEW Aloe Fusion | **Cherry Hill** -

Andaman | **Morristown** 23

Aroma Royal Thai | **Franklin Pk** 22

Bamboo Leaf | **multi.** 24

Bangkok Garden | **Hackensack** 24

Chao Phaya | **multi.** 23

Z Far East Taste | **Eatontown** 26

Ginger Thai | **Freehold Twp** 15

Mie Thai | **Woodbridge** 25

New Main Taste | **Chatham** 23

Z Origin | **multi.** 26

Pad Thai | **Highland Pk** 22

Penang | **multi.** 20

Siam | **Lambertville** 21

Siam Garden | **Red Bank** 23

Sirin | **Morristown** 22

Siri's | **Cherry Hill** 25

Somsak/Taan | **Voorhees** 23

Spice Cuisine | **Bloomfield** -

Sri Thai | **Hoboken** 24

Thai Chef | **multi.** 21

Thai Kitchen | **multi.** 23

Thai Thai | **Stirling** 25

NEW Thai Tida | **Lambertville** -

Tuptim | **Montclair** 22

Wondee's Thai | **Hackensack** -

TURKISH

NEW Anatolia's | **Cliffside Pk** -

Beyti Kebab | **Union City** 24

Bosphorus | **Lake Hiawatha** 22

Dayi'nin Yeri | **Cliffside Pk** -

Kaptan | **Hackettstown** __|

Lalezar | **Montclair** __|

Lodos | **New Milford** 21|

Marmara | **Manalapan** __|

Samdan | **Cresskill** 22|

Seven Hills | **Highland Pk** 21|

VEGETARIAN

(* vegan)

Chand Palace | **Parsippany** 22|

Kaya's Kitchen* | **Belmar** __|

Little Saigon | **A.C.** __|

Tuptim | **Montclair** 22|

NEW Zen Palate | **Princeton** __|

VIETNAMESE

Bamboo Leaf | **multi.** 24|

Little Saigon | **A.C.** __|

Saigon R./Mo' Pho | **multi.** 24|

Nha Trang Pl. | **Jersey City** 24|

Pho Binh | **Jersey City** __|

Locations

Includes restaurant names, cuisines and Food ratings. **Z** indicates places with the highest ratings, popularity and importance.

Metro New York Area

ALLENDALE

Allendale B&G	*Pub*	16
Restaurant L	*Continental*	-

BELLEVILLE

Belmont Tavern	*Italian*	24

BERKELEY HEIGHTS

NEW Divino	*Italian*	-
Trap Rock	*Amer.*	21

BLOOMFIELD

Holsten's	*Amer.*	-
NEW Prana	*Indian/Mideastern*	-
Senorita's	*Mex.*	20
Spice Cuisine	*Eclectic*	-

CALDWELL

Nori	*Pan-Asian*	22

CARLSTADT

Il Villaggio	*Italian*	23
Tina Louise	*Asian*	24

CEDAR GROVE

Lu Nello	*Italian*	25

CLIFFSIDE PARK

NEW Anatolia's	*Turkish*	-
Dayi'nin Yeri	*Turkish*	-
Z It's Greek To Me	*Greek*	18

CLIFTON

Belvedere	*Italian*	19
Chengdu 46	*Chinese*	24
Jamie's	*Italian*	-
Tick Tock	*Diner*	17

CLOSTER

Harvest Bistro	*French*	22

CRANFORD

NEW A Toute Heure	*Amer.*	-
Garlic Rose	*Eclectic*	21

CRESSKILL

Samdan	*Turkish*	22

EAST NEWARK

Pic-Nic	*Portug./Spanish*	-

EAST RUTHERFORD

Z Park/Orchard	*Eclectic*	22

EDGEWATER

Z Baumgart's Café	*Amer./Pan-Asian*	19
Brooklyn's Pizza	*Pizza*	22
Fleming's	*Steak*	22
Magic Pot	*Fondue*	19
Rebecca's	*Cuban*	24
Z River Palm	*Steak*	25
Roberto's II	*Italian*	19

EMERSON

Z Arthur's	*Steak*	18

ENGLEWOOD

Akai Lounge	*Japanese*	23
Z Baumgart's Café	*Amer./Pan-Asian*	19
Z It's Greek To Me	*Greek*	18
Saigon R./Mo' Pho	*Viet.*	24
Smoke Chophse.	*Seafood/Steak*	22
Solaia	*Italian*	20
Tapas de Espana	*Spanish*	20
Wild Ginger	*Japanese*	25

ENGLEWOOD CLIFFS

Assembly	*Steak*	16
Cafe Italiano	*Italian*	18
Grissini	*Italian*	22

FAIRFIELD

NEW Merchant Hse.	*Amer.*	-

FAIR LAWN

Oceanos	*Seafood*	-
Z River Palm	*Steak*	25

LOCATIONS

FORT LEE

Doo Rae Myun Ok | *Korean*	21
Z It's Greek To Me | *Greek*	18
Saigon R./Mo' Pho | *Viet.*	24
Sally Ling | *Chinese*	19

FRANKLIN LAKES

Z Chef's Table | *French*	28

GARFIELD

GoodFellas | *Italian*	-

GLEN ROCK

Rocca | *Italian*	22

HACKENSACK

Bangkok Garden | *Thai*	24
Brooklyn's Pizza | *Pizza*	22
Z Cheesecake Factory | *Amer.*	19
Cubby's BBQ | *BBQ*	17
Five Guys | *Burgers*	-
Lotus Cafe | *Chinese*	24
Z McCormick/Schmick | *Seafood*	20
Morton's Steak | *Steak*	24
Restaurant | *Italian*	21
Sea Shack | *Seafood*	20
Solari's | *Italian*	21
Stony Hill Inn | *Continental/Italian*	23
Thai Chef | *Thai*	21
Wondee's Thai | *Thai*	-

HARRINGTON PARK

Roman Cafe | *Italian*	19

HAWTHORNE

Sabor | *Nuevo Latino*	22

HOBOKEN

Ali Baba | *Mideast.*	20
Z Amanda's | *Amer.*	26
Anthony David's | *Eclectic/Italian*	25
Z Arthur's | *Steak*	18
Z Augustino's | *Italian*	26
Baja | *Mex.*	20
Benny Tudino's | *Pizza*	21
Brass Rail | *Amer.*	19
Charrito's | *Mex.*	24
City Bistro | *Amer.*	19
Court Street | *Continental*	21
Z Cucharamama | *S Amer.*	26
Cup Joint | *Amer.*	20
Elysian Cafe | *French*	21
Frankie & Johnnie | *Steak*	23
Gaslight | *Amer./Italian*	20
Grimaldi's Pizza | *Pizza*	25
India on Hudson | *Indian*	19
Z It's Greek To Me | *Greek*	18
Z Karma Kafe | *Indian*	25
Z La Isla | *Cuban*	26
Lola's | *Spanish*	22
Lua | *Pan-Latin*	22
Madison B&G | *Amer.*	21
Margherita's | *Italian*	22
Melting Pot | *Fondue*	19
Oddfellows | *Cajun/Creole*	19
Onieal's | *Amer.*	19
Robongi | *Japanese*	25
Sri Thai | *Thai*	24
Sushi Lounge | *Japanese*	24
3 Forty Grill | *Amer.*	21
Zafra | *Pan-Latin*	24

HO-HO-KUS

Ho-Ho-Kus Inn | *Continental/Italian*	21

JERSEY CITY

Amiya | *Indian*	21
Azúcar | *Cuban*	19
Baja | *Mex.*	20
Casa Dante | *Italian*	22
Charrito's | *Mex.*	24
Hard Grove | *Amer./Cuban*	14
Z It's Greek To Me | *Greek*	18
Komegashi | *Japanese*	24
Liberty House | *Amer.*	20
Light Horse | *Amer.*	22
Madame Claude | *French*	23
Marco & Pepe | *Amer.*	22
Nha Trang Pl. | *Viet.*	24
NEW Ox | *Amer.*	-
Pho Binh | *Viet.*	-
Porto Leggero | *Italian*	23

⚡ South City Grill	*Amer.*	23
Suez Canal	*Seafood*	-
Taqueria	*Mex.*	20

KENILWORTH

⚡ Le Rendez-Vous	*French*	26
Tosca	*Italian*	20

LITTLE FALLS

Tomo's Cuisine	*Japanese*	-

LIVINGSTON

⚡ Baumgart's Café	*Amer./Pan-Asian*	19
Eppes Essen	*Deli*	18
NEW Hale/Hearty	*Sandwiches/Soup*	-
⚡ It's Greek To Me	*Greek*	18
Nero's Grille	*Steak*	17
Strip House	*Steak*	23

MAHWAH

Boulevard Grille	*Amer.*	18
⚡ River Palm	*Steak*	25

MAPLEWOOD

⚡ Lorena's	*French*	27
NEW Luke's	*Amer.*	-
Verjus	*French*	25

MIDLAND PARK

Arturo's	*Italian*	22

MILLBURN

⚡ Basilico	*Italian*	23
Five Guys	*Burgers*	-
La Campagna	*Italian*	24
restaurant.mc	*Amer./Eclectic*	-

MONTCLAIR

⚡ Aozora	*French/Japanese*	25
Blu	*Amer.*	25
Corso 98	*Italian*	21
Cuban Pete's	*Cuban*	17
⚡ CulinAriane	*Amer.*	27
Egan & Sons	*Irish*	17
Epernay	*French*	21
⚡ Fascino	*Italian*	26
Indigo Smoke	*BBQ*	22

Lalezar	*Turkish*	-
NEW Next Door	*Amer.*	-
Nori	*Pan-Asian*	22
Nouveau Sushi	*Pan-Asian*	25
Osteria Giotto	*Italian*	25
Passionne	*French*	23
Raymond's	*Amer.*	21
Richie Cecere's	*Italian*	21
Table 8	*Amer.*	23
Taro	*Pan-Asian*	21
Thai Chef	*Thai*	21
Tuptim	*Thai*	22

MONTVALE

Aldo & Gianni	*Italian*	21

MOONACHIE

Bazzarelli	*Italian*	22
Segovia	*Portug./Spanish*	22

MOUNTAINSIDE

Raagini	*Indian*	22
Spanish Tavern	*Spanish*	22

NEWARK

Adega Grill	*Portug./Spanish*	24
Brasilia	*Brazilian*	23
Casa Vasca	*Spanish*	24
Don Pepe	*Portug./Spanish*	21
⚡ Fernandes Steak	*Steak*	26
⚡ Fornos of Spain	*Spanish*	23
Iberia	*Portug./Spanish*	21
Je's	*Soul Food*	26
Maize	*Amer.*	21
Mompou	*Spanish*	20
Spain	*Portug./Spanish*	21
Spanish Tavern	*Spanish*	22
Theater Sq. Grill	*Amer./Continental*	20
Tony Da Caneca	*Portug./Spanish*	24

NEW MILFORD

Lodos	*Med./Turkish*	21

NEW PROVIDENCE

Aquila Cucina	*Italian*	21
Jose's Cantina	*Mex.*	19

LOCATIONS

NORTH BERGEN

Sabor | *Nuevo Latino* — 22
Tapas de Espana | *Spanish* — 20

NORTHVALE

Madeleine's | *Continental/French* — 24

OAKLAND

Cenzino | *Italian* — 24
Portobello | *Italian* — 20
Ruga | *Amer.* — 20

PALISADES PARK

So Moon Nan Jip | *Korean* — 23

PARAMUS

Z Chakra | *Amer.* — 21
El Cid | *Spanish* — 21
Z Legal Sea Foods | *Seafood* — 20
Napa Valley | *Amer.* — 22

PARK RIDGE

Esty Street | *Amer.* — 23
Park Steak | *Seafood/Steak* — 24

PATERSON

E & V | *Italian* — 24

RAHWAY

Z David Drake | *Amer.* — 27

RAMSEY

Z Cafe Panache | *Eclectic* — 28
Ginger & Spice | *Asian* — –
Kinchley's Tavern | *Pizza* — 21
Look See | *Chinese* — 19
Varka Fish Hse. | *Greek/Seafood* — 25

RIDGEFIELD PARK

Habana Latin | *Cuban/Mex.* — –
Luka's | *Italian* — 22

RIDGEWOOD

Z Baumgart's Café | *Amer./Pan-Asian* — 19
Bazzini | *Amer.* — 21
Brooklyn's Pizza | *Pizza* — 22
Country Pancake | *Amer.* — 19
Dim Sum Dynasty | *Chinese* — 21
Gazelle Café | *Amer.* — –
Z It's Greek To Me | *Greek* — 18
Joel's Malibu | *Eclectic* — –
Z Latour | *French* — 27
Marra's | *Italian* — 20
Radicchio | *Italian* — 23
Sakura-Bana | *Japanese* — 25
Silver Oak Bistro | *Amer./Southern* — 23
Village Green | *Amer.* — 25

ROCHELLE PARK

Z South City Grill | *Amer.* — 23

RUTHERFORD

Z Cafe Matisse | *Eclectic* — 27
Mignon Steak | *Steak* — 23
Village Gourmet | *Eclectic* — 21

SADDLE RIVER

Z Saddle River Inn | *Amer./French* — 27

SCOTCH PLAINS

503 Park | *Eclectic* — 20
Stage Hse. | *Amer.* — 23

SECAUCUS

Bareli's | *Italian* — 23

SHORT HILLS

Benihana | *Japanese* — –
Z Legal Sea Foods | *Seafood* — 20
Terrace Rest. | *Med.* — 22

SOUTH HACKENSACK

Aldo & Gianni | *Italian* — 21

SOUTH ORANGE

Cafe Arugula | *Italian* — 20
Neelam | *Indian* — 18
Niecy's | *Southern* — 20

SPRINGFIELD

Cathay 22 | *Chinese* — 23
Hunan Spring | *Chinese* — 19

SUMMIT

Brix 67 | *Eclectic/Japanese* — 18
DabbaWalla | *Indian* — 19

Fiorino	*Italian*	23
Hunt Club	*Seafood/Steak*	20
🛛 Huntley Taverne	*Amer.*	22
La Focaccia	*Italian*	24
La Pastaria	*Italian*	19
Monster Sushi	*Japanese*	19
Roots Steak	*Steak*	-
Soufflé	*French*	23

TEANECK

Amarone	*Italian*	21
Bistro En	*French*	22
East	*Japanese*	18

TENAFLY

Axia Taverna	*Greek*	21

TOTOWA

Sushi Lounge	*Japanese*	24

UNION

Ristorante Benito	*Italian*	25

UNION CITY

Beyti Kebab	*Turkish*	24
Charrito's	*Mex.*	24
NEW Park Ave.	*Amer./Pan-Latin*	-

UPPER MONTCLAIR

Alan@594	*Italian*	20
Dai-Kichi	*Japanese*	22
Orbis Bistro	*Amer.*	22

VERONA

Amazing Hot Dog	*Hot Dogs*	22

WALLINGTON

Krakus	*Polish*	-

WANAQUE

Berta's Chateau	*Italian*	22

WASHINGTON TOWNSHIP

Bacari Grill	*Amer.*	21

WAYNE

🛛 Cheesecake Factory	*Amer.*	19

WEEHAWKEN

Arthur's Landing	*Amer.*	20
🛛 Chart House	*Amer./Seafood*	20
🛛 Ruth's Chris	*Steak*	24

WESTFIELD

Acquaviva	*Italian*	23
🛛 Chez Catherine	*French*	27
Isabella's	*Amer.*	22
🛛 Mojave Grille	*SW*	24
Theresa's	*Italian*	23
WindMill, The	*Hot Dogs*	-

WEST NEW YORK

🛛 P.F. Chang's	*Chinese*	21

WEST ORANGE

🛛 Highlawn	*Amer.*	24
🛛 Manor	*Amer.*	23
Primavera	*Italian*	20

WESTWOOD

🛛 It's Greek To Me	*Greek*	18
Melting Pot	*Fondue*	19

Central

BASKING RIDGE

Bombay Curry	*Indian*	-
🛛 3 West	*Amer.*	23
Vine	*Amer./Med.*	22

BEDMINSTER

🛛 Pluckemin Inn	*Amer.*	25

BERNARDSVILLE

🛛 Bernards Inn	*Amer.*	26
NEW Due Terre	*Italian*	-
NEW Equus	*Amer.*	-
Grill 73	*Amer.*	22
Le Petit Chateau	*French*	25
Tsuki	*Japanese*	22

BOONTON

Il Michelangelo	*Italian*	21
Reservoir Tavern	*Italian*	22

BOUND BROOK

Amazing Hot Dog	*Hot Dogs*	22
Girasole	*Italian*	25

LOCATIONS

BRANCHBURG

Cafe Cucina | *Italian* — 23

BRIDGEWATER

Cafe Emilia | *Italian* — 22

🄩 McCormick/Schmick | *Seafood* — 20

Thai Kitchen | *Thai* — 23

CHATHAM

New Main Taste | *Thai* — 23

🄩 Scalini Fedeli | *Italian* — 27

🄩 Serenade | *French* — 27

Taste of Asia | *Malaysian* — 21

CHESTER

Benito's | *Italian* — 24

CONVENT STATION

Rod's Steak | *Seafood/Steak* — 21

CRANBURY

Cranbury Inn | *Amer.* — 17

DENVILLE

Cafe Metro | *Eclectic* — 21

Hunan Taste | *Chinese* — 23

Midori | *Japanese* — 24

Rattlesnake Ranch | *SW* — 16

DOVER

Quiet Man | *Pub* — 22

EAST BRUNSWICK

Bombay Gardens | *Indian* — 22

Gusto Grill | *Amer.* — -

Shogun | *Japanese/Steak* — 18

Wasabi | *Japanese* — 24

EAST HANOVER

Luigi's | *Italian* — 19

Mr. Chu | *Chinese* — 22

Penang | *Malaysian/Thai* — 20

Saffron | *Indian* — 23

EDISON

Akbar | *Indian* — 18

Benihana | *Japanese* — -

🄩 Cheesecake Factory | *Amer.* — 19

Five Guys | *Burgers* — -

Grand Shanghai | *Pan-Asian* — 21

Jack Cooper's | *Deli* — 19

LouCás | *Italian* — 24

Meemah | *Chinese/Malaysian* — 24

Ming | *Chinese/Indian* — 23

Moghul | *Indian* — 24

Moksha | *Indian* — 22

Penang | *Malaysian/Thai* — 20

Skylark Diner | *Amer.* — 19

Wonder Seafood | *Chinese* — 24

FLANDERS

Silver Spring | *French* — 23

FRANKLIN PARK

Aroma Royal Thai | *Thai* — 22

GILLETTE

Meyersville Inn | *Amer.* — -

GLADSTONE

Gladstone Tavern | *Amer.* — -

Opah Grille | *Seafood* — 24

GREEN BROOK

Shogun | *Japanese/Steak* — 18

HIGHLAND PARK

Pad Thai | *Thai* — 22

Pithari Taverna | *Greek* — -

Seven Hills | *Turkish* — 21

HILLSBOROUGH

Cafe Graziella | *Italian* — 22

🄩 CoccoLa | *Amer./Italian* — 22

🄩 Old Man Rafferty's | *Amer.* — 19

Pheasants Land. | *Amer./Continental* — 17

Thai Kitchen | *Thai* — 23

ISELIN

Casa Giuseppe | *Italian* — 24

Chowpatty | *Indian* — -

KENDALL PARK

Shogun | *Japanese/Steak* — 18

LAKE HIAWATHA

Bosphorus | *Turkish* — 22

LONG VALLEY

NEW Splash | *Seafood* | - |

MADISON

Garlic Rose | *Eclectic* | 21 |
Z Il Mondo | *Italian* | 25 |
Shanghai Jazz | *Chinese* | 21 |
Soho 33 | *Eclectic* | 19 |

MANVILLE

GRUB Hut | *BBQ* | - |

MENDHAM

Black Horse | *Pub Food* | 19 |
Dante's | *Italian* | 21 |
NEW KC's | *Belgian/French* | - |
Sammy's Cider | *Steak* | 21 |

METUCHEN

NEW Aglio | *Italian* | - |
Alessio 426 | *Continental* | 20 |
Metuchen Inn | *Amer.* | 22 |

MEYERSVILLE

Casa Maya | *Mex.* | 20 |

MIDDLESEX

NEW Mi Sueño | *Continental* | - |

MILLTOWN

Fresco Steak | *Seafood/Steak* | 23 |

MONROE TOWNSHIP

Europa/Monroe | *Med.* | - |

MONTVILLE

Columbia Inn | *Pizza* | 20 |

MORRIS PLAINS

Z Arthur's | *Steak* | 18 |
Hunan Chinese | *Chinese* | 23 |
NEW Tabor Rd. | *Amer.* | - |

MORRISTOWN

Andaman | *French/Thai* | 23 |
Copeland | *Amer.* | 25 |
Z Grand Cafe | *French* | 25 |
La Campagna | *Italian* | 24 |
Mehndi | *Indian* | - |
Ming II | *Pan-Asian* | - |

Z Origin | *French/Thai* | 26 |
Pamir | *Afghan* | 21 |
Pierre's | *French* | 23 |
Settebello | *Italian* | 22 |
Sirin | *Thai* | 22 |
Sushi Lounge | *Japanese* | 24 |
Tashmoo | *Pub* | - |
Tim Schafer's | *Amer.* | 25 |

MOUNTAIN LAKES

Z South City Grill | *Amer.* | 23 |

NEW BRUNSWICK

Z Catherine Lombardi | *Italian* | 21 |
Clydz | *Amer.* | 23 |
NEW Daryl | *Amer.* | - |
Delta's | *Southern* | 22 |
Z Frog/Peach | *Amer.* | 26 |
NEW Hotoke | *Pan-Asian* | - |
Makeda | *Ethiopian* | 23 |
Nova Terra | *Pan-Latin* | 22 |
Old Bay | *Cajun/Creole* | 17 |
Z Old Man Rafferty's | *Amer.* | 19 |
Panico's | *Italian* | 24 |
Piquant Bread | *Indian* | - |
SoHo on George | *Amer.* | 23 |
Z Stage Left | *Amer.* | 26 |
Verdigre | *Amer.* | 22 |

NORTH BRUNSWICK

Z Arthur's | *Steak* | 18 |
NEW Indigo | *Indian* | - |
Noodle Hse. | *Asian* | 19 |
Rupee Room | *Indian* | - |

OLD BRIDGE

A Tavola | *Italian* | 23 |
Big Ed's BBQ | *BBQ* | 17 |
Pine Tavern | *Amer.* | 22 |

PARSIPPANY

Chand Palace | *Indian* | 22 |
Eccola | *Italian* | 23 |
Five Guys | *Burgers* | - |
Z Ruth's Chris | *Steak* | 24 |

PEAPACK

Café Azzurro | *Italian* | - |
Limestone Cafe | *Amer.* | 22 |

PERTH AMBOY

Portuguese Manor | *Portug./Spanish* | 21

PINE BROOK

Don Pepe | *Portug./Spanish* | 21
Don Pepe's Steak | *Steak* | 22

PISCATAWAY

Al Dente | *Italian* | 23
Chand Palace | *Indian* | 22
Malabar House | *Indian* | -

RANDOLPH

La Strada | *Italian* | 22

RARITAN

Acqua | *Italian* | 21
Espo's | *Italian* | 21

RIVERDALE

Rosemary & Sage | *Amer.* | 26

ROCKY HILL

One 53 | *Amer.* | -

SKILLMAN

Ya Ya Noodles | *Chinese* | -

SOMERSET

Chao Phaya | *Thai* | 23
Sophie's Bistro | *French* | 22

SOMERVILLE

NEW Bank 34 | *Pan-Asian* | -
Chao Phaya | *Thai* | 23
da Filippo | *Italian/Seafood* | 24
La Scala | *Italian* | 22
Martino's | *Cuban* | 21
Melting Pot | *Fondue* | 19
Z Origin | *French/Thai* | 26
Shumi | *Japanese* | 25
Verve | *Amer./French* | 23
Wasabi | *Japanese* | 24

SOUTH AMBOY

Morgan Fishery | *Seafood* | -

SOUTH BRUNSWICK

Sens Asian | *Asian* | 22

STIRLING

Thai Thai | *Thai* | 25

WARREN

Jose's Cantina | *Mex.* | 19
NEW Stonehouse | *Amer.* | -

WATCHUNG

Five Guys | *Burgers* | -

WHIPPANY

Cinque Figlie | *Italian* | 21
Il Capriccio | *Italian* | 26
Melting Pot | *Fondue* | 19
Nikko | *Japanese* | 24

WOODBRIDGE

Five Guys | *Burgers* | -
Mie Thai | *Thai* | 25

North Shore

ABERDEEN

Mahzu | *Japanese* | 22

ALLENTOWN

Black Forest | *German* | 19

ASBURY PARK

Z Bistro Olé | *Portug./Spanish* | 25
Brickwall Tavern | *Amer.* | 19
Carmine's Asbury Pk | *Italian* | -
NEW D & L BBQ | *BBQ* | -
Harrison | *Amer.* | 24
Jimmy's | *Italian* | 24
La Tapatia | *Mex.* | -
Mkt. in the Middle | *Eclectic* | 23
Z Moonstruck | *Amer./Med.* | 24
Z Old Man Rafferty's | *Amer.* | 19
Posillipo | *Italian* | 22
NEW Salt Water | *Amer.* | -
Sister Sue's | *Carib.* | 21
Z Taka | *Japanese* | 26

ATLANTIC HIGHLANDS

Copper Canyon | *SW* | 25
Gianna's | *Italian* | 25
Memphis Pig Out | *BBQ* | 19
Sapo Verde | *Mex.* | -

AVON-BY-THE-SEA

Avon Pavilion | *Amer.* 18

BAY HEAD

Bay Head Bistro | *Amer.* 21

Grenville | *Amer.* 21

BEACH HAVEN

🆉 Gables, The | *Eclectic* 26

Harvey Cedars | *Seafood* 22

Roberto's | *Italian* 22

Tuckers | *Amer.* 18

BELMAR

Brandl. | *Amer.* 24

Casa Solar | *Pan-Latin* 25

Kaya's Kitchen | *Veg.* -

Klein's Fish Mkt. | *Seafood* 20

Matisse | *Amer.* 22

Surf Taco | *Mex.* 20

🆕 Vivas | *Nuevo Latino* -

WindMill, The | *Hot Dogs* -

BRADLEY BEACH

Bamboo Leaf | *Thai/Viet.* 24

Bella Sogno | *Italian* 21

La Nonna | *Italian* 18

Vic's | *Pizza* 20

BRICK

Five Guys | *Burgers* -

Ikko | *Japanese* 22

Mexico Lindo | *Mex.* 28

Villa Vittoria | *Italian* 22

WindMill, The | *Hot Dogs* -

BRIELLE

Shipwreck Grill | *Amer.* 25

COLTS NECK

Christopher's | *Amer.* 21

I Cavallini | *Italian* 25

EATONTOWN

🆉 Far East Taste | *Chinese/Thai* 26

SAWA Steak | *Japanese* 22

FAIR HAVEN

Le Fandy | *French* 26

🆉 Nauvoo Grill | *Amer.* 16

Raven & Peach | *Amer.* 24

FREEHOLD

🆉 Cheesecake Factory | *Amer.* 19

El Familiar | *Colombian/Mex.* -

🆉 El Meson | *Mex.* 24

Federici's | *Pizza* 21

La Cipollina | *Italian* 23

Main St. Bistro | *Amer.* 21

Metropolitan Cafe | *Asian/Eclectic* 22

Oyako Tso's | *Japanese* 21

🆉 P.F. Chang's | *Chinese* 21

🆕 South St. Steak | *Steak* -

WindMill, The | *Hot Dogs* -

FREEHOLD TOWNSHIP

Aangan | *Indian* 23

Cafe Coloré | *Italian* 21

Ferrari's | *Italian* 22

Frankie Fed's | *Italian* 20

Ginger Thai | *Thai* 15

Mahzu | *Japanese* 22

My Little Greek | *Greek* -

HARVEY CEDARS

Caneel Bay | *Carib.* 17

Harvey Cedars | *Seafood* 22

Plantation | *Amer.* 19

HAZLET

Aligado Asian | *Japanese/Thai* 23

HIGHLANDS

Bahrs Landing | *Seafood* 15

🆉 Bay Ave. | *Amer./Italian* 28

Chilangos | *Mex.* 21

Doris & Ed's | *Amer./Seafood* 25

🆕 Havana | *Cuban* -

Inlet Café | *Seafood* 19

Neil's Oyster | *Amer./Seafood* -

Windansea | *Seafood* 20

HOLMDEL

🆉 It's Greek To Me | *Greek* 18

K.O.B.E. | *Japanese* 25

HOWELL

Bamboo Leaf | *Thai/Viet.* 24

Cabin | *Amer.* 18

Christie's	*Italian*	24
Juanito's	*Mex.*	23
Sushi by Kazu	*Japanese*	28

JACKSON

Java Moon	*Amer.*	19
NEW Scorpio's Steak	*Steak*	-
Solo Bella	*Italian*	21
Surf Taco	*Mex.*	20

KEYPORT

Drew's Bayshore	*Amer.*	28

LAVALLETTE

Crab's Claw	*Seafood*	17

LINCROFT

Lincroft Inn	*Continental*	18

LITTLE SILVER

Ray's	*Seafood*	23
Table	*Amer.*	-

LONG BEACH TOWNSHIP

daddy O	*Amer.*	18

LONG BRANCH

Z Avenue	*French*	22
Charley's	*Amer.*	19
Z It's Greek To Me	*Greek*	18
McLoone's	*Amer.*	17
NEW Pearl/Lisbon	*Portug.*	-
Richard's	*Deli*	20
Rooney's	*Seafood*	18
SAWA Steak	*Japanese*	22
Z Sirena	*Italian*	23
Tuzzio's	*Italian*	21
WindMill, The	*Hot Dogs*	-

MANAHAWKIN

Mud City	*Seafood*	21

MANALAPAN

Java Moon	*Amer.*	19
Konbu	*Japanese*	25
Marmara	*Turkish*	-
Michael's Cucina	*Italian*	19
Spargo's Grille	*Amer.*	25

MANASQUAN

Bayou Cafe	*Cajun/Creole*	23
Mahogany Grille	*Amer.*	23
Squan Tavern	*Italian*	19
Surf Taco	*Mex.*	20

MARLBORO

Brioso	*Italian*	23
Crown Palace	*Chinese*	22
Jerry & Harvey's	*Deli*	18
Pino's	*Italian*	18

MATAWAN

Aby's	*Mex.*	22
Buttonwood Manor	*Amer.*	18
West Lake	*Chinese*	25

MIDDLETOWN

Anna's Italian	*Italian*	22
China Palace	*Taiwanese*	-
Crown Palace	*Chinese*	22
Neelam	*Indian*	18
Z Nicholas	*Amer.*	29
Sono Sushi	*Japanese*	26

MILLSTONE

Luchento's	*Italian*	20

MONMOUTH BEACH

Sallee Tee's	*Amer./Eclectic*	21

NAVESINK

Navesink Fishery	*Seafood*	24

NEPTUNE CITY

Brennen's	*Steak*	22
Pete & Elda's	*Pizza*	-

NORMANDY BEACH

Labrador	*Eclectic*	23
NEW Pop's Garage	*Mex.*	-

OAKHURST/OCEAN TOWNSHIP

Manhattan Steak	*Steak*	22
Takara	*Japanese*	25

OCEAN GROVE

WindMill, The	*Hot Dogs*	-

POINT PLEASANT

Capt'n Ed's | *Seafood/Steak* — 19
Clark's Landing | *Amer.* — 17

POINT PLEASANT BEACH

BayPoint Prime | *Steak* — 24
Europa South | *Portug./Spanish* — 20
Latitude 40N | *Seafood* — 23
Red's Lobster | *Seafood* — 24
Spike's | *Seafood* — 22
Surf Taco | *Mex.* — 20

RED BANK

Basil T's | *Amer./Italian* — 20
Bienvenue | *French* — 24
Bistro at Red Bank | *Eclectic* — 21
Danny's Steak | *Steak* — -
Dish | *Amer.* — 22
Echo | *Eclectic* — 19
Eurasian Eatery | *Eclectic* — 20
Gaetano's | *Italian* — 19
Juanito's | *Mex.* — 23
La Pastaria | *Italian* — 19
Melting Pot | *Fondue* — 19
Molly Pitcher | *Amer.* — 22
Osteria Dante | *Med.* — 19
Red | *Amer.* — 20
Savanna | *Spanish* — 20
Siam Garden | *Thai* — 23
NEW Siena Grille | *Italian* — -
Sogno | *Italian* — 23
Teak | *Pan-Asian* — 23
Thyme Square | *Med.* — 21
2Senza | *Med.* — 20
WindMill, The | *Hot Dogs* — -

RUMSON

Barnacle Bill's | *Hamburgers* — 21
Z David Burke | *Amer.* — 26
Salt Creek | *Amer.* — 20
NEW Undici | *Italian* — -
What's Your Beef? | *Steak* — 20

SEA BRIGHT

Anjelica's | *Italian* — 25
Harry's Lobster | *Seafood* — 22
McLoone's | *Amer.* — 17
Yumi | *Pan-Asian* — 26

SEA GIRT

Rod's Olde Irish | *Pub* — 19

SHIP BOTTOM

La Spiaggia | *Italian* — 26
Raimondo's | *Italian* — 23

SHREWSBURY

Java Moon | *Amer.* — 19
Pasta Fresca | *Amer.* — 22
San Remo | *Italian* — 22

SOUTH SEASIDE PARK

Atlantic B&G | *Amer./Seafood* — 24
Berkeley | *Seafood* — 18
Surf Taco | *Mex.* — 20

SPRING LAKE

Black Trumpet | *Amer.* — 23
Island Palm Grill | *Amer.* — 18
Z Whispers | *Amer.* — 27

SPRING LAKE HEIGHTS

Jose's | *Mex.* — 22
Mill/Spring Lake | *Amer.* — 20

STAFFORD

Octopus's Gard. | *Seafood* — 22

SURF CITY

Blue | *Amer./Eclectic* — 23
Yellow Fin | *Amer.* — 25

TINTON FALLS

Asia Star Cafe | *Pan-Asian* — -
NEW Kanji Steak |
   Japanese/Steak — -
Portofino | *Italian* — 25

TOMS RIVER

Bistro 44 | *Amer./French* — 25
Five Guys | *Burgers* — -
NEW Queen Victoria | *Tea* — -
Surf Taco | *Mex.* — 20

TOMS RIVER TOWNSHIP

Aamantran | *Indian* — 23
El Familiar | *Colombian/Mex.* — -
Nobi | *Japanese* — 25
Shogun | *Japanese/Steak* — 18

WALL

Scarborough Fair | *Amer.* — 20
Shogun | *Japanese/Steak* — 18
Sumo | *Japanese* — ⌐

Delaware Valley

ALLAMUCHY

Mattar's | *Amer./Eclectic* — 24

FLEMINGTON

Blue Fish | *Seafood* — 20
California Grill | *Eclectic* — 20
NEW 55 Main | *Amer.* — ⌐
NEW Fusion | *Asian Fusion* — ⌐
Market Roost | *Eclectic* — 22
Matt's Rooster | *Amer.* — 25
Shaker Cafe | *Amer./Eclectic* — ⌐

FRENCHTOWN

Frenchtown Inn | *Eclectic/French* — 23

HACKETTSTOWN

Kaptan | *Turkish* — ⌐

HAMBURG

Restaurant Latour | *Amer.* — ⌐

HAMILTON

Z Rat's | *French* — 24

HAMILTON TOWNSHIP

Tattoni's | *Italian* — ⌐

HIGH BRIDGE

Casa Maya | *Mex.* — 20
Circa | *French* — 20

HOPE

Inn at Millrace | — 21
    Amer./Continental

HOPEWELL

Z Blue Bottle | *Amer.* — 27
Brothers Moon | *French* — 22

LAMBERTVILLE

Anton's/Swan | *Amer.* — 22
Bell's | *Amer./Italian* — 19
De Anna's | *Italian* — ⌐

Full Moon | *Eclectic* — 17
Hamilton's | *Med.* — 24
Inn/Hawke | *Amer.* — 18
Lambertville Station | *Amer.* — 17
Lilly's/Canal | *Eclectic* — 21
Manon | *French* — 25
No. 9 | *Amer.* — 24
Ota-Ya | *Japanese* — 23
Rick's | *Italian* — ⌐
Siam | *Thai* — 21
NEW Thai Tida | *Thai* — ⌐

LAWRENCEVILLE

Acacia | *Amer.* — 25
Elements Asia | *Pan-Asian* — 23
Fedora Cafe | *Eclectic* — 19
Java Moon | *Amer.* — 19
Passage to India | *Indian* — 23
Simply Radishing | *Amer.* — 18

MILFORD

Milford Oyster Hse. | *Seafood* — ⌐
Ship Inn | *Pub* — 19

NEWTON

Z André's | *Amer.* — 27
Krave Café | *Amer.* — ⌐

OLDWICK

Tewksbury Inn | *Amer.* — 22

PENNINGTON

Edo Sushi | *Chinese/Japanese* — 20

PHILLIPSBURG

NEW Thyme Rest. | *Amer.* — ⌐
Union Station | *Amer.* — ⌐

PRINCETON

Z Ajihei | *Japanese* — 26
Alchemist/Barrister | *Amer.* — 16
Z Blue Point | *Seafood* — 25
Conte's | *Pizza* — ⌐
Z Ferry Hse. | *Amer./French* — 25
Ichiban | *Japanese* — 17
Lahiere's | *Continental/French* — 21
Main St. Euro-Amer. | — 18
    Amer./Continental

Mediterra | *Med.*	20
Salt Creek | *Amer.*	20
Teresa Caffe | *Italian*	21
Tortuga's | *Mex.*	21
Tre Piani | *Italian/Med.*	21
Triumph Brewing | *Eclectic*	18
Underground Café | *E Euro.*	13
Witherspoon Grill | *Seafood/Steak*	-
Yankee Doodle | *Amer.*	14
NEW Zen Palate | *Veg.*	-

RINGOES

Harvest Moon | *Amer.*	24

ROBBINSVILLE

Z DeLorenzo's | *Pizza*	28

ROSEMONT

Cafe at Rosemont | *Amer.*	22

SERGEANTSVILLE

Sergeantsville Inn | *Amer.*	23

SPARTA

Z Zoe's | *French*	26

STANHOPE

Bell's Mansion | *Amer.*	18
Z Black Forest Inn | *Continental/German*	23

STOCKHOLM

Savannah's | *Eclectic*	-

STOCKTON

Meil's | *Amer.*	23

TRENTON

Amici Milano | *Italian*	22
Blue Danube | *E Euro.*	22
Z DeLorenzo's | *Pizza*	28
Homestead Inn | *Italian*	23
John Henry's | *Seafood*	21

UNION TOWNSHIP

Grand Colonial | *Eclectic*	25
Z Perryville Inn | *Amer.*	26

WALLPACK CENTER

Walpack Inn | *Amer.*	19

WEST WINDSOR

Penang | *Malaysian/Thai*	20
Sunny Gdn. | *Chinese*	22

South Shore

ATLANTIC CITY

Angelo's | *Italian*	20
Bobby Flay Steak | *Steak*	24
Buddakan | *Pan-Asian*	-
Capriccio | *Italian*	25
Carmine's | *Italian*	20
Chef Vola's | *Italian*	26
Continental | *Amer.*	-
Corky's | *BBQ*	16
Cuba Libre | *Cuban*	21
Dock's Oyster | *Seafood*	26
Gallagher's Steak | *Steak*	22
Girasole | *Italian*	25
House of Blues | *Southern*	16
Irish Pub | *Irish*	18
Little Saigon | *Viet.*	-
Los Amigos | *Mex./SW*	23
Melting Pot | *Fondue*	19
Mia | *Italian*	26
Old Homestead | *Steak*	25
Z Ombra | *Italian*	25
Palm | *Steak*	24
Z P.F. Chang's | *Chinese*	21
Phillips Seafood | *Seafood*	-
Red Square | *Eclectic/Russian*	-
Z Ruth's Chris | *Steak*	24
Z SeaBlue | *Seafood*	27
Sonsie | *Amer.*	-
Specchio | *Italian*	25
Tony Luke's | *Sandwiches*	-
Tony's | *Pizza*	-
Tun Tavern | *Amer.*	18
Waterfront Buffet | *Eclectic*	17
Z White Hse. | *Sandwiches*	27
Wolfgang Puck | *Amer.*	23

AVALON

Cafe Loren | *Amer.*	25

BRIGANTINE

Laguna Grill | *Amer./Eclectic* 22

CAPE MAY

Alexander's | *French* 24
Axelsson's | *Seafood* 22
Blue Pig Tavern | *Amer.* 20
Copper Fish | *Amer./Seafood* 20
Cucina Rosa | *Italian* 23
🟦 Ebbitt Room | *Amer.* 27
🟦 410 Bank St. | *Creole* 27
Frescos | *Italian/Med.* 24
Lobster Hse. | *Seafood* 20
Lucky Bones | *Amer.* 18
Mad Batter | *Amer.* 21
Merion Inn | *Amer.* 20
🟦 Peter Shields | *Amer.* 26
Tisha's | *Amer.* 25
Ugly Mug | *Amer.* 16
🟦 Union Park | *Amer.* 26
🟦 Washington Inn | *Amer.* 26

CLERMONT

Karen & Rei's | *Amer.* 27

EGG HARBOR

Renault Winery | *Amer.* 22
Tre Figlio | *Italian* 24

GALLOWAY

🟦 Ram's Head Inn | *Amer.* 26

GALLOWAY TOWNSHIP

Athenian Gdn. | *Greek* 23

HAMMONTON

NEW Mr. Bill's | *Deli* -

LINWOOD

Barrel's | *Italian* 19

MARGATE

Barrel's | *Italian* 19
Bobby Chez | *Seafood* 25
Dune | *Seafood* -
NEW Manna | *Amer.* -
Steve & Cookie's | *Amer.* 25
Tomatoes | *Calif./Eclectic* 24
Ventura's | *Italian* 17

MAYS LANDING

Inn at Sugar Hill | *Amer.* -

NORTHFIELD

NEW Tap Rm. | *Amer.* -

NORTH WILDWOOD

Claude's | *French* 25

OCEAN CITY

Nag's Head | *Amer.* 26

SEA ISLE CITY

Busch's Seafood | *Seafood* 19

SMITHVILLE

Smithville Inn | *Amer.* 18

SOMERS POINT

Crab Trap | *Seafood* 21
NEW Inlet, The | *Amer.* -
Tucker's Steak | *Seafood/Steak* 19

VENTNOR

NEW Sage | *Med.* -

WEST CAPE MAY

🟦 Black Duck | *Eclectic* 26
Vanthia's | *Seafood* -

WILDWOOD

Marie Nicole's | *Amer.* 23

Suburban Philly Area

BERLIN

Filomena | *Italian* 20

BORDENTOWN

NEW Alstarz | *Eclectic* -
Farnsworth Hse. | *Continental* 21
Mastoris | *Diner* 19

BURLINGTON

Café Gallery | *Continental* 21

CAMDEN

NEW Victor's Pub | *Pub* -

CHERRY HILL

Alisa Cafe | *French* 22
NEW Aloe Fusion | *Thai* -
Bahama Breeze | *Carib.* 16
Bobby Chez | *Seafood* 25

NEW Brio	*Italian*	-
Caffe Aldo	*Italian*	23
Z Cheesecake Factory	*Amer.*	19
NEW Dream Café	*French*	-
Elephant/Castle	*Pub*	10
NEW Embers Grill	*Amer.*	-
Five Guys	*Burgers*	-
Kibitz Room	*Deli*	24
Kuzina by Sofia	*Greek*	-
La Campagne	*French*	24
Z McCormick/Schmick	*Seafood*	20
Megu Sushi	*Japanese*	22
Z Mélange	*Creole*	26
Mikado	*Japanese*	22
NEW Mirabella	*Italian*	-
Norma's	*African/Mideast.*	21
Oasis Grill	*Med./Moroccan*	25
P.J. Whelihan's	*Pub Food*	17
Ponzio's	*Diner*	16
Sakura Spring	*Chinese/Japanese*	23
Siri's	*French/Thai*	25

CINNAMINSON

NEW Tokyo Bleu	*Japanese*	-

CLEMENTON

Filomena	*Italian*	20
NEW 947 B&G	*Amer.*	-

COLLINGSWOOD

Barone's	*Italian*	20
NEW Blackbird	*Amer.*	-
Bobby Chez	*Seafood*	25
Casona	*Cuban*	24
NEW Dockhoppers	*Seafood*	-
Nunzio	*Italian*	23
Pop Shop	*Amer.*	18
Z Sagami	*Japanese*	26
Sapori	*Italian*	24
Tortilla Press	*Mex.*	23
Water Lily	*Asian/French*	24
Word of Mouth	*Amer.*	24

DEPTFORD

Filomena	*Italian*	20

GIBBSBORO

Chophouse	*Seafood/Steak*	23

HADDONFIELD

NEW Fuji	*Japanese*	-
NEW Javier's	*Amer.*	-
Little Tuna	*Seafood*	20
P.J. Whelihan's	*Pub Food*	17

HADDON HEIGHTS

Anthony's	*Italian*	23
Elements	*Amer.*	21
Kunkel's	*Seafood/Steak*	20

LINDENWOLD

La Esperanza	*Mex.*	24

MAPLE SHADE

Mikado	*Japanese*	22
P.J. Whelihan's	*Pub Food*	17
Tacconelli's	*Pizza*	24

MARLTON

Food/Thought	*Amer.*	24
Gagan Bistro	*Indian*	-
Joe's Peking	*Chinese*	23
Mexican Food	*Mex.*	18
Mikado	*Japanese*	22
Z P.F. Chang's	*Chinese*	21
Pizzicato	*Italian*	20
Redstone	*Amer.*	-

MEDFORD

Beau Steak	*Seafood/Steak*	22
Braddock's	*Amer.*	22
Ted's on Main	*Amer.*	-

MEDFORD LAKES

P.J. Whelihan's	*Pub Food*	17

MOORESTOWN

Barnacle Ben's	*Seafood*	19
Barone's	*Italian*	20

MOUNT EPHRAIM

Five Guys	*Burgers*	-

MOUNT HOLLY

High St. Grill	*Amer.*	23
Robin's Nest	*Amer.*	22

LOCATIONS

MOUNT LAUREL

Bobby Chez | *Seafood* — 25
El Azteca | *Mex.* — 17

NEW GRETNA

Allen's Clam | *Seafood* — -

PENNSAUKEN

Benihana | *Japanese* — -
Pub | *Steak* — 18
NEW Tortilla Press Cantina | *Mex.* — -

SEWELL

Blue Eyes | *Steak* — 20
Bobby Chez | *Seafood* — 25
Creole Cafe | *Cajun/Creole* — 27
P.J. Whelihan's | *Pub Food* — 17

VOORHEES

Bobby Chez | *Seafood* — 25
Catelli | *Italian* — 24
Chez Elena Wu | *Asian/French* — 24
Coconut Bay | *Asian* — 21
Laceno Italian | *Italian/Seafood* — 25
Little Café | *Eclectic* — 25
Ritz Seafood | *Pan-Asian/Seafood* — 24
Somsak/Taan | *Thai* — 23

WEST BERLIN

Los Amigos | *Mex./SW* — 23

WESTMONT

Cork | *Amer.* — 21
Giumarello's | *Italian* — 25
Kitchen 233 | *Amer.* — 22

Special Features

Listings cover the best in each category and include restaurant names, locations and Food ratings. Multi-location restaurants' features may vary by branch. ☒ indicates places with the highest ratings, popularity and importance.

ADDITIONS

(Properties added since the last edition of the book)

Aglio | **Metuchen**
Aloe Fusion | **Cherry Hill**
Alstarz | **Bordentown**
Anatolia's | **Cliffside Pk**
A Toute Heure | **Cranford**
Bank 34 | **Somerville**
Benihana | **multi.**
Blackbird | **Collingswood**
Brio | **Cherry Hill**
Café Azzurro | **Peapack**
Carmine's Asbury Pk | **Asbury Pk**
D & L BBQ | **Asbury Pk**
Danny's Steak | **Red Bank**
Daryl | **New Bruns.**
Divino | **Berkeley Hts**
Dockhoppers | **Collingswood**
Dream Café | **Cherry Hill**
Due Terre | **Bernardsville**
Dune | **Margate**
Embers Grill | **Cherry Hill**
Equus | **Bernardsville**
55 Main | **Flemington**
Five Guys | **multi.**
Fuji | **Haddonfield**
Fusion | **Flemington**
Gladstone Tavern | **Gladstone**
Hale/Hearty | **Livingston**
Havana | **Highlands**
Holsten's | **Bloomfield**
Hotoke | **New Bruns.**
Indigo | **N Brunswick**
Inlet, The | **Somers Point**
Javier's | **Haddonfield**
Kanji Steak | **Tinton Falls**
KC's | **Mendham**
Krave Café | **Newton**
Kuzina by Sofia | **Cherry Hill**
Luke's | **Maplewood**

Manna | **Margate**
Merchant Hse. | **Fairfield**
Ming II | **Morristown**
Mirabella | **Cherry Hill**
Mi Sueño | **Middlesex**
Morgan Fishery | **S Amboy**
Mr. Bill's | **Hammonton**
Next Door | **Montclair**
947 B&G | **Clementon**
Ox | **Jersey City**
Park Ave. | **Union City**
Pearl/Lisbon | **Long Branch**
Pop's Garage | **Normandy Bch**
Prana | **Bloomfield**
Queen Victoria | **Toms River**
Redstone | **Marlton**
Rupee Room | **N Brunswick**
Sage | **Ventnor**
Salt Water | **Asbury Pk**
Scorpio's Steak | **Jackson**
Siena Grille | **Red Bank**
South St. Steak | **Freehold**
Splash | **Long Valley**
Stonehouse | **Warren**
Tabor Rd. | **Morris Plains**
Tap Rm. | **Northfield**
Tattoni's | **Hamilton Twp**
Ted's on Main | **Medford**
Thai Tida | **Lambertville**
Thyme Rest. | **Phillipsburg**
Tokyo Bleu | **Cinnaminson**
Tony's | **A.C.**
Tortilla Press Cantina | **Pennsauken**
Undici | **Rumson**
Union Station | **Phillipsburg**
Vanthia's | **W Cape May**
Victor's Pub | **Camden**
Vivas | **Belmar**
WindMill, The | **multi.**

SPECIAL FEATURES

Witherspoon Grill	**Princeton**	⌐
Zen Palate	**Princeton**	⌐

BREAKFAST

(See also Hotel Dining)

Avon Pavilion	**Avon-by-Sea**	18
Christopher's	**Colts Neck**	21
Country Pancake	**Ridgewood**	19
Eppes Essen	**Livingston**	18
Full Moon	**Lambertville**	17
Java Moon	**multi.**	19
Je's	**Newark**	26
Market Roost	**Flemington**	22
Meil's	**Stockton**	23
Ponzio's	**Cherry Hill**	16
Zafra	**Hoboken**	24

BRUNCH

☑ Amanda's	**Hoboken**	26
Anthony David's	**Hoboken**	25
Braddock's	**Medford**	22
Brothers Moon	**Hopewell**	22
Cafe at Rosemont	**Rosemont**	22
Café Gallery	**Burlington**	21
☑ Chart House	**Weehawken**	20
Court Street	**Hoboken**	21
Crown Palace	**multi.**	22
Frenchtown Inn	**Frenchtown**	23
Gladstone Tavern	**Gladstone**	⌐
Grenville	**Bay Hd.**	21
Grill 73	**Bernardsville**	22
Harvest Bistro	**Closter**	22
Labrador	**Normandy Bch**	23
La Campagne	**Cherry Hill**	24
Lambertville Station	**Lambertville**	17
Madame Claude	**Jersey City**	23
Marco & Pepe	**Jersey City**	22
Molly Pitcher	**Red Bank**	22
Napa Valley	**Paramus**	22
☑ Rat's	**Hamilton**	24
Restaurant	**Hackensack**	21
Taqueria	**Jersey City**	20
Terrace Rest.	**Short Hills**	22
Tortilla Press	**Collingswood**	23
Verjus	**Maplewood**	25
Zafra	**Hoboken**	24

BUFFET SERVED

(Check availability)

Aamantran	**Toms River Twp**	23
Aangan	**Freehold Twp**	23
Akbar	**Edison**	18
Alessio 426	**Metuchen**	20
Allendale B&G	**Allendale**	16
Amiya	**Jersey City**	21
Assembly	**Englewood Cliffs**	16
☑ Black Forest Inn	**Stanhope**	23
Bombay Curry	**Basking Ridge**	⌐
Bombay Gardens	**E Brunswick**	22
Café Gallery	**Burlington**	21
Chand Palace	**Parsippany**	22
Copeland	**Morristown**	25
NEW Embers Grill	**Cherry Hill**	⌐
Gagan Bistro	**Marlton**	⌐
House of Blues	**A.C.**	16
Hunt Club	**Summit**	20
India on Hudson	**Hoboken**	19
☑ Karma Kafe	**Hoboken**	25
Kaya's Kitchen	**Belmar**	⌐
Lambertville Station	**Lambertville**	17
Madeleine's	**Northvale**	24
Madison B&G	**Hoboken**	21
☑ Manor	**W Orange**	23
Matisse	**Belmar**	22
McLoone's	**multi.**	17
Mehndi	**Morristown**	⌐
Mill/Spring Lake	**Spring Lake Hts**	20
Moghul	**Edison**	24
Moksha	**Edison**	22
Molly Pitcher	**Red Bank**	22
Neelam	**multi.**	18
Noodle Hse.	**N Brunswick**	19
☑ Old Man Rafferty's	**New Bruns.**	19
Passage to India	**Lawrenceville**	23
Pierre's	**Morristown**	23
Raagini	**Mountainside**	22
Rod's Steak	**Convent Station**	21
Rupee Room	**N Brunswick**	⌐
Saffron	**E Hanover**	23
Salt Creek	**Rumson**	20
Savannah's	**Stockholm**	⌐

Shanghai Jazz | **Madison**	21
Smithville Inn | **Smithville**	18
Strip House | **Livingston**	23
Terrace Rest. | **Short Hills**	22
Waterfront Buffet | **A.C.**	17

BUSINESS DINING

NEW Aglio | **Metuchen**	–
Assembly | **Englewood Cliffs**	16
Benihana | **multi.**	–
Café Azzurro | **Peapack**	–
Z Chez Catherine | **Westfield**	27
Copeland | **Morristown**	25
NEW Daryl | **New Bruns.**	–
Z David Burke | **Rumson**	26
NEW Divino | **Berkeley Hts**	–
NEW Due Terre | **Bernardsville**	–
NEW Embers Grill | **Cherry Hill**	–
NEW Equus | **Bernardsville**	–
Z Fascino | **Montclair**	26
NEW 55 Main | **Flemington**	–
Fiorino | **Summit**	23
NEW Fuji | **Haddonfield**	–
Gallagher's Steak | **A.C.**	22
Gladstone Tavern | **Gladstone**	–
Z Highlawn | **W Orange**	24
Ho-Ho-Kus Inn | **Ho-Ho-Kus**	21
I Cavallini | **Colts Neck**	25
Jamie's | **Clifton**	–
Kitchen 233 | **Westmont**	22
K.O.B.E. | **Holmdel**	25
Lu Nello | **Cedar Grove**	25
Manhattan Steak | **Oakhurst**	22
Z McCormick/Schmick | **Cherry Hill**	20
Mill/Spring Lake | **Spring Lake Hts**	20
NEW Mi Sueño | **Middlesex**	–
Moksha | **Edison**	22
Morton's Steak | **Hackensack**	24
Old Homestead | **A.C.**	25
Panico's | **New Bruns.**	24
Passage to India | **Lawrenceville**	23
Phillips Seafood | **A.C.**	–
Pierre's | **Morristown**	23
Z Pluckemin Inn | **Bedminster**	25
Portofino | **Tinton Falls**	25

Raven & Peach | **Fair Haven**	24
Z River Palm | **multi.**	25
Roots Steak | **Summit**	–
Z Sirena | **Long Branch**	23
Smoke Chophse. | **Englewood**	22
Specchio | **A.C.**	25
NEW Stonehouse | **Warren**	–
Stony Hill Inn | **Hackensack**	23
NEW Tabor Rd. | **Morris Plains**	–
NEW Thyme Rest. | **Phillipsburg**	–
Union Station | **Phillipsburg**	–
NEW Victor's Pub | **Camden**	–
Vine | **Basking Ridge**	22
Wasabi | **Somerville**	24

BYO

Aamantran | **Toms River Twp**	23
Aangan | **Freehold Twp**	23
Aby's | **Matawan**	22
Acacia | **Lawrenceville**	25
NEW Aglio | **Metuchen**	–
Z Ajihei | **Princeton**	26
Alan@594 | **Upper Montclair**	20
Aldo & Gianni | **S Hackensack**	21
Alessio 426 | **Metuchen**	20
Alexander's | **Cape May**	24
Ali Baba | **Hoboken**	20
Aligado Asian | **Hazlet**	23
Alisa Cafe | **Cherry Hill**	22
Allen's Clam | **New Gretna**	–
Amazing Hot Dog | **Verona**	22
NEW Anatolia's | **Cliffside Pk**	–
Andaman | **Morristown**	23
Anjelica's | **Sea Bright**	25
Anna's Italian | **Middletown**	22
Anthony David's | **Hoboken**	25
Anthony's | **Haddon Hts**	23
Z Aozora | **Montclair**	25
Aquila Cucina | **New Providence**	21
Asia Star Cafe | **Tinton Falls**	–
A Tavola | **Old Bridge**	23
Athenian Gdn. | **Galloway Twp**	23
NEW A Toute Heure | **Cranford**	–
Avon Pavilion | **Avon-by-Sea**	18
Bamboo Leaf | **multi.**	24

🆕 Bank 34 | **Somerville**	‑
Barnacle Ben's | **Moorestown**	19
Barone's | **multi.**	20
Barrel's | **multi.**	19
☑ Basilico | **Millburn**	23
☑ Baumgart's Café | **multi.**	19
☑ Bay Ave. | **Highlands**	28
Bay Head Bistro | **Bay Hd.**	21
Bayou Cafe | **Manasquan**	23
BayPoint Prime | **Pt. Pleas. Bch**	24
Bazzini | **Ridgewood**	21
Bella Sogno | **Bradley Bch**	21
Benito's | **Chester**	24
Bienvenue | **Red Bank**	24
Bistro at Red Bank | **Red Bank**	21
Bistro 44 | **Toms River**	25
☑ Bistro Olé | **Asbury Pk**	25
🆕 Blackbird | **Collingswood**	‑
☑ Black Duck | **W Cape May**	26
Black Forest | **Allentown**	19
Black Trumpet | **Spring Lake**	23
Blu | **Montclair**	25
Blue | **Surf City**	23
☑ Blue Bottle | **Hopewell**	27
Blue Fish | **Flemington**	20
☑ Blue Point | **Princeton**	25
Bobby Chez | **multi.**	25
Bombay Curry | **Basking Ridge**	‑
Bombay Gardens | **E Brunswick**	22
Bosphorus | **Lake Hiawatha**	22
Boulevard Grille | **Mahwah**	18
Brandl. | **Belmar**	24
Brasilia | **Newark**	23
Brioso | **Marlboro**	23
Brix 67 | **Summit**	18
Brooklyn's Pizza | **multi.**	22
Brothers Moon | **Hopewell**	22
Cafe Arugula | **S Orange**	20
Cafe at Rosemont | **Rosemont**	22
Café Azzurro | **Peapack**	‑
Cafe Coloré | **Freehold Twp**	21
Cafe Graziella | **Hillsborough**	22
Cafe Loren | **Avalon**	25
☑ Cafe Matisse | **Rutherford**	27
Cafe Metro | **Denville**	21
☑ Cafe Panache | **Ramsey**	28
California Grill | **Flemington**	20
Caneel Bay | **Harvey Cedars**	17
Capt'n Ed's | **Pt. Pleas.**	19
Casa Maya | **multi.**	20
Casa Solar | **Belmar**	25
Casona | **Collingswood**	24
Chand Palace | **Parsippany**	22
Chao Phaya | **multi.**	23
Charrito's | **multi.**	24
☑ Chef's Table | **Franklin Lakes**	28
Chef Vola's | **A.C.**	26
Chez Elena Wu | **Voorhees**	24
Chophouse | **Gibbsboro**	23
Chowpatty | **Iselin**	‑
Christie's | **Howell**	24
Christopher's | **Colts Neck**	21
Claude's | **N Wildwood**	25
Coconut Bay | **Voorhees**	21
Copeland | **Morristown**	25
Copper Canyon | **Atlantic H.**	25
Corso 98 | **Montclair**	21
Creole Cafe | **Sewell**	27
Cuban Pete's | **Montclair**	17
Cucina Rosa | **Cape May**	23
☑ CulinAriane | **Montclair**	27
Cup Joint | **Hoboken**	20
DabbaWalla | **Summit**	19
da Filippo | **Somerville**	24
Dai-Kichi | **Upper Montclair**	22
🆕 D & L BBQ | **Asbury Pk**	‑
Dante's | **Mendham**	21
Dayi'nin Yeri | **Cliffside Pk**	‑
☑ DeLorenzo's | **multi.**	28
Dim Sum Dynasty | **Ridgewood**	21
Doo Rae Myun Ok | **Fort Lee**	21
🆕 Dream Café | **Cherry Hill**	‑
Drew's Bayshore | **Keyport**	28
🆕 Due Terre | **Bernardsville**	‑
Dune | **Margate**	‑
Edo Sushi | **Pennington**	20
El Azteca | **Mt Laurel**	17
Elements Asia | **Lawrenceville**	23
Elements | **Haddon Hts**	21
El Familiar | **Toms River Twp**	‑
☑ El Meson | **Freehold**	24
Epernay | **Montclair**	21

Eppes Essen | **Livingston**	18
Eurasian Eatery | **Red Bank**	20
Z Far East Taste | **Eatontown**	26
Z Fascino | **Montclair**	26
Fedora Cafe | **Lawrenceville**	19
Ferrari's | **Freehold Twp**	22
Z Ferry Hse. | **Princeton**	25
NEW 55 Main | **Flemington**	–
Five Guys | **Watchung**	–
503 Park | **Scotch Plains**	20
Food/Thought | **Marlton**	24
Z 410 Bank St. | **Cape May**	27
Frankie Fed's | **Freehold Twp**	20
Frescos | **Cape May**	24
Fresco Steak | **Milltown**	23
NEW Fuji | **Haddonfield**	–
Full Moon | **Lambertville**	17
NEW Fusion | **Flemington**	–
Z Gables, The | **Beach Haven**	26
Gaetano's | **Red Bank**	19
Gagan Bistro | **Marlton**	–
Gallagher's Steak | **A.C.**	22
Garlic Rose | **Madison**	21
Gazelle Café | **Ridgewood**	–
Gianna's | **Atlantic H.**	25
Ginger & Spice | **Ramsey**	–
Ginger Thai | **Freehold Twp**	15
Girasole | **Bound Brook**	25
Gladstone Tavern | **Gladstone**	–
Grill 73 | **Bernardsville**	22
GRUB Hut | **Manville**	–
Habana Latin | **Ridgefield Pk**	–
Hamilton's | **Lambertville**	24
Harvey Cedars | **multi.**	22
Hunan Spring | **Springfield**	19
Ichiban | **Princeton**	17
Ikko | **Brick**	22
Z Il Mondo | **Madison**	25
Indigo Smoke | **Montclair**	22
Isabella's | **Westfield**	22
Island Palm Grill | **Spring Lake**	18
Z It's Greek To Me | **multi.**	18
Jack Cooper's | **Edison**	19
Java Moon | **multi.**	19
NEW Javier's | **Haddonfield**	–
Jerry & Harvey's | **Marlboro**	18

Joel's Malibu | **Ridgewood**	–
Joe's Peking | **Marlton**	23
Jose's | **Spring Lake Hts**	22
Jose's Cantina | **multi.**	19
Juanito's | **multi.**	23
NEW Kanji Steak | **Tinton Falls**	–
Kaptan | **Hackettstown**	–
Karen & Rei's | **Clermont**	27
Kaya's Kitchen | **Belmar**	–
NEW KC's | **Mendham**	–
Kibitz Room | **Cherry Hill**	24
K.O.B.E. | **Holmdel**	25
Konbu | **Manalapan**	25
Krave Café | **Newton**	–
Kunkel's | **Haddon Hts**	20
Kuzina by Sofia | **Cherry Hill**	–
Labrador | **Normandy Bch**	23
La Campagna | **multi.**	24
La Campagne | **Cherry Hill**	24
Laceno Italian | **Voorhees**	25
La Cipollina | **Freehold**	23
La Focaccia | **Summit**	24
Z La Isla | **Hoboken**	26
La Pastaria | **multi.**	19
La Scala | **Somerville**	22
La Spiaggia | **Ship Bottom**	26
Latitude 40N | **Pt. Pleas. Bch**	23
Z Latour | **Ridgewood**	27
Le Fandy | **Fair Haven**	26
Z Le Rendez-Vous | **Kenilworth**	26
Lilly's/Canal | **Lambertville**	21
Limestone Cafe | **Peapack**	22
Little Café | **Voorhees**	25
Little Saigon | **A.C.**	–
Little Tuna | **Haddonfield**	20
Lodos | **New Milford**	21
Look See | **Ramsey**	19
Z Lorena's | **Maplewood**	27
Lotus Cafe | **Hackensack**	24
LouCás | **Edison**	24
Luchento's | **Millstone**	20
Luka's | **Ridgefield Pk**	22
Madame Claude | **Jersey City**	23
Mad Batter | **Cape May**	21
Madeleine's | **Northvale**	24
Magic Pot | **Edgewater**	19

Mahzu	**multi.**	22
Main St. Bistro	**Freehold**	21
Malabar House	**Piscataway**	–
🆕 Manna	**Margate**	–
Manon	**Lambertville**	25
Margherita's	**Hoboken**	22
Market Roost	**Flemington**	22
Marmara	**Manalapan**	–
Marra's	**Ridgewood**	20
Martino's	**Somerville**	21
Matisse	**Belmar**	22
Matt's Rooster	**Flemington**	25
Meemah	**Edison**	24
Megu Sushi	**Cherry Hill**	22
Meil's	**Stockton**	23
🅉 Mélange	**Cherry Hill**	26
Mexico Lindo	**Brick**	28
Meyersville Inn	**Gillette**	–
Michael's Cucina	**Manalapan**	19
Midori	**Denville**	24
Mie Thai	**Woodbridge**	25
Mignon Steak	**Rutherford**	23
Mikado	**multi.**	22
Ming	**Edison**	23
🆕 Mirabella	**Cherry Hill**	–
🆕 Mi Sueño	**Middlesex**	–
Moghul	**Edison**	24
🅉 Mojave Grille	**Westfield**	24
Monster Sushi	**Summit**	19
Saigon R./Mo' Pho	**multi.**	24
Morgan Fishery	**S Amboy**	–
Mr. Chu	**E Hanover**	22
Mud City	**Manahawkin**	21
My Little Greek	**Freehold Twp**	–
Navesink Fishery	**Navesink**	24
Neelam	**multi.**	18
New Main Taste	**Chatham**	23
🆕 Next Door	**Montclair**	–
Nha Trang Pl.	**Jersey City**	24
Niecy's	**S Orange**	20
Nobi	**Toms River Twp**	25
No. 9	**Lambertville**	24
Noodle Hse.	**N Brunswick**	19
Nori	**multi.**	22
Norma's	**Cherry Hill**	21
Nouveau Sushi	**Montclair**	25

Nunzio	**Collingswood**	23
Oasis Grill	**Cherry Hill**	25
Octopus's Gard.	**Stafford**	22
Orbis Bistro	**Upper Montclair**	22
🅉 Origin	**multi.**	26
Osteria Dante	**Red Bank**	19
Osteria Giotto	**Montclair**	25
Ota-Ya	**Lambertville**	23
Oyako Tso's	**Freehold**	21
Pamir	**Morristown**	21
Passionne	**Montclair**	23
Pasta Fresca	**Shrewsbury**	22
Penang	**multi.**	20
🅉 Peter Shields	**Cape May**	26
Pho Binh	**Jersey City**	–
Piquant Bread	**New Bruns.**	–
Pithari Taverna	**Highland Pk**	–
Pizzicato	**Marlton**	20
Pop Shop	**Collingswood**	18
Raagini	**Mountainside**	22
Radicchio	**Ridgewood**	23
Raimondo's	**Ship Bottom**	23
Raymond's	**Montclair**	21
Ray's	**Little Silver**	23
Rebecca's	**Edgewater**	24
Red's Lobster	**Pt. Pleas. Bch**	24
Restaurant L	**Allendale**	–
Richard's	**Long Branch**	20
Rick's	**Lambertville**	–
Ritz Seafood	**Voorhees**	24
Roberto's	**Beach Haven**	22
Robongi	**Hoboken**	25
Rocca	**Glen Rock**	22
Roots Steak	**Summit**	–
Rosemary & Sage	**Riverdale**	26
Ruga	**Oakland**	20
Rupee Room	**N Brunswick**	–
🅉 Ruth's Chris	**multi.**	24
Sabor	**N Bergen**	22
🅉 Saddle River Inn	**Saddle R.**	27
Saffron	**E Hanover**	23
🅉 Sagami	**Collingswood**	26
🆕 Sage	**Ventnor**	–
Sakura-Bana	**Ridgewood**	25
Sakura Spring	**Cherry Hill**	23
Salt Creek	**Princeton**	20

San Remo | **Shrewsbury**	22
Sapori | **Collingswood**	24
Sapo Verde | **Atlantic H.**	-
Savanna | **Red Bank**	20
SAWA Steak | **multi.**	22
Sens Asian | **S Brunswick**	22
☑ Serenade | **Chatham**	27
Settebello | **Morristown**	22
Seven Hills | **Highland Pk**	21
Shaker Cafe | **Flemington**	-
Shanghai Jazz | **Madison**	21
Shogun | **Wall**	18
Shumi | **Somerville**	25
Siam | **Lambertville**	21
Siam Garden | **Red Bank**	23
Silver Oak Bistro | **Ridgewood**	23
Simply Radishing | **Lawrenceville**	18
☑ Sirena | **Long Branch**	23
Sirin | **Morristown**	22
Siri's | **Cherry Hill**	25
Sister Sue's | **Asbury Pk**	21
Smoke Chophse. | **Englewood**	22
Sogno | **Red Bank**	23
Soho 33 | **Madison**	19
Solo Bella | **Jackson**	21
Somsak/Taan | **Voorhees**	23
Sono Sushi | **Middletown**	26
Sophie's Bistro | **Somerset**	22
Soufflé | **Summit**	23
NEW South St. Steak | **Freehold**	-
Spargo's Grille | **Manalapan**	25
Spike's | **Pt. Pleas. Bch**	22
Sri Thai | **Hoboken**	24
Sumo | **Wall**	-
Sunny Gdn. | **W Windsor**	22
Surf Taco | **multi.**	20
Sushi by Kazu | **Howell**	28
Sushi Lounge | **Totowa**	24
Table 8 | **Montclair**	23
Tacconelli's | **Maple Shade**	24
☑ Taka | **Asbury Pk**	26
Taqueria | **Jersey City**	20
Taro | **Montclair**	21
Taste of Asia | **Chatham**	21
Tattoni's | **Hamilton Twp**	-

Ted's on Main | **Medford**	-
Thai Chef | **Montclair**	21
Thai Kitchen | **multi.**	23
Thai Thai | **Stirling**	25
NEW Thai Tida | **Lambertville**	-
Theresa's | **Westfield**	23
Thyme Square | **Red Bank**	21
Tim Schafer's | **Morristown**	25
Tina Louise | **Carlstadt**	24
Tisha's | **Cape May**	25
NEW Tokyo Bleu | **Cinnaminson**	-
Tomo's Cuisine | **Little Falls**	-
Tortilla Press | **Collingswood**	23
Tortuga's | **Princeton**	21
Tsuki | **Bernardsville**	22
Tuptim | **Montclair**	22
Underground Café | **Princeton**	13
☑ Union Park | **Cape May**	26
Vanthia's | **W Cape May**	-
Village Gourmet | **Rutherford**	21
Village Green | **Ridgewood**	25
NEW Vivas | **Belmar**	-
Wasabi | **E Brunswick**	24
Water Lily | **Collingswood**	24
West Lake | **Matawan**	25
☑ Whispers | **Spring Lake**	27
Wild Ginger | **Englewood**	25
Wondee's Thai | **Hackensack**	-
Wonder Seafood | **Edison**	24
Word of Mouth | **Collingswood**	24
Ya Ya Noodles | **Skillman**	-
Yellow Fin | **Surf City**	25
Yumi | **Sea Bright**	26
Zafra | **Hoboken**	24

CATERING

Aamantran | **Toms River Twp**	23
Aangan | **Freehold Twp**	23
☑ Amanda's | **Hoboken**	26
Andaman | **Morristown**	23
☑ André's | **Newton**	27
Anjelica's | **Sea Bright**	25
Anthony David's | **Hoboken**	25
Athenian Gdn. | **Galloway Twp**	23
☑ Augustino's | **Hoboken**	26
Barone's | **multi.**	20

Ⓩ Bernards Inn | **Bernardsville**	26
Bombay Gardens | **E Brunswick**	22
Brioso | **Marlboro**	23
Brothers Moon | **Hopewell**	22
Cafe Loren | **Avalon**	25
Ⓩ Cafe Matisse | **Rutherford**	27
Ⓩ Cafe Panache | **Ramsey**	28
Caffe Aldo | **Cherry Hill**	23
Casa Dante | **Jersey City**	22
Catelli | **Voorhees**	24
Chowpatty | **Iselin**	-
Ⓩ Cucharamama | **Hoboken**	26
da Filippo | **Somerville**	24
Dock's Oyster | **A.C.**	26
Doris & Ed's | **Highlands**	25
Eppes Essen | **Livingston**	18
Esty Street | **Park Ridge**	23
Ⓩ Far East Taste | **Eatontown**	26
Ⓩ Ferry Hse. | **Princeton**	25
Filomena | **Berlin**	20
Ⓩ Frog/Peach | **New Bruns.**	26
Ⓩ Gables, The | **Beach Haven**	26
Girasole | **Bound Brook**	25
Ⓩ Grand Cafe | **Morristown**	25
Hamilton's | **Lambertville**	24
Harvest Moon | **Ringoes**	24
Joe's Peking | **Marlton**	23
Kibitz Room | **Cherry Hill**	24
La Campagne | **Cherry Hill**	24
Le Petit Chateau | **Bernardsville**	25
Limestone Cafe | **Peapack**	22
Little Café | **Voorhees**	25
Little Tuna | **Haddonfield**	20
Makeda | **New Bruns.**	23
Market Roost | **Flemington**	22
Mattar's | **Allamuchy**	24
Ming | **Edison**	23
Moghul | **Edison**	24
Ⓩ Moonstruck | **Asbury Pk**	24
Morton's Steak | **Hackensack**	24
Mud City | **Manahawkin**	21
Ⓩ Nicholas | **Middletown**	29
No. 9 | **Lambertville**	24
Norma's | **Cherry Hill**	21
Ⓩ Ombra | **A.C.**	25
Ⓩ Origin | **multi.**	26

Ⓩ Ram's Head Inn | **Galloway**	26
Rebecca's | **Edgewater**	24
Robongi | **Hoboken**	25
Rosemary & Sage | **Riverdale**	26
Saigon R./Mo' Pho | **Englewood**	24
Siri's | **Cherry Hill**	25
Squan Tavern | **Manasquan**	19
Stage Hse. | **Scotch Plains**	23
Ⓩ Stage Left | **New Bruns.**	26
Tim Schafer's | **Morristown**	25
Tina Louise | **Carlstadt**	24
Ⓩ Washington Inn | **Cape May**	26
Ⓩ Whispers | **Spring Lake**	27
Zafra | **Hoboken**	24

CELEBRITY CHEFS

Anton's/Swan | *Chris Connors* | **Lambertville**	22
Ⓩ Avenue | *Antonio Mora* | **Long Branch**	22
Ⓩ Bay Ave. | *Joe Romanowski* | **Highlands**	28
BayPoint Prime | *Dennis Foy* | **Pt. Pleas. Bch**	24
Ⓩ Bernards Inn | *Corey Heyer* | **Bernardsville**	26
Blu | *Zod Arifai* | **Montclair**	25
Bobby Flay Steak | *Bobby Flay* | **A.C.**	24
Ⓩ Cafe Panache | *Kevin Kohler* | **Ramsey**	28
Ⓩ Chef's Table | *Claude Baills* | **Franklin Lakes**	28
Copeland | *Thomas Ciszak* | **Morristown**	25
Ⓩ Cucharamama | *Maricel Presilla* | **Hoboken**	26
NEW Daryl | *David Drake* | **New Bruns.**	-
Ⓩ David Burke | *David Burke* | **Rumson**	26
Ⓩ David Drake | *David Drake* | **Rahway**	27
Ⓩ Fascino | *Ryan DePersio* | **Montclair**	26
NEW Fuji | *Matt Ito* | **Haddonfield**	-
Karen & Rei's | *Karen Nelson* | **Clermont**	27

Kitchen 233 | *Chris Painter* | **Westmont** | 22

☑ Latour | *Michael Latour* | **Ridgewood** | 27

Le Petit Chateau | *Scott Cutaneo* | **Bernardsville** | 25

☑ Lorena's | *Humberto Campos* | **Maplewood** | 27

☑ Mélange | *Joe Brown* | **Cherry Hill** | 26

Mia | *G. Perrier, C. Scarduzio* | **A.C.** | 26

☑ Nicholas | *Nicholas Harary* | **Middletown** | 29

Nunzio | *Nunzio Patruno* | **Collingswood** | 23

☑ Ombra | *James Hennessey* | **A.C.** | 25

Orbis Bistro | *Nancy Caballes* | **Upper Montclair** | 22

☑ Perryville Inn | *Paul Ingenito* | **Union Twp** | 26

Porto Leggero | *M. Cetrulo, A. Stella* | **Jersey City** | 23

☑ Scalini Fedeli | *Michael Cetrulo* | **Chatham** | 27

☑ SeaBlue | *Michael Mina* | **A.C.** | 27

☑ Serenade | *James Laird* | **Chatham** | 27

Silver Oak Bistro | *Gary Needham* | **Ridgewood** | 23

Specchio | *James Hennessey* | **A.C.** | 25

Wolfgang Puck | *Wolfgang Puck* | **A.C.** | 23

Zafra | *Maricel Presilla* | **Hoboken** | 24

CHILD-FRIENDLY

(Alternatives to the usual fast-food places; * children's menu available)

Aby's* | **Matawan** | 22

Alisa Cafe | **Cherry Hill** | 22

☑ Amanda's | **Hoboken** | 26

☑ André's | **Newton** | 27

Anjelica's | **Sea Bright** | 25

Axelsson's* | **Cape May** | 22

Bahama Breeze* | **Cherry Hill** | 16

Bamboo Leaf | **Bradley Bch** | 24

Bareli's | **Secaucus** | 23

Barone's* | **multi.** | 20

☑ Baumgart's Café* | **multi.** | 19

Bazzini* | **Ridgewood** | 21

Bell's | **Lambertville** | 19

Bell's Mansion* | **Stanhope** | 18

Beyti Kebab | **Union City** | 24

Big Ed's BBQ* | **Old Bridge** | 17

☑ Black Duck | **W Cape May** | 26

☑ Black Forest Inn | **Stanhope** | 23

Blue | **Surf City** | 23

☑ Blue Point* | **Princeton** | 25

Bobby Chez | **multi.** | 25

Bombay Gardens | **E Brunswick** | 22

Braddock's* | **Medford** | 22

Brioso | **Marlboro** | 23

Cabin* | **Howell** | 18

Cafe Loren | **Avalon** | 25

Capriccio | **A.C.** | 25

Casa Dante | **Jersey City** | 22

Casa Giuseppe | **Iselin** | 24

Casa Vasca | **Newark** | 24

Catelli | **Voorhees** | 24

Cenzino | **Oakland** | 24

Chao Phaya | **Somerville** | 23

☑ Cheesecake Factory | **multi.** | 19

Chengdu 46 | **Clifton** | 24

Christie's* | **Howell** | 24

Clydz | **New Bruns.** | 23

Copper Fish* | **Cape May** | 20

☑ Cucharamama | **Hoboken** | 26

da Filippo | **Somerville** | 24

Dock's Oyster* | **A.C.** | 26

E & V | **Paterson** | 24

El Azteca* | **Mt Laurel** | 17

Elements | **Haddon Hts** | 21

Elephant/Castle* | **Cherry Hill** | 10

☑ El Meson* | **Freehold** | 24

Espo's* | **Raritan** | 21

Esty Street | **Park Ridge** | 23

☑ Far East Taste | **Eatontown** | 26

Filomena* | **multi.** | 20

Food/Thought* | **Marlton** | 24

☑ Fornos of Spain | **Newark** | 23

☑ 410 Bank St. | **Cape May** | 27

Frankie Fed's* | **Freehold Twp** | 20

Frenchtown Inn | **Frenchtown** | 23

☑ Grand Cafe | **Morristown**	25
Harvest Moon | **Ringoes**	24
Homestead Inn | **Trenton**	23
Ikko* | **Brick**	22
Inn/Hawke* | **Lambertville**	18
☑ It's Greek To Me* | **multi.**	18
Java Moon* | **multi.**	19
Kibitz Room* | **Cherry Hill**	24
La Campagne* | **Cherry Hill**	24
Laceno Italian | **Voorhees**	25
La Esperanza* | **Lindenwold**	24
La Scala | **Somerville**	22
☑ Legal Sea Foods* | **multi.**	20
Little Tuna | **Haddonfield**	20
Lu Nello | **Cedar Grove**	25
☑ Manor | **W Orange**	23
Margherita's | **Hoboken**	22
Meil's | **Stockton**	23
☑ Mélange | **Cherry Hill**	26
Mexican Food* | **Marlton**	18
Mexico Lindo* | **Brick**	28
Midori | **Denville**	24
Mie Thai | **Woodbridge**	25
Mikado | **Cherry Hill**	22
Ming | **Edison**	23
Moghul | **Edison**	24
Mud City* | **Manahawkin**	21
Nag's Head* | **Ocean City**	26
Navesink Fishery | **Navesink**	24
New Main Taste | **Chatham**	23
No. 9 | **Lambertville**	24
Norma's* | **Cherry Hill**	21
Nunzio* | **Collingswood**	23
Opah Grille* | **Gladstone**	24
Ota-Ya | **Lambertville**	23
Panico's | **New Bruns.**	24
☑ Park/Orchard* | **E Rutherford**	22
Passage to India | **Lawrenceville**	23
☑ P.F. Chang's | **Marlton**	21
Pierre's | **Morristown**	23
Pizzicato* | **Marlton**	20
Ponzio's* | **Cherry Hill**	16
Pop Shop* | **Collingswood**	18
Pub* | **Pennsauken**	18
Raimondo's* | **Ship Bottom**	23

☑ Ram's Head Inn* | **Galloway**	26
☑ Rat's | **Hamilton**	24
Rebecca's | **Edgewater**	24
Reservoir Tavern | **Boonton**	22
Ristorante Benito | **Union**	25
Ritz Seafood | **Voorhees**	24
Robongi | **Hoboken**	25
Rosemary & Sage | **Riverdale**	26
Ruga | **Oakland**	20
Sabor | **N Bergen**	22
Saffron | **E Hanover**	23
☑ Sagami | **Collingswood**	26
Saigon R./Mo' Pho | **Englewood**	24
SAWA Steak* | **Eatontown**	22
Shipwreck Grill | **Brielle**	25
Shumi | **Somerville**	25
Siri's | **Cherry Hill**	25
Sister Sue's | **Asbury Pk**	21
Sogno | **Red Bank**	23
SoHo on George | **New Bruns.**	23
Somsak/Taan | **Voorhees**	23
Sono Sushi* | **Middletown**	26
Steve & Cookie's | **Margate**	25
Surf Taco* | **multi.**	20
Sushi by Kazu | **Howell**	28
Thai Kitchen | **multi.**	23
Thai Thai | **Stirling**	25
Theresa's* | **Westfield**	23
Tina Louise | **Carlstadt**	24
Tomatoes | **Margate**	24
Tortilla Press* | **Collingswood**	23
Tre Figlio* | **Egg Harbor**	24
Tuckers* | **Beach Haven**	18
Verjus | **Maplewood**	25
Wasabi | **multi.**	24
West Lake | **Matawan**	25
☑ White Hse. | **A.C.**	27
Wild Ginger | **Englewood**	25
Word of Mouth | **Collingswood**	24
Zafra | **Hoboken**	24
☑ Zoe's | **Sparta**	26

DANCING

Acqua | **Raritan**	21
NEW Alstarz | **Bordentown**	-
Azúcar | **Jersey City**	19

Baja | **Jersey City**	20
Brickwall Tavern | **Asbury Pk**	19
Busch's Seafood | **Sea Isle City**	19
Cabin | **Howell**	18
Casa Dante | **Jersey City**	22
✓ CoccoLa | **Hillsborough**	22
Cuba Libre | **A.C.**	21
Delta's | **New Bruns.**	22
Echo | **Red Bank**	19
Filomena | **Berlin**	20
Hunt Club | **Summit**	20
Laguna Grill | **Brigantine**	22
Madeleine's | **Northvale**	24
✓ Manor | **W Orange**	23
Mill/Spring Lake | **Spring Lake Hts**	20
Mompou | **Newark**	20
Portuguese Manor | **Perth Amboy**	21
✓ Rat's | **Hamilton**	24
Restaurant | **Hackensack**	21
Sabor | **N Bergen**	22
Savannah's | **Stockholm**	–
✓ South City Grill | **multi.**	23
Verdigre | **New Bruns.**	22
Windansea | **Highlands**	20

DELIVERY/TAKEOUT

(D=delivery, T=takeout)

Aamantran | D, T | **Toms River Twp**	23
Aby's | D, T | **Matawan**	22
Alisa Cafe | T | **Cherry Hill**	22
Athenian Gdn. | T | **Galloway Twp**	23
Bahama Breeze | T | **Cherry Hill**	16
✓ Baumgart's Café | T | **multi.**	19
Bayou Cafe | D | **Manasquan**	23
Bell's | T | **Lambertville**	19
Belmont Tavern | T | **Belleville**	24
Beyti Kebab | T | **Union City**	24
Big Ed's BBQ | T | **Old Bridge**	17
Blue Danube | T | **Trenton**	22
Bobby Chez | T | **multi.**	25
Brooklyn's Pizza | T | **multi.**	22
Cafe at Rosemont | T | **Rosemont**	22
California Grill | T | **Flemington**	20

Casa Maya | T | **Meyersville**	20
Chao Phaya | T | **Somerville**	23
Chilangos | T | **Highlands**	21
Crown Palace | T | **multi.**	22
✓ DeLorenzo's | T | **Trenton**	28
El Familiar | T | **Toms River Twp**	–
✓ El Meson | T | **Freehold**	24
Eppes Essen | T | **Livingston**	18
✓ Far East Taste | T | **Eatontown**	26
Federici's | T | **Freehold**	21
Filomena | T | **multi.**	20
Frankie Fed's | T | **Freehold Twp**	20
Full Moon | T | **Lambertville**	17
Grimaldi's Pizza | D | **Hoboken**	25
Harvey Cedars | T | **Beach Haven**	22
Hunan Chinese | T | **Morris Plains**	23
India on Hudson | D | **Hoboken**	19
Indigo Smoke | T | **Montclair**	22
✓ It's Greek To Me | T | **multi.**	18
Java Moon | T | **multi.**	19
Je's | D, T | **Newark**	26
Joe's Peking | T | **Marlton**	23
Juanito's | T | **multi.**	23
✓ Karma Kafe | D | **Hoboken**	25
Komegashi | D, T | **Jersey City**	24
Limestone Cafe | T | **Peapack**	22
Los Amigos | T | **multi.**	23
Lotus Cafe | D | **Hackensack**	24
Madison B&G | T | **Hoboken**	21
Mahzu | T | **Aberdeen**	22
Margherita's | D | **Hoboken**	22
Market Roost | T | **Flemington**	22
Mastoris | T | **Bordentown**	19
Meemah | T | **Edison**	24
Meil's | T | **Stockton**	23
Memphis Pig Out | T | **Atlantic H.**	19
Mexico Lindo | T | **Brick**	28
Mie Thai | T | **Woodbridge**	25
Mikado | T | **Cherry Hill**	22
Moghul | T | **Edison**	24
New Main Taste | T | **Chatham**	23
Niecy's | T | **S Orange**	20
Nobi | T | **Toms River Twp**	25

Noodle Hse. | T | **N Brunswick** <u>19</u>

Norma's | T | **Cherry Hill** <u>21</u>

Z Old Man Rafferty's | T | <u>19</u>
multi.

Ota-Ya | T | **Lambertville** <u>23</u>

Pad Thai | T | **Highland Pk** <u>22</u>

Passage to India | T | <u>23</u>
Lawrenceville

Penang | D, T | **multi.** <u>20</u>

Z P.F. Chang's | T | **multi.** <u>21</u>

Raagini | T | **Mountainside** <u>22</u>

Reservoir Tavern | T | **Boonton** <u>22</u>

Richard's | T | **Long Branch** <u>20</u>

Robongi | D, T | **Hoboken** <u>25</u>

Saffron | D | **E Hanover** <u>23</u>

Saigon R./Mo' Pho | T | <u>24</u>
Englewood

Sakura-Bana | T | **Ridgewood** <u>25</u>

Seven Hills | T | **Highland Pk** <u>21</u>

Shogun | T | **multi.** <u>18</u>

Shumi | T | **Somerville** <u>25</u>

Siam | T | **Lambertville** <u>21</u>

Sono Sushi | T | **Middletown** <u>26</u>

Spike's | T | **Pt. Pleas. Bch** <u>22</u>

Sri Thai | D | **Hoboken** <u>24</u>

Sunny Gdn. | T | **W Windsor** <u>22</u>

Sushi Lounge | D, T | **Hoboken** <u>24</u>

Taste of Asia | T | **Chatham** <u>21</u>

Thai Chef | T | **multi.** <u>21</u>

Thai Kitchen | T | **multi.** <u>23</u>

Tina Louise | T | **Carlstadt** <u>24</u>

Tortuga's | T | **Princeton** <u>21</u>

Tuzzio's | T | **Long Branch** <u>21</u>

Vic's | T | **Bradley Bch** <u>20</u>

Wasabi | D, T | **multi.** <u>24</u>

West Lake | T | **Matawan** <u>25</u>

Z White Hse. | T | **A.C.** <u>27</u>

Wonder Seafood | T | **Edison** <u>24</u>

DESSERT

Aquila Cucina | **New Providence** <u>21</u>

Z Baumgart's Café | **multi.** <u>19</u>

Z Chakra | **Paramus** <u>21</u>

Z Cheesecake Factory | **multi.** <u>19</u>

Copeland | **Morristown** <u>25</u>

Z Fascino | **Montclair** <u>26</u>

Fedora Cafe | **Lawrenceville** <u>19</u>

Karen & Rei's | **Clermont** <u>27</u>

Z Old Man Rafferty's | **multi.** <u>19</u>

Raymond's | **Montclair** <u>21</u>

Robin's Nest | **Mt Holly** <u>22</u>

ENTERTAINMENT

(Call for days and times of
performances)

Atlantic B&G | jazz | <u>24</u>
S Seaside Pk

Bahama Breeze | Caribbean | <u>16</u>
Cherry Hill

Z Bernards Inn | piano | <u>26</u>
Bernardsville

Beyti Kebab | belly dancing | <u>24</u>
Union City

Blue Eyes | singer | **Sewell** <u>20</u>

Z Blue Point | jazz | **Princeton** <u>25</u>

Catelli | band | **Voorhees** <u>24</u>

da Filippo | piano | **Somerville** <u>24</u>

Dock's Oyster | piano | **A.C.** <u>26</u>

Z Ebbitt Room | jazz | <u>27</u>
Cape May

Filomena | varies | **multi.** <u>20</u>

Food/Thought | piano | **Marlton** <u>24</u>

Z Grand Cafe | piano | <u>25</u>
Morristown

Harvest Moon | piano | **Ringoes** <u>24</u>

Il Capriccio | piano | **Whippany** <u>26</u>

Indigo Smoke | jazz/R&B | <u>22</u>
Montclair

Lalezar | belly dancing | <u>-</u>
Montclair

Le Petit Chateau | varies | <u>25</u>
Bernardsville

Mattar's | piano | **Allamuchy** <u>24</u>

Makeda | funk/jazz | <u>23</u>
New Bruns.

Matisse | jazz | **Belmar** <u>22</u>

McLoone's | jazz/rock | <u>17</u>
Sea Bright

Molly Pitcher | piano | **Red Bank** <u>22</u>

Mompou | varies | **Newark** <u>20</u>

Z Moonstruck | jazz/piano | <u>24</u>
Asbury Pk

Norma's | belly dancing | <u>21</u>
Cherry Hill

Nova Terra | Latin | **New Bruns.** <u>22</u>

☑ Peter Shields	piano	**Cape May**	26
Pub	jazz	**Pennsauken**	18
☑ Ram's Head Inn	piano	**Galloway**	26
☑ Rat's	varies	**Hamilton**	24
Raven & Peach	guitar/piano	**Fair Haven**	24
Sabor	DJ	**multi.**	22
Shanghai Jazz	jazz	**Madison**	21
Shipwreck Grill	jazz	**Brielle**	25
Steve & Cookie's	varies	**Margate**	25
Tortilla Press	guitar	**Collingswood**	23
Tre Figlio	varies	**Egg Harbor**	24
Verve	varies	**Somerville**	23
Windansea	varies	**Highlands**	20

FAMILY-STYLE

Adega Grill	**Newark**	24
Carmine's	**A.C.**	20
Chef Vola's	**A.C.**	26
Cinque Figlie	**Whippany**	21
Joe's Peking	**Marlton**	23
Michael's Cucina	**Manalapan**	19
Pad Thai	**Highland Pk**	22
☑ P.F. Chang's	**multi.**	21
Spanish Tavern	**Mountainside**	22

FIREPLACES

Acqua	**Raritan**	21
Adega Grill	**Newark**	24
☑ Amanda's	**Hoboken**	26
Anna's Italian	**Middletown**	22
Anton's/Swan	**Lambertville**	22
☑ Arthur's	**N Brunswick**	18
☑ Avenue	**Long Branch**	22
Axia Taverna	**Tenafly**	21
Bareli's	**Secaucus**	23
Beau Steak	**Medford**	22
☑ Bernards Inn	**Bernardsville**	26
Berta's Chateau	**Wanaque**	22
☑ Black Forest Inn	**Stanhope**	23
Black Horse	**Mendham**	19
Black Trumpet	**Spring Lake**	23
Blue Pig Tavern	**Cape May**	20

Braddock's	**Medford**	22
Cabin	**Howell**	18
Casona	**Collingswood**	24
☑ Catherine Lombardi	**New Bruns.**	21
Chophouse	**Gibbsboro**	23
Christopher's	**Colts Neck**	21
Clark's Landing	**Pt. Pleas.**	17
Clydz	**New Bruns.**	23
Cork	**Westmont**	21
Crab's Claw	**Lavallette**	17
Cranbury Inn	**Cranbury**	17
☑ Ebbitt Room	**Cape May**	27
Eccola	**Parsippany**	23
Elephant/Castle	**Cherry Hill**	10
Europa/Monroe	**Monroe Twp**	–
Filomena	**multi.**	20
☑ Gables, The	**Beach Haven**	26
Giumarello's	**Westmont**	25
Gladstone Tavern	**Gladstone**	–
☑ Grand Cafe	**Morristown**	25
Grenville	**Bay Hd.**	21
Harry's Lobster	**Sea Bright**	22
Harvest Bistro	**Closter**	22
Harvest Moon	**Ringoes**	24
High St. Grill	**Mt Holly**	23
☑ Huntley Taverne	**Summit**	22
Il Michelangelo	**Boonton**	21
Inlet Café	**Highlands**	19
Inn at Millrace	**Hope**	21
Inn at Sugar Hill	**Mays Landing**	–
Inn/Hawke	**Lambertville**	18
Jamie's	**Clifton**	–
Karen & Rei's	**Clermont**	27
Kitchen 233	**Westmont**	22
Kunkel's	**Haddon Hts**	20
La Campagne	**Cherry Hill**	24
Laguna Grill	**Brigantine**	22
Mad Batter	**Cape May**	21
Mahogany Grille	**Manasquan**	23
Main St. Euro-Amer.	**Princeton**	18
Mastoris	**Bordentown**	19
McLoone's	**Sea Bright**	17
NEW Merchant Hse.	**Fairfield**	–
Metuchen Inn	**Metuchen**	22
Meyersville Inn	**Gillette**	–

Molly Pitcher | **Red Bank**	22
Nag's Head | **Ocean City**	26
Z Nauvoo Grill | **Fair Haven**	16
Neil's Oyster | **Highlands**	-
Nero's Grille | **Livingston**	17
NEW Park Ave. | **Union City**	-
Z Perryville Inn | **Union Twp**	26
Z Peter Shields | **Cape May**	26
Pheasants Land. | **Hillsborough**	17
P.J. Whelihan's | **Medford Lakes**	17
Plantation | **Harvey Cedars**	19
Z Pluckemin Inn | **Bedminster**	25
Portobello | **Oakland**	20
Posillipo | **Asbury Pk**	22
Pub | **Pennsauken**	18
Z Ram's Head Inn | **Galloway**	26
Z Rat's | **Hamilton**	24
Restaurant | **Hackensack**	21
Richie Cecere's | **Montclair**	21
Roberto's | **Beach Haven**	22
Roman Cafe | **Harrington Pk**	19
Salt Creek | **Princeton**	20
Savannah's | **Stockholm**	-
Scarborough Fair | **Wall**	20
Z Serenade | **Chatham**	27
Sergeantsville Inn | **Sergeantsville**	23
Settebello | **Morristown**	22
Seven Hills | **Highland Pk**	21
Shanghai Jazz | **Madison**	21
Smithville Inn | **Smithville**	18
Solaia | **Englewood**	20
Stage Hse. | **Scotch Plains**	23
Z Stage Left | **New Bruns.**	26
Steve & Cookie's | **Margate**	25
NEW Stonehouse | **Warren**	-
Sushi Lounge | **Totowa**	24
NEW Tabor Rd. | **Morris Plains**	-
NEW Tap Rm. | **Northfield**	-
Z 3 West | **Basking Ridge**	23
NEW Thyme Rest. | **Phillipsburg**	-
Tosca | **Kenilworth**	20
Trap Rock | **Berkeley Hts**	21
Tuckers | **Beach Haven**	18
NEW Undici | **Rumson**	-
Z Union Park | **Cape May**	26
Walpack Inn | **Wallpack**	19
Z Washington Inn | **Cape May**	26
Z Whispers | **Spring Lake**	27
Wolfgang Puck | **A.C.**	23
Yankee Doodle | **Princeton**	14

HISTORIC PLACES

(Year opened; * building)

1682 | Farnsworth Hse.* | **Bordentown**	21
1685 | Grand Colonial* | **Union Twp**	25
1697 | Lincroft Inn* | **Lincroft**	18
1734 | Sergeantsville Inn* | **Sergeantsville**	23
1737 | Stage Hse.* | **Scotch Plains**	23
1742 | Black Horse* | **Mendham**	19
1750 | Cranbury Inn* | **Cranbury**	17
1785 | Meyersville Inn* | **Gillette**	-
1787 | Smithville Inn* | **Smithville**	18
1790 | Ho-Ho-Kus Inn* | **Ho-Ho-Kus**	21
1800 | Bell's Mansion* | **Stanhope**	18
1800 | Cafe at Rosemont* | **Rosemont**	22
1800 | Robin's Nest* | **Mt Holly**	22
1800 | Tewksbury Inn* | **Oldwick**	22
1805 | Frenchtown Inn* | **Frenchtown**	23
1818 | Stony Hill Inn* | **Hackensack**	23
1823 | Braddock's* | **Medford**	22
1840 | David Drake* | **Rahway**	27
1840 | Milford Oyster Hse.* | **Milford**	-
1840 | Washington Inn* | **Cape May**	26
1843 | Metuchen Inn* | **Metuchen**	22
1847 | Gladstone Tavern* | **Gladstone**	-
1850 | Delta's* | **New Bruns.**	22
1850 | Light Horse* | **Jersey City**	22
1856 | Equus* | **Bernardsville**	-

1856 | High St. Grill* | **Mt Holly**	23
1856 | Il Michelangelo* |	21
Boonton	
1860 | Inn/Hawke* |	18
Lambertville	
1863 | Lambertville Station* |	17
Lambertville	
1864 | Renault Winery* |	22
Egg Harbor	
1865 | Park Ave.* | **Union City**	-
1868 | Rick's* | **Lambertville**	-
1870 | Silver Spring* | **Flanders**	23
1874 | Saddle River Inn* |	27
Saddle R.	
1879 | Ebbitt Room* | **Cape May**	27
1880 | Claude's* | **N Wildwood**	25
1880 | 410 Bank St.* | **Cape May**	27
1880 | Moonstruck* |	24
Asbury Pk	
1882 | Busch's Seafood |	19
Sea Isle City	
1882 | Mad Batter* | **Cape May**	21
1883 | Alexander's* | **Cape May**	24
1890 | Gables, The* |	26
Beach Haven	
1890 | Grenville* | **Bay Hd.**	21
1890 | Matt's Rooster* |	25
Flemington	
1890 | Red* | **Red Bank**	20
1890 | Whispers* | **Spring Lake**	27
1895 | Amanda's* | **Hoboken**	26
1895 | Elysian Cafe* | **Hoboken**	21
1895 | Limestone Cafe* |	22
Peapack	
1895 | Queen Victoria* |	-
Toms River	
1897 | Dock's Oyster | **A.C.**	26
1897 | Tap Rm. | **Northfield**	-
1900 | Athenian Gdn.* |	23
Galloway Twp	
1900 | Doris & Ed's* | **Highlands**	25
1900 | Scarborough Fair* | **Wall**	20
1903 | Columbia Inn* |	20
Montville	
1905 | Casona* | **Collingswood**	24
1906 | Onieal's* | **Hoboken**	19
1909 | Highlawn* | **W Orange**	24
1910 | Stage Left* | **New Bruns.**	26

1912 | Grill 73* | **Bernardsville**	22
1917 | Bahrs Landing |	15
Highlands	
1919 | Lahiere's | **Princeton**	21
1920 | 947 B&G* | **Clementon**	-
1920 | Ugly Mug* | **Cape May**	16
1921 | Chef Vola's | **A.C.**	26
1921 | Federici's | **Freehold**	21
1926 | Iberia | **Newark**	21
1926 | Spike's | **Pt. Pleas. Bch**	22
1927 | Berta's Chateau* |	22
Wanaque	
1928 | Molly Pitcher* |	22
Red Bank	
1929 | Hunt Club | **Summit**	20
1929 | Posillipo* | **Asbury Pk**	22
1930 | Anthony's* | **Haddon Hts**	23
1930 | Pheasants Land.* |	17
Hillsborough	
1932 | Lobster Hse. | **Cape May**	20
1932 | Spanish Tavern | **Newark**	22
1933 | Harry's Lobster |	22
Sea Bright	
1933 | Sammy's Cider |	21
Mendham	
1935 | Allendale B&G |	16
Allendale	
1935 | Angelo's | **A.C.**	20
1936 | Reservoir Tavern |	22
Boonton	
1936 | Steve & Cookie's* |	25
Margate	
1937 | Kinchley's Tavern |	21
Ramsey	
1937 | Yankee Doodle |	14
Princeton	
1938 | Mill/Spring Lake |	20
Spring Lake Hts	
1939 | Bell's | **Lambertville**	19
1939 | Holsten's | **Bloomfield**	-
1939 | Homestead Inn | **Trenton**	23
1939 | Solari's | **Hackensack**	21
1940 | La Spiaggia* |	26
Ship Bottom	
1941 | Conte's | **Princeton**	-
1941 | Walpack Inn* | **Wallpack**	19
1942 | Tuzzio's* | **Long Branch**	21
1945 | Berkeley | **S Seaside Pk**	18

1946	White Hse.*	A.C.	27
1947	DeLorenzo's	multi.	28
1947	Vic's	Bradley Bch	20
1948	Tick Tock*	Clifton	17
1950	Main St. Euro-Amer.*	Princeton	18
1951	Pub	Pennsauken	18
1951	Rod's Steak	Convent Station	21
1956	Arthur's	Morris Plains	18
1956	Manor	W Orange	23
1957	Eppes Essen	Livingston	18

HOTEL DINING

Alexander's Inn
   Alexander's | Cape May — 24

Blue Bay Inn
   Copper Canyon | Atlantic H. — 25

Borgata Hotel, Casino & Spa
   Bobby Flay Steak | A.C. — 24
   Old Homestead | A.C. — 25
   Z Ombra | A.C. — 25
   Z SeaBlue | A.C. — 27
   Specchio | A.C. — 25
   Tony Luke's | A.C. — -
   Wolfgang Puck | A.C. — 23

Caesars on the Boardwalk
   Mia | A.C. — 26

Carroll Villa Hotel
   Mad Batter | Cape May — 21

Clarion Hotel
   Elephant/Castle | Cherry Hill — 10

Congress Hall Hotel
   Blue Pig Tavern | Cape May — 20

Crowne Plaza Cherry Hill
   NEW Embers Grill | Cherry Hill — -

Crystal Springs Resort
   Restaurant Latour | Hamburg — -

daddy O
   daddy O | Long Beach — 18

Grand Summit Hotel
   Hunt Club | Summit — 20

Green Gables Inn
   Z Gables, The | Beach Haven — 26

Grenville Hotel
   Grenville | Bay Hd. — 21

Hewitt Wellington Hotel
   Z Whispers | Spring Lake — 27

Hilton at Short Hills
   Terrace Rest. | Short Hills — 22

Hilton Hotel
   Z Ruth's Chris | Parsippany — 24

Ho-Ho-Kus Inn
   Ho-Ho-Kus Inn | Ho-Ho-Kus — 21

Madison Hotel
   Rod's Steak | Convent Station — 21

Molly Pitcher Inn
   Molly Pitcher | Red Bank — 22

Nassau Inn
   Yankee Doodle | Princeton — 14

Ocean Club Condos
   Girasole | A.C. — 25

Ramada Inn
   NEW Indigo | N Brunswick — -

Resorts Atlantic City Casino
   Capriccio | A.C. — 25
   Gallagher's Steak | A.C. — 22

Robert Treat Hotel
   Maize | Newark — 21

Sandpiper Inn
   Black Trumpet | Spring Lake — 23

Sheraton Hotel
   Tun Tavern | A.C. — 18

Swan Hotel
   Anton's/Swan | Lambertville — 22

Quarter at the Tropicana
   Carmine's | A.C. — 20
   Cuba Libre | A.C. — 21

Victoria on Main
   NEW Queen Victoria | Toms River — -

Virginia Hotel
   Z Ebbitt Room | Cape May — 27

Westin Governor Morris
   Copeland | Morristown — 25

Westminster Hotel
   Strip House | Livingston — 23

Wilshire Grand
   Primavera | W Orange — 20

JACKET REQUIRED

Z Highlawn | **W Orange**	24
Z Manor | **W Orange**	23
Molly Pitcher | **Red Bank**	22

LATE DINING

(Weekday closing hour)

Allendale B&G | 1 AM | **Allendale**	16
Basil T's | 12 AM | **Red Bank**	20
Benny Tudino's | 12:45 AM | **Hoboken**	21
Brickwall Tavern | 1 AM | **Asbury Pk**	19
Carmine's | 12 AM | **A.C.**	20
Clydz | 1:30 AM | **New Bruns.**	23
Cuban Pete's | 12 AM | **Montclair**	17
Elephant/Castle | varies | **Cherry Hill**	10
House of Blues | 12 AM | **A.C.**	16
Iberia | 1:30 AM | **Newark**	21
Irish Pub | 24 hrs. | **A.C.**	18
Kinchley's Tavern | 12 AM | **Ramsey**	21
Lucky Bones | 1 AM | **Cape May**	18
Marie Nicole's | 12 AM | **Wildwood**	23
Mastoris | 1 AM | **Bordentown**	19
NEW 947 B&G | 12 AM | **Clementon**	–
NEW Park Ave. | 2 AM | **Union City**	–
Pete & Elda's | 12 AM | **Neptune City**	–
Z P.F. Chang's | varies | **A.C.**	21
P.J. Whelihan's | 2 AM | **multi.**	17
Ponzio's | 1 AM | **Cherry Hill**	16
Skylark Diner | 1 AM | **Edison**	19
So Moon Nan Jip | 3 AM | **Palisades Pk**	23
Surf Taco | varies | **Jackson**	20
Tick Tock | 24 hrs. | **Clifton**	17
Tony's | 3 AM | **A.C.**	–
Tun Tavern | varies | **A.C.**	18
NEW Victor's Pub | varies | **Camden**	–
WindMill, The | varies | **multi.**	–

MEET FOR A DRINK

Acqua | **Raritan**	21
Adega Grill | **Newark**	24
Arturo's | **Midland Pk**	22
Atlantic B&G | **S Seaside Pk**	24
Z Avenue | **Long Branch**	22
Barnacle Bill's | **Rumson**	21
Basil T's | **Red Bank**	20
Bell's | **Lambertville**	19
Black Horse | **Mendham**	19
Blue Pig Tavern | **Cape May**	20
Brickwall Tavern | **Asbury Pk**	19
Cenzino | **Oakland**	24
Charley's | **Long Branch**	19
Chilangos | **Highlands**	21
Circa | **High Bridge**	20
Clark's Landing | **Pt. Pleas.**	17
Continental | **A.C.**	–
Copper Canyon | **Atlantic H.**	25
Crab's Claw | **Lavallette**	17
Cuba Libre | **A.C.**	21
Z Cucharamama | **Hoboken**	26
daddy O | **Long Beach**	18
Danny's Steak | **Red Bank**	–
NEW Daryl | **New Bruns.**	–
Z David Burke | **Rumson**	26
Z David Drake | **Rahway**	27
NEW Divino | **Berkeley Hts**	–
NEW Due Terre | **Bernardsville**	–
Echo | **Red Bank**	19
NEW Embers Grill | **Cherry Hill**	–
NEW Equus | **Bernardsville**	–
Espo's | **Raritan**	21
Frankie & Johnnie | **Hoboken**	23
Gaslight | **Hoboken**	20
Gladstone Tavern | **Gladstone**	–
NEW Hotoke | **New Bruns.**	–
House of Blues | **A.C.**	16
Hunt Club | **Summit**	20
Z Huntley Taverne | **Summit**	22
NEW Indigo | **N Brunswick**	–
Inlet Café | **Highlands**	19
Inn/Hawke | **Lambertville**	18
Irish Pub | **A.C.**	18
Kitchen 233 | **Westmont**	22
Los Amigos | **multi.**	23

Lua | **Hoboken**	22
Marco & Pepe | **Jersey City**	22
Mkt. in the Middle | **Asbury Pk**	23
🔢 McCormick/Schmick | **Cherry Hill**	20
McLoone's | **Sea Bright**	17
Mediterra | **Princeton**	20
NEW Merchant Hse. | **Fairfield**	–
Metropolitan Cafe | **Freehold**	22
Mia | **A.C.**	26
Mompou | **Newark**	20
Neil's Oyster | **Highlands**	–
NEW 947 B&G | **Clementon**	–
Oddfellows | **Hoboken**	19
Old Bay | **New Bruns.**	17
🔢 Old Man Rafferty's | **multi.**	19
Onieal's | **Hoboken**	19
Opah Grille | **Gladstone**	24
NEW Ox | **Jersey City**	–
NEW Park Ave. | **Union City**	–
Pine Tavern | **Old Bridge**	22
P.J. Whelihan's | **multi.**	17
Plantation | **Harvey Cedars**	19
Quiet Man | **Dover**	22
Redstone | **Marlton**	–
Restaurant | **Hackensack**	21
Rod's Olde Irish | **Sea Girt**	19
Sallee Tee's | **Monmouth Bch**	21
Salt Creek | **Rumson**	20
Ship Inn | **Milford**	19
🔢 South City Grill | **multi.**	23
🔢 Stage Left | **New Bruns.**	26
NEW Stonehouse | **Warren**	–
Sushi Lounge | **Hoboken**	24
NEW Tabor Rd. | **Morris Plains**	–
Teak | **Red Bank**	23
Tewksbury Inn | **Oldwick**	22
NEW Thyme Rest. | **Phillipsburg**	–
NEW Tokyo Bleu | **Cinnaminson**	–
NEW Tortilla Press Cantina | **Pennsauken**	–
Trap Rock | **Berkeley Hts**	21
Triumph Brewing | **Princeton**	18
Tuckers | **Beach Haven**	18
Tun Tavern | **A.C.**	18

Ugly Mug | **Cape May**	16
NEW Undici | **Rumson**	–
Union Station | **Phillipsburg**	–
NEW Victor's Pub | **Camden**	–
Vine | **Basking Ridge**	22
Windansea | **Highlands**	20
Witherspoon Grill | **Princeton**	–
Wolfgang Puck | **A.C.**	23
Yankee Doodle | **Princeton**	14

MICROBREWERIES

Basil T's | **Red Bank**	20
Egan & Sons | **Montclair**	17
Ship Inn | **Milford**	19
Trap Rock | **Berkeley Hts**	21
Triumph Brewing | **Princeton**	18

OFFBEAT

Aangan | **Freehold Twp**	23
Aby's | **Matawan**	22
Akai Lounge | **Englewood**	23
Ali Baba | **Hoboken**	20
NEW Anatolia's | **Cliffside Pk**	–
Bangkok Garden | **Hackensack**	24
🔢 Baumgart's Café | **multi.**	19
Bayou Cafe | **Manasquan**	23
Beyti Kebab | **Union City**	24
Blue | **Surf City**	23
Blue Danube | **Trenton**	22
Bombay Curry | **Basking Ridge**	–
Casa Solar | **Belmar**	25
Chand Palace | **Parsippany**	22
Chao Phaya | **Somerville**	23
Charrito's | **Jersey City**	24
Chef Vola's | **A.C.**	26
Chilangos | **Highlands**	21
China Palace | **Middletown**	–
🔢 Cucharamama | **Hoboken**	26
DabbaWalla | **Summit**	19
Dayi'nin Yeri | **Cliffside Pk**	–
Doo Rae Myun Ok | **Fort Lee**	21
Elements Asia | **Lawrenceville**	23
🔢 El Meson | **Freehold**	24
🔢 Far East Taste | **Eatontown**	26
Fedora Cafe | **Lawrenceville**	19
Garlic Rose | **multi.**	21
Ginger & Spice | **Ramsey**	–

Grand Shanghai | **Edison**	21
Hard Grove | **Jersey City**	14
NEW Hotoke | **New Bruns.**	–
Z It's Greek To Me | **multi.**	18
Je's | **Newark**	26
Kaptan | **Hackettstown**	–
Z Karma Kafe | **Hoboken**	25
NEW KC's | **Mendham**	–
K.O.B.E. | **Holmdel**	25
Krakus | **Wallington**	–
La Esperanza | **Lindenwold**	24
Z La Isla | **Hoboken**	26
Little Café | **Voorhees**	25
Madame Claude | **Jersey City**	23
Mad Batter | **Cape May**	21
Makeda | **New Bruns.**	23
Malabar House | **Piscataway**	–
Manon | **Lambertville**	25
Marmara | **Manalapan**	–
Martino's | **Somerville**	21
Meemah | **Edison**	24
Meil's | **Stockton**	23
Mexico Lindo | **Brick**	28
Mie Thai | **Woodbridge**	25
Ming | **Edison**	23
Moghul | **Edison**	24
Moksha | **Edison**	22
Mompou | **Newark**	20
Navesink Fishery | **Navesink**	24
New Main Taste | **Chatham**	23
Nha Trang Pl. | **Jersey City**	24
Niecy's | **S Orange**	20
Norma's | **Cherry Hill**	21
Old Bay | **New Bruns.**	17
Ota-Ya | **Lambertville**	23
Pamir | **Morristown**	21
Z Park/Orchard | **E Rutherford**	22
Passage to India | **Lawrenceville**	23
Penang | **Edison**	20
Piquant Bread | **New Bruns.**	–
Pop Shop | **Collingswood**	18
Pub | **Pennsauken**	18
Raagini | **Mountainside**	22
Z Rat's | **Hamilton**	24
Rupee Room | **N Brunswick**	–
Saffron | **E Hanover**	23

Saigon R./Mo' Pho | **Englewood**	24
Sens Asian | **S Brunswick**	22
Seven Hills | **Highland Pk**	21
Shaker Cafe | **Flemington**	–
Siam | **Lambertville**	21
Siam Garden | **Red Bank**	23
Siri's | **Cherry Hill**	25
Sister Sue's | **Asbury Pk**	21
Somsak/Taan | **Voorhees**	23
Suez Canal | **Jersey City**	–
Sunny Gdn. | **W Windsor**	22
Z Taka | **Asbury Pk**	26
Taro | **Montclair**	21
Taste of Asia | **Chatham**	21
Teak | **Red Bank**	23
Tina Louise | **Carlstadt**	24
Water Lily | **Collingswood**	24
West Lake | **Matawan**	25
Wild Ginger | **Englewood**	25
Ya Ya Noodles | **Skillman**	–
Yumi | **Sea Bright**	26

OUTDOOR DINING

(G=garden; P=patio;
S=sidewalk; T=terrace)

Anthony David's | S | **Hoboken**	25
Anton's/Swan | P | **Lambertville**	22
Arthur's Landing | T | **Weehawken**	20
Atlantic B&G | P | **S Seaside Pk**	24
Avon Pavilion | T | **Avon-by-Sea**	18
Axelsson's | G | **Cape May**	22
Bahama Breeze | T | **Cherry Hill**	16
Bamboo Leaf | S | **Bradley Bch**	24
Barone's | P, S | **multi.**	20
Z Bernards Inn | T | **Bernardsville**	26
Blue | P | **Surf City**	23
Z Blue Point | P | **Princeton**	25
Bobby Chez | P | **Margate**	25
Brothers Moon | S | **Hopewell**	22
Café Gallery | T | **Burlington**	21
Z Cafe Matisse | G | **Rutherford**	27
Caffe Aldo | P | **Cherry Hill**	23
Z Cucharamama | S | **Hoboken**	26
Danny's Steak | S | **Red Bank**	–

Elysian Cafe | P, S | **Hoboken**	21
Filomena | P | **Berlin**	20
Frenchtown Inn | P | **Frenchtown**	23
☑ Frog/Peach | P | **New Bruns.**	26
☑ Gables, The | P | **Beach Haven**	26
Girasole | P | **A.C.**	25
Girasole | P | **Bound Brook**	25
Giumarello's | P | **Westmont**	25
☑ Grand Cafe | P | **Morristown**	25
Hamilton's | P | **Lambertville**	24
Harvest Moon | G | **Ringoes**	24
India on Hudson | S | **Hoboken**	19
Inn/Hawke | P | **Lambertville**	18
Klein's Fish Mkt. | P, T | **Belmar**	20
La Campagne | G, T | **Cherry Hill**	24
☑ Latour | S | **Ridgewood**	27
☑ Le Rendez-Vous | S | **Kenilworth**	26
Lilly's/Canal | P | **Lambertville**	21
Matisse | T | **Belmar**	22
☑ Mélange | P | **Cherry Hill**	26
Mexican Food | P | **Marlton**	18
Mill/Spring Lake | T | **Spring Lake Hts**	20
☑ Moonstruck | T | **Asbury Pk**	24
Nag's Head | P | **Ocean City**	26
☑ Perryville Inn | P | **Union Twp**	26
☑ Peter Shields | T | **Cape May**	26
☑ Rat's | T | **Hamilton**	24
Raven & Peach | P | **Fair Haven**	24
Rebecca's | P | **Edgewater**	24
Robin's Nest | T | **Mt Holly**	22
Robongi | S | **Hoboken**	25
☑ Ruth's Chris | S | **Weehawken**	24
Ship Inn | S | **Milford**	19
Shipwreck Grill | T | **Brielle**	25
Stage Hse. | G | **Scotch Plains**	23
☑ Stage Left | P | **New Bruns.**	26
Tisha's | P | **Cape May**	25
Tuckers | P | **Beach Haven**	18
Village Green | S | **Ridgewood**	25
Windansea | T | **Highlands**	20
Word of Mouth | P | **Collingswood**	24

Zafra | P | **Hoboken**	24
☑ Zoe's | P | **Sparta**	26

PEOPLE-WATCHING

Benihana | **Pennsauken**	-
☑ Bernards Inn | **Bernardsville**	26
Bobby Flay Steak | **A.C.**	24
NEW Brio | **Cherry Hill**	-
Brix 67 | **Summit**	18
Buddakan | **A.C.**	-
Caffe Aldo | **Cherry Hill**	23
Catelli | **Voorhees**	24
☑ Chart House | **Weehawken**	20
Clark's Landing | **Pt. Pleas.**	17
Clydz | **New Bruns.**	23
Continental | **A.C.**	-
Copeland | **Morristown**	25
Cuba Libre | **A.C.**	21
☑ Cucharamama | **Hoboken**	26
daddy O | **Long Beach**	18
NEW Daryl | **New Bruns.**	-
☑ David Drake | **Rahway**	27
Delta's | **New Bruns.**	22
NEW Dream Café | **Cherry Hill**	-
Eccola | **Parsippany**	23
Echo | **Red Bank**	19
NEW Embers Grill | **Cherry Hill**	-
NEW Equus | **Bernardsville**	-
NEW Hotoke | **New Bruns.**	-
☑ Huntley Taverne | **Summit**	22
NEW Indigo | **N Brunswick**	-
NEW Javier's | **Haddonfield**	-
Kitchen 233 | **Westmont**	22
Lambertville Station | **Lambertville**	17
Limestone Cafe | **Peapack**	22
Lua | **Hoboken**	22
Makeda | **New Bruns.**	23
☑ McCormick/Schmick | **Cherry Hill**	20
NEW Merchant Hse. | **Fairfield**	-
Mia | **A.C.**	26
Molly Pitcher | **Red Bank**	22
Mompou | **Newark**	20
NEW 947 B&G | **Clementon**	-
NEW Ox | **Jersey City**	-
NEW Park Ave. | **Union City**	-

subscribe to ZAGAT.com

☑ Pluckemin Inn | **Bedminster**	25
Ponzio's | **Cherry Hill**	16
Pop Shop | **Collingswood**	18
Pub | **Pennsauken**	18
Salt Creek | **Rumson**	20
Sammy's Cider | **Mendham**	21
☑ South City Grill | **Jersey City**	23
NEW Tabor Rd. | **Morris Plains**	-
Tapas de Espana | **N Bergen**	20
Teak | **Red Bank**	23
☑ 3 West | **Basking Ridge**	23
Tortilla Press | **Collingswood**	23
NEW Tortilla Press Cantina | **Pennsauken**	-
NEW Undici | **Rumson**	-
NEW Victor's Pub | **Camden**	-
Witherspoon Grill | **Princeton**	-
Wolfgang Puck | **A.C.**	23
☑ Zoe's | **Sparta**	26

POWER SCENES

☑ Basilico | **Millburn**	23
BayPoint Prime | **Pt. Pleas. Bch**	24
☑ Bernards Inn | **Bernardsville**	26
Bobby Flay Steak | **A.C.**	24
☑ Cafe Panache | **Ramsey**	28
Caffe Aldo | **Cherry Hill**	23
Casa Dante | **Jersey City**	22
Catelli | **Voorhees**	24
☑ Catherine Lombardi | **New Bruns.**	21
☑ Chakra | **Paramus**	21
☑ Chez Catherine | **Westfield**	27
Cuba Libre | **A.C.**	21
NEW Daryl | **New Bruns.**	-
☑ David Burke | **Rumson**	26
NEW Embers Grill | **Cherry Hill**	-
☑ Fascino | **Montclair**	26
☑ 410 Bank St. | **Cape May**	27
Gallagher's Steak | **A.C.**	22
Hunt Club | **Summit**	20
☑ Il Mondo | **Madison**	25
☑ McCormick/Schmick | **Cherry Hill**	20
McLoone's | **Sea Bright**	17
Morton's Steak | **Hackensack**	24
Old Homestead | **A.C.**	25

Opah Grille | **Gladstone**	24
Phillips Seafood | **A.C.**	-
Pierre's | **Morristown**	23
Ponzio's | **Cherry Hill**	16
Redstone | **Marlton**	-
☑ Saddle River Inn | **Saddle R.**	27
☑ SeaBlue | **A.C.**	27
☑ Serenade | **Chatham**	27
Solari's | **Hackensack**	21
Table | **Little Silver**	-
NEW Undici | **Rumson**	-
☑ Washington Inn | **Cape May**	26
Wolfgang Puck | **A.C.**	23

PRE-THEATER DINING

(Call for prices and times)

Arthur's Landing | **Weehawken**	20
Maize | **Newark**	21
Theater Sq. Grill | **Newark**	20
2Senza | **Red Bank**	20

PRIVATE ROOMS

(Restaurants charge less at off times; call for capacity)

☑ Amanda's | **Hoboken**	26
☑ André's | **Newton**	27
Barone's | **Moorestown**	20
☑ Bernards Inn | **Bernardsville**	26
☑ Bistro Olé | **Asbury Pk**	25
☑ Black Duck | **W Cape May**	26
☑ Cafe Matisse | **Rutherford**	27
Caffe Aldo | **Cherry Hill**	23
Catelli | **Voorhees**	24
☑ Chakra | **Paramus**	21
☑ Chez Catherine | **Westfield**	27
Chez Elena Wu | **Voorhees**	24
☑ Ebbitt Room | **Cape May**	27
☑ Fascino | **Montclair**	26
Food/Thought | **Marlton**	24
☑ Gables, The | **Beach Haven**	26
Girasole | **Bound Brook**	25
Giumarello's | **Westmont**	25
Hamilton's | **Lambertville**	24
Harvest Bistro | **Closter**	22
Karen & Rei's | **Clermont**	27
Mattar's | **Allamuchy**	24
☑ Nauvoo Grill | **Fair Haven**	16
☑ Nicholas | **Middletown**	29

SPECIAL FEATURES

☑ Perryville Inn | **Union Twp**	26
Porto Leggero | **Jersey City**	23
Pub | **Pennsauken**	18
☑ Serenade | **Chatham**	27
Stage Hse. | **Scotch Plains**	23
☑ Stage Left | **New Bruns.**	26
Tomatoes | **Margate**	24
☑ Washington Inn | **Cape May**	26
☑ Zoe's | **Sparta**	26

PRIX FIXE MENUS

(Call for prices and times)

☑ André's | **Newton**	27
Anthony David's | **Hoboken**	25
☑ Bernards Inn | **Bernardsville**	26
Cafe at Rosemont | **Rosemont**	22
☑ Cafe Matisse | **Rutherford**	27
☑ Cafe Panache | **Ramsey**	28
☑ Chez Catherine | **Westfield**	27
☑ David Drake | **Rahway**	27
☑ Ebbitt Room | **Cape May**	27
☑ Fascino | **Montclair**	26
Frenchtown Inn | **Frenchtown**	23
☑ Frog/Peach | **New Bruns.**	26
☑ Gables, The | **Beach Haven**	26
☑ Latour | **Ridgewood**	27
Manon | **Lambertville**	25
Mattar's | **Allamuchy**	24
☑ Nicholas | **Middletown**	29
Norma's | **Cherry Hill**	21
Nunzio | **Collingswood**	23
☑ Perryville Inn | **Union Twp**	26
☑ Rat's | **Hamilton**	24
Rosemary & Sage | **Riverdale**	26
☑ Scalini Fedeli | **Chatham**	27
☑ Serenade | **Chatham**	27
Sono Sushi | **Middletown**	26
Stage Hse. | **Scotch Plains**	23
☑ Stage Left | **New Bruns.**	26
Verjus | **Maplewood**	25
Village Green | **Ridgewood**	25
☑ Zoe's | **Sparta**	26

QUICK BITES

Aby's | **Matawan**	22
Alchemist/Barrister | **Princeton**	16
Amazing Hot Dog | **Verona**	22

Bobby Chez | **multi.**	25
Buttonwood Manor | **Matawan**	18
Continental | **A.C.**	-
Cubby's BBQ | **Hackensack**	17
NEW Dockhoppers | **Collingswood**	-
Doo Rae Myun Ok | **Fort Lee**	21
Full Moon | **Lambertville**	17
GRUB Hut | **Manville**	-
Irish Pub | **A.C.**	18
Jack Cooper's | **Edison**	19
Jerry & Harvey's | **Marlboro**	18
Kibitz Room | **Cherry Hill**	24
La Tapatia | **Asbury Pk**	-
Mastoris | **Bordentown**	19
NEW Merchant Hse. | **Fairfield**	-
Mexican Food | **Marlton**	18
Morgan Fishery | **S Amboy**	-
NEW Mr. Bill's | **Hammonton**	-
Neil's Oyster | **Highlands**	-
Nha Trang Pl. | **Jersey City**	24
Noodle Hse. | **N Brunswick**	19
NEW Ox | **Jersey City**	-
Pic-Nic | **E Newark**	-
Ponzio's | **Cherry Hill**	16
Pop Shop | **Collingswood**	18
Shaker Cafe | **Flemington**	-
Simply Radishing | **Lawrenceville**	18
Takara | **Ocean Twp**	25
Tashmoo | **Morristown**	-
Tick Tock | **Clifton**	17
Tony Luke's | **A.C.**	-
NEW Tortilla Press Cantina | **Pennsauken**	-
NEW Victor's Pub | **Camden**	-
Windansea | **Highlands**	20
Witherspoon Grill | **Princeton**	-
NEW Zen Palate | **Princeton**	-

QUIET CONVERSATION

NEW Aglio | **Metuchen**	-
Braddock's | **Medford**	22
☑ Chez Catherine | **Westfield**	27
☑ David Drake | **Rahway**	27
Farnsworth Hse. | **Bordentown**	21
NEW 55 Main | **Flemington**	-

Fiorino | **Summit**	23
Food/Thought | **Marlton**	24
Frenchtown Inn | **Frenchtown**	23
NEW KC's | **Mendham**	-
Krave Café | **Newton**	-
NEW Luke's | **Maplewood**	-
Mahogany Grille | **Manasquan**	23
Melting Pot | **Westwood**	19
Meyersville Inn | **Gillette**	-
NEW Mi Sueño | **Middlesex**	-
Molly Pitcher | **Red Bank**	22
Z Pluckemin Inn | **Bedminster**	25
Z Rat's | **Hamilton**	24
Rupee Room | **N Brunswick**	-
Soufflé | **Summit**	23
NEW Splash | **Long Valley**	-
NEW Stonehouse | **Warren**	-
Ted's on Main | **Medford**	-
NEW Thyme Rest. | **Phillipsburg**	-
Union Station | **Phillipsburg**	-
Village Green | **Ridgewood**	25
Z Whispers | **Spring Lake**	27

RAW BARS

Z Avenue | **Long Branch**	22
Bahrs Landing | **Highlands**	15
BayPoint Prime | **Pt. Pleas. Bch**	24
Beau Steak | **Medford**	22
Berkeley | **S Seaside Pk**	18
Blue Eyes | **Sewell**	20
Z Blue Point | **Princeton**	25
Cafe Arugula | **S Orange**	20
Caffe Aldo | **Cherry Hill**	23
Carmine's Asbury Pk | **Asbury Pk**	-
Catelli | **Voorhees**	24
Circa | **High Bridge**	20
Clark's Landing | **Pt. Pleas.**	17
Z CoccoLa | **Hillsborough**	22
Copeland | **Morristown**	25
NEW Dockhoppers | **Collingswood**	-
Dock's Oyster | **A.C.**	26
Fresco Steak | **Milltown**	23
Grand Colonial | **Union Twp**	25
Grill 73 | **Bernardsville**	22

Harvey Cedars | **multi.**	22
Klein's Fish Mkt. | **Belmar**	20
Kunkel's | **Haddon Hts**	20
La Focaccia | **Summit**	24
Z Legal Sea Foods | **multi.**	20
Liberty House | **Jersey City**	20
Little Tuna | **Haddonfield**	20
Lobster Hse. | **Cape May**	20
Z McCormick/Schmick | **Hackensack**	20
McLoone's | **multi.**	17
Milford Oyster Hse. | **Milford**	-
Morgan Fishery | **S Amboy**	-
Neil's Oyster | **Highlands**	-
Nero's Grille | **Livingston**	17
Old Homestead | **A.C.**	25
Plantation | **Harvey Cedars**	19
Red's Lobster | **Pt. Pleas. Bch**	24
Sallee Tee's | **Monmouth Bch**	21
Shipwreck Grill | **Brielle**	25
Solaia | **Englewood**	20
Z South City Grill | **multi.**	23
Spike's | **Pt. Pleas. Bch**	22
Steve & Cookie's | **Margate**	25
Varka Fish Hse. | **Ramsey**	25

ROMANTIC PLACES

Acquaviva | **Westfield**	23
NEW Aglio | **Metuchen**	-
Z Amanda's | **Hoboken**	26
Anton's/Swan | **Lambertville**	22
Atlantic B&G | **S Seaside Pk**	24
Beau Steak | **Medford**	22
NEW Blackbird | **Collingswood**	-
Z Cafe Matisse | **Rutherford**	27
Catelli | **Voorhees**	24
Z Catherine Lombardi | **New Bruns.**	21
Creole Cafe | **Sewell**	27
Z CulinAriane | **Montclair**	27
Z David Burke | **Rumson**	26
Z David Drake | **Rahway**	27
Z Ebbitt Room | **Cape May**	27
NEW Equus | **Bernardsville**	-
NEW 55 Main | **Flemington**	-
Frenchtown Inn | **Frenchtown**	23
NEW Fuji | **Haddonfield**	-

SPECIAL FEATURES

Ⓩ Gables, The | **Beach Haven** _26_

Gaslight | **Hoboken** _20_

Giumarello's | **Westmont** _25_

Ⓩ Grand Cafe | **Morristown** _25_

Grenville | **Bay Hd.** _21_

Harvest Moon | **Ringoes** _24_

I Cavallini | **Colts Neck** _25_

Il Capriccio | **Whippany** _26_

NEW Indigo | **N Brunswick** _-_

Inn at Millrace | **Hope** _21_

Jose's Cantina | **multi.** _19_

NEW KC's | **Mendham** _-_

K.O.B.E. | **Holmdel** _25_

Krave Café | **Newton** _-_

La Cipollina | **Freehold** _23_

Le Petit Chateau | **Bernardsville** _25_

Ⓩ Le Rendez-Vous | **Kenilworth** _26_

Lilly's/Canal | **Lambertville** _21_

Melting Pot | **Westwood** _19_

Metuchen Inn | **Metuchen** _22_

Mia | **A.C.** _26_

NEW Mi Sueño | **Middlesex** _-_

Molly Pitcher | **Red Bank** _22_

NEW Park Ave. | **Union City** _-_

Ⓩ Perryville Inn | **Union Twp** _26_

Ⓩ Peter Shields | **Cape May** _26_

Pino's | **Marlboro** _18_

Plantation | **Harvey Cedars** _19_

Ⓩ Ram's Head Inn | **Galloway** _26_

Ⓩ Rat's | **Hamilton** _24_

Raven & Peach | **Fair Haven** _24_

Rebecca's | **Edgewater** _24_

Rod's Steak | **Convent Station** _21_

Rupee Room | **N Brunswick** _-_

Savanna | **Red Bank** _20_

Ⓩ Scalini Fedeli | **Chatham** _27_

Scarborough Fair | **Wall** _20_

Ⓩ SeaBlue | **A.C.** _27_

Sergeantsville Inn | **Sergeantsville** _23_

NEW Stonehouse | **Warren** _-_

Stony Hill Inn | **Hackensack** _23_

Ⓩ Taka | **Asbury Pk** _26_

Ted's on Main | **Medford** _-_

Tewksbury Inn | **Oldwick** _22_

NEW Thyme Rest. | **Phillipsburg** _-_

Ⓩ Washington Inn | **Cape May** _26_

Water Lily | **Collingswood** _24_

Ⓩ Whispers | **Spring Lake** _27_

SENIOR APPEAL

NEW Aglio | **Metuchen** _-_

Asia Star Cafe | **Tinton Falls** _-_

Athenian Gdn. | **Galloway Twp** _23_

Bahrs Landing | **Highlands** _15_

Berkeley | **S Seaside Pk** _18_

NEW Blackbird | **Collingswood** _-_

NEW Brio | **Cherry Hill** _-_

Buttonwood Manor | **Matawan** _18_

Café Azzurro | **Peapack** _-_

California Grill | **Flemington** _20_

Capt'n Ed's | **Pt. Pleas.** _19_

Carmine's | **A.C.** _20_

Ⓩ Catherine Lombardi | **New Bruns.** _21_

Chophouse | **Gibbsboro** _23_

Christopher's | **Colts Neck** _21_

Crab Trap | **Somers Point** _21_

NEW Dockhoppers | **Collingswood** _-_

Don Pepe | **multi.** _21_

Don Pepe's Steak | **Pine Brook** _22_

E & V | **Paterson** _24_

El Cid | **Paramus** _21_

NEW Embers Grill | **Cherry Hill** _-_

NEW 55 Main | **Flemington** _-_

Ⓩ Fornos of Spain | **Newark** _23_

Gagan Bistro | **Marlton** _-_

Gallagher's Steak | **A.C.** _22_

Grenville | **Bay Hd.** _21_

Iberia | **Newark** _21_

Jack Cooper's | **Edison** _19_

Java Moon | **multi.** _19_

NEW KC's | **Mendham** _-_

Kibitz Room | **Cherry Hill** _24_

Kitchen 233 | **Westmont** _22_

Klein's Fish Mkt. | **Belmar** _20_

Krave Café | **Newton** _-_

Kuzina by Sofia | **Cherry Hill** _-_

Lahiere's | **Princeton** _21_

Ⓩ Legal Sea Foods | **Short Hills** _20_

Little Tuna | **Haddonfield** _20_

Lobster Hse. | **Cape May** _20_

LouCás | **Edison**	24
NEW Luke's | **Maplewood**	-
Z McCormick/Schmick | **multi.**	20
Meyersville Inn | **Gillette**	-
Mill/Spring Lake | **Spring Lake Hts**	20
NEW Mi Sueño | **Middlesex**	-
NEW Mr. Bill's | **Hammonton**	-
Oceanos | **Fair Lawn**	-
Octopus's Gard. | **Stafford**	22
Pete & Elda's | **Neptune City**	-
Pop Shop | **Collingswood**	18
Portobello | **Oakland**	20
Portuguese Manor | **Perth Amboy**	21
Pub | **Pennsauken**	18
Z SeaBlue | **A.C.**	27
Sea Shack | **Hackensack**	20
Smithville Inn | **Smithville**	18
NEW Splash | **Long Valley**	-
NEW Stonehouse | **Warren**	-
Ted's on Main | **Medford**	-
NEW Thyme Rest. | **Phillipsburg**	-
Tucker's Steak | **Somers Point**	19
Union Station | **Phillipsburg**	-
Varka Fish Hse. | **Ramsey**	25
Villa Vittoria | **Brick**	22
Waterfront Buffet | **A.C.**	17
Water Lily | **Collingswood**	24
Wolfgang Puck | **A.C.**	23
NEW Zen Palate | **Princeton**	-

SINGLES SCENES

Acqua | **Raritan**	21
Atlantic B&G | **S Seaside Pk**	24
Blue Pig Tavern | **Cape May**	20
Brickwall Tavern | **Asbury Pk**	19
Brooklyn's Pizza | **Ridgewood**	22
Buddakan | **A.C.**	-
Cenzino | **Oakland**	24
Circa | **High Bridge**	20
City Bistro | **Hoboken**	19
Clark's Landing | **Pt. Pleas.**	17
Clydz | **New Bruns.**	23
Continental | **A.C.**	-
Copper Canyon | **Atlantic H.**	25

Corky's | **A.C.**	16
Cuba Libre | **A.C.**	21
Z Cucharamama | **Hoboken**	26
NEW Daryl | **New Bruns.**	-
Grissini | **Englewood Cliffs**	22
Gusto Grill | **E Brunswick**	-
House of Blues | **A.C.**	16
Inlet Café | **Highlands**	19
La Nonna | **Bradley Bch**	18
Lua | **Hoboken**	22
McLoone's | **Sea Bright**	17
Metropolitan Cafe | **Freehold**	22
Mia | **A.C.**	26
Mompou | **Newark**	20
NEW 947 B&G | **Clementon**	-
Nova Terra | **New Bruns.**	22
Z Old Man Rafferty's | **multi.**	19
NEW Ox | **Jersey City**	-
NEW Park Ave. | **Union City**	-
Piquant Bread | **New Bruns.**	-
P.J. Whelihan's | **multi.**	17
Plantation | **Harvey Cedars**	19
Quiet Man | **Dover**	22
Red | **Red Bank**	20
Redstone | **Marlton**	-
Restaurant | **Hackensack**	21
Rooney's | **Long Branch**	18
NEW Sage | **Ventnor**	-
Sallee Tee's | **Monmouth Bch**	21
Savannah's | **Stockholm**	-
Shipwreck Grill | **Brielle**	25
Sister Sue's | **Asbury Pk**	21
Z South City Grill | **Jersey City**	23
Sushi Lounge | **multi.**	24
Teak | **Red Bank**	23
Tomatoes | **Margate**	24
Trap Rock | **Berkeley Hts**	21
Verve | **Somerville**	23
Windansea | **Highlands**	20
Witherspoon Grill | **Princeton**	-

SLEEPERS

(Good to excellent food, but little known)

Aamantran | **Toms River Twp**	23
Aby's | **Matawan**	22
Alessio 426 | **Metuchen**	20

Alexander's | **Cape May** 24
Aligado Asian | **Hazlet** 23
Anna's Italian | **Middletown** 22
Bay Head Bistro | **Bay Hd.** 21
Bayou Cafe | **Manasquan** 23
BayPoint Prime | **Pt. Pleas. Bch** 24
Bella Sogno | **Bradley Bch** 21
Bistro 44 | **Toms River** 25
Blue Danube | **Trenton** 22
Blue Fish | **Flemington** 20
Bosphorus | **Lake Hiawatha** 22
Cafe Loren | **Avalon** 25
Chilangos | **Highlands** 21
Circa | **High Bridge** 20
Claude's | **N Wildwood** 25
Copper Fish | **Cape May** 20
Creole Cafe | **Sewell** 27
Cup Joint | **Hoboken** 20
Doo Rae Myun Ok | **Fort Lee** 21
Drew's Bayshore | **Keyport** 28
503 Park | **Scotch Plains** 20
Gianna's | **Atlantic H.** 25
Grand Shanghai | **Edison** 21
Harrison | **Asbury Pk** 24
Harry's Lobster | **Sea Bright** 22
High St. Grill | **Mt Holly** 23
Homestead Inn | **Trenton** 23
Ikko | **Brick** 22
Je's | **Newark** 26
Jose's | **Spring Lake Hts** 22
Karen & Rei's | **Clermont** 27
Kitchen 233 | **Westmont** 22
K.O.B.E. | **Holmdel** 25
Konbu | **Manalapan** 25
Kunkel's | **Haddon Hts** 20
La Esperanza | **Lindenwold** 24
Laguna Grill | **Brigantine** 22
La Spiaggia | **Ship Bottom** 26
Lodos | **New Milford** 21
Marie Nicole's | **Wildwood** 23
Market Roost | **Flemington** 22
Mattar's | **Allamuchy** 24
Megu Sushi | **Cherry Hill** 22
Mexico Lindo | **Brick** 28
Moksha | **Edison** 22
Mompou | **Newark** 20
Nag's Head | **Ocean City** 26
Nha Trang Pl. | **Jersey City** 24
Niecy's | **S Orange** 20
Nobi | **Toms River Twp** 25
Oasis Grill | **Cherry Hill** 25
Octopus's Gard. | **Stafford** 22
Passionne | **Montclair** 23
Pasta Fresca | **Shrewsbury** 22
Sakura Spring | **Cherry Hill** 23
Sens Asian | **S Brunswick** 22
Silver Spring | **Flanders** 23
Sister Sue's | **Asbury Pk** 21
Solo Bella | **Jackson** 21
So Moon Nan Jip | **Palisades Pk** 23
Sushi by Kazu | **Howell** 28
Takara | **Ocean Twp** 25
Taqueria | **Jersey City** 20
Thyme Square | **Red Bank** 21
Verdigre | **New Bruns.** 22
West Lake | **Matawan** 25
Wonder Seafood | **Edison** 24

SPECIAL OCCASIONS

NEW Aglio | **Metuchen** -
Bacari Grill | **Washington Twp** 21
Beau Steak | **Medford** 22
Z Blue Bottle | **Hopewell** 27
Bobby Flay Steak | **A.C.** 24
Z Cafe Matisse | **Rutherford** 27
Z Cafe Panache | **Ramsey** 28
Catelli | **Voorhees** 24
Z Chakra | **Paramus** 21
Z Chart House | **Weehawken** 20
Z Chef's Table | **Franklin Lakes** 28
Chengdu 46 | **Clifton** 24
Z Chez Catherine | **Westfield** 27
Z Cucharamama | **Hoboken** 26
NEW Daryl | **New Bruns.** -
Doris & Ed's | **Highlands** 25
NEW Due Terre | **Bernardsville** -
NEW Equus | **Bernardsville** -
Z Ferry Hse. | **Princeton** 25
NEW 55 Main | **Flemington** -
Food/Thought | **Marlton** 24
Frenchtown Inn | **Frenchtown** 23
Gallagher's Steak | **A.C.** 22

subscribe to ZAGAT.com

Giumarello's | **Westmont**	25
Z Grand Cafe | **Morristown**	25
Harvest Moon | **Ringoes**	24
Z Highlawn | **W Orange**	24
NEW Hotoke | **New Bruns.**	-
Il Capriccio | **Whippany**	26
NEW Indigo | **N Brunswick**	-
Karen & Rei's | **Clermont**	27
NEW KC's | **Mendham**	-
K.O.B.E. | **Holmdel**	25
Z Latour | **Ridgewood**	27
Madeleine's | **Northvale**	24
Maize | **Newark**	21
Z Manor | **W Orange**	23
Mattar's | **Allamuchy**	24
NEW Mi Sueño | **Middlesex**	-
Napa Valley | **Paramus**	22
Z Nicholas | **Middletown**	29
No. 9 | **Lambertville**	24
Nunzio | **Collingswood**	23
Z Peter Shields | **Cape May**	26
Posillipo | **Asbury Pk**	22
Z Ram's Head Inn | **Galloway**	26
Z Rat's | **Hamilton**	24
Raven & Peach | **Fair Haven**	24
Rebecca's | **Edgewater**	24
Robin's Nest | **Mt Holly**	22
Rod's Steak | **Convent Station**	21
Rupee Room | **N Brunswick**	-
Z Saddle River Inn | **Saddle R.**	27
Z SeaBlue | **A.C.**	27
Z Serenade | **Chatham**	27
Shanghai Jazz | **Madison**	21
Specchio | **A.C.**	25
Stage Hse. | **Scotch Plains**	23
NEW Stonehouse | **Warren**	-
Stony Hill Inn | **Hackensack**	23
Taro | **Montclair**	21
Z 3 West | **Basking Ridge**	23
NEW Thyme Rest. | **Phillipsburg**	-
Z Washington Inn | **Cape May**	26
Wild Ginger | **Englewood**	25
Witherspoon Grill | **Princeton**	-
Wolfgang Puck | **A.C.**	23
Z Zoe's | **Sparta**	26

TASTING MENUS

Anthony David's | **Hoboken**	25
Bella Sogno | **Bradley Bch**	21
Z Bernards Inn | **Bernardsville**	26
Bienvenue | **Red Bank**	24
Black Trumpet | **Spring Lake**	23
Z Cafe Panache | **Ramsey**	28
Z Chez Catherine | **Westfield**	27
Copeland | **Morristown**	25
Z David Drake | **Rahway**	27
NEW Due Terre | **Bernardsville**	-
Z Ebbitt Room | **Cape May**	27
Z Fascino | **Montclair**	26
NEW Fuji | **Haddonfield**	-
Island Palm Grill | **Spring Lake**	18
La Campagne | **Cherry Hill**	24
Z Latour | **Ridgewood**	27
Le Petit Chateau | **Bernardsville**	25
Z Le Rendez-Vous | **Kenilworth**	26
Z Lorena's | **Maplewood**	27
Z Mélange | **Cherry Hill**	26
Z Nicholas | **Middletown**	29
Norma's | **Cherry Hill**	21
Nouveau Sushi | **Montclair**	25
Nunzio | **Collingswood**	23
Z Ombra | **A.C.**	25
Passionne | **Montclair**	23
Z Perryville Inn | **Union Twp**	26
Z Rat's | **Hamilton**	24
Renault Winery | **Egg Harbor**	22
Restaurant Latour | **Hamburg**	-
Rosemary & Sage | **Riverdale**	26
Z Serenade | **Chatham**	27
Spargo's Grille | **Manalapan**	25
Stage Hse. | **Scotch Plains**	23
Z Stage Left | **New Bruns.**	26
Village Green | **Ridgewood**	25
Vine | **Basking Ridge**	22
Z Zoe's | **Sparta**	26

TRANSPORTING EXPERIENCES

Anton's/Swan | **Lambertville**	22
Avon Pavilion | **Avon-by-Sea**	18
Blue Danube | **Trenton**	22
Z Chakra | **Paramus**	21
Chao Phaya | **Somerville**	23

SPECIAL FEATURES

🆉 Cucharamama | **Hoboken**	_26_
🆉 Ebbitt Room | **Cape May**	_27_
Epernay | **Montclair**	_21_
🆉 Fascino | **Montclair**	_26_
Hamilton's | **Lambertville**	_24_
K.O.B.E. | **Holmdel**	_25_
La Campagne | **Cherry Hill**	_24_
🆉 Lorena's | **Maplewood**	_27_
Makeda | **New Bruns.**	_23_
Manon | **Lambertville**	_25_
Ming | **Edison**	_23_
Moksha | **Edison**	_22_
Pamir | **Morristown**	_21_
🆉 Perryville Inn | **Union Twp**	_26_
🆉 Pluckemin Inn | **Bedminster**	_25_
🆉 Rat's | **Hamilton**	_24_
🆉 Saddle River Inn | **Saddle R.**	_27_
Seven Hills | **Highland Pk**	_21_
Shanghai Jazz | **Madison**	_21_
Silver Oak Bistro | **Ridgewood**	_23_
Siri's | **Cherry Hill**	_25_
Sister Sue's | **Asbury Pk**	_21_
Taro | **Montclair**	_21_
Walpack Inn | **Wallpack**	_19_

TRENDY

Anna's Italian | **Middletown**	_22_
🆕 A Toute Heure | **Cranford**	_-_
Axelsson's | **Cape May**	_22_
🆕 Bank 34 | **Somerville**	_-_
🆉 Basilico | **Millburn**	_23_
🆉 Bistro Olé | **Asbury Pk**	_25_
Blu | **Montclair**	_25_
Blue | **Surf City**	_23_
🆉 Blue Bottle | **Hopewell**	_27_
Bobby Flay Steak | **A.C.**	_24_
Brickwall Tavern | **Asbury Pk**	_19_
Buddakan | **A.C.**	_-_
🆉 Cafe Matisse | **Rutherford**	_27_
Casona | **Collingswood**	_24_
🆉 Chakra | **Paramus**	_21_
Chef Vola's | **A.C.**	_26_
Conte's | **Princeton**	_-_
Continental | **A.C.**	_-_
Cuba Libre | **A.C.**	_21_
🆉 Cucharamama | **Hoboken**	_26_

daddy O | **Long Beach**	_18_
🆕 Daryl | **New Bruns.**	_-_
🆉 David Burke | **Rumson**	_26_
🆉 DeLorenzo's | **Trenton**	_28_
Delta's | **New Bruns.**	_22_
Dock's Oyster | **A.C.**	_26_
Doris & Ed's | **Highlands**	_25_
Drew's Bayshore | **Keyport**	_28_
🆕 Equus | **Bernardsville**	_-_
🆉 Far East Taste | **Eatontown**	_26_
🆉 Fascino | **Montclair**	_26_
Federici's | **Freehold**	_21_
Frescos | **Cape May**	_24_
🆕 Fusion | **Flemington**	_-_
Gaetano's | **Red Bank**	_19_
Garlic Rose | **multi.**	_21_
Girasole | **Bound Brook**	_25_
Harvest Moon | **Ringoes**	_24_
🆉 Highlawn | **W Orange**	_24_
Homestead Inn | **Trenton**	_23_
🆕 Hotoke | **New Bruns.**	_-_
🆉 Il Mondo | **Madison**	_25_
🆕 Indigo | **N Brunswick**	_-_
Joel's Malibu | **Ridgewood**	_-_
🆕 KC's | **Mendham**	_-_
K.O.B.E. | **Holmdel**	_25_
Labrador | **Normandy Bch**	_23_
La Campagna | **Morristown**	_24_
🆉 Latour | **Ridgewood**	_27_
Lobster Hse. | **Cape May**	_20_
🆉 Lorena's | **Maplewood**	_27_
Lua | **Hoboken**	_22_
Mad Batter | **Cape May**	_21_
Mahzu | **Aberdeen**	_22_
Makeda | **New Bruns.**	_23_
Marco & Pepe | **Jersey City**	_22_
Martino's | **Somerville**	_21_
Matt's Rooster | **Flemington**	_25_
🆉 Mélange | **Cherry Hill**	_26_
Mia | **A.C.**	_26_
🆉 Mojave Grille | **Westfield**	_24_
Mud City | **Manahawkin**	_21_
Niecy's | **S Orange**	_20_
Nikko | **Whippany**	_24_
🆕 947 B&G | **Clementon**	_-_
No. 9 | **Lambertville**	_24_

Nunzio | **Collingswood**	23
Old Homestead | **A.C.**	25
Z Origin | **Somerville**	26
NEW Ox | **Jersey City**	-
Z Park/Orchard | **E Rutherford**	22
NEW Park Ave. | **Union City**	-
Pete & Elda's | **Neptune City**	-
Pine Tavern | **Old Bridge**	22
Piquant Bread | **New Bruns.**	-
Plantation | **Harvey Cedars**	19
Z Pluckemin Inn | **Bedminster**	25
Z Rat's | **Hamilton**	24
Rebecca's | **Edgewater**	24
Reservoir Tavern | **Boonton**	22
Z River Palm | **multi.**	25
Rod's Olde Irish | **Sea Girt**	19
Rosemary & Sage | **Riverdale**	26
Rupee Room | **N Brunswick**	-
Z Sagami | **Collingswood**	26
NEW Sage | **Ventnor**	-
Saigon R./Mo' Pho | **Englewood**	24
Z Scalini Fedeli | **Chatham**	27
Z SeaBlue | **A.C.**	27
Shaker Cafe | **Flemington**	-
Shanghai Jazz | **Madison**	21
Siam | **Lambertville**	21
Siri's | **Cherry Hill**	25
Sister Sue's | **Asbury Pk**	21
Steve & Cookie's | **Margate**	25
NEW Tabor Rd. | **Morris Plains**	-
Taste of Asia | **Chatham**	21
Teak | **Red Bank**	23
Theresa's | **Westfield**	23
Z 3 West | **Basking Ridge**	23
Tim Schafer's | **Morristown**	25
NEW Tokyo Bleu | **Cinnaminson**	-
Tony Luke's | **A.C.**	-
2Senza | **Red Bank**	20
NEW Undici | **Rumson**	-
Verve | **Somerville**	23
Vic's | **Bradley Bch**	20
Z White Hse. | **A.C.**	27
Witherspoon Grill | **Princeton**	-
Wolfgang Puck | **A.C.**	23
Yellow Fin | **Surf City**	25
Zafra | **Hoboken**	24

TWENTYSOMETHINGS

Akai Lounge | **Englewood**	23
Avon Pavilion | **Avon-by-Sea**	18
Baja | **Hoboken**	20
Basil T's | **Red Bank**	20
Blue Pig Tavern | **Cape May**	20
Brickwall Tavern | **Asbury Pk**	19
Buddakan | **A.C.**	-
Caneel Bay | **Harvey Cedars**	17
City Bistro | **Hoboken**	19
Conte's | **Princeton**	-
Continental | **A.C.**	-
Cuba Libre | **A.C.**	21
Cubby's BBQ | **Hackensack**	17
Z Cucharamama | **Hoboken**	26
NEW Daryl | **New Bruns.**	-
NEW Fusion | **Flemington**	-
House of Blues | **A.C.**	16
Inlet Café | **Highlands**	19
Los Amigos | **multi.**	23
Mexican Food | **Marlton**	18
Mia | **A.C.**	26
Mompou | **Newark**	20
Oddfellows | **Hoboken**	19
Old Bay | **New Bruns.**	17
Z Old Man Rafferty's | **multi.**	19
NEW Ox | **Jersey City**	-
NEW Park Ave. | **Union City**	-
Pine Tavern | **Old Bridge**	22
Pithari Taverna | **Highland Pk**	-
Z Pluckemin Inn | **Bedminster**	25
Rattlesnake Ranch | **Denville**	16
Red | **Red Bank**	20
Z South City Grill | **multi.**	23
Squan Tavern | **Manasquan**	19
Surf Taco | **multi.**	20
Sushi Lounge | **Hoboken**	24
NEW Tabor Rd. | **Morris Plains**	-
Tacconelli's | **Maple Shade**	24
Tapas de Espana | **N Bergen**	20
Teresa Caffe | **Princeton**	21
Triumph Brewing | **Princeton**	18
NEW Undici | **Rumson**	-
Witherspoon Grill | **Princeton**	-
Wolfgang Puck | **A.C.**	23
Yankee Doodle | **Princeton**	14

SPECIAL FEATURES

VIEWS

VISITORS ON EXPENSE ACCOUNT

Manhattan Steak	**Oakhurst**	22
Z McCormick/Schmick | **Cherry Hill**		20
Mia | **A.C.**		26
Morton's Steak | **Hackensack**		24
Z Nicholas | **Middletown**		29
Old Homestead | **A.C.**		25
Panico's | **New Bruns.**		24
NEW Park Ave. | **Union City**		-
Z Pluckemin Inn | **Bedminster**		25
Portofino | **Tinton Falls**		25
Z Ram's Head Inn | **Galloway**		26
Ristorante Benito | **Union**		25
Z Scalini Fedeli | **Chatham**		27
Z SeaBlue | **A.C.**		27
Z Sirena | **Long Branch**		23
Smoke Chophse. | **Englewood**		22
Specchio | **A.C.**		25
Z Stage Left | **New Bruns.**		26
NEW Stonehouse | **Warren**		-
Table | **Little Silver**		-
Z 3 West | **Basking Ridge**		23
NEW Undici | **Rumson**		-
Witherspoon Grill | **Princeton**		-
Wolfgang Puck | **A.C.**		23

WARM WELCOME

Z Amanda's | **Hoboken**	26
Angelo's | **A.C.**	20
Benito's | **Chester**	24
Berta's Chateau | **Wanaque**	22
Z Blue Point | **Princeton**	25
Casa Giuseppe | **Iselin**	24
Z Chez Catherine | **Westfield**	27
Z Cucharamama | **Hoboken**	26
da Filippo | **Somerville**	24
Z Far East Taste | **Eatontown**	26
Labrador | **Normandy Bch**	23
Z Le Rendez-Vous | **Kenilworth**	26
Madeleine's | **Northvale**	24
Nunzio | **Collingswood**	23
Opah Grille | **Gladstone**	24
Plantation | **Harvey Cedars**	19
Quiet Man | **Dover**	22
Ristorante Benito | **Union**	25
Rod's Olde Irish | **Sea Girt**	19

| Sister Sue's \| **Asbury Pk** | 21 |
| Taqueria \| **Jersey City** | 20 |

WATERSIDE

Atlantic B&G | **S Seaside Pk**	24
Z Avenue | **Long Branch**	22
Avon Pavilion | **Avon-by-Sea**	18
Axelsson's | **Cape May**	22
Bahrs Landing | **Highlands**	15
Barnacle Bill's | **Rumson**	21
Z Baumgart's Café | **Edgewater**	19
Café Gallery | **Burlington**	21
Capriccio | **A.C.**	25
Z Chart House | **Weehawken**	20
Chophouse | **Gibbsboro**	23
Crab Trap | **Somers Point**	21
Hamilton's | **Lambertville**	24
NEW Inlet, The | **Somers Point**	-
Inlet Café | **Highlands**	19
Inn at Sugar Hill | **Mays Landing**	-
Z It's Greek To Me | **Long Branch**	18
Klein's Fish Mkt. | **Belmar**	20
Komegashi | **Jersey City**	24
Lambertville Station | **Lambertville**	17
Liberty House | **Jersey City**	20
Lilly's/Canal | **Lambertville**	21
Lua | **Hoboken**	22
Matisse | **Belmar**	22
McLoone's | **multi.**	17
Mill/Spring Lake | **Spring Lake Hts**	20
Molly Pitcher | **Red Bank**	22
Neil's Oyster | **Highlands**	-
Z Peter Shields | **Cape May**	26
Z Rat's | **Hamilton**	24
Red's Lobster | **Pt. Pleas. Bch**	24
Robin's Nest | **Mt Holly**	22
Rooney's | **Long Branch**	18
Sallee Tee's | **Monmouth Bch**	21
NEW Salt Water | **Asbury Pk**	-
Z Sirena | **Long Branch**	23
3 Forty Grill | **Hoboken**	21
Tisha's | **Cape May**	25
Tuckers | **Beach Haven**	18
Z Union Park | **Cape May**	26

SPECIAL FEATURES

Ventura's | **Margate**	17
Windansea | **Highlands**	20
Z Zoe's | **Sparta**	26

WINNING WINE LISTS

Beau Steak | **Medford**	22
Z Bernards Inn | **Bernardsville**	26
Berta's Chateau | **Wanaque**	22
Z Black Forest Inn | **Stanhope**	23
Bobby Chez | **Sewell**	25
Bobby Flay Steak | **A.C.**	24
Brass Rail | **Hoboken**	19
Z Catherine Lombardi | **New Bruns.**	21
Z Chakra | **Paramus**	21
Chengdu 46 | **Clifton**	24
Court Street | **Hoboken**	21
Crab's Claw | **Lavallette**	17
Z Cucharamama | **Hoboken**	26
NEW Daryl | **New Bruns.**	-
Z David Burke | **Rumson**	26
Z David Drake | **Rahway**	27
Doris & Ed's | **Highlands**	25
NEW Due Terre | **Bernardsville**	-
NEW Embers Grill | **Cherry Hill**	-
NEW Equus | **Bernardsville**	-
Esty Street | **Park Ridge**	23
Z Frog/Peach | **New Bruns.**	26
Gladstone Tavern | **Gladstone**	-
Harvest Moon | **Ringoes**	24
Kitchen 233 | **Westmont**	22
Le Petit Chateau | **Bernardsville**	25
Z Manor | **W Orange**	23
Mediterra | **Princeton**	20
NEW Merchant Hse. | **Fairfield**	-
Mia | **A.C.**	26
Napa Valley | **Paramus**	22
Z Nicholas | **Middletown**	29
Z Ombra | **A.C.**	25
NEW Ox | **Jersey City**	-
Z Park/Orchard | **E Rutherford**	22
NEW Park Ave. | **Union City**	-
Z Pluckemin Inn | **Bedminster**	25
Z Rat's | **Hamilton**	24
Restaurant Latour | **Hamburg**	-
Salt Creek | **Rumson**	20

Z Scalini Fedeli | **Chatham**	27
Z SeaBlue | **A.C.**	27
Z Serenade | **Chatham**	27
Specchio | **A.C.**	25
NEW Splash | **Long Valley**	-
Stage Hse. | **Scotch Plains**	23
Z Stage Left | **New Bruns.**	26
NEW Stonehouse | **Warren**	-
NEW Tabor Rd. | **Morris Plains**	-
Z 3 West | **Basking Ridge**	23
Tre Figlio | **Egg Harbor**	24
Tre Piani | **Princeton**	21
Z Washington Inn | **Cape May**	26
Witherspoon Grill | **Princeton**	-
Wolfgang Puck | **A.C.**	23

WORTH A TRIP

Atlantic City	
Dock's Oyster	26
Z SeaBlue	27
Z White Hse.	27
Basking Ridge	
Z 3 West	23
Bedminster	
Z Pluckemin Inn	25
Bernardsville	
Z Bernards Inn	26
Brant Beach	
daddy O	18
Cape May	
Z Ebbitt Room	27
Z 410 Bank St.	27
Frescos	24
Z Peter Shields	26
Chatham	
Z Scalini Fedeli	27
Z Serenade	27
Cherry Hill	
La Campagne	24
Clermont	
Karen & Rei's	27
Clifton	
Chengdu 46	24
Collingswood	
Nunzio	23
Z Sagami	26

SPECIAL FEATURES

Wine Vintage Chart

This chart, based on our 0 to 30 scale, is designed to help you select wine. The ratings (by **Howard Stravitz,** a law professor at the University of South Carolina) reflect the vintage quality and the wine's readiness to drink. We exclude the 1991–1993 vintages because they are not that good. A dash indicates the wine is either past its peak or too young to rate. Loire ratings are for dry white wines.

Whites

	88	89	90	94	95	96	97	98	99	00	01	02	03	04	05	06
French:																
Alsace	-	25	25	24	23	23	22	25	23	25	27	25	22	24	25	-
Burgundy	-	23	22	-	28	27	24	22	26	25	24	27	23	27	26	24
Loire Valley	-	-	-	-	-	-	-	-	24	25	26	23	24	27	24	
Champagne	24	26	29	-	26	27	24	23	24	24	22	26	-	-	-	-
Sauternes	29	25	28	-	21	23	25	23	24	24	28	25	26	21	26	23
California:																
Chardonnay	-	-	-	-	-	-	-	24	23	26	26	25	27	29	25	
Sauvignon Blanc	-	-	-	-	-	-	-	-	-	-	27	28	26	27	26	27
Austrian:																
Grüner Velt./Riesling	-	-	-	-	25	21	26	26	25	22	23	25	26	25	26	-
German:	25	26	27	24	23	26	25	26	23	21	29	27	24	26	28	-

Reds

	88	89	90	94	95	96	97	98	99	00	01	02	03	04	05	06
French:																
Bordeaux	23	25	29	22	26	25	23	25	24	29	26	24	25	24	27	25
Burgundy	-	24	26	-	26	27	25	22	27	22	24	27	25	25	27	25
Rhône	26	28	28	24	26	22	25	27	26	27	26	-	25	24	25	-
Beaujolais	-	-	-	-	-	-	-	-	24	-	23	25	22	28	26	
California:																
Cab./Merlot	-	-	28	29	27	25	28	23	26	22	27	26	25	24	24	23
Pinot Noir	-	-	-	-	-	-	24	23	24	23	27	28	26	25	24	-
Zinfandel	-	-	-	-	-	-	-	-	-	25	23	27	24	23	-	
Oregon:																
Pinot Noir	-	-	-	-	-	-	-	-	-	-	27	25	26	27	-	
Italian:																
Tuscany	-	-	25	22	24	20	29	24	27	24	27	20	25	25	22	24
Piedmont	-	27	27	-	23	26	27	26	25	28	27	20	24	25	26	-
Spanish:																
Rioja	-	-	-	26	26	24	25	22	25	24	27	20	24	25	26	24
Ribera del Duero/Priorat	-	-	-	26	26	27	25	24	25	24	27	20	24	26	26	24
Australian:																
Shiraz/Cab.	-	-	-	24	26	23	26	28	24	24	27	27	25	26	24	-
Chilean:	-	-	-	-	-	-	24	-	25	23	26	24	25	24	26	-